A Certain Club

A Certain Club

Club

One Hundred Years of
The Players

New York · 1888-1988

JOHN TEBBEL

Library of Congress Cataloging-in-Publication Data

Tebbel, John William, 1912–
   A certain club.

   1. Players (Club)   2. Acting—Societies, etc.—History.
3. Actors—United States—Biography.   4. Booth, Edwin,
1833–1893.   5. New York (N.Y.)—Clubs—History.   I. Title.
PN2016.P53T43   1988   792'.06'07471   88-33827
ISBN 0-914373-17-X

Printed in the United States of America

Produced by Wieser & Wieser, Inc.
118 East 25th Street, New York, NY 10010.

Contents

PART THREE: Modern Times

PART FOUR: Icons and Institutions

Preface

WRITING THIS BOOK HAS BEEN A JOYOUS AND REWARDING EXPERIENCE. I am immensely grateful to the Executive Committee, the Library Board, and all those who chose me for the task, making it possible for me to write what has turned out to be as much a love letter as it is a history.

My thanks also to Louis Rachow, the Club's curator, who made available to me the storehouse of records which form the basis of this work. They include the bound volumes of annual Board of Directors' reports from the beginning until 1921. At that point the *Bulletin* takes over, and I have read its files from that date until the *Brief Chronicles* of the present, besides two collections marking the fiftieth and seventy-fifth anniversaries of the Club.

Beyond all these, I have drawn on Walter Oettel's *Sketch Book*, the four volumes of Albert Bigelow Paine's *Autobiography of Mark Twain*, plus other volumes about Twain in my own library, as well as Edward Anthony's *O Rare Don Marquis*, and still other relevant works as they occur in the text. My thanks, also, to Robert Giroux for making available to me the material on Henry James's visits to the Club.

JOHN TEBBEL
Southbury, Connecticut
March 28, 1988

A Certain Club

Ah, dead done! Forever dead and done
The mellow dusks, the friendly dusks and dim,
When Charley shook the cocktails up, or Tim—
Gone are ten thousand gleaming moments, gone
Like fireflies twinkling toward oblivion!
Ah, how the bubbles used to leap and swim,
Breaking in laughter round the goblet's brim,
When Walter pulled a cork for us, or John!
I have seen ghosts of men I never knew—
Great, gracious souls, the golden hearts of earth—
Look from the shadows in those rooms we love,
Living a wistful instant in our mirth:
I have seen Jefferson smile down on Drew,
And Booth pause, musing, on the stair above.

—Don Marquis

PART ONE

Early Years

CHAPTER 1

Edwin Booth and His Dream

WHEN EDWIN BOOTH DIED IN 1893 HE LEFT BEHIND HIM THE RECORD OF a life in the theater—the greatest American Hamlet of his time, or perhaps any other—and the bitter memory of an innocent association with one of the most somber tragedies in American history, the assassination of Abraham Lincoln by his brother John Wilkes Booth. His work on the stage, distinguished as it was, is no more than a theatrical icon today, severed from living memory. His own name has long since been removed from association with the despised name of his brother. But he left behind him an enduring monument to both his art and his transcendent humanity in the club he founded in 1888, The Players, which still glows on the south side of Gramercy Park in New York City as it did a century ago.

At least three biographers have told us the details of Booth's life, as tortured in private as it was splendid in the theater, but many of The Players who now cherish his Club have only a dim sense of the man who created it, and of how it was created. A brief prologue, then, before the historical play begins.

What kind of man was Booth? Not an easy question, because he was as complex as many of the characters he played. To early Players who had known him, memories were often conflicting. He was a tragedian on and off the stage, said some; not at all, he was humorous, with a smile for

3

everyone, said others. On a single point there was agreement: he was the most lovable man any of his friends had ever known. In all the many observations of Booth, it is virtually impossible to find anything discreditable that he ever said or did, even though that may be hard to believe in a cynical age.

Traveling Americans today can get a sense of his beginnings if they visit his restored birthplace, Tudor Hall, in Bel Air, Harford County, Maryland. Booth and his brother John were born there in a log cabin while the main house was being built (Booth in 1833). Tudor Hall was a two-story white brick building surrounded by pastures and giant trees, which their father, Junius Brutus Booth, another noted Shakespearean actor, constructed. The original house had twelve rooms, with bricks and glass that Junius imported from his native England. Later he added a wing with English Tudor leaded casements. There were double back-to-back fireplaces on each floor.

Theater annals give us several different places where Booth first appeared on the stage, but historians now agree that his initial performance was given only three miles from Bel Air, in a homemade production at the Harford County Circuit Court House. It was his gateway to the world.

Donald Seawell, a Player of our time, believes that to understand Booth properly, we need to view his unique position in the theater in 1864 at the peak of his fame, and that may well be true. But to appreciate the kind of man who survived an incredible series of personal tragedies to illuminate the lives of his own and future generations, we need to recall something of what he was before the peak.

As a great tragedian, Booth must also have had an inner sense of comedy or he would not have been able to survive a boyhood spent as a nursemaid to Junius, his father, whose boozy exploits were a scandal in theater circles, yet who, once the curtains parted, played Shakespeare with a genius only his son could surpass. Booth took care of Junius, loved him and acted with him while they toured the country, enduring physical suffering and the frequent scorn of a citizenry that held actors in contempt. Like so many in the theater, Booth more than paid his dues before he became famous. Sometimes he was near starvation; success was often followed by devastating setbacks.

Life on the road with Junius was highly educational, if nothing else. On a one-night stand when Booth was only ten years old, he was helping his father prepare for Act V of *Richard III,* buckling on his armor while simultaneously trying to hide a bottle from him, when Edwin Forrest burst into the dressing room. Young Booth had been named for him (and for the Irish actor Tom Flynn, whose name he soon dropped). Junius and Forrest were public rivals in print, but offstage they were close friends. On this night they embraced each other and Forrest drew out his own bottle. As they warmed up to it, Forrest began a little dance in which Junius joined him, spurred on by young Edwin's rendition of "Old Zip Coon" on his banjo. The room had begun to shake when the stage manager rushed in shouting, "Mr. Booth, it's Bosworth Field!"

Richard III proved to be a fateful play in Edwin's life. He had seen his father perform it so often that he knew the role by heart, and when his first opportunity to play a major part in a play arrived unexpectedly one night in Marysville, California, he was ready. At 8 o'clock that evening a packed house was waiting to see his father play Richard, but Junius could not go on. Charitable biographers have said he was too ill, but it seems more likely he was too drunk. The theater manager was in a state of panic, not wanting to lose a profitable audience and pay refunds. Consequently, he listened when the stage manager told him young Booth could play the part.

No announcement was made. Booth simply went on for his father. The audience appeared not to notice the difference, except that its applause was much more enthusiastic than even Junius was accustomed to hearing. The next day members of the company said the father never saw the day when he could do as well. Edwin went on later to play Richard all over the United States and it proved to be his greatest success after Hamlet.

He was playing in Chicago on an April night in 1879 when a man rose in the first balcony and fired two shots at Booth, one of which struck him. Booth looked up at the balcony, and seeing the would-be assassin raising his gun for a third shot, walked slowly into the wings. The wound was superficial, and after order had been restored, he came back on and finished the act. A demented man named Mark Gray had fired the shot and when the bullet was removed from Booth's body, he had it mounted in a gold cap and engraved "From Mark Gray to Edwin Booth."

Theater people have their particular superstitions and Booth had some of his own. He was convinced that the only reason he had escaped death in Chicago was because he had been born with a caul. He also attached importance to the influence of the numeral 3 in his life. He was born on November 13, 1833, was shot at three times (Gray did fire his third shot, harmlessly), and the attempted assassination took place on Shakespeare's birthday, April 23; he lost the mother of his only child on February 9, 1863; dedicated The Players on December 31, and died in 1893.

It was never superstitious fear that induced Booth's habitual melancholy, however, but the continuing tragic events of his life, which would have been enough to overwhelm most people. Yet Laurence Hutton, one of his closest friends, wrote in his *Talks in a Library* that Booth was "often cheerful and happy, tradition to the contrary notwithstanding." Certainly there was nothing of the "gentle, melancholy man" of tradition in the exuberant letter young Edwin, only 29 then, wrote from London to a friend on December 9, 1861, describing the horrendous circumstances of his daughter's birth:

> This has been an eventful day for me. At one a.m. I was cast adrift in my nightgown and slippers to find a doctor. At 2 a.m. I was several miles out of my reckoning, and up to my knees in mud, the night being stormy and I a stranger. 3 a.m. found me back by my wife's side with a strange M.D.— whom I had found in the mud somewhere—on t'other side of my wife's bed, when our own doctor arrived. 4 a.m. found me on the verge of agony, and 5 a.m. found me Farther—the joke is in Father, of course—a Father I am of a girl, and you will be pleased to know—a Happy One!

Something of the great love Booth had for his daughter, Edwina, is evident in the bronze casting of her hand in his, which members and visitors can see on the table in the room where he died.

Less than two years later, however, the worst period of Booth's life began. Mary Devlin, the lovely young actress he had married, the mother of Edwina, died suddenly. A crushing despair settled on the man whom Edwina would later describe as "affected almost to hysteria by some humorous incident or anecdote. And he must be careful, for too much laughing hurts his asthma." These interludes of laughter were rare indeed after the dramatic episode of April 14, 1865, when Booth's brother Johnny seared the family name into the nation's historical memory with the shot that killed Abraham Lincoln. It was like a knife thrust to Booth, at what seemed then to be a superb climax to his career. Early in 1864 he had played Shylock at Ford's Theater to an acclaiming audience including the president himself. Lincoln observed later that it had been "a great performance, but I'd a thousand times rather read it at home if it were not for Booth's playing."

Only a month before the assassination, in a bizarre coincidence, Booth had saved the life of Robert Todd Lincoln, the president's son. Robert, then a student at Harvard, had been on his way to Washington, changing trains in Jersey City. Near midnight he was about to board in order to get a berth in the sleeping car. To have the car level with the platform was a new thing to him (as it was for many travelers then), and he was unprepared when the train suddenly began to move slowly, causing a movement in the crowd of waiting passengers which pressed young Lincoln tightly against the car. The surge swept him off his feet and dropped him down into the narrow space between car and platform as the train suddenly stopped. A hand reached down, seized him by the collar, and brought him safely back to the platform. Robert turned to thank the rescuer who had saved his life, and at once saw that it was Booth, whom he had often seen on the stage. The memory of that rescue comforted Booth in his later life.

Nothing could comfort him, however, when the news of Lincoln's assassination reached him in Boston, where he was playing Sir Edward Mortimer in *The Iron Chest, or, The Mysterious Murder*. He wrote later: "Oh how little did I dream . . . when on Friday night I was as Sir Edward Mortimer exclaiming, 'Where is my honor now? Mountains of shame are piled upon me!', that I was not acting but uttering the fearful truth."

For the moment, all he could say was, "Not Johnny, not Johnny!" Booth had seldom seen his brother, then 26, since boyhood days in Baltimore. To an inquirer he recalled: "Johnny was a rattle-pated fellow, filled with Quixotic notions. . . . We used to laugh at his patriotic froth whenever secession was discussed. That he was insane on that one point, no one who knew him well can doubt. . . . He was of gentle, loving disposition, very boyish and full of fun—his mother's darling—and his deed and death crushed her spirit. He possessed rare dramatic talent, and would have made a brilliant mark in the theatrical world. . . . All his theatrical friends speak of him as a poor, crazy boy, and such his family think of him."

Booth's dignified and immensely touching letter of apology to the nation for his brother's act rests in the Club's library today, a testimonial to his strength in the face of disaster. And it *was* a disaster, not only for those involved, but for all actors. Unreasoning mobs gathered in the street, and the first fury of mass reaction to the president's assassination was directed at Booth's family. Then it was expanded to include theaters and actors in general. Most theaters had to close for a time, not only out of respect, but because the public plainly regarded them as places of evil. For a time, actors lost the respectability they had only just begun to achieve, and were reviled as they never had been before. There are those who believe the idea for such a club as The Players was born out of Booth's acute sense of responsibility for his profession in this darkest of times.

To understand the profound reversal that had taken place literally overnight in 1865, it is necessary to remember that the year before, the 300th anniversary of Shakespeare's death, had been an extraordinary year in the history of the New York theater. Never before had there been so much public interest and excitement—an unprecedented public concern for the stage never equaled since. In such a climate, producers did not have to capitalize on the anniversary by reviving Shakespeare. The bard was already the stock-in-trade of theaters in America, England, and all of Europe. German, French, Russian, and Italian stars could appear in English or American companies, speaking their native tongues, and be sure that audiences would know what they were saying, so great was the theater-going public's familiarity with the plays.

To the advantage, and sometimes disadvantage, of Booth and his fellow performers, audiences knew the actors as well as they did the plays and followed them with the same avidity rock stars command today. They would go to the same play on successive nights just to compare the acting of various stars. Actors sometimes switched roles to take advantage of such devotion, as Booth and Kean had done in *Othello,* and Booth would do later with Henry Irving.

In 1864 the chief observance of Shakespeare's anniversary was a fund-raising Shakespearean series to raise money for a statue of the bard in Central Park, then no more than a piece of rural landscape. Booth was a natural leader in this endeavor, and on the birthday itself played Romeo at the Winter Garden (the playbill is in the Club library), then at Broadway and Bond streets.

On November 25, a historic conjunction of stars appeared when Junius's three sons appeared together in *Julius Caesar*—Edwin as Brutus, Junius the younger as Cassius, and John Wilkes Booth as Marc Antony. This playbill is in the Club dining hall. John got much of the early applause, particularly from his mother, who was in the audience. During the play there was a fire in the theater and firemen abruptly appeared, but Booth came down to the footlights, and according to contemporary accounts, put down rising panic by sheer force of his personality. When the play resumed, the depth of his performance was so powerful that he eclipsed John.

On the following night there began the outstanding success of his career—or that of any other actor, some believe. Booth opened in his finest role, Hamlet, expecting that it might run from two to four weeks. Instead, it went on for a hundred nights before audiences completely enthralled by his acting. It would not have ended except for Booth's exhaustion after performances that drew ecstatic notices from everyone. The *New York Times* called it "a part in which he has no living equal." William Winter, perhaps his closest friend, asserted that Booth's Hamlet was "the simple absolute realization of Shakespeare's haunted prince." Even brother Johnny, jealous as he was but with his mind on other matters at the moment, had to declare, "There's but one Hamlet in my mind; that's my brother Edwin. You see, between ourselves, he *is* Hamlet—melancholy and all."

As Donald Seawell has observed, Booth "became Hamlet when he walked upon the stage through a full understanding of the character. Perhaps he was helped in that understanding by his own troubled life, but it is an affront to his greatness to credit his performance to a melancholy nature and an affinity for adversity. It also ignores his triumphs in other and varied roles. Two recordings of his voice in the Harvard Theatre Collection show the clarity, naturalness and magnetism of his voice."

It was a voice stilled for a time by Lincoln's death, at the peak of Booth's career, and at one of the theater's highest moments as well, when actors, those "rogues and vagabonds," became socially acceptable for the first time. Momentarily it all became suspended in historic time after that fateful night in Ford's theater. Edwin Booth was ony thirty-two but already he had run the spectrum from drunkenness and despair to an acclaim surpassed by no other actor. Ahead of him lay twenty-seven years in which, first, he had to undergo the vilification that followed Lincoln's death, escape his own attempted assassination, go bankrupt, and lose his only son, born to his second wife, Mary McVicker, whom he married in 1869. He never loved her as he had Mary Devlin, but nevertheless it was a blow to lose their son, Edgar, who lived only a few hours after birth, and then to lose the second Mary, who slipped into periods of psychotic behavior and, after lingering for years, died in 1881.

In spite of it all, Booth seemed to find himself once more as an actor in the late 1860s, came out of his self-imposed seclusion, and rose to perhaps even greater heights on the stage, becoming the acknowledged foremost actor in America. He regained his fortune, paid off his debts, and re-established the family honor.

The theory that Booth's idea for The Players originated during the period of disgrace after Lincoln's death is at least partially substantiated by an 1886 letter he wrote to his friend Albert Palmer, in which he speaks about a house he had bought in 1869 at 14 West 24th Street. "An actors' club," Booth wrote, "combining the convenience and advantages that you speak of has been a dream of mine for many years, and I had the house in question in my mind's eye for the purpose of some far-off future day." But he had turned over the house on 24th Street to his daughter and her husband. He suspected they would want an even higher figure for it if they cared to sell. In any case, Edwina was ill at the moment and he was not inclined even to discuss the matter with her. Meanwhile, he could dream. As he wrote to Palmer, "Having quite a number of theatrical books, pictures, etc. etc., I have dreamed of furnishing such an establishment with them some day. When I step aside, and before I go, I hope to accomplish something of the kind."

As the idea broadened in his mind during the next few months, Booth began to see it in broader terms than his original conception of "an actors' club." His full purpose is embodied in the language of his Deed of Gift, in the Corporate Charter, and in the Club constitution itself:

The promotion of social intercourse between the representative members of the Dramatic profession and the kindred professions of Literature, Painting, Sculpture, and Music and the Patrons of the Arts; the creation of a library relating especially to the history of the American stage and the preservation of pictures, bills of the play, photographs, and curiosities, connected with such history.

Slowly Booth began to move toward realizing his dream. With his troupe he traveled around the country by train, often accompanied by Edwina, in a private "hotel car," equipped with a piano and a small library; the other actors lived in an adjoining Pullman. Sometimes Edwina played the piano and members of the troupe sang to her accompaniment.

In 1885 Booth lost Edwina's company on tour when she married Ignatius Grossman, a Hungarian professor and stockbroker. That left her father feeling more alone than ever. Passing by him in Boston one day, the famous Harvard professor Charles Townsend Copeland ("Copey," as his devoted students called him) thought Booth seemed "to be looking in, not out, with the curious introverted gaze of his own Hamlet. . . . I thought then that I had never seen so sad a face." All that remained were the marvelous eyes, the ones Ellen Terry declared were the most beautiful she had ever seen in a human head.

By this time it was generally acknowledged what Booth had done to transform the American theater. He had changed forever the old style of bellowing, by speaking to give the impression of natural speech, though not progressing as far in that direction as we know today. Moreover, his art enabled him to give a variety of tone, inflection, and meaning even to lines that were thrice familiar. Off the stage as well, his voice was a thrilling sound to hear.

At this late stage of his career in 1885 his health was already failing, although he was only 52. Kitty Maloney, an actress who toured with him, tells in her memoirs of a day in Minnesota when Booth took the ladies of the company on an excursion to Minnehaha Falls. The day turned out to be strenuous, and when the expedition returned to the hotel late in the afternoon Miss Maloney watched Booth walk to his room, and wrote: "It was an old man I saw, dragging his feet down the hall. But in three hours there sprang upon the stage—literally sprang, his step was so light—a Beautiful Fiend, Iago, young as lean saplings swaying in the wind."

His generosity and his concern for his fellow actors were already legendary. Once on the last tour he was visited by Elizabeth Saunders, known as "the oldest living actress," who had fallen on hard times. She had played Lady Anne to Junius's Richard II, at a time when 14-year-old Edwin was playing Tressell. The aged actress and Booth laughed together, recalling how Edwin, in the play, confronted his terrifying father, saying, "Stand back, my lord, and let the coffin pass." After a long afternoon of reminiscence, Miss Saunders rose to leave and asked Booth to sign her book. He took it to a corner, wrote, returned it and said good-bye. Later, when she opened it again, Miss Saunders found a check for a thousand dollars.

On the stage he was as versatile as ever, capable of playing any one of twenty-two star parts. He also endured gracefully whatever had to be endured, and never lost the sense of humor with which he was not often credited. Playing *Macbeth* one night with Charlotte Cushman, an actress of formidable proportions, he muttered to another actor, "I often feel like saying, 'Why don't *you* kill Duncan—you're bigger than I am.'" In the wings he stood and told stories to the others, breaking off at just the right moment to go on stage again. As his co-star and close friend, Lawrence Barrett, put it, "He never shrouded himself in the dread mantle of art-absorption after he left a scene."

Over him constantly appeared to hang the memory of his family's great disgrace. George Middleton, one of the earliest Players, who had met Booth at his father's home, recalled coming upon him accidentally in the Chicago park where Augustus Saint-Gaudens's statue of Lincoln had recently been unveiled. Booth had driven alone in a carriage to see it. Getting out, he did not notice Middleton and, looking around, observed no one else. With bared head, he contemplated Lincoln's sorrowful face for a long time, then plucked a flower from his buttonhole and placed it at the statue's feet. Returning to his carriage, he turned and made a gesture of sorrow and infinite regret, climbed in and drove away.

There had been little to console him except, perhaps, that moment on January 3, 1866, less than a year after the assassination, when he returned to the stage, not knowing how he would be received. There had been threats of reprisals in the newspapers. The play was *Hamlet,* and when the curtain rose on the Danish court, the lights came up slowly and Booth could be seen, seated, in somber costume. The audience seemed not to recognize him for a moment, but then the applause started, and it grew until everyone was on his feet, giving Booth one of the most stirring ovations ever accorded an actor. His eyes filled with tears, he rose slowly, bowed deeply to the audience, and sank back in his chair.

From that night on he had risen to new heights, but in 1885 Booth was conscious that he could not go on much longer, and more than ever he thought of the Club he had dreamed of creating for so long. When he played in London he had seen the Garrick, that comfortable old rendezvous for actors, and savoring its pleasures, he felt more than ever that it was his duty, as well as his private pleasure, to found such a club. He had sold his house in Boston, and now felt he had no real home. A club, he believed, could be his real and final home.

Booth discussed his plans from time to time with his friends William Bispham and Albert Palmer, and they encouraged him. Bispham was instructed to look for a site, and the search began. Meanwhile, Booth and his troupe set off for his next-to-last transcontinental tour. Fortunately, we have a firsthand account of that trip from Kitty Maloney (quoted previously), a member of the company who later became the wife of George P. Goodale, drama critic of the Detroit *Free Press* for more than fifty years. Kitty was only eighteen when Lawrence Barrett, who engaged and directed the supporting company, hired her for the season of 1886–87. Now she was riding in Booth's private car, aptly called the David Garrick, with some of the other women in the company. In her memoirs, *Behind the Scenes with Edwin Booth,* she tells about life en route, demonstrating those social qualities "expected to keep the revered tragedian in good spirits" during the long trips, when he was given to melancholy.

Kitty recalls one evening as the train pulled itself over the Rockies when Booth began to speak of the Club, as though it were already an accomplished fact, and instructed W. H. Magonigle, his brother-in-law and treasurer of the company, to bring several actors from their Pullman just ahead into the Garrick's smoking room so they could discuss the project. Kitty asked if she might come too, and Booth graciously agreed. Apparently, she made notes because she quotes Booth directly and in some detail in her description of what followed.

"We do not mingle enough with minds that influence the world," Booth told his fellow actors when they were assembled, according to Kitty. "We should measure ourselves through personal contact with outsiders. I do not want my Club to be the gathering place of freaks who come to look upon another sort of freak. I want real men there, who will be able to realize what real men actors are! I want my Club to be a place where actors are away from the glamor of the theater."

The search for a house went on during all that season, but a place had not been found when Booth went out again on his last coast-to-coast tour in 1887–88. For a time, a building on the east side of Madison Square had been considered, but for some reason it was ruled unsuitable. Nothing else had turned up in the summer of 1887, when Booth's friend and financial adviser, Commodore Elias C. Benedict, invited the actor and several of his friends on a July cruise aboard his yacht, the *Oneida*. It proved to be a historic journey.

The destination was Newfoundland, but apparently the yacht got no farther than Boothbay Harbor, Maine, where the guests luxuriated on the deck and Edwin began to talk seriously once more about banding them all together as a club, the Club he had been dreaming about. Among those present besides Booth and the host were Lawrence Barrett, Thomas Bailey Aldrich, Laurence Hutton, William Bispham, and Parke Godwin—a mixed bag of actors, writers, editors, and businessmen. Everyone enthusiastically supported Booth's idea, and it was Aldrich who suggested the new Club be called The Players, from the "All the world's a stage" speech in *As You Like It*.

The key man in this group was not one of its celebrated members. Elias Benedict, the "Commodore," as he liked to call himself, was a financier whom Booth had known for a long time. He lived in a big house on Indian Harbor, in Greenwich, later owned by William Zeckendorf, and it was there Booth had met him by accident years before, when he was living momentarily in Westchester County. Booth had found himself in need of a new heating system, and the plumber he engaged took him to see a system of the kind he wanted to install, already in action. With permission, the plumber was showing off the system he hoped to sell Booth when the owner of the house appeared. It was, of course, the Commodore, who struck up a quick friendship with Booth that lasted until the actor died.

Not only did they become good friends, but Benedict managed Booth's money, and at the time the Club was being born, he had made a handsome profit of $150,000 in Chicago Gas as an addition to Booth's respectable fortune. This was the money Booth used to buy and renovate the house that became the Club.

On the *Oneida* Benedict joined the others in discussing with Booth what the Club should be. Its membership must include those in the other arts, they agreed, and it must be strictly private. The constitution should guarantee that no testimonial dinner be given to any individual, no matter how eminent he might be. (At the time such dinners had become scandalous vehicles for personal and political publicity.) It must be a place, as Booth had conceived it from the start, where actors could meet in easy fellowship with those working in the other arts.

Before he went on tour in September of 1887 with Barrett, Booth consulted with two of his close friends, Augustin Daly, a playwright and theater manager, and Albert M. Palmer, manager of the Union Square Theatre, and made the final decision that he would assume the cost of housing The Players. Returning briefly at the end of December for a week at the Academy, Booth met at breakfast with both managers and Barrett. It was agreed to combine the drama library Palmer had been talking about, establishing it in connection with the Actors Fund, with the theater library both had been discussing as the centerpiece of the Club.

On the following Friday afternoon, January 6, 1888, at the Red Room in Delmonico's, Daly gathered Booth and fifteen of his friends for the purpose of incorporating The Players. They were a distinguished lot. Among the fifteen incorporators there were six actors besides Booth: Joseph Jefferson, John Drew, Lawrence Barrett, James Lewis, Henry Edwards, and John A. Lane (a banker turned actor). Two of the group, Albert Palmer and Augustin Daly, were theater managers, and two others were lawyers, Daly and Stephen H. Olin. There was one businessman, William Bispham; Professor Brander Matthews, a distinguished member of the Columbia University faculty; two authors, Laurence Hutton and Samuel L. Clemens, far better known as Mark Twain; and a most unlikely figure, General William Tecumseh Sherman.

Booth and his friends signed the application that day and next day it was sent up to Albany, where it was duly approved. Meanwhile Bispham, who had been entrusted with the task of finding a home for the new Club, was still looking. Booth had left the day after he signed the incorporation application for Philadelphia, where he and Barrett were to begin a four-month tour through the southern states and on across the country to San Francisco, then back to Omaha, followed by one-night stands in eight states, ending the season at Williamsburg on May 14.

By now the subject of the Club was uppermost in his mind. He wrote to Bispham about the kind of house he wanted and the sort of location. As for Bispham, frustrated at first, he had called for help on Stanford White, who had been invited to join as a charter member. This brilliant young architect, only thirty-five at the time, lived on the north side of Gramercy Park. Bispham asked White what he thought about No. 16 Gramercy Park, one of three houses with Gothic porches and cast-iron verandas which had been built about 1844–45 for Elihu Townsend, a New York banker. It was owned by the widow of Clarkson Potter, a Democratic congressman from New York in the 1870s, but it was occupied by the socially prominent Louis Lorillard family.

Bispham knew this house well and had had his eye on it from the beginning. He had often been entertained there by the Lorillards, and was sure Booth would approve its purchase, but he relied on the advice of White, who had been described by one newspaper as the "art partner, so to speak," of that rising firm of architects, McKim, Mead & White. From his own house at the corner of Lexington Avenue on the north side of the park, White had often thought about the possibilities of No. 16, and when Bispham asked his advice, he said, "Buy it."

On April 17, Bispham made an offer for the house, advising Booth of what he had done. The tourist replied from Indianapolis (in some accounts it is St. Joseph, Missouri) that he was delighted, and added, "Our engagements have lost interest for us in the more absorbing matter of the house." No. 16 was, he said, "one of the spots Barrett and I thought was desirable." The deed was passed on May 20, Bispham wrote a check to Mrs. Potter for $75,000, and The Players had their home. The news was greeted with mixed emotions by the other residents of the houses around the park.

To understand how these comfortable people felt about the invasion of actors, we need only to look at the history of this bucolic Manhattan spot we know as Gramercy Park. It was originally the farm of James Duane, a judge, member of the Continental Congress, and mayor of New York for six years. He called it Gramercy Seat. In 1831 Samuel B. Ruggles, a Connecticut Yankee who had graduated from Yale at fourteen, bought the farm from Duane's heirs. At the time it was not much more than a large morass, awash in cattails.

Ruggles knew something about the history of this farm. He knew, for instance, that Duane had begun to assemble the property in 1761 by acquiring a small parcel of it from Gerardus Stuyvesant, a grandson of the redoubtable peg-legged Peter Stuyvesant, last governor of New Netherlands, and original owner of the old Stuyvesant farm, lying east of Bowery Road between what is now 19th and 20th Streets. In 1763 Duane added ten more acres bought from John Watts, lying east and north of his original purchase, and thus became owner of the land on which Gramercy Park stands today.

Why "Gramercy"? On old maps, the Duane farm is called "Krom Massie." Since the soil was mostly red clay, and since "cramoisy" is a word meaning "red," common to French, Dutch and English, the plausible conclusion is that "Gramercy" is an Anglicized derivative. Other etymologists, however, believe it comes from the Dutch words "Krom Moesrasje," meaning crooked little swamp, referring to the large marsh created by a brook called Crummashie, rising west of what would be Madison Square, forming a pond, then crossing what is now Fourth Avenue, skirting Kip's Bay Hill, and emptying at last into the East River, near Bellevue Hospital.

There are still other possibilities. Duane's farm was shaped like a shoemaker's knife so "Gramercy" could be derived from the Dutch "Krom," meaning crooked, and "mesje," meaning knife. Or perhaps Duane, out of gratitude for acquiring such a handsome piece of property, may have bethought himself of an Old English word, derived from Old French—"gramercy," meaning "great thanks." It was a word used commonly by Elizabethans.

In any case, Samuel B. Ruggles, a lawyer who knew his own mind, also knew what he wanted to do with this property. There were much larger matters on his mind (keeping Unitarians from becoming physical science professors at Columbia, and paving the way for the Erie Canal), but what he wanted to do with the old Duane farm was to set up a trust that would create an Arcadian park. To that end, when he bought the farm (he was only 31 and already rich), he conveyed a section of the property to three men, including two prominent lawyers, creating an area 520 feet by 184 feet between what would be 20th and 21st Streets. An iron fence would be built around this square, and on it a park would be laid out for the benefit of those who wanted to build houses around it. Sixty-six lots were provided for that purpose, and the trust provided that the owners alone would have access to the park when it was built.

In the spring of 1888 when Booth acquired No. 16, Ruggles's vision had come true. The splendid houses rested quietly behind their privet hedges. Old elms and willows lined the square and grew in the park inside the iron fence Ruggles had decreed should enclose it. Inside the fence, children played and nursemaids wheeled carriages, even as they do today. In the afternoon, barouches shepherded by coachmen pulled up before high stoops, down whose stairs descended elegant ladies. At night, hansom cabs brought these ladies home from the theater or the opera. In the houses the residents gossiped about the dinners the Lorillards or others were giving. They spoke of new books by Mark Twain and Aldrich, and of the superb performances by Mr. Booth and Mr. Barrett, not contemplating that these admired personages would soon arrive in the neighborhood to stay.

When they did learn that Virginia Potter had sold No. 16, some were aghast at the prospect of having actors and God knew what other kind of artistic humanity in their midst. They had nothing against those engaged in the arts, to be sure, but surely not in their backyard. All they desired was that nothing would be changed in their best of all possible worlds.

But nothing could stop Booth now. On the tour that spring he had been buying pictures for his new Club. When he returned to New York in May, he toured the house from top to bottom in the company of White and several members of the Club. As they went from basement to fourth floor, White kept up a running commentary on the changes he wanted to make, and Booth enthusiastically agreed. In the end he gave White carte blanche to do whatever he liked in the house, a dream commitment for any architect.

Richardson Wright, a Player who made a detailed study of what was done, wrote later that no one knows exactly what condition the house was in when Booth bought it, but judging by the cost of the alterations, White's renovation was substantial. On the park side of the building he took down a high brownstone front stoop, something he had done for another resident of the park five years earlier. Then he rearranged the front windows, created a new entrance door, and constructed the two-story brownstone colonnade across the front which is so familiar to us today. He decorated the colonnade with the Club's symbol, tragic and comic masks designed by White and Kempton, and flanked the entrance with two projecting lanterns.

All this was observed by Gramercy residents with some alarm, as a contemporary newspaper account tells us:

> When the club was entirely finished, two features concerning it gave the conservative element considerable pain. The architect of the building saw fit to embellish its exterior with two huge lanterns of a highly decorative design, which diffused their genial glow at night over the space in front of the main entrance. In the areaway were also placed evergreen trees in square green boxes. The conservative element groaned in spirit at these decorations. To them they strongly suggested the German summer beer garden, and a petition was immediately circulated for signatures, requesting the mamagement of the club to do away with these objectionable features. Their wishes as to the evergreen trees have been observed, but Mr. Stanford White's lanterns will remain as beacon lights to the tired thespian after his evening's work of unremitting mental and physical toil.

Those controversial lanterns still glow, one of the few gas fixtures remaining in New York, and they somehow reflect the imaginative taste of Stanford White and his love of the theater, of whom Commodore Benedict once said, "He was a first nighter, an every nighter—and an all nighter." There was, of course, one first night too many for White, who was shot from behind and killed by Harry K. Thaw, the eccentric Pittsburgh millionaire, as he watched the summer opening of the Madison Square Garden Roof. The object of their mutual affection was Thaw's wife, Evelyn Nesbit, a *Floradora* chorus girl, known forever after in scandalous history as "The Girl in the Red Velvet Swing."

Evelyn was far ahead in White's future as he went about rebuilding the interior of No. 16. He had volunteered to rehabilitate the house without charge, as a labor of love and as a new member of the Club that would occupy it. White did everything. As John S. Phillips recalled in a Founder's Night address many years later, he "made special designs for fixtures and interiors of rooms, selected tiles for the grill fireplace, hunted out this beautiful marble mantelpiece, for which Mr. Booth sent the motto while on tour. White drove the workers tirelessly, consulting with other artists and members of taste, and of course with Mr. Booth during his summer's leisure. Edwin Booth wanted the house prepared as a beautiful garment, suitable for the offspring of his imagination."

The new interior was essentially what it would be until further renovations began in the Twenties, to be followed by additional changes in the

Thirties and beyond, yet it would still be recognizable to any current Player. Going downstairs from the entrance hall to the basement, a billiard room occupied the space where the bar now stands, and the present billiard (or more often, pool) room was a nearly empty space leading to the lavatories, as it does today. Upstairs from the entrance was the Main Hall, as it was called then, now the Great Hall. On the ceiling was a gilded device of leaves and rosettes, a favorite device of White's; he had used it a few years earlier on a cover he designed for *Scribner's* magazine. In a corner of this handsome room was the office, with a wine room sandwiched between one of its safes and the pantry. A skylight brought in an occasional burst of sunshine.

To visualize what White called the grill room, which Players know now as the dining room, would be difficult for younger members today because it ended where the two columns stand now. Beyond it was a sort of back porch, or piazza, overlooking a garden with a fountain in the middle. The porch was later extended on both sides and it became a favorite place to dine in fine weather. All this was built over in time to lengthen the dining room and provide a stage for entertainments, especially Pipe Nights.

In White's reconstruction, the grill room had two end fireplaces, and a large bay window overlooking the porch and garden. At the east end was a serving bar, which may also have been used for drinks.

Over the huge fireplace in the main hall was the motto selected by Booth for the Club (of which, more later). He chose it and adapted it himself, insisting that White use lettering that could be read easily. There were mottoes, in fact, all over the house—in that age of mottoes—from men's room to bedroom. It is not clear whether White or someone else inspired them, particularly those in the men's room, whose two urinals are surmounted by a Shakespearean quotation, "Nature her custom holds, let shame say what she will," and a much later proletarian observation, "More haste, less speed."

Newspaper accounts of the Club called the furniture "unique," which may have been an understatement. There were several superb pieces and White may have designed some of them. Many others were gifts from original members.

On the second floor the library contained the collections that Booth, Palmer, and Daly had agreed to desposit there: a thousand of Booth's books, along with pictures and other theatrical relics; the playbill collections of Palmer and Daly; and with them Hutton's collection of death masks and manuscripts. As Brander Matthews described it three years later, "Above the shelves, where dust settles on their biographies and on the comedies and tragedies they acted, are portraits of the players of the past." Overlooking it all was a card admonishing "Silence." In the small room next door, now the library office, were a few comfortable chairs and a sofa; it was called the conversation room.

The third floor was reserved as living quarters for Booth. The Deed of Gift specified that he, his friends and his servants, would have lifetime use of that floor, although they were free to wander about the building as they chose. Barrett was Booth's guest there, living part of 1889 in the quarters now occupied by the business offices.

On the fourth floor were bedrooms occupied over the years by both the great and obscure. E. H. Sothern gave the Club a huge paneled bed, with testers and curtains, that lay in storage for years until a conscientious treasurer insisted it be brought into the Club and installed in one of the bedrooms. A member who had lingered too long at the bar was sheltered in this bed one night, but his protests next day over its claustrophobic wooden walls and thick curtains were so eloquent that the bed got a bad name in the Club and members refused to sleep in it until it was hauled away into storage again for the next forty years. Its subsequent fate is unknown.

There were no additions or changes inside until February 1889, when Booth and White discussed a private dining room on the second floor, and the new Club president told his architect, "If $2,000 will give you a suitable dining room, I would rather have it built at my expense than tax the members with any cost whatever. Figure the cost to its utmost limit and let me know as soon as possible." It was done, and White built what is now called the card room, with a bay window above the east end of the grill room. He added paneling and corner niches, one of which held a columnar steel radiator, the other a serving table.

It was remarkable that a house could be transformed in only seven months into so warm and inviting a place. As Professor Matthews observed, "The house appeared to be mellow from the very beginning," and thanks to Booth's generosity, it came into being "fully armed for the struggle for existence—not enfeebled by debts and deficiencies."

On the night of the formal opening, December 31st, 1888, the *New York World* reported: "A rapid procession of white-tied men, many without mustaches, were passing up the dainty white marble steps on which a menial with a scrubbing brush was in constant attendance for the purpose of keeping them, like the good reputation of those who were to walk on them, unspotted from the world."

Since that was written, more than 4,000 members of The Players have climbed those marble steps, a list that reads like a *Who's Who* of the arts in America, along with many others less well known who were nonetheless just as devoted to the Club that Edwin Booth founded. The Players, in fact, illuminated a New York neighborhood that, before and since, holds the richest cultural heritage in the city. Samuel J. Tilden lived next door in No. 15. Peter Cooper, William Steinway, and Cyrus Field were near neighbors. Hart Crane, Herman Melville, Henry James, Winslow Homer, and Edith Wharton lived in the environs of the Park. *The Pirates of Penzance* was completed there, and Crane finished his *Red Badge of Courage* in a shared room on Twenty-third Street, not far from where much later Nathanael West managed the Hotel Kenmore. On nearby Irving Place, O. Henry lived and drank at Healy's Cafe (now Pete's Tavern), while Ernest Boyd lived around the corner, and down the street Washington Irving resided in a house still standing. Teddy Roosevelt played in the park as a child, and so did John F. Kennedy.

Into this rich and graceful land of all the arts came the 143 original members of The Players on that historic New Year's Eve of 1888 to witness Booth's presentation of the Deed of Gift, a ceremony which has been celebrated in its essential details ever since. Of those gathered there that night, twenty-five were actors, "the worthy ones of my profession," as Booth called them. By far the largest group, 75, had no connection with the arts except as patrons—bankers, lawyers, physicians, government officials, merchants, capitalists. Eleven were theater managers, twenty-one represented literature and journalism, and eleven others were painters, architects, or sculptors.

At 11:40, as the New Year approached (the clock in the Great Hall was stopped at midnight), Booth stood in front of the fireplace mantel, under the portrait of his father, and spoke:

> Gentlemen: Although our vocations are various, I greet you all as brother Players. At this supreme moment of my life, it is my happy privilege to assume the character of host, to welcome you to the house wherein I hope that we for many years, and our legitimate successors for at least a thousand generations, may assemble for friendly intercourse and intellectual recreation. Especially for the worthy ones of my profession am I desirous that this association shall be the means of bringing them, regardless of their theatrical rank, in communion with those who, ignorant of their personal qualities hidden by the mask and motley of our calling, know them as actors only. Frequent intercourse with gentlemen of other arts and professions, who love the stage and appreciate the value of the drama as an aid to intellectual culture, must inspire the humblest player with a reverence for his vocation as one among the first of "fine arts"—which too many regard as merely a means to the gratification of vanity and selfishness. Such is the object of this club.
>
> For many years I have cherished the hope that I might be able to do something for my profession of a more lasting good than mere almsgiving, but could not determine what course to pursue. Our several benevolent institutions for the relief of poor and disabled actors . . . great as their good

work is, do not afford the social advantages so necessary for what is termed "the elevation of the stage."

Not until after many conversations with numerous friends of the theater on this subject, and while discussing it with Messrs. Barrett, Daly, and Palmer (a club of this character being suggested as the best means to the good end), did I resolve to act, to do my utmost in furtherance of the scheme proposed. This is the first step toward the accomplishment of our purpose. To our treasurer, Mr. William Bispham, we owe the wise selection of our house, to Mr. Stanford White its admirable reconstruction and embellishment, while to the poet Aldrich we are indebted for the choice of our appropriate and comprehensive title, the world being but a stage where man must "play his part." Mine just now, as the New Year dawns, is a very happy one, since it permits me to present to you by the hands of our vice-president, Mr. Daly, your title deed to this property.

Having done so, I am no longer your host. I resign the role with profound thanks for your prompt and generous cooperation in a cause so dear to me, so worthy of all well-wishers of the theater and of the Player who "struts and frets his hour upon the stage."

With that, Booth handed the Deed of Gift to Daly, although there was a slight moment of confusion when the Founder, in the emotion of the moment, caught himself giving a copy of his speech to Daly instead of the deed. Daly then gave a short speech of acceptance, saying in part: "Most nobly has our honored host followed out the instructions which, as Hamlet, he has uttered to Polonius a thousand and a thousand times himself—to 'see the players well disposed'; and truly has he used them 'after his own honor and dignity.' . . . I am not a speechmaker. Would that I were—that I might do justice to this exceptional occasion! That justice, however, will be done hereafter in the grateful recollection of every player on the world's broad stage who crosses this hospitable threshold, in which will be cherished the remembrance of Edwin Booth, while a stone stands one upon another to recall the loving companionship which actuated the giver of this noble gift."

Then Barrett read a letter from Edwina, asking him to crown her father with a wreath of laurel he held in his hand, and he did so, after which a poem written by T. W. Parsons, of Boston, was read.

With that, the solemn moment passed, and Booth said cheerfully, "Though somewhat past the season, let us now fire the Yule log sent from Boston by my daughter with the request that it be burned as her offering of love, peace, and good will to The Players. While it burns, let us drink from the loving cup bequeathed by William Warren of loved memory to our no less valued Jefferson, and by him to us. From this cup and this souvenir of long ago, my father's flagon, let us now, beneath his portrait, and on the anniversaries of the occasion hereafter, drink: To The Players' Perpetual Prosperity."

And so it was done, the cup passing from lip to lip of all those present, as it has on Founder's Night ever since. For the first time, flames leaped up brightly in the great fireplace, Booth muttering in an aside to Barrett that he had been a little worried whether the chimney would draw. The remainder of the night, as one of the newspapers observed, "was spent in conviviality."

The next day Booth wrote a letter for the first time on Club stationery. Naturally, it went to his beloved Edwina, and gives us a more human description of that scene Booth had played so well. He spoke of "last night's delightful success, the culmination of my professional hopes. . . . the success of everything—except my speech. I broke down toward the close, but it passed off with eclat . . . White, the architect, went into ecstasies and exclaimed 'even the log burned without smoking.' . . . The papers were full of it, but I've not yet had a chance to read them . . . Barrett and I got to bed about 5 a.m. . . . Since I rose at one, I've been busy packing my things to bring over here; we both concluded to pass the balance of the week 'at home' [they opened in Pittsburgh six days later]. . . . Judge Daly has just interrupted me, sends his love, and has ordered his lunch. Several of the best men in New York are here, and it will no doubt be a rendezvous of the choicest. Some are in the library reading. . . . It really seems as if we had been going for years instead of one day. . . . The walls are filled with pictures, mostly mine. My books make one section of the cases which soon will be entirely filled. Every day some gift comes; things come from strangers. . . . The list is ever full and we must go slowly now, lest we exclude the actors we want."

Daniel Frohman was the last survivor of that inaugural night, dying in 1941, but the reenactment of the ceremony year after year has insured that members will be reminded annually of the solemn undertaking Edwin Booth made then on behalf of his fellows in the arts, actors and others alike.

THE BOOTH ROOM. The chair John Barrymore used in *Hamlet* is on the left.

THE BOOTH ROOM, facing northwest.

EDWIN BOOTH'S CHAISE LONGUE in corner by window.

CARVED VASE *(opposite, top)* on window sill near chaise is inscribed "1888." Wooden box is inlaid with mother-of-pearl. SKULL OF YORICK *(opposite, below)*, reportedly used by Junius Brutus Booth and son Edwin in *Hamlet*. Pewter mug is inscribed "Players 1892."

BRONZE INCENSE BURNER, in shape of goose, is from Japan.

BOOTH'S COLLECTION OF PIPES *(opposite)* and other memorabilia.

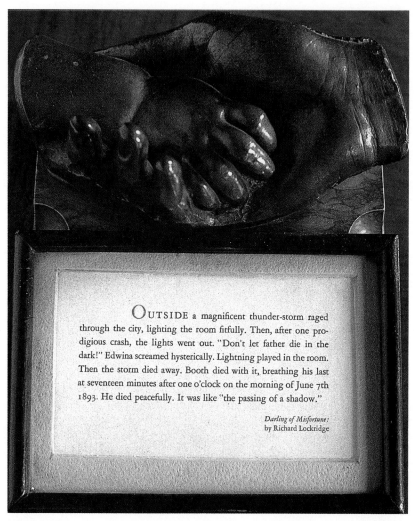

OUTSIDE a magnificent thunder-storm raged through the city, lighting the room fitfully. Then, after one prodigious crash, the lights went out. "Don't let father die in the dark!" Edwina screamed hysterically. Lightning played in the room. Then the storm died away. Booth died with it, breathing his last at seventeen minutes after one o'clock on the morning of June 7th 1893. He died peacefully. It was like "the passing of a shadow."

Darling of Misfortune:
by Richard Lockridge

BRONZE CAST OF BABY HAND of daughter Edwina, done in 1865, rests on table with framed account of Booth's death in the early morning hours of June 7, 1893. The account records the legend that just before the actor's death, the lights in the Club went out. "Don't let Father die in the dark!" Edwina is reported to have cried.

CHAPTER 2

Booth at the Club

AS THE CLUB BEGAN TO GROW AND TAKE SHAPE IN 1889, BOOTH hovered over it like the proverbial mother hen. Now that the dream had become reality, he wanted nothing that might hamper its future as he had conceived it. Watching the list of new candidates in the first few months, for example, he was disturbed by the lack of young recruits, and so he sought the help of Louis Aldrich, president of the New York branch of the Actors' Order of Friendship (Edwin Forrest had founded the parent lodge in Philadelphia, of which Booth himself was a member). "The club must have young actors," he wrote to Aldrich, "and I don't know them, but you, Louis, are in a position to reach them and choose the worthiest ones. Bring me fifty names of those you can vouch for and I'll pay their initiation fees and dues."

This plea for help was answered, and in the summer of 1889, seventy-seven actors were proposed. Club records do not show which successful candidates had their dues paid by Booth, but he must have been a little discouraged by the number of those who failed to qualify. According to the earliest candidate book (one of five issued in the first fifty years), only thirty-seven of the summer's crop of proposals, most of them by John Malone and Harry Edwards, were actually elected. Twenty-six were withdrawn and twenty-four failed to qualify after election. As a member observed later, it was much easier to get actors into the Club than to keep them there.

Even worse, a large number of members either resigned or were dropped (usually for nonpayment of dues) after a short time. These

23

defections were not confined to any single category. There are some distinguished names on the first year's list who either declined election or failed to qualify, among them William Dean Howells (Twain's friend); George Brush, the painter, and Charles Coghland, an admired actor of his time. Walter Damrosch and Maurice Barrymore were among those who withdrew their candidacies but were proposed and elected later. J. H. Stoddard was proposed twice and elected twice, while Joseph Wheelock, who had twice failed to qualify, was given a third chance.

In the written nominations recorded by the candidate books, the effort to be explicit produced some remarkable identifications: Grover Cleveland, lawyer; Peter Cooper Hewitt, manufacturer; and Lt. Com. Leonard Chenery, USN, mariner. Edmund C. Stedman, although he was an eminent scholar and poet, was proposed as a banker, which he also was. A variety of other occupations appeared, including jeweler, coal operator, auctioneer, and "milk business." Several were listed as having "no occupation," and two others were given as simply "gentleman." One book records the nomination and withdrawal of Rudyard Kipling. Owen Johnson, Jr., the novelist's infant son, was proposed, his occupation noted as "reserved."

Even without a proper quantity of young actors, The Players was not a collection of graybeards, as some have supposed. Booth was only 54, Jefferson and a few others were older, but most of the incoming members were much younger. Most were in their thirties and forties, including Stanford White and John Drew, 34; Saint-Gaudens, about 40; and Richard Watson Gilder, the Century's editor, 44. Several were in their late twenties, including Langdon Mitchell, Clyde Fitch, Oliver Herford, Richard Harding Davis, and Charles Dana Gibson.

While no effort was made to regulate it, the proportion of actors did not vary much from year to year, then or later. It was 17 percent at the beginning, 15 percent in mid-1889, and 18 percent a year later. By 1938 the figure had increased to 22 percent, and it has not varied significantly since then.

Meanwhile, the total membership increased satisfactorily, rising to 558 by the end of May 1890, reaching 673 a year later, 750 the following year, and in May 1893 the directors reported that all classes were full (they were limited at the beginning) and more than a hundred were on the waiting list. Membership in The Players has surpassed 1,000 in 1923, in 1928, and once or twice in modern times, but for the past twenty-five years or more it has never been much above or much below a thousand.

Booth's practical vision led him to seek out men of wealth who might become members and contribute their financial support as recruits to that often debated category, patron of the arts. To Booth, "patron" was the operative word, consequently it is not surprising to find names like J. P. Morgan and Cornelius Vanderbilt in the early lists. Many, if not most, of these rich patrons seldom appeared at the Club, but they paid their dues regularly for years and liked to think of themselves as belonging to it.

The board had decided at the beginning that a patron of the arts must be a gentleman who had won real distinction in a field outside the arts, and who was able to demonstrate an understanding of a club like The Players and express his sympathy with its nature. He would not have to be as famous as Morgan, it was agreed, but his achievements should be more than ordinarily worthy, and he must have a good character (which would have excluded Jay Gould) and possess an interesting mind. Some of the patrons admitted had much more interesting minds than others. The first board agreed that there should never be many patrons of the arts in the Club, probably no more than 75 at one time, but this view was considerably modified later.

Leading members of the Club were inclined to be a little defensive on this subject. Brander Matthews, for instance, writing in the *Century* for November 1891 about The Players, spoke eloquently of the young club's prestigious membership, especially its great names in the arts, but he appeared to minimize, intentionally, the category of patrons. "The mere outsider," he wrote, "admitted under an elastic definition of a patron or connoisseur of the arts is in a minority. . . . Of millionaires there are perhaps a sparse dozen on the rolls of the club, but it is a rarity to see one within the doors."

It was, in fact, as late as 1963 before the Club came to believe that it had reached and maintained a proper balance of actors, members of the allied arts, and patrons of the arts, although interpretations of the latter continued to arise from time to time.

In any case, as the Club concluded its first year, Booth could look about with satisfaction and feel that he had satisfactorily answered those who had looked on his Club's debut with some cynicism. The critic (Booth always called them "crickets") of the *Dramatic Mirror*, for instance, had written sourly just after the Club's opening: "Let's wait and see of what moral use it's going to be to the profession. The actors have been seeing as much of each other in the past as is good for 'em. They don't need any gilded halls and hammered brass grill rooms to make 'em acquainted or better their condition. And as for tiger skin rugs and tiled fireplaces making a man's soul bigger, or making a bum actor more of a gentleman, go to! Thou speakest rot!" Obviously, the gentleman from the *Dramatic Mirror* had completely missed the point of what was happening on Gramercy Park.

If he had been permitted inside the doors of No. 16 as a member—and that would have been impossible because critics were rigorously excluded until our own time, for obvious reasons—he would have found an atmosphere that would have eliminated any doubts, and companionship of a kind not found in any other New York club, except perhaps for the Century. There were some people who held memberships in both clubs, as is still the case.

Booth and his comrades at The Players lived by an unwritten code that went beyond the constitution and the bylaws. It was a code of freedom, as John Phillips once explained, that was modified only by "a sort of spiritual etiquette. . . . Our basic bill of rights parallels the legal code of King Fausole's realm, which had just two articles. 1. Harm no man. 2. Then do as you please. . . . In the earliest days of The Players, Stephen Olin said: 'In that house shall there be virtue, but there shall also be abundant cakes and ale.'"

The presence of Edwin Booth was everywhere, visible and invisible. It was, of course, his home for the remaining five years he lived. On the third floor, which he shared with Barrett when his old colleague was in town, he found some of the peace and happiness which had so long eluded him. He loved sitting in his bedroom overlooking the park, reading. On summer nights he liked to have supper on the porch in back, then come up to his room and lie on the sofa by an open window, listening to the night sounds below. He slept badly and sometimes sat looking out into the park all night. He called those his "vulture hours." A well-meaning friend asked him why he didn't travel, and Booth answered, "I've been traveling all my life. What I want now is to stay in one place with things I like around me. . . . Here is my bed, and here is the fire, and here are my books. . . . I suppose I shall wear out here."

In the Club, however, he still could not escape his fame, even if he wanted to. His image looked down from every wall in the place, in every kind of artistic translation, and when someone offered to present the Club with still another portrait of him, he could only protest: "Please don't. Even now I can't go anywhere in the house without bumping into a Booth."

He was very much a part of club life. Booth always sat with other members in the grill, and dined with them. As Augustin Daly remembered, he presided at the monthly meetings "and enjoyed having to be constantly prompted in parliamentary rules, and after innumerable repetitions, his fun was to have never quite got the hang of it."

Although he presided as president, Booth did not intend to weigh himself down with details. Far more than the board meetings, he enjoyed the supper given in the private dining room after each one. Once, when

Laurence Hutton had been absent from one of these sessions, he saw Booth next day and asked him, "What sort of meeting did you have?"

"Oh," Booth said, "the supper was cold, but the champagne was warm."

That was typical of Booth's casual approach to life outside the theater. As Guy Nichols remembered, "He cared nothing for dress. When I knew him, his wife used to buy his clothes, also his neckties. . . . He never had a valet. . . . When he occasionally wanted help in dressing here in the Club, he would send down for one of the boys. On one occasion he had lost his collar button and sent for Walter [Oettel, of whom much more later], who found it; and when Walter looked askance at the very ragged neckband of a somewhat dilapidated shirt, Mr. Booth smiled and said, 'Oh, that's all right.'

"He was the kind of man who liked old clothes and old clothes liked him. He liked old friends, too, and old times and old places. I never saw him dressed up but once. The last time I met him he was coming out of the Garfield Bank on 23rd Street. He wore a gray frock suit and a silk hat, and I couldn't help thinking how much better he looked in his old and somewhat shabby smoking jacket."

Those who did not know him as well, and were awed by his fame, were inclined to treat him with more deference than he wanted. When some members were singing and creating general noisy merriment at the bar one night, a member of the House Committee who happened by was horrified and stopped them. Mr. Booth had gone to bed, he explained, and must not be disturbed. But next day, when Booth saw a friend in the Club, he remarked, "The boys were singing last night. Why did they stop?"

"The house committee thought it would annoy you," the friend said.

"Annoy me!" Booth exclaimed. "Good Lord, I had opened my door to listen; now it seems like a club, said I."

In fact, Booth liked music of an unspectacular kind. His favorites were Stephen Foster's songs, particularly "Beautiful Dreamer." He told a friend it always consoled him because it reminded him of the happiness he had known with Mary Devlin.

Stories of his generosity (filtering down from the recipients, never from him of course) further endeared him to everyone, if that were possible. Barrett left the Club to find larger quarters in the old Windsor Hotel and died there soon after, leaving his affairs in chaotic shape. All the contracts for that last season had been made out in his name, with the usual two weeks' notice clause, and Booth came out of his retirement long enough to play the two weeks, his last appearances on the stage, saving the money for Barrett's estate.

One day Booth invited to the Club for luncheon a man with whom he had business dealings, and who now owed him nearly $13,000. After they had gone back up to Booth's room and sat, smoking and chatting, the host suddenly rose, went to his desk, took out the notes, tore them up and threw them in the fire, remarking, "I don't want to leave these behind me."

Stories about him circulated among the members. Arthur Byron, an actor friend, recalled years later the day he visited the Club to have lunch with the great man, and was talking with other friends on the couch facing the stairway when Booth appeared.

"Well, young man," he said, greeting Byron, "how are you getting on in your chosen profession?"

"I'm struggling along," Byron said.

"And I suppose when you're not hard at work in the theater, you're practicing fencing and dancing and studying Hamlet's soliloquy, or the Seven Ages," Booth pursued, smiling.

"I'm sorry, but I'm afraid I don't," Byron admitted.

Booth's smile broadened, "That's very interesting," he said. "When your father and I were your age, we didn't either."

His guest was inclined to doubt it.

Booth entertained a wide variety of guests at the Club, both members and nonmembers. They were often astonished by the breadth of his knowledge beyond the theater—exactly what he hoped to instill in his fellow actors. Having tea one day with Bishop Henry Codman Potter (who later became a member), he fell into a friendly dispute with this amiable prelate about a passage in First Corinthians, Chapter XIII, the bishop claiming he knew the exact phrasing. A Bible was called for, but a diligent search disclosed there was none in the Club, and Booth sent Walter Oettel out to find one. Walter, always resourceful, hurried to his own house, a block away, and brought back his own copy, open at the proper place. Booth, it turned out, had been right.

"Think of that," the Bishop marveled, "The actor knows the Bible better than the bishop does."

It is reasonable to assume that Booth knew this part of the Bible better than other chapters because of its familiar passage, "but when I became a man I put away childish things." Booth had been forced to put away childhood at a very early age. But he was also fond of the phrase, "for now we see through a glass darkly," and the thirteenth verse was another favorite, with its admonition, "and now abideth faith, hope, and charity, but the greatest of these is charity." No one could have exemplified that teaching more than Booth.

His first charity was the Club itself, wherever help was needed. Having served a full-course dinner for fifty cents from the beginning, the dining room found itself pinched in 1891, and the house committee told Booth they were losing money on the table d'hote, and believed the price would have to be raised.

"No, don't do that," Booth protested. "Give me the amount of the loss and I'll pay it. We mustn't raise the rate."

Booth's own eating habits were sometimes unusual. When he did not have breakfast in his room, he came down and sat at the small righthand corner table near the entrance to the grill room, which was always reserved for him, just as the table opposite the entrance was his for lunch and dinner. His appetite in these last years was small, and he could not eat all the things he ordered, but he ordered them anyway because, as he said, he wanted to encourage the kitchen staff, and in any case it helped boost the Club's receipts.

People both in and out of the Club constantly sought Booth's autograph. Walter Oettel was once asked by an employee to speak to the Founder for one on his behalf, and a few minutes later, Booth came downstairs and sat down at the writing table in the reception hall, near the foot of the stairs. Before Walter could present the employee's request Booth asked for a telegraph blank and wrote on it a message for Edwina. It didn't suit him, however, and he crumpled the paper in his hand and threw it in the wastebasket, immediately writing another one which Walter sent off.

The devoted Oettel was somehow reluctant to petition Booth on the employee's behalf, but he asked the man to empty the basket, giving him the opportunity to retrieve the crumpled paper with the coveted signature on it. Two weeks later, walking by a Third Avenue curio shop, Walter saw the telegram in the window, along with other celebrated autographs, for sale. The employee confessed that he had been pressed for money and sold it for $2. It was the kind of sacriligious act Walter could never forgive.

His devotion was equaled, if not surpassed, by Booth's old friends, who treated his presence in the Club with something approaching religious awe. When a workman appeared at the bar one day to improve its surface, he had the misfortune to arrive moments after Booth had rested his arm and hand on it while he enjoyed a drink of some kind before he departed upstairs, something he rarely did (he never drank spirits). As the carpenter began to apply his plane, an outraged member stopped him. "Don't you dare touch the place where that great man's hand has rested," he shouted. The carpenter retreated in confusion.

In these last years Booth began to change greatly. In 1893 he was only 59, but already he seemed an old man. His hair had turned white, he used a heavy cane, and when he walked it was slowly, with caution. He was suffering recurring attacks of vertigo, which had struck him first during his last tour. He had rheumatism in his right arm; it had been broken several times and he could not lift it higher than his chest. In his last appearance in Rochester he had suffered a slight stroke after his first vertigo attack. More and more he stayed in his room, going out only for his usual walk around the park, circuits that became slower and slower. No one wanted to think about it, but clearly he was dying.

All his life he had lived with visions and premonitions. While he was not a confessed spiritualist, like Joe Jefferson, he had experienced premonitions before. In a letter to a friend he wrote: "Two nights before Mrs. Booth's death in 1863, she came to me in New York, she being at that time in Dorchester, Mass. I heard her distinctly say, 'Come to me, my darling, I am almost frozen.' And when I was speeding to her on the train, not dreaming that she was seriously ill, each time I looked from the car window I saw Mrs. Booth dead, with a white cloth around her head and chin. I arrived in Dorchester to find her in her coffin."

On Founder's Night in 1892, his last, at which Grover Cleveland gave the address, Booth turned to his friend Jefferson and said in a low voice, "You drink tonight to my health, Joe. A year from tonight you will drink to my memory." Jefferson protested, but Booth gave him a sad smile, shaking his head.

He had been moved a few moments earlier by Cleveland's brief remarks:

This is one of the occasions which remind me that the best things in life are not found in struggle and turmoil, not in the sad pursuit of a favorite phantom. It is most fortunate that we are not allowed to forget that without a [word missing] of mind and body there is something within our reach more valuable, more satisfying, more ennobling, than all that wealth, or social distinction, or political honor, or even professional success can give us.

I speak of the continuation of disinterested friendships and the enjoyment of sincere relations, which cost nothing but loyalty to the best instincts of our nature and watchfulness against their persuasion.

At this hour, which ushers in a day of congratulations and kindly greetings, we have met to enjoy the friendliness and companionship which our organization so happily promotes. We have met too in the observance of a custom particularly our own, which touches our hearts with a lively sense of gratitude, thus adding to our pleasure. Above all, we rejoice that the opportunity is here and now afforded us to express our love and admiration for our Founder, whose name is a sacred word within these walls, and of whose fame, we, as his brothers and associates and his beneficiaries, are doubly proud.

You honor us all, Mr. Booth, and you know how affectionately and heartily we wish you a "Happy New Year."

As Cleveland's words died and were lost in the fervent chorus of acclaim that followed, Booth turned away, his eyes wet. He knew that it would be the last time he could expect to hear those greetings, or drink from the cup.

After the ceremony he walked over to his old friend, Charles Walcott, and said he wanted to retire. With Walcott supporting his left arm and Cleveland on his right, he walked to the elevator. With his fine sense of theater, he turned and waved to the assembled members who were watching him. "With all the suffering there was a smile," Timothy Frawley, who was there, wrote forty years later, "and we all felt the fear behind that smile—for he knew it was his good-bye to us."

There were a few moments remaining. With or without the nurse's consent, he made a brief excursion to the front room fireplace on Saturday nights, after the theater crowd had returned to the Club, and there he passed a few happy times with such friends as Nat Goodwin, John Drew, Henry Dixey, Otis Skinner, Maurice Barrymore, and Wilton Lackey.

But soon he had to be confined to his bed, and as Walter remembered, the laughter was over; only the smile remained. His last good times came when Edwina brought the grandchildren to see him. As he lay dying, a deep hush appeared to fall on the Club. His doctor, St. Clair Smith, issued bulletins from time to time and they were posted on the board near the Club's entrance, where the small black-bordered obituary cards now appear, with their Hamlet quotation, "The rest is silence." The death watch of reporters from the city's newspapers had already gathered to read the bulletins.

In the early morning of June 7, 1893, the end came at last. Earlier that night he had been reading a volume of verse by his old friend, William Winter—a dear friend even though he was a "cricket." He put the book down and looked about the room, where the memories of his life were scattered. Family portraits hung on the walls: Junius Brutus, his father; Mary Devlin (he had carried that picture of her on his tours); Edwina, of course; and even brother Johnny, whose picture hung beside his bed. There was no fire in the black marble fireplace, with its coal-burning Franklin stove, brought from his Chestnut Street home in Boston.

After the room was refurbished in 1958 (it had been allowed to sink into dust and decay) other artifacts were added, and it is not known how many of them were there the night Booth died. No one, for example, knows exactly why Charlotte Cushman's shawl is draped across the chaise lounge, or how the actress's rustic staff, which she carried in *Guy Manner-*

ing, happens to be standing in a corner. Nor are the *two* skulls which lay on the bookcase for years explained; there is only one now. Most Players who show off the room believe they were Booth's Hamlet skulls, but no proof exists. The table in the center beneath the chandelier bears Edwina's bronze-cast baby hand resting in her father's, done in 1865. Booth's humidor lies there too. His slippers, with their upturned Turkish toes, lie beside the bed, and one of his leather vests hangs on a chair. For years, a night cloakroom attendant at The Players, when asked for the key to the Booth room by a member wanting to show it, always admonished, with a smile, "Don't wake up Mr. Booth," and so it has always seemed.

That was the setting for Booth's last scene, and like so much of his life it was played with a drama which has become Club legend. Like all legends, it has its variations, and more recently has acquired at least one skeptic. Everyone agrees that the night was troubled, and about midnight or a little later, a fierce thunderstorm broke over Gramercy Park. A few members had gathered beside the great fireplace, talking somberly in low tones, waiting for word from upstairs. One of them was Edward Simmons, Emerson's distinguished first cousin. With him was George Buchanan Fife, of the *New York World.* The other reporters on the death watch were sitting in the park across the street, sending one of their number over periodically to ask for news.

As Simmons and Fife talked in the shadowy room, all the lights in the house suddenly went out. Percy Mackaye described, half a century later, what followed: "In the abrupt dark, both were too startled to speak. The silence tingled. From far up, through the stairway space, they felt a faint sound, as of a door gently shutting. Slowly then—while their hearts knocked at their ribs—occasionally they heard a muffled creak, as of descending footsteps, that paused at each landing. Listening, they hardly breathed, till—as sudden as the dark—all at once the lights leapt again into glare. Where their eyes were focused on the last landing, there stood a tall figure in black—the form of Walter. Quietly, scarcely audible, he said 'Gentlemen, Mr. Booth has just died.' Upstairs the stopped clock registered—and still registers—1:17 a.m."

Or was it 1 a.m., as other witnesses said? Particularly Charlie Connelly, second only to Walter in the chronicle of devoted employees, who became an honorary Player himself. Charlie, who was not there, wrote long after that the lights went out at 1 a.m., and remained out for five minutes. His story was confirmed by Dennis O'Brien, who was a 14-year-old page boy that night and remembered it all in 1954, when he was 75.

Three years later, however, in 1957, a skeptic appeared who cast considerable doubt on this favorite legend of all Players. Samuel Hopkins Adams had read Charlie's story about Dennis O'Brien's account of the dreadful night, noting that Dennis was presented as the only surviving person who had been there. Not so, said Sam; he was there too, as a reporter on the death watch, representing the *Sun,* and sitting with the others in the Park. He recalled that, beginning about 11 o'clock, they had been sending a reporter over to the Club from time to time to ask if there was any change. A few minutes after one, he recalled, a member opened the door and told them, "Mr. Booth is dead."

Did the lights go out in a tremendous flash of lightning and thunder as Booth died? Sam begged leave to doubt it. If that had happened, he said, the assembled reporters would certainly have noticed it, since they had their eyes constantly on No. 16. Nor was this alleged phenomenon mentioned in any of the fifteen dailies published in New York at the time. And there was still another doubt. Booth's room had both gas and electric light. Even if the storm had caused a power failure, the gas lights would have been on. His chandelier had six electric sockets, and the same number of gas jets, with glass bells.

It was all beside the point at the time. The hard fact was that Edwin Booth had died, and for days No. 16 lay dim and silent. The life had gone out of it.

After the funeral his body was taken for burial to Mt. Auburn Cemetery, in Cambridge, Massachusetts. He was buried beneath a comparatively simple monolith, standing on a hill and forming a natural stage. On one side of the memorial stone is an inset bas-relief head of Booth, in bronze, showing him as he appeared in his last years. Beneath it are words from the thirty-first chapter of Jeremiah: "For I will turn their mourning into joy, and will comfort them and make them rejoice from their sorrow."

On the stone itself are chiseled the Club's masks, of comedy and tragedy, and below it are lines from *Much Ado About Nothing,* chosen by Edwina and several of Booth's friends. They come from the longest of the Friar's speeches in the fourth act's first scene, where he has his say after Claudio has been tricked into renouncing the innocent Hero at the marriage altar. In these lines, the Friar predicts the state of Claudio's mind if he is compelled to believe that disgrace has killed Hero. The mourners made a slight alteration in the passage, substituting "thy," "my," and "thou" for "her," "his," and "she," so that the lines read:

The idea of thy life shall sweetly creep
Into my study of imagination;
And every lovely organ of thy life
Shall come apparelled in more precious habit,
More moving delicate and full of life,
Into the eye and prospect of my soul,

Than when thou liv'st indeed.

One other poem was written to commemorate Edwin Booth, read on
his 104th birthday, November 13, 1937. It was written by a poet Player,
Edgar Lee Masters, and it read:

These more than forty years since he whose bronze
Stands in Gramercy Park, while seasons range,
Passed to his sleep, but not oblivion's
Forgetfulness, have we despite all change,
We of The Players come to lay a wreath
Upon this pedestal, and speak our praise
Of Edwin Booth, whom neither time nor death,
Nor fashion, nor the moods of lesser days
Have taken from our hearts. Once as a youth
I heard his voice, I saw his eye which cast
A searching light on Brutus. I heard Booth
Enunciate, "Be patient till the last."
Why lives he in our loves while years depart?
It was his gentleness, his matchless art.

CHAPTER 3

Early Days and Early Players

AS THE PLAYERS BEGAN A RENEWED LIFE AFTER THE SHOCK OF BOOTH'S death had passed, it was clear that the directors would have to play a dominant role in the Club's further progress. The new president, Joe Jefferson, was highly popular with the members, a superb storyteller who loved to sit and spin tales at early versions of the Round Table during his off hours. But he suffered from the same problem that beset John Drew later, Walter Hampden in his time, and every other president to some degree. The demands of his profession required him to be out of town frequently, particularly since he was one of the most sought after actors on the American stage, consequently the time he could spare for the Club's affairs was limited.

The board was ready and able to take up the slack and they confronted a major problem at once. It was plain that Stanford White's design for the Club, which had seemed more than satisfactory at the beginning, was not adequate for a growing membership and the social life it generated.

The Club could afford charges. There was a balance of $21,000 in the treasury that year and financial conditions were improving rapidly. By the end of the following year there was a total of nearly $175,000 in the Club's accounts, with outstanding debts amounting to less than $50.

Consequently, board meetings were held in an atmosphere of general satisfaction and conviviality. There was no problem in obtaining a quorum. In addition to the little suppers that followed meetings, so much enjoyed by Booth, drinks were on the house. Conviviality was not unlimited, however. A few early arrivals at one meeting inquired, "What can we have for drinks?" and were told by a member of the house committee, "Anything you wish." "In that case we'll have champagne," the early birds agreed. It was served, but a line was drawn thereafter.

Demands for more space were heard soon after the turn of the century. One day Bishop Henry Codman Potter invited forty-five of his fellow prelates to the Club for luncheon, and it was discovered that there was not enough space in the private dining room. Since guests could not be admitted to the grill room without a card of admission, and it would not be possible for the Bishop to obtain forty-five cards in his name, a crisis arose. It was solved by a special meeting of the board, suspending the rules for one meal and shifting the luncheon to the grill room—the only body of high churchmen ever seen there. This and other incidents led to further alterations in 1904 and 1906, designed by McKim, Mead and White. A bay window was added to the dining room at the back, as noted earlier, and the covered porch was extended around three sides of the rear yard, leaving a tree growing through the deck in one spot.

The board could now turn its attention to other matters but they were of much less moment, judging by early records. On July 11, 1911, for example, a letter from Harrison Blake Hodges, Club secretary, to President John Drew was read to the meeting: "I have informed you by telegram, which you have acknowledged, of the successful visit of Madame Bernhardt to The Players. The expenses in connection with this were trifling, $17.80, but the board felt that under the constitution it could not defray these expenses which it had authorized acting for you in your capacity as host of Madame Bernhardt. However, the board as individuals, desired to meet this expense and the house committee was instructed to levy a $2 charge against each of the nine directors and have the same put in their bills."

This was truly Boothian generosity. Having recorded it, the board went on briskly to something more serious. It moved that a member named Harold Binney be summoned to answer disorderly conduct charges for firing a revolver several times out of a Club window. The minutes do not explain what drove Binney to this extraordinary action. He was expelled, of course, but at a subsequent meeting the Board reconsidered its action and, as an act of extreme mercy, permitted him to resign.

At an earlier meeting that year, on May 15, a new cause for concern was discussed. Another member, Richard Barry, had written what was termed a libelous article for *Pearson's Magazine,* making derogatory statements about members of the theatrical profession, and the board had given him thirty days notice to answer the charge at this May meeting. Barry chose not to appear, but sent a letter denying the board's authority to take any action, pointing out that he had not mentioned The Players by name, nor intended his remarks to apply to members. However, sixteen of those members had written letters asking that he be dismissed, and the board expelled him. His lawyer then subpoenaed the board to appear in State Supreme Court to answer a demand for his reinstatement. This became a momentary *cause célèbre,* since its outcome could affect other clubs as well, but the court upheld the board.

The early records of board meetings disclose an occasional incident at the Club somewhat remote from the spirit of fraternal love Booth had hoped to establish there. At the meeting of July 17, 1902, for example, a letter from an outraged member was read, reporting "a most unprovoked and thoroughly unjustified insult placed on the writer last night by a member of this club, before four others on the piazza dining room of the club. The circumstances are as follows . . ." And he explained them, using "Mr.———" for all those involved, but promising to supply names on request.

It appeared that just before midnight on a July night the writer had arrived at the Club and asked the page boy at the door "what gentlemen were in the house." Informed that one present was a man he had not seen for more than six months, he hastened to find him. His friend was on the piazza, in company with three other men, with one of whom the late arrival had recently had "a slight misunderstanding" when both were members of the Henrietta Crosman Company. The "plaintiff" (so to call him, in making sense of this welter of anonymity) greeted everyone but the "enemy" (again, for convenient shorthand). His friend, noting the omission, said to the enemy, "Oh, don't you know Mr. Plaintiff?" To which the enemy replied, "No, and I don't want to know him," to which the plaintiff responded feistily, "Same to you and many of 'em!"

Still trying to smooth things over, the friend proposed a drink and the plaintiff accepted, but when the proposer made the same offer to the enemy, this offender rose from the table, and as he passed the plaintiff on the way out, said, "No, thank you. I don't want to drink with this ——— ———." The plaintiff's eloquent blanks in his letter left no doubt. He added that the enemy had applied "vile epithets" and "made derogatory remarks" to and about him at the Club when he was not there. "I have no other alternative but to put it before the directors with a respectful demand for an investigation and the necessary protection from such insults from the member in question."

Unfortunately, the records do not disclose how this affair ended. It would have been instructive to know how the board treated this gross violation of the Booth spirit, particularly since it was so uncharacteristic of life at the Club in these early days—or later. The place was buzzing, as the new century began, with all kinds of efforts that were exactly what Booth had had in mind.

Not all of these were successful. In February 1900, H. H. Macdowell gave a dinner at the Club for a selected group of other members to organize The Society of Arts and Letters, whose primary aim was to give every new play a tryout in New York before a chosen audience. This would give the producers a chance to see what its prospects might be, and how it could be improved. As a test site, the Society obtained Proctor's Twenty-Third Street Theater. No one now recalls what the name of the first play was, but it is recorded that Eugene Presbrey, one of seventy-three Players who belonged to the Society, was stage director. He had a splendid idea which proved to be a mistake. Walter Oettel was persuaded, reluctantly, to appear on stage in one scene. He had no lines. All he was required to do was to walk on, take orders from people at tables in a restaurant scene, serve them, and retire.

But when Walter walked on stage for the first and last time in his life, a large contingent of Players in the audience recognized him at once and a wave of laughter swept the house. Walter's stage career was as short-lived as the Society's.

As the Club's major domo, Walter did not record this appearance as one of the red letter events in Club history, set down in his memoirs. Far more important, he believed, was the Club's participation in the Actors' Fund Fair at the Metropolitan Opera in May 1907, a resounding success largely through the efforts of The Players. Another red letter day, Walter noted, was the enfranchisement of all actor members in 1908, meaning that nonresident actor members were given the same status as those who lived in the city.

There was even one clandestine activity at the Club. In what was then known as the Booth Library—the front room on the second floor, now the Library's office—a small group met during the first three months of 1913. A plaque celebrates what they did: "In this room . . . there met without permission the small committee of four or five which ultimately led to the formation of the Actors' Equity Association."

More commonplace, and permitted, events were taking place in these first years of the new century. Dues were raised for the first time in 1904, to meet rising costs. They were lifted from $40 to $50 for residents, and from $20 to $25 for nonresidents, creating an additional $7,000 in revenue. When something needed doing, however, and the board was unwilling or unable to do it, members simply subscribed whatever funds were required. That was how in 1904 several members were able to get the veranda (as the piazza came to be called) enclosed and heated so it could be used all year.

Most of 1910, in fact, was devoted to repairs and improvements. A new mosaic floor was laid in the entrance hall, and carpeting appeared on the stairs leading up to it, as well as in the main hall itself, while the reading room was also thoroughly repaired and recovered. New water pipes assured the Club an abundance of hot water from top to bottom, and the directors laid out money for an electric vacuum cleaner. There was a new range in the kitchen, additional washtubs in the laundry, and more letter boxes in the pool room. Total cost, $1,394.

For a Club whose Pipe Nights became celebrated, it is odd to note that no provision was made for a smoking room at the beginning, and in fact pipe smoking was not permitted except in the billiard room until 1908, when eleven members petitioned the house committee to permit it above the lowest floor. The petition was granted for the main hall, or alternately the reception room, but gradually pipes invaded the reading room, the writing room, the library, and at last the dining room. Booth himself, pipe-smoking members recalled, was one of their number, indulging himself at intermissions, where fire laws were less stringent, and in his own rooms at the Club. He scrupulously avoided lighting up anywhere else in the building. The bars were not lowered in his time.

Except for this restriction, however, life at the Club was unconfined, particularly where eating and drinking were concerned. Scenes of gastronomy and oenophilia were enacted there in those early years that were never to be repeated, as the Club changed with the times, and with the city itself.

It was a time when gastronomy, at least among the more affluent, made New York the nation's capital for good food and good wine. It was the time of Delmonico's, the great Supper on Horseback, the magnificent hotel dining rooms, and the feats of such celebrated gourmands as Diamond Jim Brady. At the Club there was constant feasting around the clock and beyond, since the day began with breakfast in the dining room and ended during the small hours at night only when all latecomers were fed.

On such holidays as Washington's birthday, Easter, Fourth of July, Thanksgiving and Christmas, the Club offered a staggering dinner menu for fifty cents: oysters, soup, entree, roast, vegetables, salad, cheese, dessert, and coffee. When regular table d'hote meals were instituted, prices were still unbelievably low. At breakfast, for thirty-five cents, members could begin the day with fruit, cereal, choice of eggs, fish, or a light meat, with tea or coffee and rolls. The price of luncheon was thirty-five cents, and included fish or eggs, a meat course with two vegetables, a dessert of pie, pudding, or cheese and jam, with milk, tea or coffee. For fifty cents at dinner, members could dine on soup, fish, roast, two vegetables, salad, cheese and crackers, dessert, and coffee.

With such food available it was hardly surprising that special social gatherings began, using the kitchen as a centerpiece. The first of these, early in the century, was the Saturday luncheon, which soon became highly popular. Where else in New York could an ordinary member go for lunch and find himself in the company of such men as Joseph Jefferson, Maurice Barrymore, Thomas Bailey Aldrich, Richard Watson Gilder, Thomas Nast, Mark Twain, Richard Harding Davis, John Drew, and Brander Matthews? A namedropper's paradise.

But then the theaters so central to the Club began to move uptown, and the luncheons were succeeded by Saturday night suppers. These proved to be even more popular. They ushered in the "Time of the Chafing Dish." Such dishes appeared on every table in the grill room after theater hours, and there members who were proud of their cooking skills presided over small, impromptu parties. It was permitted, and customary, for arriving Players to attach themselves to whatever chef they most admired. Stanford White, for instance, operated one of the most popular chafing dishes; his specialty was a rarebit to which oysters were added.

The Club's treasurer, Jack Stowe, a character straight out of Dickens, constantly asserted his superiority at the chafing dish. He was known as "Stringy," because that was how he characterized every rarebit he hadn't made. Players would not forget the night he passed a full plate of his best rarebit to a waiter, asking that it be taken to a friend at another table. But as the waiter began to bear it away, Stowe moved his chair to get up—too soon, grazing the waiter's elbow just enough to topple the whole concoction onto himself, while the room burst into applause.

Even into the late hours other goodies poured out of the kitchen to satisfy the hunger of those who wanted something more substantial than chafing dish concoctions. Large quantities of buckwheat cakes and sausages were consumed, and always there was a demand for Gramercy Stew. This quintessential Players concoction was born of a request to the chef to invent something that would be typical of Players' appetites. The success of the dish he produced was both instantaneous and lasting. It was made from two pounds of cold lamb and beef, flour, stock, two carrots, two turnips, four onions, two stalks of celery, salt, pepper, bay leaves, mushroom catsup, and chili pepper. At the last moment two dozen oysters were added.

An out-of-town guest was so enchanted with Gramercy Stew that he ordered it next night at his hotel, not knowing its origins, and supposing it was a New York staple. The hotel chef had never heard of it, quite naturally, and came out of the kitchen to inquire where this strange dish had been discovered. Informed of its birthplace, he sent a minion over to the Club to get the recipe.

It should be noted that Gramercy Stew, and all the other dishes, were washed down principally with ale on draught, and on those Saturday nights when the chafing dish was supreme, every mug in the Grill Room was in constant use. But in time the chafing dish turned out to be more of a fad than an institution, attendance began to dwindle, and it was into this vacuum that Pipe Nights were born, sometime during 1905.

No one presided at these first events, which would soon become one of the most cherished of Player institutions. Churchwarden pipes and tobacco were distributed, and a keg of free beer was provided. Members sat at tables, telling stories and sometimes singing. An individual member might rise and tell a story or sing a song for everyone's benefit. There were always popular songs—"Good-bye Dolly Gray," "When I Fit for General Grant," and "Everybody Drinks in Our House," among others. There were popular entertainers, too, among them De Wolf Hopper, Raymond Hitchcock, and David Bispham.

The Pipe Night grew to be so popular that at last a chairman was appointed for each occasion. Theodore Steinway loaned a piano to the Club to aid the singers and an attempt was made at organization. The Pipe Nights sputtered along intermittently for nearly a decade, and died away briefly during the First World War. They were not revived until 1922 when the entertainment committee reinstated them as Sunday night dinners, with guest speakers and other entertainers, within and without the Club membership.

There were other attempts to bring congenial spirits together in the early days. In 1908 invitations to a Sunday morning breakfast were sent out to about twenty-five or thirty members by Charles H. Genung and F. B. Opper. The occasion was such a success that others followed, with the numbers held to about the same figure. Those invited expressed their pleasure a year later by giving a special breakfast for the original sponsors of the idea. But it, too, was a custom that faded with time. Only the Pipe Night survived these early experiments in conviviality, along with Ladies' Day, which began almost as soon as the Club itself, and whose history will be related in later pages.

There were always, of course, dinners in the private dining room, where such distinguished visitors as Sir J. Forbes-Robertson, Henry Van Dyke, Harry Lauder, and Lord Northcliffe were entertained. In 1911 Isaac Marcosson gave a dinner there for Frank Hitchcock, then Postmaster General of the United States. Ike arranged for a miniature airplane, with a mailbag suspended from it, to be floated over the table. Later, a guest deep in his liquor boldly predicted that airmail delivery might be expected no later than the middle of the twentieth century. His prediction was greeted with expressions of sympathy for his condition.

Not all Players were confined to the Club for their relaxation. While pool remained the great indoor sport, with its own lore and traditions (as we shall see), golf was a preoccupation with some members, who held handicap tournaments for six consecutive summers between 1911 and 1916. The prevailing mode was match play at eighteen holes. Grantland Rice, the dean of all sports writers, was among the winners.

There appeared to be only one problem with the tournaments. Players were likely to be so involved in their professional activities, whether on the stage or elsewhere, that they often had to cancel appearances. Only five out of nineteen matches on the average were ever played. Henry Hering was considered to be the Club's best player. He won two of the six tournaments, and was a finalist in two or three more. The contestants were drawn by lot and handicapped by their golf club ratings, if they had any, and if not, by what was trustfully accepted as truthful confession. Pairs played wherever they liked, and posted the results on the score sheet at the Club.

There were attempts to install chess as a Club sport, but it could not compete with pool, and later on with bridge. The last chess tournament was in 1917, won by John Philip Sousa, but in the continuing competitions, Gelett Burgess proved to be the cup winner. Poker was considered the black sheep of games, banished from the Club as a possible breeder of trouble. There were those devotees, however, particularly Franklin P. Adams, who regularly migrated to the Algonquin and elsewhere for games. As for bridge, it began as bridge whist, and moved with the times to auction and contract, played in what had been the private dining room.

There may have been Club baseball players in these early times, but no record of them exists, and indeed only one Players' baseball story is extant. It concerns a British visitor to the Club, Alfred Noyes, who expressed during lunch with Walter Hampden, then president, a desire to see a baseball game—as exotic to him as cricket is to Americans. Hampden and Clayton Hamilton obliged, seating their guest in a box seat behind third base and trying to explain the game as it went along. Noyes was fascinated but baffled. He was especially concerned by the activities of the third-base coach, who was trying to distract the pitcher. "I say!" Noyes exclaimed, "That's derision, isn't it?"

In the Club, if the benevolent shade of Booth happened to be peering down from the stairs, as Don Marquis imagined in his poem, the spectacle of life in those rooms could only have delighted him. The Players appeared to be working out much as he had dreamed. Ideas for plays, illustrations, poems, novels, sculpture, and all the other arts flourished in the atmosphere that had been created. Sitting together at lunch on the back porch, Henry Bacon and Charles Platt conceived the basic design for the Lincoln Memorial in Washington, which Bacon executed. Similarly, the Freer Art Gallery was born there, and the Adams Memorial in Washington's Rock Creek Cemetery. The latter emerged from the daily conversations at the Round Table, where Stanford White, who designed the pedestal, and Saint-Gaudens, who executed the sculpture, first discussed Henry Adams's orginal conception of the work.

These projects did not emerge from business meetings, forbidden in any case by house rules, but from the ideas generated by creative minds in the intimate, relaxed atmosphere of the Club. And there appeared to be no end to these minds. When the famous group calling themselves Ten American Painters first exhibited at the Montross Gallery in 1898, nine of them were Players.

A new member could not help but be awed at first by the atmosphere of the Club. Clayton Hamilton, the Columbia scholar, remembered years later how overwhelmed he was by his first dinner at the Club as a member. Arriving at six o'clock he found the dining room nearly empty, since the actors, who made up a large part of the diners and ate at five so they could get to the theater, had already left; other members did not arrive until seven or after. One man was in the Grill Room, sitting with his back to the door.

"Are you dining alone?" he inquired, looking up and seeing Hamilton standing uncertainly in the doorway. Hamilton said he was. "So am I," the solitary diner said. "Won't you sit down and have dinner with me?" It was Grover Cleveland.

That dinner was a memorable initiation for Hamilton, who at twenty-one was the youngest member of the Club, and remained so until Edwin Booth Grossmann, the founder's grandson, was elected on his twenty-first birthday. George Middleton, just twenty-two, came in with Hamilton, and Arthur Goodrich, who had become a member only the year before, was twenty-four. They were part of a drive for young members, following Booth's original intent, and the average age of those who came in about the time of Clayton's admission was less than twenty-five. The year was 1903. Joseph Jefferson was president, and ten of the incorporators were still alive and active. Nearly half the members had been Booth's personal friends.

Once the initial shyness had worn off, Clayton plunged into Club life with enthusiasm. Coming in for luncheon, as he described it later, he might see "Mark Twain, returned recently from Bermuda and still wearing the white suit which in those days was regarded as astonishingly unconventional. Seated at his right might be Augustus Saint-Gaudens, dubbed by Stevenson (quoting a phrase from the poetry of Emerson) as 'the godlike sculptor.' Whenever he turned his face a little and you saw it clearly in profile, you noticed tht it was carved by nature like a cameo." Hamilton admired the sculptor's "long, slender, astonishingly tactile, and almost unbelievably beautiful hands."

On the other side of Twain (they called him "Mark" at the Club rather than "Sam") might be Edmund Clarence Stedman, the poet. As Hamilton described him: "Stedman looked magnificent while sitting down, but when he arose from his chair, you were disappointed by the fact that his legs were not quite long enough to reach to the floor." Stedman was a banker when he wasn't writing poetry.

Stanford White was nearly always there. Hamilton describes him: "He was a man of stupendous physical and mental vigor. Wherever he went, he always carried in his pocket a hundred ordinary postcards addressed to himself. Whenever an idea occurred to him, at any hour of the day or night, he would jot it down on the back of one of those postcards and consign it to the mail. The next day, whenever he turned up at his office, he might find piled upon his desk a score of postcards to remind him of the ideas that had occurred to him the day before."

Another regular member at luncheon was Richard Watson Gilder, editor of the *Century,* whose offices were just around the corner. Hamilton remembered him as "a mouselike little man, neat-footed and deft-fingered, with deep-set, sharp, and penetrating eyes. He did not look especially impressive when he slid silently into a chair at the Round Table, but he appeared as an almost overpowering personage on those more frequent occasions when he marched in for luncheon at the head of the entire staff of the *Century.* . . ."

Hamilton described in his usual vivid style some of the artist regulars: "There was Robert Reid, who looked like one of the great Assyrian bulls in the British Museum; there was Edward Simmons, a nephew of Ralph Waldo Emerson, who in his early boyhood used to go on fishing expeditions with Thoreau; there was the burly and self-confident J. Alden Weir; there was William Metcalfe, who, subsequent to his lifelong resolve to ride upon the water wagon, always told the utter truth about everything whatever, regardless of where the chips might fall. There was Childe Hassam, a great artist who remained always a very simple child."

Other habitués included Mayo W. Hazeltine, who contributed an entire page to the New York *Sun* every week—literary essays which were followed lovingly by a large audience year after year. He signed these contributions simply "M.W.H." The reading public never knew his name. There was also, of course, Newton Booth Tarkington, called "Tark," a young Princetonian elected in 1900, and Dr. S. Weir Mitchell, of Philadelphia, one of the most noted American physicians, whose son, Langdon Mitchell, a playwright, was also a much-loved member of the Club.

There was never a shortage of actors, and most of the best were members. Hamilton, as a young recruit, stood in the presence of such as Richard Mansfield, E. H. Sothern, William Gillette, James K. Hackett, William Faversham, and David Warfield. From time to time, English members appeared: Sir Henry Irving, Sir Johnstone Forbes-Robertson, Sir Harry Lauder, Sir Herbert Tree, later Sir Cedric Hardwicke, and Maurice Evans, not yet knighted.

Among all these famous people it was perhaps inevitable that the one member capable of standing out would be the wittiest, and that was true as time went on. In these early years, the title would have gone without contest to Oliver Herford—poet, humorist, sharp-tongued observer of men and events, and a legend in Club annals. Julian Street has given us a memorable description of him:

"He was frail and gnomelike. His clothing hung from his shoulders with the empty look of clothing on a coat-hanger, and by contrast with his meager body and spindly neck his head looked large. This disproportion gave him the appearance of a baby robin, and the suggestion was enhanced by the great, astonished eyes behind his glasses, and by the nimbus of fine, soft hair, like pinfeathers on a half-bald birdling.

"Yet there was a certain style about him. His writings and drawings were full of style and he could wear an old gray homespun suit in a way that made it look newer and better than it was. . . . He wore enormously tall, starched turnover collars of a style I remember from half a century ago, spats in cool weather, and a monocle which usually hung on a black ribbon against his vest. His voice was low, his diction distinct—as befitted the son of an English clergyman—and his smile was slow and misty. He almost never laughed aloud; a smile was usually the best he gave; the rest of us, who listened to him, did the laughing."

Herford was considered to be the foremost wit of his time, and his reputation grew over a long life that did not end until 1935. Those who bought his sketches and watercolors or the small, delightful books he wrote and illustrated, found they possessed collectors' items. His work appeared in every anthology of humor, and some Herfordisms became a part of the language, as "My wife has a whim of iron," and "I don't know your face, but your manner is familiar." Yet Herford never made a conscious effort to amuse people; he had no buildups or pat routines. His humor was spontaneous, and gently devastating.

One of his favorite targets at the Club was Edward Simmons, the painter, who was known as the Club Bore because his conversation, although well informed and lively, was inclined to be endless and eventually tedious. He simply could not stop talking, once started. For his benefit, Herford put up a sign near the door, "Exit, In Case of Simmons." When Simmons asked him to write an introduction for his autobiography, Oliver did so and titled it, "Interruption."

Simmons approached Herford indignantly one day, and said, "Oliver, what do you think of this for a thing to happen to a man in his own club? Yesterday a member said to me, 'Simmons, if you'll resign from this club, I'll give you five hundred dollars.'"

Oliver regarded him earnestly. "Don't you do it, old man," he advised. "You're bound to get a much better offer."

One of Herford's most ingenious inventions was the Farragut Club, which he assured prospective members at The Players was the most exclusive in the world. He would persuade unsuspecting friends to permit him the pleasure of putting their names up for membership. After they agreed, and a suitable interval had passed, he would inform them sorrowfully that they had been blackballed; he couldn't explain why. Oliver, of course, constituted the entire membership of the Farragut Club, which he had named for its meeting place—the park bench under the statue of Admiral Farragut in Madison Square.

Julian Street asked Herford what had put the idea for the club in his head. He had organized it, Oliver said, for the sole purpose of blackballing Richard Harding Davis who was not a favorite of his, or of many other Players. It was this kind of ingenuity that caused Childe Hassam to say of his friend, "Oliver is one of the few men you call a genius without making an ass of yourself."

Herford stories were repeated endlessly and with delight by his fellow Players. Sitting with a half-dozen of his friends one evening on the spacious divan in Drunkard's Corner, a name given to the ten-foot sofa at the top of the side stairs leading to the basement, he was approached by an acquaintance who called out jovially, "I see you are surrounded by your coterie."

"No, no," Oliver protested, "not only by my coterie, but my vesterie and even my panterie. Come join us."

Witter Bynner recalled a hot summer day when everything on the Club's main floor was being removed for general cleaning, and David Garrick's bust had wound up temporarily backed against the fireplace. Bynner was alone in the room, writing a letter at the desk just above the coatroom, when Herford came in, and stopped dead when he saw Garrick.

"Well," he exclaimed, "that's the first time I ever saw a man without any behind warming his behind in front of a fireplace without any fire."

About 1913 magazines began to make themselves larger, and initiated the now universal practice of continuing stories on inside pages, to run beside advertising. It was a change that outraged Oliver, whose indignation was surpassed only by his ferocious antipathy to William Randolph Hearst. He came into the Club one day, brandishing a copy of *Cosmopolitan*, one of Hearst's several magazines, which had just begun to follow the new fashion.

"What do you think of this?" Oliver demanded of the first member he saw.

"What do *you* think of it?" the member returned cautiously.

"I think," said Herford, "that it looks like a louse magnified a thousand times."

Showing a visiting hard-to-impress author around the Club one day, Oliver thought to pique his interest, at least, with Richard Sheridan's death mask.

"Sheridan certainly looks mighty dour for a celebrated humorist," the author observed disdainfully.

"You must bear in mind," Oliver reminded him, "that he was not at his best when this mask was made."

For reasons that remain obscure, Oliver had a fondness for animals outside the usual cat-and-dog categories. He did, in fact, own a small bear. It was not a happy relationship. Oliver was forever having to rescue his bear from various crimes and misdemeanors, until at last he had to donate the animal to a zoo. A friend at the Club asked him how he had ever happened to acquire the bear. "Well," said Oliver, "I unexpectedly came into possession of quite a large sum of money, and I was so afraid I might spend it foolishly that I bought the bear."

The Club has in its possession a photograph of Herford with a year-old lion cub, whose head he is patting rather gingerly. It was taken in the studio of Herbert Adams sometime between 1894 and 1899. At the time Oliver appeared to be enamored of a lady lion-tamer, whose work in the cage he spent many hours watching. He struck up a friendship with her, although she may not have been flattered to learn that it was her animals he was really interested in. He begged her to let him be photographed with a lion cub, and she consented. On a Sunday morning the lady and the cub arrived at Adams's studio in a hansom cab, with the lion sitting up, looking out the window, his paws on the door, and a trail of small boys spilling out for more than a block behind. Pleading an engagement with a lawyer downtown, the lady left her cub with Oliver and the photographer, promising to return soon. A historic, although puzzling, photograph was the result.

For all of his nonsense and quick witticisms, Oliver Herford had a deep sense of loyalty and a fierce adherence to certain ideals. He felt intensely about the First World War, for instance, and the question of America's entry. A strong-minded interventionist from the beginning, he brought a photograph to the Club one day showing a high diplomatic representative of the Kaiser's government enjoying life on the beach at Atlantic City, standing between two charming young women with an arm around each. Oliver was not indignant about anything the picture might imply. What irritated him was the puritanical attitude of New York publishers, as he saw it, who had adamantly refused to print it under his caption, "The Son of the Beach."

President Woodrow Wilson, with his "he kept us out of war" campaign slogan in 1916, did not endear himself to an interventionist like Oliver. The President, however, greatly admired him and often quoted a line from him in his speeches. When Herford's book *This Giddy Globe* appeared, Herford dedicated it "To President Wilson (With all his faults he quotes me still)."

As he grew older, Oliver ate less and less. Never robust, to say the least, he dwindled away until he could merit the description of "an intelligence on legs." When a friend saw him walking into the Club one day in 1935, appearing frail and moving slowly, he asked Oliver solicitously how he was feeling. "I know what's the matter with me," Herford said. "I'm just fading out." It was true; the laughter had to stop at last. A week later he was dead, and the familiar black-bordered card on the bulletin board announced it.

There were those who remembered his remark when he saw that card for his friend George Barr McCutcheon, the novelist who discovered the mysterious kingdom of Graustark, posted in the same place. "When I look out of my studio window," he said, "and see the club flag at half-mast [a custom in those days], I hurry over and look at the bulletin board to see who it is, but it's always the wrong man." A few days after Oliver's death, someone who remembered that judgment penciled on his card: "Always the wrong man."

After a noon funeral a group of the pallbearers, all Players, went back to the Club for lunch. The atmosphere was unrelieved gloom at first, but then someone told a Herford story, and that reminded a friend of another, until it seemed that everyone had a favorite and wanted to tell it. The luncheon ended in hilarity. So it was ever after among those who loved him most.

* * *

As the Club membership sorted itself out in the early years, it divided into several distinct coteries. First to emerge, oddly enough, was a group of ten prominent businessmen, who formed the original Round Table. The table itself was made especially for this group and its luncheon meetings. Instead of signing separate checks, they had a rubber stamp made up with all their names on it, and this was stamped on the bill. Each man paid a tenth.

Another coterie consisted of painters and sculptors. The nine members who virtually constituted the Ten American Painters belonged to it, and they often invited sympathetic patrons of the arts to join them. Later, two more Round Tables were formed, one comprising a luncheon group of literary men and illustrators, the other consisting of actors, who, quite naturally, met mostly at night.

These divisions were not symptoms of a caste system, however. One of the Club's most distinctive characteristics was its atmosphere of total democracy, in which every member was deemed to be equal. In Club life, as in real life, this could not be taken too literally; no one pretended to be Twain's equal, for instance. But the tone of the place was a leveling one, and celebrities seemed to enjoy being treated like one of the boys. As Corey Ford once observed, "Cutting people down to size is a time-honored tradition at The Players. Members revere their clubhouse, but they show no reverence for one another. No one is a celebrity inside these doors, and affectation or pretense cannot survive long here."

Thus Mark Twain, appearing in his perennial white linen suit, could expect to hear the jocular inquiry, "Where's your streetcleaner's broom?" Franklin P. Adams, known to newspaper readers as F.P.A. and to members as Frank, was a great deflater of egos, in the tradition of Herford. On a night when a long-winded member ended an interminable story with a cliché, "Well, to make a long story short," Adams cut in. "Too late," he said. On another occasion, when a group at the bar were discussing a fellow Player who tended to be obnoxious when drunk, someone argued in his defense, "At least he's his own worst enemy."

Adams was not having it. "Not while I'm around," he quipped.

Sometimes the humor had an edge, as when Frank Sullivan described patrons of the arts: "The main qualification of a patron of the arts should be solvency, in case any of the real members need a touch." It was not true, but Sullivan couldn't resist.

Actors sometimes had their own intramural put-down sessions. Jacob (Jac) Wendell, a much admired member, was rehearsing the part of the dog in *The Bluebird,* and had worked out a remarkable repertory of barks, growls, tail-wagging, and other doggy trademarks of which he was quite proud. Dropping into the Club after rehearsal one day, he encountered an

English actor who had seen him work and tactlessly sought to correct his interpretation.

"My dear fellow," he said. "After all, you know, no dog would ever make such peculiar sounds as those. It barks in this manner." And he did a dog imitation calculated to make an animal agent happy.

Jac listened until he was finished, and then observed mildly, "Yes, yours is much more like a real dog, but," he added apologetically, "you see, I had to learn mine."

Leveling was only a facet of Club life, however. Much more common was the enveloping feeling of camaraderie that swept up nearly every member, leading to lifelong friendships—exactly what the Founder had dreamed. Witter Bynner has described the feeling vividly without making a sentimental point of it.

"It was about this period," he wrote, meaning the early 1900s, "that I used to walk from 16 Gramercy Park to the Marlborough Arms on West 10th Street, where I was rooming with Saint-Gaudens. These walks often occurred as late as one or two in the morning and, if there was a light in Mark Twain's room at 21 Fifth Avenue, I would stop for an hour or two to chat with him. Or I would walk back with O. Henry from a favorite small restaurant of his on the West Side below 14th Street for a powwow at his quarters on Irving Place, ending for me with supper at The Players around the corner.

"On one of these occasions as we were strolling back from dinner, I whistling as we passed the Union Square office of the *Century* editors, Gilder and Johnson, O'Henry admonished me in a whisper, 'Sh, Bill, you'll wake the *Century*,' He continued, 'You know, Bill, after I met the editors with you at The Players the other day, they invited me to the *Century* office and in every window there was a canary bird and under the case a stenographer with corkscrew curls.'"

At the luncheon O'Henry referred to, the *Century* editors had been in a panic because they had just acquired a second serial by Miriam Michelson, whose book *In the Bishop's Carriage* they had serialized the year before. They were about to print the first installment, and in describing it at lunch, they disclosed that the heroine was named Split. O'Henry raised his eyebrows and gravely explained that the word had another, and in the street slang of those days, an obscene meaning. The editors were aghast. They hurried back to the office and, over the indignant protests of the author, who didn't understand and to whom they could not explain, held up the issue until the heroine's name was changed. At the time, magazine and book editors had such powers, sometimes without bothering to consult the author. Even Twain had once been subjected to such treatment at the hands of Harper & Brothers.

Bynner himself worked for the *Century* between 1902 and 1907, and often took authors to lunch at The Players. He could be seen with such writers as Rex Beach, H. G. Wells, O. Henry, or Henry James in tow. These occasions were not always happy ones. Beach, for example, had just arrived from the Klondike when he came to the Club one day with Bynner, Gilder, and Robert Underwood Johnson, another of the magazine's editors. These hosts were shocked when Beach, looking about for the cuspidors that were part of the furnishings in the Great North, found none and spat several times over the back of a sofa.

Bynner first brought Henry James to the Club in the blistering summer of 1904, during the sultry last days of August. James had not been in New York for twenty years, and as he wrote later, was "absolutely overwhelmed with the heat of the city and its other terrors. It was not at all the place I had known as a boy." He found shelter at The Players with Bynner, had a satisfactory lunch, and his host showed him about the Club, which reminded James of the Garrick in London. In the library he was particularly struck by a case of daguerreotypes, "full of faces so many of which were familiar to me, that I realized I must have been fortunate enough as a boy to be in the hands of parents who were fond of the theater. . . ."

Among the old pictures he saw, "Leaning stiffly on pillars, for instance, there were two girls with long hair, the Bateman sisters, whom I used to see on the stage. I remember them, of course, the better in having known them, since those times, as two very charming women in England. But there were others, such as the Florences, who once impressed me with their singing; Maggie Mitchell, over whom I went fantastically mad, though she was undoubtedly a barbarian and would nowadays be taken for such; and there was one woman with the face and curls of a schoolmistress, draped in some ghastly pseudo-classic hanging short at her shapeless knees, whom I indubitably once took with admiring seriousness. . . ."

James had more prosaic memories of his visit. "During that day or two in New York before I left for Boston," he wrote later, "I had . . . in the Players . . . a dish that I have not tasted in over sixteen years and remember, not only as an American food but, if I mistake not, as an idiosyncrasy of New York—brandied peaches!"

After that first luncheon James went off to Boston, as he said, but when he returned, Bynner secured a card for him at the Club, as a guest member, and James returned the compliment by acting as host at late lunches. They had to be late—"very mercifully until two o'clock," he wrote Bynner, "and then we can make out a genial hour together." James considered The Players "a corner of calm," he wrote, and particularly enjoyed the "relics of mummers" which lined its walls.

His visit to America stretched into 1905, and on the eve of his departure, July 2, he wrote to Bynner:

> I return to my bad habit of protracted absence (from this great country) tomorrow, & I have many notes to write tonight (to the accompaniment of premature patriotic explosions) but I wish not to fail of making you this sign of farewell & of telling you how sorry I was that everything went to pieces in New York under stress of opening summer & I lived the victim of heat & hospitality (I mean I was in the hands of controlling friends) till I got away altogether. Otherwise I certainly should have tried to lay hands on you long enough to make up for the outrage I more or less condemned you to in the form of that second luncheon at The Players—when, gracefully, *I* shld. have been the host & ministrant. The sense that I wasn't, hadn't been, haunted me afterwards—to the degree of its taking all my force of intellect to remember that the reason of my failure so to figure was in my having disconcertively discovered, while I waited for you, that my invitation to the Club had expired—or appeared to have—the day before. That I could therefore really take no liberties. I *dreamed* subsequently, of feasting you later (after you had so kindly renewed my card) & leading you on to some biggest show afterwards; but all opportunities melted away from me—I am now spent & finished, at my rope's end & barely able to form these lines. I must get back to rest & work—work *being* for me the only rest. But this will not be so diligent that I shall not be delighted to see you if some day you look in on me through a gap—for you must have that dinner. Come and demand it as your right & believe me yours ever, Henry James.

Bynner gave at least one of his James letters to the Club, where it rests today in the archives. In other missives, James told his friend that The Players was one of the two or three places he most enjoyed visiting in America. "Whatever peace and privacy I may be finding in my rustic corner here," he wrote from London in October 1905, I have lost no echo of that kindly buzz of The Players, no moment of my immersion in which failed to fall on my ear like genial music—so that I wish you would kindly take upon yourself to be the obliging distributor of my faithful remembrance to those two anonymous young men who were so beautifully hospitable to yours and theirs very constantly."

James was extremely perceptive about comparing clubs in London and New York, as one might expect of him. "In The Players Club, as in other New York clubs (and there are so many!)," he wrote, "I was impressed with the sociability of club life here in America. The clubs in London, as I at least have observed them, serve purposes rather of utility and political coagulation than of consociation. Men take meals at their clubs in London, it strikes me, much as they would eat in a small and absolutely nice hotel, whereas here I noticed that you eat in groups and have altogether amiable chatty times together. That's the point—you are more gregarious, more sociable at your clubs, more *en famille*."

He was right about The Players. If it was nothing else, it was gregarious, sociable, and *en famille*. Where else, for instance, could one find so distinguished a literary scholar as Brander Matthews, sitting at the Round Table or elsewhere, dispensing tales of every imaginable kind? This was particularly true in his later years, when he had more time for his two favorite clubs—Monday at The Players, Tuesday at the Century. From his home near Columbia, he drove down to No. 16 in one of New York's last horse-drawn vehicles to have lunch with his friends. There, in more or less intimate conversation, he could say things he would not allow himself on the printed page, telling stories from his immense fund of historical and literary lore.

One of the things Matthews liked to talk about was his theory of "germ plasma" and its influence on world history. He had an illustrative notion about the real paternity of Louis XIV, whose father, he asserted, was not Louis XIII but the Duke of Buckingham. Similarly, he was fond of rehearsing the arguments about the paternity of Napoleon III. On the other side of that coin, he said, one had to consider the existence of a petty office holder in the provinces, whose life was drab and uneventful, yet whose mother was the famous actress Rachel, and his father Duke Aalewski, and whose grandparents were Napoleon himself and the Polish Countess Walewska. How could such a tremendous "germ plasma" heritage go so far wrong, he wanted to know.

One of Matthews's favorite stories was about his entering the Club one day to pick up his mail. He found an urgent tailor's dun in his box, addressed to someone else, and returned it to the proper slot. Just at that moment another member came up, the one for whom the bill was intended. He took the notice, examined it hastily, and feeling uncertain whether Matthews had seen it, shook his head and said loudly, "Poor silly little girl."

A more familiar figure at the Club was Childe Hassam, one of the finest painters of his time, considered in the early days as a wildly non-objective artist, but a great one nevertheless. He was a large, formidable looking man, childlike in nature, and loved by everyone. His best friend was Oliver Herford, whom he sometimes teased in a mock rough way when he had a few drinks. On one of these occasions he backed Oliver into a corner and pretended to be outraged at the cats in Herford's drawings.

"Everything I see of yours has got a cat in it," he charged.

Oliver was not intimidated. "Yes, you're right about the cats," he said, "but I don't call 'em landscapes."

Late one night he joined other members at the bar, and it was clear before long that he had taken too much. That made his friends nervous. They knew that Hassam could change under the influence of alcohol from a charming companion into a cantankerous, quarrelsome danger. That night he seemed bent on trouble. He shot arrows of sarcastic wit at random, and as the hours went by grew more and more difficult.

He resisted urgings to go home, or even to sit quietly somewhere. His friends tempered these urgings cautiously, seeing him on the verge of an explosion. They conferred in whispers about what to do. It was decided that they must send for John (another noted painter member, about whose name the Club records are silent). Someone remembered that John was on the wagon, but someone else said, "He'll come—for Childe. And he's the only man in the world who can do anything with him when he gets this way."

John was duly called from his bed, although it was after one o'clock. He protested loudly about coming out on a rescue mission. "Quite so," said the member who had called him. "Then we'll look for you in half an hour."

As his friends had predicted, Childe gave in quickly when John arrived and addressed a few stern words to him. He permitted John to help him upstairs and into bed on the top floor, although he protested all the way. Returning to the bar, and accepting the acclaim of all those still present, John declared that it had been too much and he would have to climb off the wagon and have a drink. But he, too, overdid, and two hours later those who had remained to celebrate with him were trying to get *him* up to bed. It was not easy; he sat in a chair by the bar, solid as the proverbial rock.

Then an apparition appeared in the doorway. It was Hassam, in bare feet and borrowed pajamas. His friends were not surprised. They had seen him make these miraculous recoveries before. With a sorrowful glance, he took in the situation at once, and like an elder brother, reproached John for his weakness, then helped the others get him up into the same bed he himself had just vacated.

They met at noon next day in the dining room, having an abstemious lunch. Those who passed by heard Childe giving John a long lecture on the virtues of temperance.

Hassam was far from being the only Player who could be difficult at times. Such a large collecton of artistic temperaments was bound to result in minor disturbances. Robert Reid, the painter, a tall man (six feet two, or more) with a huge frame and a Mephistophelian beard, was well liked by his fellow members, but sometimes he could be moody and difficult. Sitting down across from him one day, Julian Street spoke to Reid and got no reply.

"Why don't you say hello?" Street wanted to know. Reid simply went on eating.

"You act as if you didn't even know me," Street pursued.

"I know you all right," Reid admitted glumly.

"Well, then, if you know me, what's my name?"

"None of your damned business," Reid said, and returned to his food.

But the tables were turned on him one night not long after. David Munro had attended a dinner of the St. Andrews Society uptown, and had brought three or four Scottish pipers back down to the Club with him in a demonstration of nationalistic fervor. They gave an impromptu concert for the benefit of a Saturday night full house. Reid encountered the chief piper a little later at the bar, and found himself looking up at a hairy giant who towered over him.

"You know, I'm Scottish myself," Reid volunteered, attempting a conversation.

The giant glowered down at him, examining him carefully. "Na," he concluded, "'tis true ye're a verra curious lookin' man, but ye're nae a Scot."

Walter Oettel recalled that Reid strolled into the Club one day on a quiet summer afternoon, examined his mail and, looking down into the billiard room, saw no one except an employee on duty.

"Dennis," he called, "is any of the crowd in?"

"No, Mr. Reid," Dennis reported, "only a few actors."

Reid proved to be a man of considerable courage. In his later years, a stroke made his right hand useless and he was compelled to learn painting again with his left. Those who accepted his work at show rooms and exhibitions considered the new canvasses the equal of any he had done before.

The Club in early times was given to vocalizing at the bar, or at dinners or Pipe Nights, or with no visible excuse. While that happy custom diminished markedly in modern times, and is now confined mostly to late Pipe Nights, it flourished during the first two decades of the century. There were such professional singer members as Thomas Chalmers, formerly of the Metropolitan Opera, and John Charles Thomas, but there were many more enthusiastic amateurs, like Lodewick Vroom, who seemed to know a thousand songs by heart. Late one night, he and other choristers entertained spontaneously at the bar into the small hours, with Vroom leading the melodious pack. Next day he presided as the newly elected chairman of the house committee, at its first meeting under his direction. The first letter he read from the pile before him, delivered only that morning, was an irate protest from an elderly member, complaining bitterly about "the unconscionable howling last night at the bar." There was no help for it. Vroom had to write himself a severe reprimand.

On a Sunday afternoon both Chalmers and Thomas happened to be at the bar, along with a half-dozen or so of the better voices among the amateurs, and simply because they felt like it, they began to sing, a variety of Irish, Scotch, and English melodies—sad songs, happy ones, comic ditties, serenades, ballads, and of course, drinking songs. The concert went on two hours or more before an audience of no more than a dozen members.

When it came to spontaneous entertainment from the actors, there were a few who always seemed to be on. One was the splendid comedian, Henry Dixey, now nearly forgotten, who seemed always to be playing a part even when he was off the stage and in the Club. Calling for his hat and cane, he would suddenly be the lordly aristocrat. Or he would pretend to be a curmudgeon, or a tottering old gaffer on the verge of senility. One day a waiter in the dining room brought him a glass of milk intended for someone else.

"What is this?" he demanded, slipping into character.

"Milk, sir," the waiter replied.

Dixey frowned. "Is it *fresh* milk?" he demanded.

"Oh yes, sir," the waiter assured him.

"Then take it away," Dixey said grandly, turning back to his newspaper.

A twice-familiar figure in the Club was Brian Hooker, whose career as a Player spanned several decades, and who won immortality (of a Club sort) as chief custodian of the cheese that has stood at one end of the bar almost from the beginning. Hooker took such devoted care of the cheese, and consumed so much of it, that in time he became known as the Connecticut Cheese Hound. Brian was not only protective of the cheese, but of any infringement on what he considered the freedom of his much loved Club. When the board contemplated passing a series of rules of conduct which he considered repressive, he wrote and circulated anonymously a limerick that read:

> The Players must always be clean,
> With nothing profane or obscene
> We can't say "b'Jesus"
> To Royal Cortissoz,
> Or ————!, if you know what I mean.

Cortissoz was the dignified art critic, for many years, of the New York *Herald Tribune,* who was not nearly as austere at the Club as he was in his magisterial pronouncements on art.

Another long-time member of the Club was Newton Booth Tarkington, who dropped the "Newton" on the books that entertained generations of Americans. In fact he dropped it at the Club, too. The rule requiring members to sign their full names on dining-room checks was not made for him, he complained, because his name was so long it was hard to get on the line provided. It was tactfully suggested that he sign simply, "Tark," as he was known to the entire Club. The office never complained.

Tark became a member in 1900 and remained one until he died in 1946, although in his later years he was too ill to visit No. 16, an absence he complained of frequently to friends in wistful letters. In those years he changed remarkably, from "a protracted adolescence," as some termed it affectionately, to an elderly, aging man, in a relatively short time.

As Robert Cortez Holliday, in the obituary he wrote for the Players *Bulletin,* described it: "Increasingly a figure of beguiling distinction, he took on the aspect of a storied ancient. . . . There had been a heart attack, which he spoke of with comical trimmings, and one of the world's most celebrated drinkers went dry. . . . His excesses henceforth were solely 'work debauches.' He divided his time between Indianapolis and Kennebunk Port (where his closest friend was Kenneth Roberts), and there the most welcome of all of the many who came visiting were Players. Seldom at the Club after 1911, he would as soon have given up his citizenship as renounce his membership. For 35 years he gladly paid his dues with only rarely a glimpse of the place."

In the last years Tark spent a good deal of time writing letters, in spite of increasing blindness, and in one of the best, written to the man who brought him into the Club, Paul Wilstach, dated September 8, 1938, he recalled in vivid detail two memorable appearances Richard Mansfield made at the Club in 1898.

On the first occasion it was a splendid dinner given for Coquelin, the noted French actor, in the dining room. At this affair, attended by both Jefferson and John Drew, among others, Mansfield made an after-dinner speech in French. Later, he gave Tark a ride in his coupé to the Holland House, where he kept rooms for use when he was out late and didn't want to drive uptown to his house on Riverside Drive.

"I see again," Tarkington wrote, "the twinkle of his eyeglasses and the sleek moonpath of light down his silk hat, and the red glimmer of his long cigar, as I sat beside him during that drive over to the Avenue and 'uptown' as far as the utmost twenties, while the brisk horse took us along too quickly for me."

Tarkington told Mansfield that he had felt that night as though he had been present at an exhibition of great men's portraits.

"Didn't you think you were the greatest man there?" Mansfield asked him.

"No, not precisely," Tark said.

"You didn't! You should have. That's the way you always ought to feel."

"I? Good heavens!"

Mansfield became serious and benevolent. "Never in my whole life since I was a child," he said, "have I once entered a room full of people without insisting to myself—so that it should be apparent to them—that I was going to be the greatest person in that room. I speak for your own good. Give it a thought."

That must be why Mansfield didn't come often to The Players, Tarkington thought. "He really was a great man, not only because of his overwhelming reputation and his wonderful and versatile mind; but the club was no place for a consciously great man—greatness had to be left off at the door, where fraternity and equality began."

Later that year, Mansfield came to the Club again, as Tark's guest this time (although he was a member). They dined in the grill room. At the time Tark was trying to write plays, and Wilstach had been urging Mansfield to do one of them. "America's foremost living actor," as he was then called, said he intended to put it on, as Tark put it, "as soon as he'd taught me how to rewrite it." The rewriting had been done at the time of the dinner, Mansfield was indeed putting it on, and it was in rehearsal. Difficulties had risen, however, and Mansfield had exhibited his celebrated temper. The dinner was an attempt to smooth things over. There would be three present: the star, the manager, and Tarkington, with Wilstach and Bogey Andrews, a Mansfield favorite in the company, invited in for coffee later.

It was a pleasant and entirely satisfactory dinner, but as it came to a close over the coffee, two large Englishmen, one an actor and both drunk, swept in noisily, sat down at a table nearby and began to talk loudly, meanwhile sopping up more liquor. Tarkington reported what followed:

"'Beasts!' Mansfield said venomously. 'Great red bulging fat purple beasts! Look at 'em! Why, my God, you can't *help* looking at 'em! Why can't such horrible animals keep to themselves? Can't gentlemen dine in peace without having to listen to their obscene roarings, without having to look at their bulbous necks, swollen abdomens, distended veins, and—'

"He was interrupted when the two of them rose and came over. One introduced himself as 'the celebrated English actor, Charles Hardcastle, and this is my great friend, Joe Little, a London banker very widely known. He's sailing tomorrow morning and we're making quite a night of it. I'd like you American boys to take us in with your little party and give us both a good time.'

"Mansfield said, 'I am not an American boy. This is not my dinner party.'

" 'Good!' said Mr. Hardcastle heartily. 'We'll just join you.'

"They pulled up chairs, helped themselves to champagne, and Hardcastle began telling self-aggrandizing and witless stories, in which he was always the hero, egged on by his friend. Mansfield was poised—I'm tempted to say venomously coiled—in his corner. There was indeed something terrible in his silence, and his complexion seemed to have turned a rusty brown with pent ill feeling; his contracted eyes glittered like the points of two bright stilettos, and we all knew that a catastrophe approached.

"Hardcastle launched on a story of how he had been invited to dine with Louis Napoleon and the Empress in the Tuileries, concluding, 'The Emperor took my father's arm to conduct him to the magnificent table and I—I, myself, gentlemen—I who am sitting with you here tonight, I, Charles Hardcastle, who am drinking with you now—I, gentlemen, *I* had the honor to conduct the Empress Eugenia to dinner! I was not nervous—'

"At that point Mansfield struck. 'What about the Empress?' he asked, 'Was *she* nervous?' He rose and left, followed by the rest of the party. By the time he was putting on his hat, cloak, and muffler at the cloakroom, he was beaming again."

As a visiting British actor, Hardcastle had no doubt been given a card to the Club, which permitted him to entertain a guest. There were other more casual visitors, probably the most distinguished of whom was Theodore Roosevelt. During the years when he was contributing editor of *The Outlook*, the magazine's offices were around the corner on Fourth Avenue. In those days, it was his habit to walk over to the National Arts Club, next door to No. 16, and have lunch.

There were a few Players who had helped him with publicity work when he was running for president on the Bull Moose ticket, and they well remembered the luncheon he had given for them and other workers at the Hotel Manhattan when the campaign was over. They thought it would be a nice gesture to invite him for luncheon at the Club, hoping he would tell them something about his recent European trip. Roosevelt accepted, on condition that no reporters were present.

Burges Johnson, one of the hosts that day, recalled what happened: "I have a vivid recollection of the moment when Roosevelt stood in the doorway of our private dining room, looking in at the circular table which was spread there. I happened to stand just behind him, and others were crowded around. Over the center of the table hung a white rose and it was characteristic of his quickness of mind that his eye caught sight of that, and he turned to us there in the doorway, with his full-toothed grin and said, 'Thank you, gentlemen, thank you.'"

Since no reporters were present, there is no detailed record of what Roosevelt said, but Johnson and others remembered that he threw off all reserve (which was always in short supply with T. R.) and gave his personal view of one European sovereign after another, along with other intimate details.

Afterward, Johnson remarked how open these monarchs had been with him, and Roosevelt said: "You have to remember that they seldom get a chance to talk with anyone as an equal. If they do, they are not allowed to discuss anything important. But I had been their equal in the sense that I had been at the head of a first-class power; and now I was not, but still socially acceptable. It was safe to talk to me."

"Yes, you were an anachronism," Johnson ventured, with a smile.

"That's it," T. R. replied, with his famous grin through clamped jaws. "An anachronism. That's what I was."

All that remains on the record of the talk Roosevelt gave at The Players that day is his report that the king of Spain proudly displayed to him the weapons would-be assassins had used against him, and two other tidbits. The king of Italy, he said, took him up to the royal nursery to see the queen mother with their children, and as Roosevelt told the Players, "the king said to me, as he introduced the young crown prince, 'We are trying to have him so trained . . .' and broke off." There was also the moment when Roosevelt was in the funeral train at a royal wake, which was held up for nearly an hour at a channel port while the entourages of two emperors quarreled about which carriage should have the place of preference next to the locomotive.

This was not Roosevelt's only visit to the Club. Earlier, when he was commissioner of police, he came frequently for luncheon, and his friends at the Club often invited him to parties, even though he had the habit of leaving before they were over. He enjoyed the Club and was asked to join more than once but never became a member. Those who wondered what led him to leave parties so early discovered that when he said, as he always did, that he had to be about his duties, he meant that he intended to walk the streets at night. He was not a commissioner of police in search of crime, but a boss observing his employees. He was watching the cops.

On another plane entirely was the single visit William S. Hart made to the Club. As a young man he had seen Booth in nearly every part he played, and emulated him as much as he could during his years on the stage before, in a moment of inspiration, he gave up the theater and went to Hollywood to make silent movie Westerns. While he was still a legitimate theater actor, he longed to be in Booth's repertory company, and even though the time was past when Booth could have made that possible, he wrote to his idol at the Club, where Booth was living by then. The Founder invited him to come and talk with him. There is no record that Hart ever joined, but the single visit must have impressed him because he left $5,000 to the Club in his will.

Hart did not entirely fail in his stage ambitions. He toured with Lawrence Barrett, even though he never had a chance to play with Booth, and he played Romeo to Julia Arthur's Juliet, comparable to playing with Helen Hayes in her prime. Moreover, he was Madame Modjeska's leading man for a time, appearing with her in the same romantic roles Booth had done. His last appearance on the stage was as Messala in *Ben Hur*.

One doubts that Hart, an extremely earnest man, would have exactly fitted in with the convivial Players. The painter, Reginald T. Birch, for example, the perfect boulevardier—his manners impeccable, his mustache carefully waxed, wearing an Inverness cape—who always seemed to be standing up wherever he happened to be in the Club, even when he happened to be napping. Seeing him thus asleep one day, John King observed, "I think he's got a lot of cabhorse blood."

John Barrymore was in and out of the Club frequently, and as all the world came to know, was just as frequently drunk. One night he came out of the Club quite deeply in his cups, as the saying goes, and climbed into a waiting cab. "Take me to the Players Club," he ordered. While the driver was trying to get more comprehensible orders, the Club doorman, John, guessed what might be happening and whispered in the driver's ear. Whereupon the cab moved majestically away, around Gramercy Park very slowly, and came to rest at the entrance of No. 16 again.

Barrymore got out, but halfway to the door, he turned and shouted back at the driver: "Young man, I have been a not unnoticed figure on the stage for 38 years, and this is positively the first occasion in my entire career when anyone has so much as hinted that my enunciation is defective."

Another not-to-be-forgotten figure was Frederic Remington. The presence of this artist in the Club seemed to generate cheerfulness and enthusiasm. Everyone in the dining room stood in awe of his gastronomic capacity. What he liked especially, he told Walter Oettel, was "a good juicy part of the cow," meaning a sirloin steak consisting of two pounds of choice beef, with a liberal portion of fried potatoes. It was accompanied by the large end of a loaf of white bread, and the whole thing was washed down with English ale. Walter often said it was a real pleasure to watch him eat.

Among the incorporators and original members, Stanford White was easily the most flamboyant. Walter described him as "a large man with red hair and mustache, and driving energy." He was not always easy for employees to deal with. There was a standing rule that no meals would be served in the grill room after 2 a.m., but just about that hour one night, White came in with a party of friends and demanded food. He ordered up his customary chafing dish and the ingredients for his favorite meal: oysters, eggs, and grated cheese.

As the clock struck two, Walter closed off these proceedings by shutting the great sliding doors leading into the main hall. But a little later, White came out and ordered more food and drinks. Walter got the drinks but he left them in the great hall outside the doors, and told White where they were. "Bring them in here," White shouted, but Walter whispered in his ear that it was against the rules to serve in the Grill Room at that hour.

"Damn the rules!" White shouted. "You serve us in here and be quick about it."

No one else in the Club would have thought of addressing Walter so peremptorily; he was a daily visible reminder of the Founder, and in this case he stood on his position and refused. For a moment, the others thought White might hit Walter, which would have been sacrilege indeed, but instead he carried the tray of drinks in himself, meanwhile hurling down curses on the house committee, of which he was a member. Next day, he not only apologized to Walter but complimented him on his defense of the rules.

Among Booth's friends who were still alive, Thomas Nast was one for whom he had always had a strong attachment. Nast usually dropped in late for lunch, and as he entered the grill room, he would call out, "Walter, here comes the chip-chop man." He referred to his favorite meal—one of the Club's specialties, an English chop, consumed with a tankard of ale in his own pewter mug.

Once the night watchman asked Nast for an autograph, and the cartoonist drew a likeness of him on the spot, as he stood holding a lantern in one hand and his keys in the other. Then, in a playful mood, Nast drew himself, showing a man unsteady on his feet, high hat tipped to one side, the forefinger of his right hand extended to push a button on the night watchman's protruding stomach, with the caption, "Let me in, please." It was Nast's custom every New Year's to send the Club a sketch of himself in some typical pose, with a warm greeting.

Another of Booth's close friends was Daniel Frohman, longest lived of the incorporators, who was the last survivor of those present on the first Founder's Night when he died at 80. Frohman was omnipresent at the Club in its early days, and for some time after. He inaugurated the *Private*

Dining Room Book for Distinguished Guests. Few members today have ever seen the two earliest books, bearing the names of distinguished visitors. Frohman was also Pipemaster at the Club's first Pipe Night, and it was at his suggestion that The Players inaugurated their pre-World War I "Home Christmas Dinner," with a "host-carved" turkey; Frohman was often the host. He was also considered one of the Club's best billiard players, preferring as a partner the character actor, Edward Kennedy, whom everyone called "E. K.".

As he was in his screen roles, Kennedy could be irritable one minute and amiable the next. In a bad mood one day, he sat down at a small table and noticed several used cups and saucers on the nearby long table. Banging his fist, he ordered Walter, "Move those cups at once. There's a sign of gross carelessness and I blame you directly for this messy sight." Walter removed them quietly, not noticing Kennedy's immediately repentant glance. Next morning he got an invitation to have dinner at the Kennedy apartment, 375 Park Avenue, that night. There he was treated like a prince, with only another Player and a Kennedy nephew present, all of them surrounded by the host's remarkable collection of Whistlers.

Albert Palmer, another of the founders, did not live to see the Club grow. He died in 1905 (the same year Jefferson left the scene) after a career as a manager in New York and on the road. Oddly, Jefferson was given a laudatory obituary in the Club's yearbook, but Palmer was allowed simply to pass away. Yet his career had been remarkable. A clergyman's son, he graduated from New York University Law School, drifted into librarianship and headed the New York Mercantile Library from 1869 to 1872 before he got into finance. In that year he took over the management of a failing variety house, the Union Square Theater, which he converted into a "home of the drama." Later he managed the Madison Square, Wallack's, and other theaters, raising standards of professional management everywhere.

Of all the founders, General William T. Sherman was unquestionably the most unlikely of Players, as far as the public was concerned. Only his fellow members understood what a hopeless theater buff he was, and that he had helped form the Club not to drink, as some cynics maintained, but because he so enjoyed the company of actors. He attended all the early meetings of the Club, and was present on every Founder's Night.

Sherman admitted that he had always been stagestruck, although he never had any desire to act himself. Going to the theater was his lifetime passion. When he heard Booth was ill, Sherman wrote to him on April 5, 1889: ". . . I don't mean to thrust advice on you—you must already be surfeited with it—but I may say to you in all sincerity that I do honestly believe that I have survived all my fellows by virtue of the Player's Art, not by medicine or medical advice. At Memphis, Vicksburg, Nashville, Savannah, whenever I could I sought diversion, amusement, recreation, sometimes not one of the highest order but enough to rest the brain overburdened with care and anxiety. As a Brother Player I prescribe some of this medicine to you."

Although Sherman's biographers have paid little attention to it, he did see as much theater as he could during the Civil War. In the winter of 1864, for example, when he was spending most of his time at the federal supply base in Nashville, preparing for the great Atlantic campaign, he went to the theater constantly. But devotion to the art didn't preclude criticism. At a traveling company's performance of Shakespeare one night which was particularly bad, Sherman's voice could be heard all over the theater, making derisive comments. The officers who were with him had to persuade him to leave before a riot ensued.

After the war he moved to New York in 1886, and lived there in retirement as General of the Armies. From his comfortable house at 75 West 71st Street, he sallied out to make speeches and appearances at banquets, so many that one of his biographers, Lloyd Lewis, wrote that his last years were "one long chicken dinner." But mostly he went to the theater. He was one of the most noted of first nighters, and could be seen at every important theatrical dinner and backstage party. His physical ailments made him so restless in his final years that he found himself unable to sit through a performance, and had to see plays in installments, part in one evening, the remainder on the next.

In the end it was the theater that killed him, so to speak. On the night of February 4, 1891, he gave a box party at the old Casino Theater. It was a cold, raw evening and Sherman caught cold. Although he was still a robust 71, he had suffered from asthma for years, and the bronchial infection he got that night was too much for him. Ten days later he was dead.

* * *

Of all the Players in those early days, however, certainly the most loved was John Drew, charter member from January 7, 1888, until his death on July 9, 1927, and president from Jefferson's death in 1905. He was known to everyone at the Club as "Uncle Jack." Otis Skinner summed him up admirably: "He stood for the things the Club stands for—fellowship, ideals, dignity, and a conservation of the tradition of what is best in private and public life, and the art of the theater, and that it was for him to carry on the precept of an illustrious name. The stage to him was more than a means of livelihood, more than a trade or profession, more even than the exercise of the joy of acting—it was a duty. Anything that tended to mar the good name was a frank affront to his pride in it and his love for it."

No member ever presided over more feasts and gatherings than did John Drew. Walter Oettel, who knew him for most of his thirty-nine years, recalled after his death that he had never heard an unkind remark about him, or even a criticism. When he came into the billiard room, a crowd of his admirers always gathered around to be with Uncle Jack. They gave him a midnight dinner and reception on February 3, 1905, when he was elected to the presidency. It was like a Founder's Night gathering, replete with eloquent speeches. He was presented with a testimonial, and everyone present was given souvenir medals.

As president, he was at the Club every day he was in the city. Affable, witty, princely, courteous, always impeccably dressed, he retained his dapper erectness, touched with a slight formality, until nearly the end of his life. All the members loved him, and he returned their love, but he was not a man to slap on the back.

In later years he was often not quite sure to whom he was talking, but he always did his best to find out. From the bar he sent a telegram to John Barrymore, who he learned had just escaped the San Francisco earthquake. It appeared that the other Jack emerged from his hotel and had been immediately seized by the military, who put him to work along with everyone else clearing wreckage from the streets. Drew wired: "Glad to hear you are all right but note with regret that it took a convulsion of nature to get you up in the morning and the United States Army to make you work."

When he was unavoidably absent on Ladies' Day, Drew always ordered a basket of roses for the table at the entrance to the reception room. It was circled with a broad satin ribbon, bearing in golden letters the legend, "To the Ladies, From the President." And the ladies loved him. A fastidious dresser, his mustache was kept carefully trimmed and he parted with it reluctantly when a role demanded it be cut, although he finally gave in to fashion and went without it.

On Ladies' Day when he could be present, he stood at the head of the stairs and greeted every visitor. As a young man he could leap up those marble steps in two bounds, so it was sad to see him in his later days, when cataracts were dimming his vision, having someone guide him up and down the stairs. Once, walking across the porch in back, he crashed into the wall between the windows, sending him almost to the floor, but he recovered his balance. For the benefit of anyone who might be watching, he exclaimed, "Drunk again, by God!"

When he left the Club for the last time, for a road tour in *Trelawney of the Wells*, Drew stopped at the foot of the stairs, stood on the first step with his hands at his side as usual, and called to Frederic Dorr Steele, one of his close friends: "Come over here, Chief. Good-bye and good luck. I may be gone a long time."

At 73, ailing and close to a planned retirement, he headed a company of sixteen on a coast-to-coast tour, playing the part of Sir William Gower, a role he had played so successfully at the Empire Theater in New York. Thousands hastened to see him, but his illness increased as he traveled, and he gave his last performance in Vancouver. Taken to San Francisco, he still had strength enough to send notes to his friends in New York, regretting profoundly that he would not get to the Club again. With great courage he fought to stay alive and never wavered until the end. Urbane and gracious to the last, he observed to a sorrowing visitor that it was "just another play," except that in this one the ending was not in doubt. To his daughter, he spoke his last words about the nurse who had been attending him: "Thank her for me."

The Club held a memorial service for John Drew in the Little Church Around the Corner on his birthday, November 13, which was also Booth's. The mourning Players moved to the church in a body after the traditional wreath-laying at the foot of Booth's statue. Otis Skinner spoke for all the Club members at the service when he said: "We are consoled by the recollection of the many hours of glorious companionship at The Players."

* * *

One of the extraordinary elements in life at The Players has been the closeness of its staff to the members. In the early years, an enduring foundation for this relationship was laid down with the coming of Walter Oettel, whose name has already appeared frequently in these pages. He wrote his own account of his many years at the Club, *Walter's Sketch Book of The Players,* privately printed by the Gotham Press in 1947. The sole remaining copy of it is in the Club library, and even though it is rich in memories, it conveys only a hint of the intimate history he could have set down if he had been a writer and less restrained by nature.

In an introduction to the book, Booth Tarkington wrote: "Walter Oettel has spent his life being thoughtful of other people's comfort; he has an untiring vigilance in thinking for other people, and during his many years at The Players he has done thinking for an uncounted number of men, esteemed great thinkers. Probably Walter has known, and thought for, more great men of the arts than has any other person in the United States. He has known them, too, as they are not ordinarily known, and has often known them, probably, better than they suspected—but Walter is charitable.

"It is impossible to think of The Players without thinking of Walter. An old member thinks first of Walter . . . [he] seems not to change. He seems to be an unalterable and unaltered fixture. . . . A painter at the Club one day spoke of those who served the members, year after year, sometimes growing up from boyhood in this service, sometimes growing from youth to middle age. 'I wonder what they think of us,' he said. 'I do wonder what they really think of us.' "

An answer was provided by Charlie Connolly, second only to Walter in years of service, and equal to him in devotion. Charlie was behind the bar one day when A. E. Thomas asked him, "Don't you ever get tired of listening to some of these hard-luck stories?"

"No, sir," Charlie said. "I hear a lot of very interesting things from a lot of very interesting men."

"Well, I should think a lot of it would be pretty tedious."

"Oh, well, sir," Charlie confided, "if that's the way of it, you can just stop listening. They don't mind and it just does them good to get it off their chests."

Walter was responsible for the presence of Charlie and many other employees during his reign over the staff. Born in Gera, a small town near Leipzig, on August 18, 1866, he traveled to England while he was still a boy, and there went into service, serving as butler in several stately homes.

It could be said that Walter was the perfect servant, of a kind seen usually only on Masterpiece Theater. Speaking a gentle, unaccented English, a devout Christian and always self-effacing, his first thought was service, and never salary.

After he became a Club legend, it was believed erroneously by younger members that he had been Booth's dresser in the theater and went with him to the Club as his valet, but that was fantasy.

In his book, Walter tells us about the first time he ever saw Booth. He had been engaged as a waiter by the Club's first superintendent, the infamous Magonigle, the Founder's brother-in-law and former treasurer of his touring company. The new waiter found himself looking at the revered Booth on almost the first day he spent in the Club's service. Booth walked "with a heavy step" into the grill room for a late breakfast, gave a cheery and reassuring "Good morning" in response to Walter's timid bow, and as the new waiter wrote many years later, "sat wearily down at one of the tables designated by an older waiter. He was not at all well dressed in the fashionable sense of the word. His dark blue suit of an old style needed pressing, his low standup collar was hitched to one side, and his bow tie was very carelessly tied. But peculiarity in dress could not take from the man his saint-like expression of love for his fellow men. I determined then and there to make myself his valet at my earliest opportunity."

That ambition was never quite realized. Walter observed that Booth did not have a valet, and since his duties extended to answering calls from the bedrooms upstairs, he soon persuaded Booth to let him assist with dressing, particularly on his bad days. It did not take much persuasion. Booth had rheumatism so badly in his right arm that often help was essential. But once the relationship was established, no other employee ever waited on Booth, and while Walter had many other duties, he drew closer and closer to the Founder.

In his *Sketch Book,* Walter contrasts Barrett, who was then living in two rooms at the rear of Booth's quarters on the third floor, with the Founder. Barrett loses easily. "The contrast in the personalities of the two men plainly showed in their habits," Walter wrote, "in their choice of food, in their furnishings, and in their taste in dress. Mr. Barrett, for instance, had a showy bed of oxodized silver, while Mr. Booth's was a simple affair of dull brass. The two men breakfasted together at times and I often made a mental comparison of them as they talked. Mr. Booth was gentle and unassuming, Mr. Barrett decidedly loud and pretentious."

Walter was soon promoted to headwaiter, then to steward, and finally to superintendent of the Club. Every detail was entrusted to him, including the hiring of new staff members, in which he showed impeccable taste, as he did in everything else. In 1897, on a trip to visit a friend of his at the Niantic Country Club, in Flushing, New York, he met a 16-year-old boy from County Donegal, Charles Connolly, and as he left, invited this recent arrival from the old country to come see him if he ever got to New York. Charlie took his time. It was two years later, on March 17, 1899 (which was not only St. Patrick's Day but the day of the great Windsor Hotel fire), that he appeared at the Club and was immediately hired by Walter as a jack-of-all-trades. As Walter moved up in the ranks, Charlie moved with him, until he became a figure as much loved and respected. It was Charlie who took over passing the cup on Founder's Night, which Walter had done for more than fifty years. He remained as Club steward for fifty-five years. The Club rewarded him by making him a lifetime honorary member.

Similarly, members never thought of Walter as an employee but as a fellow Player—a counselor, confidant, and friend. For many years he lived near the Club, on East 21st Street. Later, when he retired to Fort Lee, New Jersey, his house there resembled the Club itself, with its walls adorned by the paintings of such members as Robert Reid, Edward Simmons, and Childe Hassam, which the artists had given out of simple fondness.

Walter stocked the Club's service roster with exceptional people. Twelve years after he brought in Charlie, on October 25, 1911, he hired a

17-year-old mountain boy from the Black Forest region of Kaiserstuhl, Switzerland. His name was Adolph Delabar, which some Players translated facetiously as "of the bar," and he became for years the beloved barman of the Club. Then, in 1911, Walter took on Arthur Sherman, a cheerful young Londoner, who by 1947 had become officer-overseer of the pool room. Only a year before, Walter had also hired an Italian named Augusto Buonasera, soon known to everyone as August, born near Pisa, who kept the woodwork clean and the brasses shining for thirty-seven years. As one member wrote of him years later, when he reached his 87th birthday, August was "the good gray guardian who silently haunts the upper corridors at late hours, and protects members from telephone calls."

August worked first at the Club as night watchman, and had been there for three years before it was discovered that he had never been given a vacation, or even a day off. But he had special and vital duties, such as being sure that a pint of gin was on hand for Jack Barrymore after the bar closed, and making certain that a cab waited for John Drew until he felt like leaving.

Through the decades he had performed these and a thousand other services for members, and was so much accepted as part of the Club landscape that a little group having cocktails one night in the bar were astonished when August appeared at the door, wearing a new suit, a homburg, and carrying a cane. He was saluted by the bar habitants, who that evening included James Cagney, on his way to Hollywood to make a film.

When they discovered that August was celebrating his 87th birthday, a riot of congratulations ensued. More drinks were produced for toasting the event, and August was given a box of cigars and several bottles of Scotch and brandy. They asked him where he was going to celebrate. August said he was on his way to the old house near the Whitestone Bridge where he lived with his sister-in-law and her sons; his wife had died recently at 82. Asked how he meant to get there, he shrugged and answered "by subway and bus," as usual.

"Not tonight, you aren't," the assemblage told him. He was sent home in Ray Vir Den's Cadillac, complete with chauffeur and birthday bundles.

Such long terms of service were not uncommon at The Players, and much of the reason was the peculiarly close relationship between staff and members. Over several decades, a series of Employees' Balls were held, where both members and employees, with the wives and friends of each, danced and gossiped and drank together.

Just as Walter and Charlie and August rose to varying degrees of eminence in this benevolent system, so did Adolph Delabar, who, as noted earlier, was acquired by Walter. He was hired on a damp October day, arriving at the Club as a tall, skinny young man, who wore pointed boots, skin-tight trousers, and a fawn thumb-length topcoat with balloon buttons. His thick dark-brown curls emerged from beneath a dark metallic derby, and he wore a pre-Hoover collar. Walter handed this unusual specimen over to Charlie, who sensed his talents at once, gave him a rag, and installed him behind the bar, where he remained for years. Eventually he became (in 1947) the Club's first steward in charge of kitchen, grill, and bar. Ten years earlier he had been given a tenth-anniversary dinner, presided over by Gene Lockhart, with speeches by such old members as Clayton Hamilton.

The length of tenure these much-loved and admired employees enjoyed made them as legendary as some of the notable men they served. In later years a young member could survey Charlie with some awe, knowing that this man had been behind the bar in the grill room when Mark Twain would stop momentarily in his pool game, snap his fingers in Charlie's direction, and be sure that Connolly would toss him another cigar, which Twain would catch in mid-air, as though he were a shortstop snagging a line drive.

One by one they vanished, these men who made the Club function. Walter was the first to go. He retired in 1932 after a slight stroke. His last message to the Club was read on Founder's Night 1946 and a few months later he was dead. To those surviving members who had known him, it was as though the curtain had come down on the first act of Edwin Booth's drama.

*   *   *

With the coming of the Great War, life at the Club changed as it did everywhere. The membership did its part. Out of a total of fewer than 1,100 Players, 125 were in uniform and more than half of the membership was in war work of one kind or another—the Red Cross, the YMCA, the Knights of Columbus, in overseas theaters, and in all the branches of government. Three were killed: two actors, Lionel Walsh and Robert Stowe Gill; and Major Willard Straight, publisher and financier.

In the days before American entry, however, the Club was as divided as the rest of the nation about what the United States should do, just as it would be in 1940, and again in the Vietnam era. President Wilson, reelected in 1916 as the man who would keep America out of war—in spite of Oliver Herford's opposition—reflected popular sentiment. But in the intellectual community, particularly in the book and magazine world, there were many writers and editors who wanted from the beginning to aid Britain and the allies. That was because so many of them saw the war as

SECOND FLOOR HALLWAY, circa 1907. The cuspidor, ubiquitous in those days of heavy cigar smoking, nestled against the wall. The chandelier, like the cuspidor, is long gone.

THE LOUNGE in 1907. Bust of Edwin Booth as Hamlet by Launt Thompson on the right. Grandfather clock which chimed out

midnight on Founder's Nights is now on the stairway. The so-called "drunk couch" is visible at center.

THE DINING ROOM
AND COURTYARD of
the Club, 1907, in
one of several photo-
graphs taken by Falk
for Actors Fund Fair.

THE GRILL ROOM,
as this part of the
dining room was
known in 1907.

THE LIBRARY in 1907. In those days, the Librarian's desk was in the library proper, at the rear of the room in this photograph.

THE READING ROOM of the Club, as photographed by Falk in 1907.

THE POOL ROOM originally faced the staircase, which led directly down from the foyer, unlike today's staircase, which curves down from glass doors.

THE READING AND WRITING ROOM *(opposite, top)* in a Falk photograph. THE PRIVATE DINING ROOM *(opposite, bottom)* on the second floor, set up for a small party. Now the Card Room.

THE CONVERSATION ROOM, now the office of the Club Librarian. A
stained glass portrait of Shakespeare above the window overlooks
Gramercy Park. Edwin Booth's personal library, given to The
Players, is in the bookcase on the right.

a contest between barbarism and Western culture, and also because they were very likely to have ties of one kind or another with Britain.

By late 1916, when isolationism was at its height, war fever among these writers and editors had led to the secret formation of the Vigilantes, whose activities were to be coordinated by Ferris Greenslet, the editor-in-chief of Houghton Mifflin, Boston's venerable publishing house, who also was the American coordinator for Wellington House, center of the British propaganda effort.

Even for wartime the short history of the Vigilantes is a strange one. It began on a November day in 1916 when a group of writers met for lunch at The Players. Herman Hagedorn, an author of German descent born in New York City, a Harvard graduate who had also spent a semester at the University of Berlin, had called the meeting. Apparently he felt guilty about his ancestry, and was compelled to express his loyalty somehow. His luncheon guests were S. Stanwood Menken, a lawyer who was president of the National Security League, a patriotic organization; Hamlin Garland; and Cleveland Moffett. Both the latter were members of the publicity committee of the American Defense Society, another preparedness group, like the League.

At their luncheon these men decided they would organize authors, artists, illustrators, publicists, editors, and others to fight "for their country's honor and their country's life." In a pamphlet issued to describe themselves and their plans they defended their choice of a name: "There has been a disposition to associate the Vigilantes with those beloved roughnecks of the early California days, who established order in the frontier towns and camps by methods distasteful to tender souls. We find no fault with this. In fact, we are rather proud of being linked up with the stern and vigorous pioneers who effectually squelched the anarchists and I.W.W. of their day."

In their operations the Vigilantes of 1916 meant to do publicly what Wellington House was already doing secretly. They intended to give wide dissemination to "the best available type of patriotic publicity" through newspapers, news syndicates, and magazines. They volunteered to "write articles, stories, or to draw cartoons, on demand, absolutely without charge: on any subject that might promote American participation in the war." The managing editor controlling this service was Charles J. Rosebault, formerly of the *Sun,* who was installed in headquarters in 505 Fifth Avenue. Theodore Roosevelt, approving this action by members of a Club he so much admired, gave the new organization a generous contribution. Several millionaires joined in with checks running to three and four figures. With this money the Vigilantes denounced pacifism and extolled preparedness in boilerplate material they syndicated by mail, free, to newspapers and magazines everywhere in the country.

An impressive roster of well-known authors, many of them Players, enlisted with the Vigilantes, including Samuel Hopkins Adams, Gertrude Atherton, George Ade, Rex Beach, Booth Tarkington, Ellis Parker Butler, Charles Hanson Towne, Julian Street, and Irvin S. Cobb. With such talent at their disposal, the new organization quickly became a potent force in shaping public opinion, helping to push the nation toward intervention.

Cobb eventually repented of the Vigilantes' activities. He confessed after the war that he regretted succumbing "to the prevalent hysteria" and writing propaganda under "the spell of that madness which we mistook for patriotism." Hagedorn, too, was a victim of postwar disillusionment, referring to the Vigilantes' "silly chants" and "little hymns of hate."

The war's end was celebrated at The Players in its customary way. There was one false start. On the day the war was declared over before that happy event occurred, thereby forever embarrassing Roy Howard and the United Press, Guy Nichols, a Player who was Club librarian, brought out the magnum of champagne he had been reserving; he had a son in the war. William Tachau, who would prove to be one of the greatest Players, joined him at the Club, with a few other friends.

After a few glasses Bill went over to Fifth Avenue to join the celebrants there, but on the way he met some friends who persuaded him to join them for dinner at the Brevoort. Returning to have a pre-dinner drink at the Club, Bill arrived just as a coal truck pulled up at No. 16, backed around, raised itself to unload, and down with the coal before Tachau's astounded eyes came Guy Nichols, a little sooty but ready for still more celebration.

How this interesting scene came about has never been satisfactorily explained, although there have been attempts. One of the most ingenious is that after Tachau departed, the celebrants left behind at the Club finished off the magnum and decided to join the celebration in the streets. But every avenue was so jammed that the side streets were choked up too. The Club celebrants decided it would be better to return to No. 16.

There was, of course, not a taxi in sight—even then. Always resourceful, in the tradition of The Players, they commandeered a large, high-sided coal truck, whose driver was even drunker than they were. In this vehicle they returned to No. 16, where everyone was able to get out of the truck except for Nichols, who found the sides too high. No one felt capable of lifting him out. The impasse was resolved by the driver. "Lookit," he said, "watch me fix it." There followed the maneuver which Tachau arrived just in time to witness, as Guy slid out on the sidewalk in a cloud of coal dust.

But then the war *did* end, and the cartoonist Clive Wood was walking toward The Players with another artist, Harry Grant Dart, hoping to repair hangovers with more hair of the dog. Dart stopped abruptly and grabbed his friend's arm. "My God," he said, "the American flag's at half-mast. What's that for?"

"It's Armistice Day," Wood informed him.

Bart breathed deeply in relief. "I thought it was for me," he said.

Players who had been in the war began to drift back. On a summer day in 1919 Walter Connolly recalled, he and Ivan Simpson, known at the pool table as Ivan the Terrible, returned to the Club on the same afternoon. As they greeted each other and began to talk, both thought it odd that the other had said nothing to him about his return from the service, and a puzzled, tentative caution rose between them.

"When did you get back?" Connolly asked at last.

"This morning," Simpson told him.

Connolly looked relieved. "So did I," he said.

With the dedication of the Booth statue in Gramercy Park on November 13, 1918, two days after the Armistice, the "early days" of The Players seemed to come to an end, along with so much else in American life. The statue had had a long and troubled history. As early as 1906 Saint-Gaudens had been asked to make a memorial for Booth, depicting him as Hamlet. But before a contract could be signed, Saint-Gaudens died, and in 1909 the commission was assigned again to Frederick MacMonnies. While he was preparing to sculpt it the Hamlet costumes were taken from their glass case on the third floor for the first and only time and placed on the figure of Howard Kyle, who was photographed in them in various poses for the sculptor's benefit.

As MacMonnies began to work, however, disagreements arose, dragged on for years, and the sculptor eventually gave up in 1913 and withdrew. At that point the Club held a competition for the commission, which was won by Edmond T. Quinn, who did everything but the pedestal, executed by Edwin S. Dodge. They were finished at last in 1917, but the railroad embargo prevailing during the war held up the granite base, which had to come from New Hampshire, so that in the end the statue was barely ready on dedication day, November 13, 1919.

The ceremony was scheduled for noon so that Club members who were actors could get to the theater on matinee day. Two small great-grandchildren of Booth's were in the audience. John Drew delivered the speech of acceptance and when he was finished Walter and Guy Nichols jointly drew away the cloth that concealed it.

Clayton Hamilton, who gave a short address before the unveiling, remarked that it was the only statue ever erected anywhere in the country of an actor in a costume of his calling, and the only statue of its kind in the world. There Booth stood at last, to be admired by successive generations of Players and other citizens. No one mourned the fact that he had displaced a graceful nineteenth-century water nymph, who had presided over the Park for more than fifty years. Her removal was a symbol of the change that was overtaking America. No. 16 would change too, but the spirit of its Founder would remain.

CHAPTER 4

Mark Twain: In and Out of the Club

NO ACCOUNT OF EARLY DAYS AT THE PLAYERS WOULD BE COMPLETE without Mark Twain, who was not only an incorporator but inevitably a leading spirit during the years he was a member—and even in the brief interval after he was expelled. As the Michelin guides so cogently put it, Mark is worth a detour.

In the autobiography edited by his friend and fellow Player, Albert Bigelow Paine, Twain quotes the letter that became his formal introduction to the Club. It was from Augustin Daly, dated January 2, 1888, who wrote: "Mr. Augustin Daly will be very much pleased to have Mr. S. L. Clemens meet Mr. Booth, Mr. Barrett, and Mr. Palmer and a few friends at lunch on Friday next, January 6 (at one o'clock in Delmonico's) to discuss the formation of a new club which it is thought will claim your interest."

Twain recalled that all the founders were present, but he cast doubt on the accepted assumption that the Club's name had already been chosen. "I remember that several names were proposed, discussed, and abandoned at the luncheon," he wrote, "that finally Thomas Bailey Aldrich suggested that compact and simple name." The discrepancy is only one of location, however; it may well have been chosen at the luncheon rather than on the *Oneida*. In any case, as Twain says, "The objections to it were easily routed and driven from the field, and the vote in its favor was unanimous."

Twain entered happily into the life of the Club; it was made for him. Only a few months after the opening, on March 30, 1889, he was among those presumed to be present at a gala midnight supper in Delmonico's, given by Daly and Albert Palmer to honor Booth for his gift to The Players of the property at No. 16. The guests included a galaxy of incorporators: besides Booth and his hosts, William Bispham, John Drew, Joseph Jefferson, Brander Matthews, Lawrence Barrett, Stephen Olin, and General Sherman, along with such figures as Nat Goodwin, the Australian actor; John Gilbert, General Porter, Constant Coquelin, Saint-Gaudens, and Chauncey Depew.

"Next morning," Twain recalled later in one of his platform speeches, "the *Times* said that toward the end of the affair, which went on till dawn, 'General Porter dropped gracefully into poetry and W. W. Winter fell into it with a dull thud, and afterward shed tears on Edward Harrigan's neck.'" The *Times* also reported that Twain was present, but in an auto-biographical dictation of December 28, 1906, he asserts that he was home ill and did not speak, despite the fact that the *Times* gave a detailed summary of his talk.

The contradiction is easily resolved. Twain was absent, but he did write a speech which someone else delivered for him. It was a notable speech, too, titled "The Long Clam," and began, "Although I am debarred from making a speech, by circumstances which I will presently explain, I yet claim the privilege of adding my voice to yours in deep and sincere welcome and homage to Edwin Booth. . . ." He went on to praise the Founder in the effluent manner of the times. Then he disclosed the reason for his absence. Apparently, he had inadvertently consumed a bad clam, which he called the Long Clam.

"You swallow the Long Clam," Twain told his fellow Players, "and history begins. . . . I would rather go on an orgy with anybody in the world than a Long Clam. I would rather never have any fun at all than try to get it out of a Long Clam. . . . It's two days now, and this is the third night, as far as I've got. In all that time I haven't had a wink of sleep that didn't have an earthquake in it, or a cyclone, or an instantaneous pho-tograph of Sheol. And so all that is left for me is a dissolving rag or two of former humanity and a fading memory of happier days; the rest is Long Clam."

Calling Booth a modest, amiable man, Twain observed what only those who knew the Founder best were aware of—that this consummate actor, superbly eloquent on the stage, was so self-effacing that when he was called upon to make a speech, he could contrive only a few halting sentences.

In and out of the Club it appeared that Twain, the rambunctious individualist, was always at the center of some kind of disturbance, trivial or more serious. There was, for example, the great Actors' Fund Fair of 1907, noted earlier, which Walter listed among the Club's "Red Letter Days." In fact, it lasted for ten days, involving not only theater people but such social leaders as Mrs. Stuyvesant Fish, Mrs. Herman Oelrichs, and Mrs. Arthur Iselin. There were bazaars, vaudeville, sideshows (an albino girl, a human skeleton, a wild man from Harlem), a polling booth where patrons could vote for the most popular actress at ten cents a vote, and a miniature racetrack where lower-case players could lose as easily as elsewhere. Douglas Fairbanks was in charge of a soap booth, which led to reports that he was leaving the stage to go into the soap business.

Twain had consented to help out with the Century Theatre Club booth, but Mrs. Sidney Rosenfeld, the club's president and a Christian Scientist, would not have him because of his well-known denunciations of that faith. There were indignation meetings and letters exchanged, until Daniel Frohman diplomatically suggested that Twain be transferred to The Players Club booth. He was also a star of the show. On May 6, after President Theodore Roosevelt had pressed a button in the Oval Office lighting up the Metropolitan Opera House for the fair's opening, Frohman, who was president of the Actors' Fund, made the first speech, and he was followed by Twain, who easily eclipsed Mrs. Rosenfeld and left her for dead on the field of battle. After his speech he moved over to The Players booth and sold autographs.

Twain especially enjoyed eating at the Club, whether the occasion was formal or casual. One of his happiest times was the dinner given by the Club on December 1, 1893, honoring John William Mackay, one of the four bonanza kings who had made fortunes from the Comstock lode in the 1870s, along with George Hearst, William Randolph's father. Mackay was the epitome of a Player—affable, unpretentious, generous, fond of music and the theater. For him, the Club kitchen had produced a menu it seemed to think was typical of miners' fare—soup, raw oysters, corned beef and cabbage. Twain arrived about midnight and was delighted to find so many old friends from his *Roughing It* days with whom he could swap stories.

It was during a memorable private dinner at the Club, given by twenty-five of his friends, that the famous Paine autobiography had its genesis.

The table decorations and favors that night were stuffed frogs, a salute to the renowned Jumping Frog of Calaveras County. Brander Matthews presided and Paine was there, a young writer who had had several books published but still was without a large success. Charles Genung, another guest, saw Paine at the Club next day and said, "Albert, I have a hunch you should be Mark Twain's biographer. And if you propose the idea to him, I'm sure it will come to pass." Paine was doubtful, but his fellow Players persuaded him to make an appointment with Twain, and the result was the four-volume autobiography, dictated to Paine, who edited and arranged it. This work was the standard until Charles Neider's rearrangement, with new material, in 1959.

During the two years he lived at the Club, Twain ate most of his meals there, sitting at a round table by the bay window in the dining room. He had the same breakfast every morning: coffee, rolls, and three softboiled eggs, served to him broken in a water tumbler because the regular egg glasses would not hold three at a time.

One morning his regular waiter, John, was late getting to work, and without even stopping for his own breakfast, hurried to prepare Twain's usual order. In his haste, he broke two eggs into a regular egg glass and kept the third for himself. Mark put down his morning paper as John served him, but before the waiter left the room, he heard Twain pounding his call bell furiously. John returned to the table.

"Just how many eggs are in this cup?" Twain wanted to know.

"Three, sir," John said, looking embarrassed.

"Hm." Twain looked straight at the waiter, "Is Walter about?"

Walter was summoned. "I want to congratulate you on your waiter," Mark said. "He really is a wonder. I've been staying in this house for several months, and I've tried over and over to get three eggs into one of these egg glasses. This young man comes along and does with ease what I have failed to do after countless efforts. I say he's a wonder."

In this case, as in others, it was difficult to know when Twain was just being Twain, or when he was really angry.

While he was living at the Club, Twain took William Bispham to the New Amsterdam Hotel to dine one night, for the sake of variety. It was an unusual occasion for Bispham. He had his home and his church, and never dined at the Club or elsewhere unless a board meeting ran over to 6 o'clock. He was a proper, rather conventional man so it was not surprising that the conversation began to lag halfway through dinner, but then Bispham noted that his companion had stopped talking entirely, quite uncharacteristic of Twain. Looking up, Bispham saw that he was staring at a lovely young woman dining alone at another table—remarkable in itself for those days.

"Mark!" Bispham exclaimed, shocked. "Don't you see that you're embarrassing her?"

"She's wonderful, William, isn't she wonderful?" Twain murmured, not shifting his eyes away.

"Yes, but you mustn't, you mustn't," Bispham said, rising in his agitation and trying to draw Twain's attention from the object of his desire.

But Twain rose too, and said with an intensity that could only have shocked poor Bispham even more, "Why, I'd rather lie down beside that young woman naked than beside General Grant in full uniform!"

Mark could forgive many things but he could not forgive a lawyer called Phineas Alvah Ludlum—or at least so called by the discreet Walter in his memoirs. Ludlum was considered a conspicuous misfit at the Club by other members as well, a man with obtrusive manners that annoyed many and infuriated Twain.

Alone in the grill room one morning having his late breakfast, Twain saw Ludlum come in, and piling up his dishes, food and all, he carried them to a small tea table in the main hall. Ludlum, however, was too obtuse to notice this obvious slight, and greeted Twain in his usual bumptious manner. Having finished breakfast in the main hall, Twain moved on into the reading room and began to absorb himself in magazines, looking up long enough to observe that it had begun to rain outside.

Meanwhile, Ludlum finished breakfast and went to the coatroom. Seeing the rain falling, he asked the attendant if there was an umbrella in the house. "I'm sorry, sir, but there isn't," the boy told him.

"I see one in there," Ludlum said impatiently.

"That belongs to Mr. Clemens. I can't give you that," the boy said.

Ludlum brushed by him and took it anyway. "Don't worry," he said, "Mark Twain is a great friend of mine. He's not likely to go out, but if he should want his umbrella, tell him that Mr. Phineas Alvah Ludlum has taken it for a few hours, as he had to go to a funeral." He departed with the umbrella.

Later, Clemens rose from his magazines and prepared to leave to keep an appointment. At the cloakroom the boy told him what had happened to his umbrella. Furious, Twain began pacing up and down on the landing, and to Walter, who was just coming up from the pool room, he roared, "Mr. Phineas Alvah Ludlum should be barred from the Club." Turning to the cloakroom boy, he added, "I hope Mr. Ludlum's damned funeral is a failure!"

For Twain, this episode had a happy ending. Only a short time later the police removed Ludlum from a bordello one night, and the lawyer made the mistake of giving his address as The Players, 16 Gramercy Park. The incident was reported in the newspapers next day and Ludlum was expelled.

On ordinary days at the Club, Twain appeared to be like any other Player. Charlie recalled that no one on the staff seemed to realize how famous a man he was. They treated him with respect, of course, as they would any other Player. Members naturally treated him as they did each other, in the leveling tradition of the Club, but it was also true that not many of them at that time realized they were in the presence of a great literary figure. To them he was a writer no more important than, say, Booth Tarkington. They saw him as a charming but sometimes irascible man in a white suit who often ordered a hot drink at the bar—Scotch, bourbon, or a rye toddy, regardless of the temperature outside.

(Bars in those days had a kettle of steaming water on tap for the benefit of hot-toddy customers, in this era preceding the time of the iced drink.)

Like any other member, Twain was also capable of the occasional gaffe. He recorded one of them himself in Neider's version of the autobiography. Drifting into the Club one night, he related, he found a half-dozen fellow Players sipping punches and talking. He joined them, and the talk soon turned to Bret Harte. A young fellow sitting at Twain's elbow began to deliver a virtual eulogy of the Harte family, particularly Mrs. Harte and her daughters, who were living alone in a small New Jersey town—a hardworking and cheerful family. To earn their living, the young man said, Mrs. Harte taught music, and the girls employed their arts of drawing, embroidery, and similar crafts to make money. Listening with the others, Twain could only applaud. "I was aware that he was speaking the truth and not overstating it," Twain said. Then the young man's enthusiastic tribute took a different turn, and Twain relates what happened:

> But presently he diverged into eulogies of the ostensible head of that deserted family, Bret Harte. He said that the family's happiness had one defect in it; the absence of Harte. He said that their love and their reverence for him was a beautiful thing to see and hear; also, their pity of him on account of his enforced exile from home. He also said that Harte's own grief, because of this bitter exile, was beautiful to contemplate; that Harte's faithfulness in writing by every steamer was beautiful too; that he was always longing to come home in his vacations but his salary was so small that he could not afford it; nevertheless, in his letters he was always promising himself this happiness in the next steamer or the next one after that one; and that it was pitiful to see the family's disappointment when the named steamers kept on arriving without him; that his self-sacrifice was an ennobling spectacle; that he was man enough and fine enough to deny himself in order that he might send to the family every month, for their support, that

portion of his salary which a more selfish person would devote to the Atlantic voyage.

Up to this time I had "stood the raise," as the poker players say, but now I broke out and called the young fellow's hand—as the poker players also say, I couldn't help it. I saw that he had been misinformed. It seemed to be my duty to set him right.

I said, "Oh, that be hanged! There's nothing in it. Bret Harte has deserted his family and that is the plain English of it. Possibly he writes to them, but I am not weak enough to believe it until I see the letters; possibly he is pining to come home to his deserted family, but no one that knows him will believe that. But there is one thing about which I think there can be no possibility of doubt—and that is, that he has never sent them a dollar and has never intended to send them a dollar. Bret Harte is the most contemptible, poor little soulless blatherskite that exists on the planet to-day. . . ."

I had been dimly aware, very vaguely aware, by fitful glimpses of the countenances around me, that something was happening. It was I that was happening but I didn't know it.

But when I had reached the middle of that last sentence somebody seized me and whispered into my ear, with energy, "For goodness sake shut up! This young fellow is Steele. He's engaged to one of the daughters."

Only something so inadvertent could rein in, momentarily, the ebullient Twain spirit, although he could be impressed into something approaching complete respect by people or things outside his sphere. He and Henry Rogers, a Standard Oil tycoon, went with a group of Players one day to watch James Corbett box, and he was excited by the sight of this fighting machine in action. Stanford White took Twain in to talk with Corbett, and Mark pronounced him later "the most perfectly and beautifully constructed human animal in the world." For Twain, that was extreme praise. His admiration for animals and disdain for much of the human race was evident in what he wrote.

Twain's *cause célèbre* at the Club was his expulsion in January 1903 for nonpayment of dues. He was not alone in the wholesale banishment that occurred then. Club records show that thirty-eight others, including Jefferson, were dropped at the same time for the same reason. Henry Miller and Wilton Lackaye, who were on the list, paid up, and were reinstated (although Walter asserts Lackaye never came back), but not Jefferson; the records are mysteriously silent about what happened in his case. He must have been reinstated almost at once. Junius Brutus Booth was also on the list, but he paid up only to become delinquent again the following year, was dropped again, and disappears from the written record.

In his autobiography, Twain gives us different versions of the story, all of them vitriolic. "Mr. Booth's bequest was a great and generous one," he writes (or dictates) at one point, "but he left two. The other one was not much of a benefaction. It was a relative of his who needed a support. As secretary (Twain was wrong; he was superintendent), he governed the club and its board of managers like an autocrat from the beginning until three or four months ago, when he retired from the position superannuated. . . ."

The superintendent was more than a brother-in-law who needed help, however; he had also been the treasurer of Booth's touring company, as noted earlier. Piecing the evidence together, it appears that during the time W. H. Magonigle reigned, some influential members of the board were either ignorant of his actions or condoned them, and all of them were toppled at the same time later.

Stories about the results of Magonigle's highhandedness, bordering on insolence, circulated in the Club from time to time. Lackaye and Miller, for example, were once treated rudely by a waiter at dinner one night, an unheardof event at the Club. They complained to a member of the House Committee who was also on the board. When they had finished, the member said, "That's your story, now I'll get the waiter's."

The two diners left the Club, indignant, and went over to the Hotel Amsterdam, on the corner of Fourth Avenue and 21st Street, where they resumed eating, having angrily left their Club dinner. This hotel was becoming a haven at that period for Players who were disgusted with the Club's administration. Dining there, Lackaye recalled how, a few years earlier, he had visited Stratford-on-Avon while he was working in the London theater and decided it would be a nice gesture if he could get some ivy there, bring it back to New York, and have it planted around the Club's piazza. A London florist preserved it for him until he could take it home, but he had to leave without it, and a fellow Player brought it back on a trip a month later. Lackaye had the ivy delivered to the House Committee and explained to Magonigle what was to be done. Instead, it was left to die on the floor in a corner of the coatroom.

Lackaye's departure from the Club after being expelled (if Walter is correct) was a matter of concern to his friend Twain and other Players because, as Walter put it, he was "a great spirit." He once introduced Childe Hassam to a friend at the Club as "Mr. Worms," adding, "You know, every Childe Hassam." As he lay dying, he heard that The Players were putting on *Troilus and Cressida,* and asked a friend to get him two tickets on the aisle. When his wife, a trained nurse, told him he could not possibly make it, he insisted and wrote out a check on the spot. His wife followed the friend from the room and told him that if Lackaye went to the theater, he would fall dead in the aisle. It took the doctor's unequivocal orders to keep him home.

To return to the main event: Twain insisted that when he went abroad in 1891 he left behind a "paymaster" with instructions to pay all his bills while he was gone, and the Club secretary (he meant Magonigle) was instructed that this was being done. When Magonigle sent him a bill in Europe, he sent it back, reminding him of the instructions. Two years later, the same thing occurred, Twain repeated his instructions, and yet the bills kept coming. Mark's ire was rising because he was now getting offensive notes from Magonigle. "These I answered profusely," he tells us.

When he returned from Europe in 1901, no bills arrived for a year. Then, as he recalled, "We took a residence at Riverdale-on-the-Hudson and straightway came a Players' bill for dues. I was aweary, aweary, and I put it in the waste basket. Ten days later the bill came again, and with it a shadowy threat. I waste-basketed it. After another ten days the bill came once more, and this time the threat was in a concreted condition. It said very peremptorily that if the bill were not paid within a week I would be expelled from the club and posted as a delinquent. This went the way of its predecessors, into the waste basket. On the named day I was posted as expelled." The date was January 12, 1903.

When the news of Twain's departure circulated in the Club, there was a spontaneous wave of sorrow, and renewed affection for him. Robert Reid, the artist, and David Munro, editor of the *North American Review,* two of his special friends, wrote anguished letters, inquiring what had happened. When he explained, they urged him to bring the matter to the attention of the board and ask for a reconsideration, but Twain declined. He did not say why, nor did he in his autobiography. In that volume he says that his friends thought things would change when Magonigle "retired from the autocracy." Retirement was not exactly what occurred, however. Magonigle's departure resulted from one of the few Club scandals in its century of existence.

What brought down Magonigle was hubris. He did the unthinkable and tried to fire Walter, but contrary to Twain's recollection, it did not occur before Mark came back to the Club; it was two years later. Howard Kyle tells the story in *Walter's Sketch Book,* since Walter would not have dreamed of telling it himself.

Kyle returned from a trip to London in 1907 and found two members awaiting him, extremely upset. Walter had been discharged by the house committee, they said. At that point the committee consisted of, among others, Nicholas Biddle, a financier; Richard Hunt, an architect; and Daniel Frohman, who was also the treasurer. Kyle went to Walter's house and, with tears in his eyes, the faithful servant would say nothing about the firing.

At that point Kyle directed his suspicions to the superintendent, recalling that when it had been his turn to have dinner with Magonigle at his house in a small New Jersey town—a member was thus entertained every Sunday night—he had observed that the house and its contents seemed quite beyond Magonigle's salary.

Confronting him now, Kyle demanded, "Did you get the House Committee to dismiss Walter?" Magonigle admitted it. "Well," Kyle said, "you'd better have his dismissal recalled if you wish to be held in esteem by the members. Telephone Biddle and get the discharge rescinded right away, if you know when you're well off." It was done. A little later, delinquent bills began turning up, and the board had to pay them out of the members' pockets, occasioning the calling of an auditor who examined the books and reported that funds were missing and the records mishandled.

The house committee resigned in a body because it had apparently not known of what was going on, although it was responsible. Magonigle escaped with a stern admonition to mend his ways, since nothing had been proved, although it was plain that he had tried to ruin Walter by making him a scapegoat. Kyle went on the house committee himself, and William Morrow was made chairman, after which the board met the deficiencies in the books, about $8,000, out of the members' own pockets, $5,000 of which came from John Drew. The whole disgraceful affair was hushed up so successfully that the fragmentary records remaining are still riddled with contradictions, and questions that can never be answered.

It took much less horrendous events to lure Twain back into the Club. A movement began among some members, mostly among those at the Round Table, to bring him home again. Munro and Reid drafted a simple appeal in verse, with no apologies to Robert Burns:

> To
> *Mark Twain*
> *from*
> *The Clansmen*

Will ye no come back again?
Will ye no come back again?
  Better lo'ed ye canna be,

Will ye no come back again?

They signed it, along with about thirty others, and sent it off. They knew he had always been moved by those lines. Soon came his reply:

"Well-Beloved—Surely those lovely verses went to Prince Charlie's heart, if he had one, & certainly they have gone to mine. I shall be glad & proud to come back again after such a moving & beautiful compliment as this from comrades whom I have loved so long. I hope you can poll the necessary vote; I know you will try, at any rate. It will be many months before I can foregather with you, for this black border is not perfunctory, not a convention; it symbolizes the loss of one whose memory is the only thing I worship. [His wife had died.] It is not necessary for me to thank you—words could not deliver what I feel, anyway. I will put the contents of your envelope in the small casket where I keep the things which have become sacred to me."

This appears in Volume 4 of Paine's version of the *Autobiography*. In Volume 2, dictated at a later time, he tells a quite different story, following his mention of the "ancient secretary's" retirement.

"The boys," he said, "thought that my return to the club would be plain and simple sailing now, but I thought differently. I was no longer a member. I could not become a member without consenting to be voted for by the board, like any other candidate, and I would not do that. The management had expelled me upon the mere statement of a clerk that I was a delinquent. They had not asked me to testify in my defense. They might properly argue from that that I had not all of a sudden become a rascal, and that I might be able to explain the situation if asked.

"The board's whole proceeding had been like *all* the board's proceedings from the beginning—arbitrary, insolent, stupid. That board's proper place, from the beginning, was the idiot asylum. I could not allow myself to be voted for again, because from my view of the matter I had never lawfully and legitimately ceased to be a member. However, a way fair and honorable to all concerned was easily found to bridge the separating crack. I was made an honorary member, and I have been glad to resume business at the old stand."

Nothing of this can be found in the Board's minutes. On the contrary, its record for December 11, 1905, says simply: "On motion the action of the Board in declaring Mr. Samuel L. Clemens as no longer a member of the Club at a meeting held Jan. 12, 1903, was reconsidered, and Mr. Clemens was thereupon reinstated as a member in good standing, past indebtedness to be cancelled by the Treas., and his dues to be remitted perpetually, and the Sec'y. was instructed to invite Mr. Clemens, on behalf of the Board, to resume his membership and to tender its congratulations on the occasion of his 70th birthday." In short, Clemens was made, not an honorary, but a life member.

Rejoicing at his return, twenty-two of his friends gave him a dinner at the Club a few days after Founder's Night in 1906. (It was the same dinner at which the stuffed frogs appeared, and Paine was nudged into doing the *Autobiography*.). Twain's own account of the affair in the first volume of that work is the great man at his most characteristic:

On this occasion Brander Matthews was chairman, and he opened the proceedings with an easy and comfortable and felicitous speech. Brander is always prepared and competent when he is going to make a speech. Then he called up Gilder, who came empty, and probably supposed he was going to be able to fill from Brander's tank, whereas he struck a disappointment. He labored through and sat down, not entirely defeated, but a good deal crippled. Frank Miller (painter) was next called up. He struggled along through his remarks, exhibiting two things—one, that he had prepared and couldn't remember the details of his preparation, and the other that his text was a poor text. In his talk the main sign of preparation was that he tried to recite two considerable batches of poetry—good poetry—but he lost confidence and turned it into bad poetry by bad recitation. Sculpture was to have been represented, and Saint-Gaudens had accepted and had promised a speech, but at the last moment he was not able to come and a man who was thoroughly unprepared had to get up and make a speech in Saint-Gaudens's place. He did not hit upon anything original or disturbing in his remarks, and, in fact, they were so tottering and hesitating and altogether commonplace that really he seemed to have hit upon something new and fresh when he finished by saying that he had not been expecting to be called upon to make a speech! I could have finished his speech for him, I had heard it so many times.

These people were unfortunate because they were *thinking*—that is, Miller and Gilder were—all the time that Matthews was speaking: they were trying to keep in mind the little preparations which they had made, and this prevented them from getting something new and fresh in the way of a text out of what Brander was saying. In the same way, Miller was still thinking about his preparation while Gilder was talking, and so he overlooked possible texts furnished by Gilder.

But as I had asked Matthews to put me last on the list of speakers, I had all the advantage possible to the occasion. For I came without a text, and these boys furnished plenty of texts to me, because my mind was not absorbed in trying to remember my preparation—they didn't exist. I spoiled, in a degree, Brander's speech, because his speech had been prepared with direct reference to introducing me, the guest of the occasion—and he had to turn that all around and get out of it, which he did very gracefully, explaining that his speech was a little lopsided and wrong end first because I had asked to be placed last in the list of speakers. I had a plenty good-enough time, because Gilder had furnished me a text: Brander had furnished me a text: Miller had furnished me a text. These texts were fresh, hot from the hat, and they produced the same eager disposition to take hold of them and talk that they would have produced in ordinary conversation around a table in a beer mill.

Unfortunately, there is no record of what Twain *did* say. No doubt it surpassed anything these loyal friends could offer in literary quality, but not their expressions of love for him.

On the few occasions Twain wrote about the club in a more serious way, he brought to his task the unsparing vision that illuminates his best work. The joking he did in the description quoted above (it was the kind of genial put-down typical of his time) was followed in the next section of the *Autobiography* by a long story about a Player named John Malone.

"Midway of the dinner," said Twain, "I got a glimpse, through a half-open door, of that pathetic figure, John Malone. There he was, left out, of course. Sixty-five years old; and his history may be summarized—his history for fifty years—in those two words, those eloquent words—'left out.' He had been left, and left out, and left out, as the years drifted by for nearly two generations. He was always expecting to be counted in. He was always pathetically hoping to be counted in; and that hope never deserted him through all those years, and yet was never in any instance realized. During all those years that I used to drop in at the Players for a game of billiards and a chat with the boys, John Malone was always there until midnight and after. He had a cheap lodging in the Square—somewhere in Gramercy Park, but the club was his real home. . . ."

Then Twain told John Malone's story. Briefly, he had been an apprentice in a weekly newspaper in Willamette, Oregon, when Booth made a one-night stand there. John emerged from the theater stagestruck. He joined the troupe and traveled with it, performing all kinds of menial chores and occasionally appearing on the stage to say something like, "My Lord, the carriage waits." In time, however, he began to get larger parts, and rose until he ranked not far below Booth himself as a tragedian, in company with John McCullough. When Booth left the stage it was understood that one of the two Johns would succeed him. A great opportunity arose when a major role was offered in Philadelphia. Malone accepted at once—and missed the train. McCullough took his place and scored a success that guaranteed him lifelong fame.

From that point on, Malone's fortunes declined steadily. The time came when he could no longer get a part, even a minor one, in the theater. Yet he always believed that some day he would get the chance, the *one* chance, that would make him famous and compel people to acknowledge that he was the rightful successor to Booth. Once he was asked to play Othello in one of the major New York theaters, but the producers canceled the project at the last minute. He spent a great deal of time at the Club, and in fact became its official historian. That was what his life had come to at the time of the Twain welcome-back dinner.

"As I was saying," Twain resumed in the *Autobiography,* "at mid-dinner that night I saw him through the half-open door. There he remained through the rest of the dinner, 'left out,' always left out. But at the end of the speeches, when a number of us were standing up in groups and chatting, he crept meekly in and found his way to the vacant chair at my side, and sat down. I sat down at once and began to talk with him. I was always fond of him—I think everyone was."

Twain relates that the president of City College came over to chat, and in an effort to include Malone in the conversations, asked him if he had ever been in Dublin, New Hampshire.

"How does it lie as regards Manchester?" Malone inquired.

The president told him, and John said, "I have never been to Dublin, but I have a sort of recollection of Manchester. I am pretty sure I was there once—but it was only a one-night stand, you know."

Twain continues: "It filled my soul with a gentle delight, a gracious satisfaction, the way he said that 'Only a one-night stand.' It seemed to reveal that in his half century of daydreaming he had been an Edwin Booth and unconscious that he was only John Malone—that he was an Edwin Booth, with a long and great and successful career behind him, in which 'one-night stands' sank into insignificance and the memory unused to treasuring such little things could not keep tally of them. He said it with the splendid indifference and serenity of a Napoleon who was making an indolent effort to remember a skirmish in which a couple of soldiers had been killed, but was not finding it really worthwhile to dig deep after such a fact."

A few days after the dinner Twain spoke to Volney Streamer, the Club librarian, about Malone. Mark's friend, David Munro, who had been one of the chief architects of the event, had been unable to attend the dinner, and so planned to give one of his own on February 6, and had told Twain that if there was anyone he wanted to invite, all he had to do was give Munro the name. Twain wanted Malone to attend, so that for once he would not be left out, and now he was asking Streamer, who knew everyone, in the most discreet way how Malone stood with the members. Twain did not want him embarrassed. But Streamer assured him that everyone liked John—and pitied him too.

Then the librarian gave Twain his own version of Malone's life, and produced two surprises. First, he was not a bachelor but had a married daughter in New York. Second, Streamer had also been a member of Booth's company at the time Malone joined it, and traveled with him for years.

A few days later Malone contributed a surprise of his own. As Twain recalled it, "Rev. Joe Twitchell arrived from Hartford to take dinner and stay all night and swap some lies, and he sat here by the bed the rest of the afternoon, and we talked, and I told him all about John Malone. Twitchell came in after breafast this morning . . . to chat again, and he brought me this, which he had cut out of the morning paper."

The clipping Twain read was headlined, "VETERAN ACTOR DEAD. John Malone was Historian of The Players' Club," and it went on: "John Malone, the historian of The Players' Club and one of the oldest actors in the country, was stricken with apoplexy yesterday afternoon in front of Bishop Greer's residence, 7 Gramercy Park, a few doors from the club. Bishop Greer saw his fall, and with the assistance of his servants, carried Mr. Malone into his house. He was unconscious, and the bishop telephoned to Police Headquarters. An ambulance was sent from Bellevue Hospital, and Mr. Malone was taken to the institution by Dr. Hawkes. Later The Players had him removed to the Post-Graduate Hospital, where he died last night.

"Mr. Malone was sixty-five years old, and supported all the notable actors of a past generation. For a long time he was associated with Booth and Barrett, He had appeared on the stage but infrequently of late years, devoting the greater part of his time to magazine work. He lived with a married daughter in West 147th Street, but visited The Players' Club nearly every day. He was on his way to the club when he was stricken."

Twain ends his account, rather sententiously for him: "While Twitchell and I were talking about John Malone he was passing from this life. His disappointments are ended. At last he is not 'left out.' It was a long wait, but the best of all fortunes is his at last."

* * *

Not much remains of Mark Twain at the Club today in a physical sense—his billiard cue beside the green table, the Gordon Stevenson portrait of him on the wall. There was also a surprising addition in 1939: Dan Beard, chief of the Boy Scouts, sent the Club one of Twain's pipes and a hunk of his tobacco to be added to the collection of Players' memorabilia. In the note accompanying his gift, Beard wrote, to "My dear boys of The Players" (which must have caused some wincing): "After Mark Twain's death, his daughter, Clara, gave me this pipe and tobacco as a souvenir of my dear friend and her father. . . . I know of no fitter place for these to rest than at my former club, The Players, where I myself have had so many enjoyable times when C. D. Gibson, Fred Remington, Charlie Reinhart, Oliver Herford, and Brander Matthews used to gather at the Round Table to cuss and discuss the art, literature, stage, and topics of the day. They were glorious times. I thought that on Mark's birthday, maybe you might want to have a little ceremony, and like the Indians, pass the pipe around and take a puff of his tobacco. To use this tobacco straight would be strong medicine, but, blended with ordinary tobacco, it gives it a pleasant kick."

Mercifully, this ceremony was never undertaken. But Beard was dead right about one thing: They were, indeed, "glorious times," those early days of The Players.

PART TWO

The Middle Years

CHAPTER 5

The Twenties

AS THOUSANDS OF HISTORIANS HAVE TOLD US, IN EVERY CONCEIVABLE way, the Twenties marked a turning point in the nation's life, a postwar era of change, the kind that great wars always produce. Even so specialized a corner of American and New York life as The Players was not immune to it.

In some ways, however, the Club did *not* change, particularly in its essential character. To Otis Skinner, in the early years of that decade, The Players remained "a shining example of the perfectly trained diaphragm. It functions without any effort, without thought. I am aware that when I step off the Gramercy Park sidewalk and enter its welcoming door that I am going to meet diverse and sundry of my co-mates who have no diaphragms at all. If they ever did have, their properties have atrophied. They do have contact with a world beyond the clubhouse walls that causes the midriff to rise at every traffic signal; but they bring them to a haven of repose where companionship, true understanding and generosity spread like a balm over all its votaries; where thought is free, conversation uncensored, laughter unchecked, vituperation a virtue, and the midriff ignored. Some men are born with midriffs, others achieve midriffs, and some midriffs are thrust upon them, but not in The Players Club." (It should be noted here that our legal name is "The Players." To add "Club" is not only superfluous but inaccurate.)

In Skinner's words there spoke the voice of the early years, surviving in a changing world that some Players continued to resist for a long time. The old one had simply been too comfortable. Many of the early leading

93

spirits were still active at No. 16, and in relating the history of these middle years there is bound to be some overlapping, although many of the older members were beginning to fade into the historic past as new spirits appeared. But several who had been overshadowed in the past were now emerging as Club personalities in their own right.

For old and new, young and old, there was a single dreadful fact that had to be confronted. With the arrival of Prohibition on January 16, 1920, New York closed up on the surface and blossomed in a different form below, behind closed doors with peepholes. By January 1922, the New York *Times* was reporting that clubs in the city had made proper adjustments to the new order: "Safety deposits for private stock are a feature of club life these days. . . . So great is the pressure for some place to keep stock where it cannot be watered down that there is hardly a well-known uptown club that does not have a special set of lockers devoted to maintaining the securities in good condition for the members . . . still plenty of good liquor to be had . . . many waiters who manage to conduct a thriving business in gin, whisky, and rum—courts are as loathe to give search warrants for clubs as they are for the ransacking of private dwellings."

At The Players, the liquor lockers were placed across from the mailboxes in the space between the pool table and the men's room. Charlie was their custodian and he was gravely aware of his responsibility because the enforcers had wasted no time in making an example of no less a public figure than John J. McGraw, who was manager and part owner of the New York Giants.

Only seven months after Prohibition went into effect, McGraw was involved in a fight at the Lambs, of which he was a member, over whether he had bought liquor in the club. Both he and the desk clerk were arrested, and McGraw was indicted for illegal possession. The authorities threatened to prosecute the club and some of its members, although this proved to be no more than a threat. Nevertheless, the incident was a clear signal to every club in New York, and they took notice, even after McGraw was acquitted by a jury under Federal Judge Learned Hand because several prosecution witnesses failed to appear.

"Taking notice," however, simply meant that clubs went to extraordinary lengths to conceal what they were doing—for a time, at least. Eventually, when it became clear that individual enforcement was relatively futile, and that the police were involved in chasing bootleggers, a more relaxed mood prevailed.

But not relaxed enough. At The Players it had been found that a mailbox could hold a flask of the proper size, and there was also a certain carelessness about bar patronage. In those days the bar was not parallel to the street as it is now, but was backed up against the west wall separating The Players from its next door neighbor, the National Arts Club. On a summer afternoon, with the windows open, sounds from the bar were inclined to drift outside if they were above a certain decibel level. They had surpassed that point one hot day and a lady sitting by an open window at the club next door could not help overhearing. Peering out, she observed an employee carrying packages through the basement door of No. 16 and came to the obvious conclusion. She called police.

They arrived, arrested a Club employee and a nearby janitor from another building, where in the basement they found enough evidence to stand up in any court. At The Players there was consternation. Someone remembered that an assistant district attorney was a member, but someone else recalled that he was under suspension at the moment for boisterous behavior. He was called immediately, however, and fences were mended with indecent speed. The attorney rushed to the precinct station, convinced the police that they had made a serious mistake which would be noted in the prosecutor's office, and the Club's employee was released. Everyone forgot about the janitor, who stayed in jail until next morning. Very little of the seized liquor was recovered. No one could remember where it had gone.

While it lasted, Prohibition produced a crop of stories that became part of Club folklore. Bispham and Charles Genung, for example, were sitting near the bar one evening, engaged in a furious whispered conversation which attracted the curious who strained to hear what was going on. After many whispers from Genung and impatient "yes, yeses" from Bispham, the conspiracy was disclosed when Bispham spoke aloud in his usual roar: "Yes, yes. But do you put the raisins in before the yeast or the yeast before the raisins?"

Typical of the charade that Prohibition became was the visit one day of a police inspector who walked down the steps to the office, which was then next to the bar, having to pass the habitués thereof who were lined up three deep. Fighting his way through the fumes, the officer informed the man on duty that the police department had been sent an anonymous letter charging that demon rum was loose in the basement of The Players. He was welcome to inspect the basement, said the clerk, and together they did so. "I see there's nothing in the charge," the officer said blandly, and left.

The police, in fact, had given up where the Club was concerned, as an incident near the end of Prohibition days made plain. Aymar Embury had planned a Christmas party and at the last minute it was discovered that a case of Scotch, necessary to the occasion, was not on hand. In a panic, Embury turned to Charlie. Yes, Charlie said, he had the Scotch; delivering it was the problem. But then he learned that, even as they spoke, the policeman who patroled the Gramercy Park district was being entertained in the Club kitchen, and Charlie approached him with the problem at once.

"Certainly," said this obliging law enforcer, "Mr. Embury must have his Scotch. I'll take it right up in the police car."

Charlie had good reason to be sure of the officer's help. Only a few nights earlier, Jules Guerin had departed from the Club with two bottles of gin making a large lump in the front of his coat, when he encountered this same patrolman.

"What's that you've got there?" the law wanted to know.

"Booze," Jules admitted, seeing no point in trying to conceal it.

"I thought so," the patrolman said. "Be on your way now."

So the good ship Prohibition sailed on over seas of hypocrisy until repeal became effective on December 5, 1933. Earlier, on April 7, beer had been restored by an act of Congress, and the house committee had acted with admirable speed to install the pumps and other equipment needed for draught beer, light or dark. When the real thing arrived, beer was forgotten and the Club *Bulletin* reported: "Sounds of hammering in the region of Charlie's office have lately signaled the passing of the Dark Ages. Gone at last are those hideous Volstead lockers, and there will be plenty of room for the bottles which free men may once more take or leave alone. Gone also is the draft beer machine."

The *Bulletin* had arrived almost with Prohibition, originating in the fall of 1921, the inspiration of Arthur Goodrich. It did not end, of course, with repeal but has continued in one form or another until the present. Goodrich turned over the editorship to George Casamajor soon after the founding, and when that member died in the summer of 1923, Lawton Mackall took the reins until February 1925, after which Frederic Dorr Steele, Henry Saylor, William Plante, George W. Stewart, editor of *The Players at 75 Years,* Jack Iams, Robert Carter and a number of other editors in between held the editorial reins. It has been an intermittent publication, with several gaps in publication, and it has assumed various forms. Nevertheless, it is unsurpassed in Club archives as a historical record.

The *Bulletin's* celebration of the end of Prohibition at the Club found an echo in the New York *Herald Tribune,* not surprising since many of its best editors and reporters were members. "Some index of the business done over the bar at The Players in Gramercy Park on the first day of legal drinking within the Club's premises," the paper reported, "may be found in the circumstance that members wore down three full-length, extra heavy lead copy pencils signing their names to bar checks. While there is no standing permitted against the bar itself of this historic club, tables have been laid out in the billiard room and the new freedom has attracted unusually large numbers during the last two days."

While the anecdotes of these and earlier times might lead one to think that the Club's existence depended largely on alcohol, that was not the case. The Players simply reflected the mores and manners of New York social life in those periods, and when that life began to change, the Club changed as well.

In the early Twenties, change was everywhere in the American air as the nation embarked on that decade known, among many other titles, as the Jazz Age, or the Era of Wonderful Nonsense. At the Club in 1921 change took on the proportions of heresy. A murmuring had arisen among some members that too many changes were taking place in the quiet old Gramercy Park neighborhood and, in any case, the theaters had moved uptown, taking social life with them. Why not follow, they wanted to know.

"Why?" John Drew replied simply, echoing the feelings of the shocked majority. "A club is a place one *goes* to." On December 18, 1921, one hundred four members met and conducted a formal debate on whether to move. Malcolm Duncan spoke for the affirmative, and that professional iconoclast, Albert J. Nock, not surprisingly took the negative. After months of investigation and argument, a meeting was called for April 10, 1922, and the question was put to a vote. The official count was 335 against moving, 185 for. The argument was settled, once and for all, but it gave the older members especially a nasty shock, and they were some time getting over it. To them, it was as though 185 members had chosen to spit on Booth's grave.

Dave McKinley, who would become a leading figure in the Club during the Twenties and Thirties, was made acutely aware of how much things were changing when, as a member of the house committee, he was asked to go through minutes of past committee meetings to see if some gems of management might be interred there. The board had decided that the constitution and bylaws needed changing, and the committee had been instructed to come up with some suggestions before the next meeting.

The earlier minutes were located in the basement, scattered among all kinds of debris. Most were uninformative. They simply recorded that the house committee, met, those present were listed, the minutes of the last meeting were read and approved, and the meeting adjourned. But there *were* gems, although not of managerial usefulness. An entire meeting was spent deciding whether a popular member should be suspended for ten or thirty days, because he had arrived at No. 16 in a hansom cab with a lady companion, whom he left outside while he went in and returned with two foaming beakers, which both consumed on the spot. In a true Solomonic judgment the committee added ten days to thirty days, divided by half, and gave the member twenty days' suspension.

Another meeting was spent deciding the fate of the goldfish in the backyard pool, much admired by the gentlemen who contemplated them from the piazza, where many preferred to dine. The question was what to do with the fish in the winter. A committee member reported that the librarian had volunteered to take care of the goldfish in his home if the Club would pay for a bowl to keep them in. A resolution was offered, thanking the librarian and accepting his offer. But then another member interposed, arguing that this action was premature since the committee hadn't appropriated any money for the bowl. Solemnly, the appropriation was duly authorized.

One of the most arcane proposals was made at a meeting involving the high cost of liquor licenses. The Technology Club, which occupied the building next door to the East, proposed that the two clubs might get away with one license for both on a fifty-fifty basis by boring a hole through the wall where the cloakroom was (and is) located. Drinks could be shoved through one way, and empty glasses returned. It was a tempting offer, considering the amount of money to be saved, but the Committee put temptation behind. The entrance would lose dignity, its members said.

As the Twenties began, sterner matters were on the table when the board and its various committees, particularly the house committee, met. First consideration had to be given to the physical condition of the clubhouse. John S. Phillips wrote years later: "My mind jumps back to the early Twenties: the kitchen in shocking condition, the porch drab and unattractive; the bar half width; the office beside it with the accounting room back on the street; bedrooms and beds shabby and uncomfortable; original plumbing fast deteriorating; heating system inadequate. Time and the neglect enforced during World War I had taken their toll. We who lived much in this house found so much of beauty in Stanford White's planning, and charm in the fading pictures, furnishings and decorations that the ensemble gave us a sense of living in a fine old mansion. . . . I have heard cosmopolitans say that they knew no club in the world like it in agreeable atmosphere."

Nevertheless, the agreeable atmosphere was in a state of imminent collapse and the first of several recurrent renovations had to be taken, coming on down to the present. Every one of them was opposed vociferously by opponents of change, and each one left the clubhouse in much better condition than it was before.

The renaissance of the Twenties began by completely changing the area below stairs, and the service arrangements adjacent to it, making improvements in conditions that had not been visible to most members. In the postwar depression, the Club itself could not afford these alterations, and $22,000 had to be raised outside. Besides the downstairs, the upstairs bedrooms were renovated and the "penthouse" built over them. Bill Tachau emerged as the Club's leader in supervising change; he was in control for two decades. He designed the porch, with its fountain in the yard below, and later changed the barroom to the welcoming spot it remains today, with its side tables and round table. He introduced a new heating plant, making the entire house warm for the first time, and installed air-conditioning on the lower level until then almost unlivable in summer.

When Phillips entered the Club after the first wave of renovation, he observed "the change from half-darkness to full light; pictures brought back to life and sight, after years of obsolescence; everywhere wholesome clearing; tasteful floor covering and upholstery replaced or renewed. . . . All this was done without touching the funds or income of the Club." Phillips had invested a good deal of his own money in these renovations; his wife noted that he had bought only one new suit in six years.

The major part of these first alterations occurred in the basement, where the kitchen and employees' quarters were greatly enlarged by cutting through the wall into the building next door to the East, thus nearly doubling facilities, adding storerooms, a service dining room, and modern dishwashing machinery. Lack of space and facilities had made it nearly a miracle to serve meals in the dining room. Now the new kitchens extended under both buildings, and were reached by stairways serving both The Players and the Technology Club. All pastry could now be made on the premises. The dishwashing that had been done by hand in a cramped pantry next to the dining room was now accomplished below by electricity. The steam table, once in the dining room, was moved to the basement, making room for more dining tables, particularly welcome on Pipe Nights. Many of these repairs should have been done years before; the Club was paying for the deterioration of the previous decade.

Upstairs, there were new beds in the bedrooms, new carpet for the library and reading room, and extensive upholstering done. For a time in 1923 the members were uprooted and had to eat and talk at the Lambs, the Harvard Club, the Century, and the National Arts Club next door, where the Round Table was temporarily removed.

Unusually successful were the efforts to beautify the backyard—or the Goldfish Den, as members called it. Ferns planted under the supervision of a caring member lasted until the yard itself and the porch surrounding it disappeared years later.

In 1926 the renovators attacked the private dining room, by then known as the card room. Dingy woodwork began to glow again. A murky canvas on one wall which some members had mistaken for a thunderstorm on the Zuyder Zee proved to be a portrait of a young woman by Thomas Sully. On the floor above, the Booth room was scoured after years of grimy disuse, and its furniture put in order. Fixtures and ornaments were brought to their original lustre, as they were throughout the clubhouse.

With the first major wave of renovation accomplished in 1926, the *Bulletin* reported that members agreed the clubhouse had never looked so attractive, all objections to the contrary. Meals were much improved, and members were coming to the Club in increasing numbers. In this first year of Walter's superintendency, all records were broken at both luncheon and dinner.

Answering some complaints, the house committee explained why it had been necessary to have new plumbing. Taller buildings had been rising around the Park, some of them fourteen stories high. Old and small water mains in the neighborhood had compelled the new apartment houses to install powerful pumps to force water up to their tanks in order to get pressure on the top floors. The plumbing at No. 16 was not equal to the strains imposed on it by these changes.

By 1928 the cost of the alterations had reached nearly $30,000, including $2,800 to make the always controversial elevator operative. It had been necessary to move the employees' toilet in the cellar to make room for the elevator's new machinery. New electric fans were installed on the roof that year, and new ones on the porch as well. The old fans had gone into the junk pile, along with the old ice machine and the fireproof doors between the clubhouse and No. 17. The Club wanted to sell this debris, but no one would buy it and it had to be carted away—expensively. All told, the house appeared to be in such good condition that no large expenditures would be needed to improve it for some time.

An unexpected complication in the renovation downstairs was the fact that the Technology Club's lease on the building next door at No. 17 expired on April 30, 1928, and that meant the cozy arrangement by which the Club shared its basement space had to come to an end. Some room could be made in No. 16's crowded basement, but obviously something else had to be done, and Bill Tachau did it by utilizing the space under the garden. Forty-eight loads of dirt were removed from it; fortunately, there was no solid rock. The result was additional space for a staff dining-room and storage.

In the center of the new garden was a smaller and lighter fountain, with an entirely new family of goldfish in the pool. Five had not survived the transfer. In each corner were an iron table and four chairs, where members could eat on warm summer days. Three steps led down into the garden from the porch, which was later enclosed.

Some members were worried about the ancient ailanthus growing in a corner of the garden, because its roots would now have less room to expand. Two eminent tree surgeons were called in to assess the situation, and reported that it would live (would anything really kill a New York ailanthus?). They ordered a supply of tree food placed about the roots and predicted it would flourish, as it did.

Although most of the money for the alterations had been raised outside the Club's budget, finances were an intermittent, often serious, worry at The Players then and later, as they were at every other club, some of which did not survive. At the beginning of the decade, in fact, treasurer Dave McKinley, who struggled with Club finances for years, reported that the Club was "heading straight for the rocks." Occasionally his agonies reached a climax, as when he emerged from the kitchen into the pool room, and addressing the astounded players assembled there, shouted: "I want to know who the hell uses up three hundred dollars worth of quill toothpicks in this joint every year."

The search for revenue in the early Twenties led to one of the most enterprising and remarkable of The Players' many activities. In 1922, acting on the inspiration of Francis Wilson, the Club launched a series of annual revivals, employing its own members and a few others. The plays went on every season, with only two interruptions, until 1940. While they failed in the end to solve the Club's financial problems, the revivals helped to mitigate a particularly difficult period, and added much to Club prestige. In the first three years the plays turned in more than $50,000 to the Club's Theatre Fund, which was considered as a reserve, and cautious management made it necessary to draw less than $4,000 to pay the bills at No. 16.

In 1922 the initial offering was *The Rivals*, which grossed more than $20,000 from reasonably priced ticket sales at $5 and $3. *School for Scandal* followed in 1923, and *She Stoops to Conquer* in 1924, which grossed more than $32,000. They could scarcely help succeeding with such casts. In *She Stoops to Conquer,* for example, Elsie Ferguson played Kate Hardcastle, Helen Hayes was seen as Constance Neville, Pauline Lord was the Maid, Margalo Gillmore the Barmaid, Dudley Digges was Squire Hardcastle, and J. M. Kerrigan played Jack Slang. Oliver Herford wrote a prologue read by Henry Dixey, impersonating Shaw. The preceding *School for Scandal* had enlisted John Drew, Lionel Barrymore, Raymond Hitchcock, O. P. Heggie, Ernest Truex, Etienne Girardot, Ethel Barrymore, and Helen Hayes.

In 1925 came *Trelawney of the Wells,* starring John Drew, who had been reluctant to join the cast, saying, "They don't want me any more." It was not true. Even in a cast full of stage idols of the day, audiences crowded in to see Drew; he was as much a magnet as ever. When he made his last exit, the play was over as far as they were concerned. Drew spoke the prologue in the following year's revival of *Henry IV, Part I,* in an acting version prepared by Brander Matthews and Frank Gillmore, with a cast that included Basil Rathbone as Prince Hal, William Courtleigh as Henry, Rosamond Pinchot as Prince John, Philip Merivale as Hotspur, Otis Skinner as Falstaff, Peggy Wood as Lady Percy, and Marie Dressler as Mistress Quickly, also played later by Blanche Ring.

After a less memorable *Julius Caesar* in 1927, the series had a real hit in *The Beaux Stratagem,* produced in 1928, directed by Howard Lindsay, with a cast including Raymond Hitchcock, Dorothy Stickney, James T. Powers, Helen Menken, Fay Bainter, Henrietta Crosman, O. P. Heggie, and Josephine Hull as a servant. It was hailed by enthusiastic reviews from Brooks Atkinson, Percy Hammond, and Stark Young, who applauded such extra touches as a prologue written by Edgar Lee Masters and delivered by Walter Hampden, and a closing epilogue written and delivered by David Belasco.

This production was so successful that it was proposed to take it on the road but, no doubt predictably, that idea was greeted with a petition from twenty-five older members who protested that "any commercial production to be billed as under the auspices of the Club" would be "unbecoming to the tradition and dignity of the Club." They were outvoted, however. The tour took place, and turned in a gratifying profit, adding to the $38,000 it had grossed in its limited one-week New York run, a record in itself.

This may have been the high point of the revival series, with most of the reviews in the nature of raves, or barely short of it, and a splendid after-theater party at the Club, with Daniel Frohman as toastmaster, and speeches that went on until 4:30 in the morning. On tour the play was seen in all the nation's principal cities. *Becky Sharp,* the 1929 revival, was a victim of the crash and did less well, but oddly enough, the 1930 bill, when conditions were worse, made more money, although the plays themselves, *Milestones* and *Little Father of the Wilderness,* were far from being classics.

As the Depression took hold, it became more of a struggle to put on these productions. *The Way of the World* did moderately well in 1931, but there was considerable doubt whether a play would be produced at all in 1932. The Play Committee had wanted to do *Trilby,* but at the last minute the copyright owners rescinded their earlier approval, and it had to be abandoned, with only two months left in a bad season. At this juncture the board decided to give up a revival that year, but twenty-five members petitioned for a reconsideration, calling for a special Club meeting, at which there were new offers of support. It was suggested that a great play could be done that would not require costly scenery. *Troilus and Cressida* seemed to be a logical choice. Henry Herbert prepared a text, then staged and directed the production.

At the bottom of the Depression, in 1933, doubts were even more prevalent, but in a spirit of "come what may," the Club decided to do the play so many members had wanted since the revivals began—*Uncle Tom's Cabin*. George L. Aiken's original script, by that time virtually forgotten, was to be used, revised by A. E. Thomas but carefully leaving the first version's general form and character, even its dialogue, virtually intact. During the discussions leading up to a final decision, it turned out that only one member of the board had ever seen the play. Although it had often (and usually) been played tongue-in-cheek, even burlesqued, it was decided to do the play straight.

Otis Skinner was Uncle Tom; he had played the role first when he was only nineteen. Ernest Glendinning was St. Clare, Thomas Chalmers appeared as Simon Legree, and the cast included Cecilia Loftus as Chloe, Elizabeth Risdon as Eliza Harris, Fay Bainter as Topsy, and Lois Shore as Little Eva.

"Bloodhounds Bay in Gramercy Park," the *Herald Tribune* headlined its story on the revival announcement, and there were those who feared the critics would bay even louder when they heard some of the original dialogue. In the first act, scene four, for instance, Eliza stands beside the tavern on the river's bank and says, "We have reached the river. Let it but roll between us and our pursuers, and we are safe! Gracious powers! The river is choked with cakes of ice!" Later on, George Gaul, playing George Shelby, was required to turn to the audience and say, as he stood on a New Orleans street, "At length my mission of mercy is nearly finished. I have now but to find the house of Mr. St. Clare, re-purchase old Uncle Tom, and convey him back to his wife and children in Old Kentucky. Someone approaches. He may perhaps be able to give me the information I require. I will accost him."

Even the stage directions in the original were challenging. For Act 6, Scene 7: "Gorgeous clouds, tinted with sunlight. EVA, robed in white, is discovered on the back of a milkwhite dove, with expanded wings, as if just soaring upward. Her hands are extended in benediction over ST. CLARE and UNCLE TOM who are kneeling and gazing up at her. Impressive music. Slow curtain."

It was a tribute to the enduring strength of Harriet Beecher Stowe's novel—still in print today and still holding the hardcover record at more than 7,000,000 copies—that audiences loved the Club's revival, as did all but the most misanthropic critics. The surefire values built into the novel, quite unconsciously, were present in the play as well, easily surviving archaic language and sometimes unbelievable stage directions.

After that the road had to be downward. There was no revival the following year, and in 1935 the Club turned to a 1913 hit, *Seven Keys to Baldpate,* written by a Player, Earle Derr Biggers, and directed by another, Sam Forrest. Its success could be attributed to the star, George M. Cohan. At the play party afterward, the Club made what it considered a gallant gesture, inviting several nonparticipating ladies to join the revelry, since there had been only four in the cast.

George Ade's *The County Chairman* was the 1936 play, first seen in 1903 at Wallach's Theatre, where it ran 266 performances and played nearly five years on the road with Maclyn Arbuckle, a Player, in the title role. Revived, it proved to be an artistic success but a financial flop, first in the series to fail at the box office. On Saturday night, there was exactly $409.50 in the till, a new low. Perhaps the most notable feature of this venture was the fact that George Ade himself had just become a member. But the play's failure at the box office was a sign that the end could not be far off.

In the spring of 1937 the board told itself that, after all, there was no law requiring it to produce a play, and if something showed up that looked like it would be successful, the Club would do it. Nothing showed in that year, or in 1938, although an attempt was made then. It had been planned to do scenes from Booth's repertoire and a cast drawn from Hollywood and Broadway had been virtually signed up, the "virtually" consisting of such hedges as, "if I'm free," "unless I have to leave town," or "if the studio schedule permits." The entire cast drowned in a sea of these qualifications by April and simply disappeared. There was one more effort, *Love for Love,* in 1940, but it was not a major success and then the war overwhelmed everything and everybody.

To look back on those years, the Twenties and Thirties, from the viewpoint of renovations in the Club and revivals to stave off financial ruin, it might appear that The Players had turned grim. That was hardly the case. It went on its occasionally outrageous and always merry way, as it had from the beginning.

New features were introduced. In 1922 a hearty Irishman named Francis S. Murphy took up a position as a taxi starter for both The Players and the National Arts Club. Whistling through his fingers, he was regarded as a primary asset by those members unable to leave Gramercy Park under their own power. A small office was built for him under the balcony overhang in front of No. 16 in 1925, providing him with a telephone and protection from the weather.

Those who believe that some things never change in New York may regard with satisfaction the *Bulletin's* 1927 description of Murphy's value: "He has the happy faculty of being able to produce a cab in the pouring rain when, as is well known and understood, all such vehicles leave the Island of Manhattan for parts unknown." This paragon died in the autumn of 1937. After an earlier operation, he had made an attempt to return to his familiar post. "I went up to the Gate," he told inquiring Players who had missed him, "and Saint Peter he says to me, 'Gwan back to Gramercy Park where ye belong. We've got too many Irish here already.'"

A few days after he returned, Murphy died and left the Club mourning him.

Among these mourners was Charlie Connolly, who was ready with an explanation later on when Murphy's taxi booth was removed in the interests of aesthetics and changing times (over the objections of Dave McKinlay, who wanted it preserved as a memorial). The removal had disclosed a mysterious array of bars, chains, and locks. What were *these?*, members wanted to know. Charlie explained. At the turn of the century, he said, few members owned motor cars (or machines, as they were called then), and most of them came to the Club on their bicycles, unless they were rich enough to own a horse and carriage. The duties of the Club doorman included relieving the arriving member of his vehicle, fastening it with a chain and lock, and keeping an eye on it until it was needed again. A legendary (but unnamed) figure was the member who arrived every night promptly at nine o'clock, spent the evening, and left again at midnight to ride all the way to Brooklyn.

In the early Twenties, Murphy was ever ready to aid those who came without vehicles of their own—most of them still did not own automobiles—and no doubt heard the distant sounds of revelry inside. But not much of it could have emanated from the great domino tournament of 1923, for which an entry fee of fifty cents was charged. At Founders Night that year, the thirty-fourth celebration of this event, a crisis arose over the traditional business of stopping the grandfather's clock at midnight in order to synchronize the stroke and the end of the speech. So many of these stoppages had succeeded in wrecking the clock. The smallest number present to date, only 104 members, did without that tradition but faithfully followed another by staying to celebrate until dawn. Changing times were affecting this ritual. Wives were beginning to object to spending New Year's Eve alone.

Efforts were still made, however, to ignore the increasingly frantic Twenties and bask in what remained of the past's warm light. The annual Christmas dinner was still one of the most popular events, and in 1925 the actor Oliver Doud Byron sat at one end of a long table, contemplating a bird weighing about twenty pounds which he was to carve. Byron dispatched this bird with ease, but a second one appeared to tire him, particularly when a swarm of latecomers arrived. The chef had to be summoned so Byron could eat his own dinner. There was a small tree in the center of the table, with presents on it for every diner. These gifts were numbered, and corresponding numbers were drawn by members from an old-fashioned basket carried by an old-fashioned Santa Claus. The presents turned out to be fifes, drums, harmonicas, bells, horns, and other noisemakers, bringing the dinner to a deafening close.

Carried away by success, some of the Scottish members asked a little later to have a special dinner of home-cooked haggis. Walter's wife, who was already celebrated for making the first plum pudding ever eaten at the Club, volunteered to cook the haggis. Only a few hardy Scots asked for a second helping; the other diners were polite about it.

Eating was a preoccupation of the members even in these middle years, when the gustatory splendors of an earlier day had all but vanished. They were still inclined to be traditional about it, particularly when it came to the cheese, which had graced one end of the bar, with attending crackers, since the Club's earliest days, and survives today, although not always in the same location. Frederic Dorr Steele wrote the poem that appeared beside it for decades, freely translated from the Shakespearean epitaph:

Good frend for cheese's sake forebeare
To digg ye cheese encloased heare;
Patience awyle and yf God please
Owre Charles may chance to change ye cheese.

Much was made, then and later, of the raids on the cheese conducted by Brian Hooker, who (as noted earlier) was known as the Connecticut Cheese Hound. A member came looking for him one day at the bar, asserting he had a letter for Hooker which had to be delivered at the earliest possible moment. An idle member, Ira Remsen, agreed to see to the delivery. Lifting the cover, he placed the letter on the cheese and waited. It was only moments later when Hooker appeared, came at once to the bar, lifted the cover, and took his letter.

As legendary as the cheese, for three decades at least, or possibly more, was Mary the Club cat. The confusion in time arises because there were several Marys over the years, all equally beloved by members except those who were dog owners. Mary's only real enemy in the Twenties was the black dog that Albert Bruning sometimes brought to the Club.

Mary accompanied August on his nightly rounds as night watchman, and it was on one of these journeys that she discovered a comfortable pile of materials in an upper room, including discarded pictures that the Art Committee had left there. On the following night August discovered that Mary had peed on these rejected treasures, a fact he reported with some dismay. When he heard of it, Bill Mackay, the Art Committee's chairman, declared, "Gentlemen, I believe the cat was right," and forthwith made her an ex-officio member of the committee.

Such frivolity was part of the Club's character. It was one with such suggestions as the plea made to the House Committee that an anteater be either bought or hired to roam the piazza during the summer season and keep down the annual invaders. At the same time, and on the coin's other side, in those hot months the rule requiring jackets to be worn on the main floor and the piazza was strictly enforced, even with the thermometer in the nineties.

Nothing in the wilder annals of the Club's history, however, could surpass its ultimate jest in the *Bulletin* of April 1, 1926, when Frederic Dorr Steele was editor. Apparently few took notice of the date. "The Bulletin proposes here," the lead article began, "what we have privately advanced for several years, an amendment to our Club constitution as follows: On the first day of May each year, one member shall be expelled from the Club, such member to be elected by written ballot of all members of the Club.

"Every member shall be required to cast his vote, under penalty of the forfeiture of his own membership. On the first day of April of each year, the Secretary shall mail to each member an engraved and numbered ballot for this purpose, which shall be filled out and returned not later than May 1. The return shall be counted under the supervision of the Board of Directors and the result announced at the annual meeting of the Club, on which date the expulsion shall take effect.

"Unquestionably it involves wounding the feelings of one man. But is it not possible that the greater good of nearly a thousand may outweigh the injury—perhaps the injustice—done to an individual? . . . Would not the consciousness of this fateful necessity, this unavoidable deletion of one of us, have a salutary effect on the daily conduct and manners of us all? The choice would be a solemn duty, not to be used as the pretext for ejecting any man for his creed, for his opinions, or even necessarily for his moral turpitude. Perhaps, with this law in effect, we all may be exalted to a higher plane so that the casting out of one may come to seem not so much the punishment of a culprit or the passing of a pest, as a kind of lofty sacrifice. . . . Meantime, how courtesy and kindness would be fostered in the Club! How many slovenly or selfish habits would be corrected! What Utopian sunshine would brighten the old house! Think it over."

They did, and an astonishing number took the proposal seriously and endorsed it. There was immediate enthusiastic support, and at least two members asserted they had been proposing such an idea for years. Others debated whether the proposal was legal. Some wondered whether hidden malice was involved, and speculated about its object. These doubters issued a circular letter which said ungrammatically in part: "We wonder who our Editor is picking on. We always have a remedy for an objectionable member, so why start discussion by this vapid idea? . . . Let him come out in the open and speak. . . . Who is this person our otherwise sane Editor desires to hit at? . . ."

Perhaps the noblest response came from Alleyne Ireland, who wrote:

> The Players may take legitimate pride in the decision of the Fates to reserve for "The Bulletin" the honor of presenting to the world of clubdom a proposal which, if put into effect, would remove from Club life a defect for which, hitherto, prayer, imprecation, and ingenuity alike have failed to provide a remedy. . . .
>
> A Club may discover that it has admitted to membership a person who, though he does not steal the silver or cut "Hatrack" out of the April issue of "The Mercury," commits nevertheless a thousand offenses against that code of manners—not less understood because it is not clearly defined—from which alone the amenities of Club life derive their charm and their tenure.
>
> Since good morals never created an association which bad manners could not disrupt, it is precisely those persons who defy the spirit of a Club whilst defying its rules who constitute the greatest danger to the cherished traditions of The Players.
>
> I avail myself of this opportunity to endorse the proposed Amendment and to make it part of our Charter. If I should be the first member expelled under the mandatory rule, I should console myself with the reflection that it was the desire to expel me which had led to the adoption of a policy so logical and salutary.

It was not long before the news of this half-serious jape began circulating beyond the Club. A new magazine in town, Harold Ross's *New Yorker,* took notice, and under the frank headline "Practical Joke," observed, in part: "It has been suggested that there are the elements of a sly joke in the pamphlet making the proposal. [The *Bulletin* editors expressed annoyance later at being passed off as producing a pamphlet.] But several clubmen [who were] observed picking it up with a smile have not set it down without at least one exclamation of serious approval. In every club there are what are called 'regrettable members,' about whom, as matters now stand, nothing can be done."

Several New York papers commented on the proposal, and the contagion spread abroad to London, where the *Observer* noted the idea with approval, and the *Evening Standard* carried a two-column article beginning: "The Players Club of New York, that spiritual home of many actors, writers, artists, and dilettantes of all nationalities, recently advanced a potent suggestion as to how to keep a club just what it was intended to be. . . ."

The *Bulletin's* outrageous proposal unexpectedly won a measure of international approval, but needless to say, nothing was ever done about it—at The Players, in London, or anywhere else.

There were, indeed, far more serious matters to consider at the Club in 1926, primary among them the death of John Drew, which made the election of a new president necessary. There were three possible candidates: Otis Skinner, the vice-president; Francis Wilson, father of the revivals and former vice-president; and E. H. Sothern. But all three asked the board to choose the foremost Shakespearean actor of the younger generation, as a gesture to the Founder. There was only one possible choice, Walter Hampden, and he was duly elected on September 26, 1927.

Whether it was Hampden's leadership, coming after a long period when "Uncle Jack" was either ailing or out of town, or whether it was the bouyant atmosphere of the late Twenties, the Club prospered as it had not done for some time. From 1924 to 1928, the total membership increased from 885 to 1,044, and the average attendance was much greater than at any other time in the forty years of its existence. Records for Pipe Nights were broken regularly, the private dining room was used more often than it had been for years, and more records were broken in the main dining room. In February 1928, thirteen new members were elected, another record for a winter month, and a hitherto unprecedented list of seventeen candidates had been proposed since February 1.

The Club itself gave much credit to Henry Watson, chairman of the house committee since 1925, and Bill Tachau, who between them had taken the decaying clubhouse and completely renovated it, as described earlier.

One of the results of this renaissance that particularly gratified most Players was the establishment of the John Drew Fund in 1928. Seeking to honor their late and beloved president, members had looked about for some worthy cause. It was Arthur Goodrich who suggested the establishment of a fund which would be used to help needy fellow Players. An appeal was sent out to all members in May, with the first subscriptions limited to not more than five dollars from any one member, unless it was made anonymously. The first response was not overwhelming, but the Board went ahead with its plan to establish a permanent capital fund. The first annual report showed $1,525 in this fund, with only the income to be used. Only a third of the members had contributed, and $1,000 of the amount had come from one member, David J. Byrne.

The subsequent history of the John Drew Fund is a story of how a seemingly lost cause can be saved by reason of common adversity. Having gotten off to a decidedly lukewarm start, the fund was quickly exhausted in the early years of the Depression. Joe Chase, its administrator, had no fund to administer, even though many Players were broke and hungry. Chase resorted to the simplest of appeals. He took one of the heavy trophy cups from the mantel over the fireplace and set it at the end of the bar, asking only for spare coins to be dropped in to benefit the fund. Hungry members who needed food were invited to take a little money out of the cup.

There was an immediate response. Members who still had incomes gave everything they could spare, either to the cup or the fund itself. In 1930 and 1931, a total of nearly $7,500 was contributed, leaving only $177.80 in the permanent fund, but by 1938 that figure had reached $15,000, and it was decided to incorporate so that contributions would be tax deductible. Annual appeals added $50,000 during the next eighteen years, and it was considered time to separate the annual fund from the permanent or capital fund. Surpluses were invested. Consulting its lawyers, the Club decided to revise the charter in 1956 so that tax-exemption could not be challenged. That was done by removing the restriction of grants and gifts to Players only, amending the charter to read that the fund could be used for broader charitable purposes. But the John Drew Fund remained, as it does today, primarily to help Players who are needy and distressed.

There were enough old members, even incorporators, still active at No. 16 in the Twenties to applaud when Edwin Booth's name led all the rest of those nominated for inclusion in the New York University Hall of Fame in 1924. This was a physical "Hall," situated on what was then the Bronx campus of the university—a curving, colonnaded, semicircular arch on a hill with a view over the city. Busts of the famous occupied spaces between the colonnade pillars.

Booth's election was nearly unanimous, and so was approval of the choice by the press, with a single exception. Heywood Broun wrote in the *World:* "The last election for the Hall of Fame achieved what seems to me a ridiculous result. Edwin Booth, who received the highest vote of all, was elected and just behind him came John Paul Jones. Walt Whitman was ninth in the list and will still not, at the present time, be admitted.

"Without doubt Booth was a great actor. . . . But an actor has nothing to offer to posterity. . . . Acting is one of the least of the arts, or at any rate it is wholly dependent upon the fleshly presence of the performer. Nothing in marble can convey to us the faintest conception of what Booth must have been. . . . No person whose judgment is in any way valuable doubts the genius of Walt Whitman. 'Who was this Booth?' will inquire the passerby one hundred years from now.

"Nor can it be argued that it would be unfair to the dead Booth to ask him to step aside in favor of Whitman. In life he earned an immeasurably greater volume of acclaim. That was his bargain. It is the bargain every actor must make. . . . Walt set down words on paper and then he had to wait. . . . Booth we paid in full while he was yet alive."

"Who was this Booth," indeed! The issue of the *Bulletin* reporting such heresy chose carefully the customary Shakespearean quotation on its title page: "A lousy knave, to have his jibes and his mockeries!" (*Merry Wives of Windsor*, Act III, Scene 3.) At that point, Heywood Broun must have seemed the least likely man to be elected a member of The Players—yet he was, only a few years before his death in 1940.

As a fitting footnote to this noncontroversy, Edmond T. Quinn, who did the statue of Booth in Gramercy Park, was chosen to execute the Hall of Fame bust. The money required was raised by subscription in the Club.

As life at No. 16 began to change slowly in the Twenties, accommodating itself reluctantly to changing times, the social atmosphere of the past demonstrated the most resistance to let go any part of what had been, and would continue to be, a good thing. Members coped with the blight of Prohibition, as described earlier, and otherwise they carried on much as they had before the Great War and the arrival of the Jazz Age interrupted their pleasures.

That could be seen in such celebrations as the one given for Walter Hampden after his election. Waiters were dressed in Shakespearean costume, and the toastmaster was flanked on either side by a guard holding aloft a four-stemmed candelabrum, complete with lighted candles. A surprised Hampden was presented with the girdle Booth had worn so often as Hamlet.

Arthur M. Blake is credited with introducing bridge to the club at some point in the Twenties; it was already becoming a national craze. Blake said he had learned the game in Italy, where he had been staying, and played it with several Italian officers who were friends of his. Returning to the card room at the Club, he found his friends there were still playing Solo Whist. "They were all glad to see me," he recalled later, "but when I told them about the new game of Auction and begged them to try a hand and see what it was like, with one accord they turned on me and said, 'We're glad to see you back, but get to hell out of here or sit quietly and don't interrupt our game.' I told them if they would only try just one hand, as a favor to me, they would never play Solo again. I almost had to go on my knees to persuade them, and lo and behold my prophecy came true, for they took to it instanter, and not another game of Solo was played in the Club from that time on.

Practical joking of the old school survived at the Club, particularly among frequenters of the bar. Jac Wendell once arranged with a fellow member to stage a mock fight for the benefit of an actor recently arrived from London, who had made the mistake of telling his friends at The Players that he had heard some wild tales about life in America, but had seen no evidence of it. The fight convinced him, but the acting was too good. The visitor, roused by the spectacle, took sides and plunged into the battle himself. No blood was shed.

Charlie Connolly often presided behind the bar, although he had many other and more important duties. In his honor Edgar Lee Masters wrote a Prohibition poem in September 1929, which appeared only in the *Bulletin*. It began:

> Grateful for gin, and full of thanks for Charley
> We who in better days despised cheap tankards,
> Stand and are served amid the daily parley,
>   We disappointed drunkards.

And it ended:

> But who's the man who served The Players better,
> Remembering what has been? And with good infusions
> Of what's commendable, till the times are wetter,
>   Stays our illusions?
> Who is it? Charley Connolly! Let our plaudits
> Ring till the Hudson and the Harlem River
> Give back his name, and let our friendly audits
>   Write him forever!

It seemed there was always music of some kind in the air of No. 16. The entire D'Oyly Carte Opera Company came to dinner at the Club one night, and the celebration thereafter went on until dawn. Harry Burleigh, the noted black composer, came down to sing spirituals of his own arranging, and Irving Berlin appeared to offer versions of ragtime in his inimitable voice. The entire Schola Cantorum, with Deems Taylor singing tenor in the front row, offered a program of student songs, among others.

And then, of course, there were the amateurs, Players with voices of various calibers. There was, for example, the Ptomaine Quartet, whose specialty was ballads of the Gay Nineties, called by F.P.A. "Brave Songs of an Elder Day." Several of the best amateurs were singing at the bar one night when, encouraged by a few more drinks than usual, they decided to cross over to New Jersey and attend a widely advertised revival meeting.

Prudently absorbing some cloves to disguise their alcoholic breaths, they migrated across on the ferry and joined the congregation in song, transforming the old hymns with such enthusiasm that women around them were crying and the men were cheering them on. With tears on his cheeks, the revivalist himself came down to thank the visitors for the true vision of Beulah Land they had provided that night.

*   *   *

So, amid customary song and mirth, life at the Club in the Twenties came to an end, on the brink of the second great change to sweep the country in this century. Members were already complaining about the cost of living in 1929. Taxi fares on the line waiting outside had gone to fifteen cents, with additions at every fifth of a mile. The cabs were also finding it hard to get to the curb because there was no back entrance for delivery on 19th Street, as the Arts Club enjoyed. There were members who thought the Club should buy No. 17, but the owners were asking $160,000, and it might cost as much as $75,000 more to renovate the building. The board said no. They pointed out that it was costing much more to run the Club because the cost of living had risen 59.4 percent since 1914, and only the two-cent stamp had remained unaltered by inflation. With the club divided about equally between residents and nonresidents, average dues were $75 a year. The budget was tight, but the outlook was good, the board said.

As we know now, they could not have been more mistaken.

CHAPTER 6

"O Rare Don Marquis"

IF OLIVER HERFORD HAD BEEN THE DOMINANT SPIRIT IN THE SOCIAL scene at the Club in the years from the turn of the century to the close of the war, Don Marquis occupied the same place in the Twenties and Thirties. There was some overlapping. Marquis joined the Club in 1916 and died on December 29, 1937, a period in which Herford also flourished, but somehow Marquis came to overshadow his friend, at least in some respects. He gave the Club much of himself and his work, not the least of which was the poem that provides this book with its title.

Like Booth's, Don Marquis's life was essentially tragic. Born in Walnut, Illinois, in 1878, he was beset with disasters from the time of his first wife's death. His son, Robert, followed and then his small daughter, Barbara. He himself was struck down by a stroke before he died early, at 59.

At The Players, however, he was the brightest of spirits. He loved the place, and once wrote about it in a novelette called *Off the Arm,* in which it was thinly disguised as "The Gramercy." The egocentric hero is seen paying the Club a visit and meeting a dozen members who appear under their own names, two of them misspelled. It was a mutual love affair between Don and The Players. Perennially in financial trouble, he was lying broke and ill in the hospital early in 1929 when his friends at the

115

Club got together and devised a way to help him. They printed a private, limited edition of one of his poems, 106 copies subscribed for at $10 each. A total of $1,060 was turned over to him. By November 1, he had given the John Drew Fund a check for $310 in part payment, and sent the remainder to the fund on November 13.

When his daughter died in November 1931, Marquis wrote to the Club, thanking the members for their flowers, and continuing: "She was a Player at heart herself. I took her into the Club one day when she was a little thing—it was raining outside and I had to stop there—and told her she was the only woman who was let in, besides Sarah Bernhardt, except on Ladies' Day and the suppers after the annual play revivals, and she was always proud of it." In Barbara's bank account Marquis found $40 earned from a little paper she had started. He sent it as a contribution to the John Drew Fund.

Marquis expressed his love for the Club in several ways, among them a limerick written in the heat of his continuing competition with F.P.A.:

> There's a certain club known as The Players
> Frequented by guys who aren't prayers
> Excepting at pool,
> Where they pray as a rule
> That their conquerors fall down the stayers.

This was not, obviously, a fair sample of Marquis's art. While his output of prose and poetry, in books and the newspaper column he wrote for the *Sun,* was prodigious, he was best known in the Club for his quips, as Herford was. They have been told and retold for decades, in many versions. A favorite was the remark he was supposed to have made as he came into the grill room after a prolonged spell on the water wagon: "I've conquered my goddam will power, gentlemen. A double Scotch, please."

On another occasion, a winter night when the air at the bar had grown smoky and foul, someone demanded the front door be opened. "If the air down here was good enough for Edwin Booth," Marquis shouted, "it's good enough for you. And it's the same air!" After air-conditioning the same story was retold as Marquis's protest against the innovation.

Marquis did, in fact, spend most of his time on the Club's lower level, among what was sometimes called "the downstairs membership." When the bar was moved he vociferously protested replacing the heavy cord, like a ship's cable, leading downstairs (often called the lifeline) with a metal rail.

Marquis was in the habit of arriving at the Club about 2 or 3 o'clock in the morning after a long evening of work. He was looking for companionship and his usual "snack," as he called it, of blueberry pie and milk. He was thus engaged one night when an actor named Jimmy arrived wearing a waistcoat of a brilliant pattern, dripping with long Angora hairs. Don eyed the garment somberly.

"For God's sake, Jimmy," he said. "Why are you wearing a vest the likes of that?"

"I'll tell you," Jimmy said agreeably. "I just had pneumonia and I don't want it again."

"Do you mean to stand there and tell me," Don said severely, "that you wouldn't rather have pneumonia than wear a vest like that?"

Jimmy assured him it was so.

"Well, I'm going to complain to the house committee," Don said. "They won't let me bring my dog into the Club and he's a lot better looking than that vest."

Jimmy had the last word. "Maybe, but he doesn't wear it as well."

That would never have been Don's opinion. He loved his Boston bull terrier, Pete, with a devotion that only another dog-lover could understand. Ed Anthony, Marquis's biographer and a fellow Player, tells of the day Jack King was about to enter the Club when he saw Don sitting on the curb outside, sharing his lunch with Pete. When he came to the Club that day, Don had checked Pete at the door, as he usually did, but when the waiter brought his lunch, a pair of superior chops, he thought of Pete sitting downstairs in the cloakroom, unfed, and decided he must share. As King came upon them, Marquis was saying to Pete, "Now it's your turn, Petey."

Dogs were not permitted at the Club, but somehow Pete seemed to be there often, in the cloakroom on a leash held patiently by what were called page boys in those days, a breed now extinct. There came a day, however, when Pete escaped and a search party found him profaning the sanctuary, Booth's bedroom, lying on The Bed itself. Or so the legend persisted in the Club. When Anthony was compiling his biography, however, Don's former secretary told him that the story was probably the product of Marquis' infinitely creative mind.

Anthony also discovered that Don was presumptuous in criticizing Jimmy's Angora vest, since he was so casual and sometimes bizarre about what he himself wore. He appeared at the Club one day in a suit with pants of one color, and a jacket of a different hue, a fashion which was then not commonplace, as it is today. Don explained that he had found a valet service on Lexington Avenue, near where he lived, which advertised it would clean and press a two-pants suit (the product of lean Depression years) for thirty-five cents. Marquis owned two such suits, and deciding that this was a bargain only a rich man would reject, he sent over one of them. The service lost both pants and sent the jacket back, with an apology.

On his way to the Club when this occurred, Don simply mismatched the jacket with the pants from his other suit in a combination then considered on the far cutting edge of men's high fashion. A fellow Player who witnessed his arrival, and had the proper connections, arranged to have a letter sent on the stationery of a New York daily, asking Don if he would consider writing a weekly men's fashion column. Marquis saw through this hoax at once and submitted a sample of such a column, in which he wrote: "Pants will be worn this year of the Depression by those who can afford them."

The Marquis legend at the Club was often fed by Don himself. In his biography Anthony questions the authenticity of the story (told here earlier) of his boasting that he had conquered his will power and could now fall off the wagon by having a drink. In fact, his biographer says, Marquis was not a heavy drinker even in those hard-drinking days of 1916, when he joined. He never drank more than lightly, and sometimes not at all. It was after one of the dry periods that he was found with a glass in his hand, and when someone took notice of it, he remarked that he was glad it had been observed because he wanted to try out the "will power" crack. The result was a story that became one of the most durable Marquis anecdotes.

Nevertheless, as Charlie Connolly recalled, Don was far from being an enemy of booze. At a Club party which Charlie believed was the most hilarious in the history of No. 16, the second floor had been converted into a replica of an oldtime Western saloon, with a long bar decorated by artificial bullet holes, a swinging-door entrance, and sawdust on the floor. Most of the members and their guests appeared, incongruously, in dinner jackets, except for the few in scanty costumes who were impersonating ladies of the evening.

It was Don's suggestion that a few others appear as Salvation Army soul-savers, waving their tambourines and trying to convert the trollops with hymns and prayers. Don himself was a bartender, along with Brian Hooker, and wore a handlebar mustache, with his hair parted in the middle. At some point in the evening, the mustache fell off into a mug of beer, but Marquis went on playing a part he had always wanted to play, drinking little himself and going home sober. Watching him leave, Charlie thought he looked worn and dispirited, like an actor after playing a part he had failed to realize.

The fact was that Don had wanted to be an actor when he was a young man and never quite got over being stagestruck, as he readily confessed to other members, who liked to kid him about it. Marquis asserted that he deeply envied actors, stood in awe of them, and declared that they were the only category of humans he felt that way about. The Club's theater people refused to take him seriously. His friend John Barrymore pretended that Don's estimation of actors was not credible to those who were in the theater, that everyone knew actors were a lowdown, shiftless lot. Why was Don exalting them? Barrymore demanded. Was he running for president of The Players?

One member *did* take him seriously, however. In 1926 Howard Lindsay planned to produce Marquis's hit play, *The Old Soak,* at the Lakewood Theater in Skowhegan, and offered Don the title role. It proved to be a disaster. Here was a man with such a remarkable memory, particularly for the theater, that F.P.A. once called him a walking Shakespearean concordance, yet when he got on the stage, in his own play, he had great difficulty remembering the lines he himself had written. Mercifully, it was a short run.

But the Skowhegan flop failed to cure Don's stage fever. Charlie recalled years later that he heard Marquis and some other members discussing the possibility of forming a company to put on a play, and having seen *The Old Soak,* the Club godfather asked if he could invest a thousand dollars of his own money in it. The members, with some reluctance, agreed. But the venture was not a success, and the play closed in spite of a few friendly reviews, leaving the backers out of pocket, including Charlie.

That disturbed Marquis. He called Charlie aside one day a little later and presented him with an envelope, saying, "Here's your money back." There was a small argument. Charlie insisted that he had taken the same chance as the others and refused a refund. Don argued that Charlie made his money the hard way, and he couldn't sleep nights if he thought this revered honorary member had suffered from the loss. "Just count it and see if it's all there," he said, brushing aside all protests. It was more than simple kindness, Charlie said later. Other people could be kind, but Don Marquis made you feel he really cared.

Charlie considered Marquis the most thoughtful man he ever knew, and it would have been next to impossible to find anyone in the Club with a bad word for him. The Players was his religion, and some of its members his closest friends. He sometimes wrote his *Sun Dial* column there, a regular feature of the New York *Sun,* and often tossed off other small pieces, including "A Certain Club." He wrote it one afternoon and it appeared in a verse section at the back of *The Old Soak* in the play's original version as a novel. He dedicated it to his friend Winfield Scott Moody, a colleague on the *Sun* who had brought him into the Club.

Don's casual quips became as famous and as much quoted as Herford's had been. Berton Braley, a well-known purveyor of light verse in the

Twenties, once heard a young actor say to Marquis that he couldn't understand why a group would melt away every time he started to talk.

"Do you think I'm a bore or something?" he asked plaintively.

"Or something," Marquis agreed.

In the Club, he spent much of his time at the pool table, where he appeared with his jacket off, displaying bright red arm garters. He played mostly with a group calling itself the Poolist Fathers. Its members included Rollin Kirby, the noted cartoonist, and the painter George Bellows, the Club's only member who defied the rules and often arrived in a turtleneck sweater. Frederic Dorr Steele, Ed Anthony, and several others also belonged to this group.

As an excuse to begin a game, if one was needed, Don would say, "I haven't earned my cab fare yet." He meant his single great extravagance, long taxi rides, particularly those he made to his home in Forest Hills. Frank Murphy, the taxi starter, and the drivers in the Club's taxi line, all knew Don and his habits. They waited for him to appear, knowing he would tip them generously and tell them stories on the way. His sister Maude, who tried to manage Don's life with no success whatever, deplored the long rides to Forest Hills and frequently scolded him. He paid no attention.

Since the stakes were so small at the pool table, it was necessary sometimes for Don to play until nearly breakfast time before he could make enough money to take a cab home, particularly because he was not one of the best players. He did win occasionally but more often than not it was the result of luck, rather than skill. However, no one was a more charming companion at the table; even his heckling was an entertainment in itself. When he made an obviously lucky shot, he liked to explain it in elaborate scientific terms.

Playing with F.P.A. one night and learning that the Conning Tower's proprietor had become a father for the first time, Don heard his fellow columnist asking for advice on how to raise his son to be a millionaire genius. "You must never forget the fundamentals," Marquis told him, "like never changing diapers in midstream."

Marquis occasionally played bridge, with even less skill, which he freely admitted. "I play conversational bridge," he said. That meant he was not in the same league with those addicts who played near the bar, but was relegated to the card room upstairs, to a group known as the Minor League. Don's problem was that he was incapable of sitting still for long periods and staring at cards. He wanted to talk.

Jack King remembered: "We always knew what to expect when we let Don into the game. There wouldn't be any serious bridge but there would be fun. Everybody loved him so we'd allow him to ramble on. You'd find yourself trying to ignore him and concentrate on your cards but he had a way of being so darned entertaining that sometimes, against your better judgment, you'd put your cards down and get into the conversation yourself—and the first thing you knew, nobody was playing bridge. Only Don, with that contagious smile and those innocent blue eyes, could have gotten away with it."

Once the actor Clive Wood asked Marquis why he bothered to play bridge at all. "My motives are purely mercenary," Don said. That puzzled Wood, who knew he usually lost. But Marquis explained that writers were always looking for new things to write about, and since bridge was such a funny game he had decided to find out why that was, and when he did, he planned to write articles about it. He wasn't joking. Both in his column and in a satiric *Collier's* piece he described how anyone could win at bridge with the Marquis System, which required, among other novelties, a physician to be in attendance at every table, or else a registered nurse capable of taking blood pressures.

Indifferent at games though he was, Marquis possessed a true competitive spirit. Having dinner one night with Lawton Mackall on the veranda, both men ordered cherry pie, and with the first mouthful, Mackall found a pit. A moment later, Don had one too and that aroused his competitive instinct.

"We've got a game going here," he said happily. "What do you say to fifty cents high man?"

The game ended with Don's three pits, and Mackall with his original single. "Good game," Don said with satisfaction, picking up the fifty cents. "We ought to play it more often."

It was all part of Don's inability to take money seriously. There was the epic day when Harold Ross encountered him at the Club, at an early stage of the *New Yorker*'s career when it was struggling. Ross repeated an earlier offer he had made to Marquis, asking him to write for the magazine at an extremely modest rate of pay per word. Don sensed immediately that a victim had been delivered to him and he went into his act.

"I'm an indigent author, Harold," he said in effect. "I'm paying alimony to three wives and I have a lot of children. I'm not even on anybody's payroll right now, and when I write I've got to have a lot more money than what you can afford to pay."

Ross, who was noted for his ability to squeeze a great deal of work from writers for minimal fees, took the high ground. He thought it was too bad that Don was willing to put mere cash above the prestige of writing for the *New Yorker,* but if he insisted on being mercenary, he would raise his offer to twenty-five cents a word.

Marquis pretended to think it over, and then said, "We can do business. But I can let you have only one word as a starter. Have you got a quarter?"

Momentarily baffled, Ross produced one. Marquis put it in his pocket and said, "Thanks."

"You're a con man," Ross said. "I'm going to see my lawyer."

"I let you off easy," Marquis told him. "If I were really greedy, I would have offered you two words as a starter." What words? Ross wanted to know. "No, thanks," Don told him. "That would have cost you fifty cents."

Marquis was not so indifferent to money, however, that he would let his disdain obscure honor. In 1934 the Depression had so depleted him that he tried to resign from the Club. In a letter to the board, he wrote: "Gentlemen: As I am busted and don't feel easy spending anything that is not absolutely necessary until I get my debts paid, I am obliged to resign from the Club. When I get straightened out again financially, I shall apply for reinstatement. Please send any current bills to the above address and have the office send mail there." In a P.S., he added characteristically, "There's no silly peeve of any kind, but the plain statement is the true one. And for Christ's sake don't fish around for any special list for me to go on, like a deferred payment plan or anything of that sort, which some clubs have, because I feel badly enough about getting out. If I stay away from the damned, dear old dive for six or eight months and get some real work done, I'll have money enough to come back in."

But the board would have none of it. It rejected his resignation unanimously, and instructed Dave McKinlay, the treasurer, to carry him on the rolls indefinitely. Marquis was a proud man, however, and he seldom appeared at the Club again. Moreover, he was not well, and it was clear to his anxious friends that the laughing would have to stop.

There had been a warning. Anthony recalls in his biography that Don had been playing pool one night with his friend Dr. Richard Hoffman, who had come into the Club the same year, when he stopped for a moment, his cue in the air, and turned to lean on a table, saying, "Who put out the lights?" He told Hoffman that he had been about to make a sensational shot, and wanted the pleasure of seeing it.

Hoffman knew at once what had happened. He put an arm around Marquis to support him and whispered, "The lights are on, Don. You've had an accident. This will be a temporary blindness." He explained matter-of-factly that Don had suffered the blockage of a cerebral vessel, and there would probably be no paralysis. He took his friend home, but his quick diagnosis was unfortunately not correct. Marquis was diagnosed as suffering from uremic poisoning and eventually had to be hospitalized. Later, paralysis did occur, leaving him all but speechless.

Rollin Kirby remembered visiting him with F.P.A. in Forest Hills not long before he died. The two visitors talked but the great conversationalist, one of the best of his time, could not respond. He could only listen, his eyes filling with tears of frustration. At last he managed to gasp out just two words, "Goddam! Goddam!" and the tears ran down his cheeks.

If religion was to be a consolation, it would have to be a personal belief. Marquis was no believer in organized religion and an enemy of what he called "Received Authority," meaning anything spiritual that he thought was cant or fraud. Yet he was in fact deeply religious himself, and wrote a moving play, *The Dark Hours,* about the crucifixion. Ironically, it was a flop.

When he died, Don Marquis left behind him a record of twenty-eight books of poetry and humor, in addition to his plays and the memory of his much admired daily column. In that, he had created the character by which he is best remembered today—"archy," the necessarily lower-case cockroach who typed out his stories on Don's typewriter in the newspaper office at night and was immortalized by Marquis in his *Archy and Mehitabel.*

Grover Loud, a Player who worked for the New York *World-Telegram,* wrote an affectionate story, picked up later by the other dailies, reporting that on Founder's Night, two days after Marquis's death, "archy" visited the bar at the Club, traversing its entire length and possibly circling the framed copy of "A Certain Club" hanging on the wall, as much as three times.

A silence fell on No. 16 for a time after Marquis died. Everyone mourned him, and Harold T. Pulsifer, one of his friends, expressed what everyone was feeling when he wrote this tribute:

Don

There is another face upon the stair
That smiles upon all Players from the dark,
Vibrant and luminous. We are aware
That we have caught a vision of the spark
That lights the world through tragedy and mirth;
That we have known a spirit who has played
A gallant part upon this stage, the earth,
And going, left his comrades unafraid.

There shall be laughter when we think of him

Poured forth in living tribute to his soul
And in Dark Hours his eyes across the brim
In joyous dalliance at the wassail bowl.
But if you loved him, guard that holy wrath
That swept all false pretenders from his path!

CHAPTER 7

The Thirties

WITH THE ENTIRE COUNTRY ON ITS ECONOMIC KNEES, IT WAS HARDLY
surprising that an enterprise so relatively marginal as a gentleman's club
should be in deep trouble when the Depression struck. From reports of
annual meetings in the early Thirties, it is clear that the board doubted in
1931 and 1932 whether the Club could survive. Similar establishments,
burdened with large mortgages and bond issues, had already gone under,
unable to weather the sudden deflation.

Because of Booth's gift, The Players was in a sounder condition than
the others, needing only enough income to pay for taxes and maintenance,
but still it was a struggle because members were resigning in droves,
unable to pay their dues. Assessments to meet deficits were obviously out
of the question. Occasional gifts helped to keep the Club afloat, but in the
end it was the courage and ingenuity of its management that not only
made survival possible, but the mid-Thirties actually resulted in another
period of necessary renovation. Even the *Bulletin,* which could manage
only one issue in 1931, produced four issues the following year.

At the core of the Club's successful fight to save itself was a deliberate
and earnest attack on expenses, begun soon after the Crash, and even
before anyone had fully realized its consequences. In the winter of 1931–
32 the board concluded that its obligation to the library and its collections
would require certain expenditures, for which money could be obtained
only by cutting expenses. It proved to be a lucky decision. As the *Bulletin*
reported in 1932, "In a panic year, in the face of slow collections and
declining receipts from dues and house charges, the relation between

income and outgo has been $12,000 better than during the preceding year. But for this, with the scanty contribution from last year's play, we could not have come this far without drawing on the capital funds which should be touched only as an emergency measure."

Three members of the house committee were largely responsible for staving off disaster—Bill Tachau, John S. Phillips, and Frank E. Mason. They not only saved money but improved Club organization at the same time, even when the Club was losing resident members at the rate of forty or fifty a year. Total savings during 1932 were $11,000, the result of drastic changes and rearrangements in personnel resulting in a more efficient system. It was a humane operation, too. Walter Oettel had retired after forty years of service, but the payroll was reduced further by $4,471 through shortened hours and firing only those who had most recently joined the staff. No salaries were reduced. The kitchen staff was re-organized under a new chef, and losses in the grill reduced by $4,300. Further economies were accomplished by competitive buying of supplies, and using members as purchasing agents when they could get special discounts.

It was astonishing how much could be done to the Club at the very bottom of the Depression. Bedrooms on the top floor were converted to steam heat rather than gas, reducing fuel bills and diminishing the danger of fire. Bookcases were installed in the Booth Room. A modern shower replaced a forty-year-old bathtub in the top-floor bathroom. Indirect lighting was installed in the card room, saving 50 percent on electric bills and gratifying the players. Bookkeeping operations were moved to the third floor, leaving space for improvements in the pool room. New radiators were installed in the enclosed dining porch, saving coal bills. Sprinklers were installed in cellar and kitchen to reduce fire hazards and, consequently, insurance bills.

One obvious source of income was to take in new members, and thus staunch the outward flow, but no one wanted that done at the expense of lowering the quality of membership. It was recommended that every member should be asked to bring in one new recruit, a device often used since in times of need. The Club never came anywhere near this goal, but the campaign did bring in such new faces as Roark Bradford, George M. Cohan, Pat O'Brien, Louis Calhern, and Whitford Kane. Even as they arrived, however, such other old members as John Philip Sousa, Tyrone Power (grandson of another Tyrone Power and father to a third), Vachel Lindsay, and David Belasco were among those taken by death.

Founders Night and Pipe Nights continued to be celebrated in spite of the lack of funds, with the price of admission to Pipe Nights lowered from $1.75 to $1.00. Between these celebrations, Players were cheered by the

Shakespearean quotations that always appeared on the first page of the *Bulletin*, such exhortations as "Cheer your hearts: Be you not troubled with the time" (*Antony and Cleopatra*, Act 3, Scene 6); "There is some soul of goodness in things evil/Would men observingly distil it out" (*Henry V*, Act 4, Scene 1); "Once more unto the breech, dear friends" (same play, Act 3, Scene 1); and "Well, whiles I am a beggar I will rail/And say there is no sin but to be rich" (*King John*, Act 2, Scene 1).

Tea was served in the main hall every day at 4:30, but the usual bountiful tray of sweets had disappeared. Looking into the park, the tea drinkers could see that in the dark Depression winter of 1932 the old square had been decorated for Christmas, the first time it had ever been done. A stately Christmas tree stood near Booth's statue, and the small trees around the square, including those in front of the Club, had been decorated with colored lights. It was as though Gramercy Park had decided to shake its fist at hard times.

Yet the realities were not denied. The Club contributed all it could to Selena Royle's Actors Dinner Club, where those out of work and desperate were able at least to eat. In 1933, during the first eleven weeks of this club, more than 21,000 dinners were served. The organization was particularly close to The Players, since it had been founded by the daughter of a member who happened also to be married to a member. When it began its work in the old Union Church, other members painted the brick walls and scrubbed its floors before operations began. Later it was moved to the Great Northern Hotel, where it served 13,363 dinners in its first five weeks.

During the bank holiday of March 1933, the Actors' Dinner Club helped alleviate the frightening realities not only with food but by making the Club one of the cheeriest places in the city. All the hostesses were actresses who did much to enliven the scene for the 300 unemployed members of the profession who ate there every night. Far from looking like a grim soup kitchen, the Club made it hard to distinguish the hosts from the guests. That was because the dollar dinners were paid for by actors who were hosts to unknown actor-guests. But in spite of gifts and hard work the operation was running about $2,000 short in the first five weeks uptown, a deficit met by contributions every week from working actors in addition to $200 a week from the Stage Relief Fund.

Players Night at the Actors Dinner Club was a sellout, with a record attendance and stellar entertainment by the Club, the highlights of which were Nina Tarasova's appearance and a duet sung by Frank Chapman, a member, with his wife, Gladys Swarthout. It was also The Players who sponsored the Barter Inn, located in Abingdon, Virginia, where actors during this time of crisis could spend the summer economically. Facilities were offered for golf, tennis, swimming, and mountain climbing. A theater was provided for actors; pianos and practice rooms for musicians; and models and easels for painters. The fee for everything, including board and room, was an astonishing $30 a month.

Inevitably the tensions of the Depression were visible in spite of every effort to reduce them. Tempers were inclined to be short, and one night at No. 16 two members began to quarrel and a fight ensued in which, as the *Bulletin* solemnly put it, "blood was spilled upon our sacred floor." The incident was reported to the board as a violation of the rules, and both combatants were suspended for two weeks.

No one familiar with Club life was surprised, however, when this decision was immediately challenged by a flood of witnesses who were prepared to swear that only one of the two was guilty, while the other had shown remarkable forbearance. The board retreated to high ground. Those witnesses should have made their views known before the suspension ruling was made, it decreed. Briefly, it was not a happy time at the Club.

But only briefly. What was remarkable in the worst Depression years was not only how the Club survived and even prospered in some ways, but how it managed to preserve and even enhance its social life. Among the "Red Letter Days" in the Club's history, as listed by Walter in his memoirs, three occurred in the Thirties.

First of these was the centenary observance of Booth's birth on November 13, 1933, at a formal dinner, with speeches by Otis Skinner, George M. Cohan, David Warfield, Royal Cortissoz, and Albert Andrews. In planning this event, a curious fact about Booth surfaced. Sydney Barton Booth, the Founder's nephew, pointed out in a letter to the *Bulletin* that his uncle's name should be pronounced as though it rhymed with "smooth." That was how Booth pronounced it, he said, and had enshrined the pronunciation in a brief poem about the family name:

How sharper than a serpent's tooth
The thankless tongue that names him "Booth"!
Till on our death bed cool and smooth
They lay us down, we'll call it "Booth."

Needless to say, The Players went right on rhyming it with tooth.

A second red letter event occurred in early November 1935, observing the centenary of Mark Twain's birth, which was actually on November 30, too close to Thanksgiving that year. Clayton Hamilton arranged the program, which featured W. W. Ellsworth, now an elderly gentleman, who had been publisher of the *Century* for many years. In his retirement he had anticipated Hal Holbrook by several decades, traveling up and down the country to celebrate Mark Twain. His was not an impersonation, however, but a lecture on his favorite author (whom he had published) complete with lantern slides. William Lyon Phelps spoke at the dinner (he was also chairman) along with William Gillette and Richard Burton. The latter two had lived in Hartford when Twain was in residence and knew him intimately.

It was the third red letter day, on November 6, 1938, that proved to be one of the most remarkable events in Club history. To celebrate its fiftieth anniversary, the Club proposed to reproduce its great hall on the Waldorf-Astoria's ballroom stage, or at least the fireplace and lounge portion, and there reenact the Founder's Night ritual. There was some grumbling from those who argued that this most intimate of Club rites should never be viewed outside the precincts of No. 16 but enthusiasm for the project was too great to be denied.

It was a memorable performance, preceded by a banquet for 1,100 guests. In the opening scene a quartet could be observed singing (a mixed piece of realism; this seldom happened in the main hall), and two Club members were to be seen trying to shut out their presence behind newspapers. With Walter Hampden presiding, assisted by Otis Skinner, a short speech about Booth and his relationship to the current theater was offered by Marc Connolly, after which Theodore Steinway introduced the noted violinist Albert Spalding, accompanied as always by Andre Benoit, who played four pieces. This was followed by two classic Shakespearean excerpts, the closet scene from *Hamlet* and the balcony scene from *Romeo and Juliet,* performed respectively by Mady Christians with Maurice Evans, and Richard Waring with Eva Le Gallienne.

Then came the Founder's Night ritual, and in spite of anticipatory fears it made a profound impression on the hushed audience. Hendrik Willem van Loon was the speaker and Otis Skinner read Booth's words. Walter, brought in from retirement for the occasion, introduced the loving cup exactly on time, and the old clock, moved uptown for the occasion, showed more punctuality in striking than it had at No. 16.

When the real ceremony occurred at the end of the month it was not the anticlimax some had thought it would be. A hundred or more members turned out (attendance was constantly decreasing then) to hear Dudley Digges give the traditional speech, a talk about the young Booth, and to watch David Warfield read the Booth speech. Walter passed the loving cup once more, noting later that he had done so on every Founder's Night except the first one.

The red-letter affairs were not the only outstanding social events of the Thirties, however. There was, for example, the dinner in 1936 for John

Gielgud, fresh from his great success as Hamlet, joined at the head table by Hampden, Skinner, and Sir John Barbirolli. Nearby sat Maurice Evans and Sir Cedric Hardwicke. Thus three generations of Hamlets were present, in person or in spirit—Booth, Hampden, Evans, and Gielgud. Skinner spoke of the touring Hamlets he had known, and Arthur Byron read Don Marquis's amusing sketch of Hamlet in rehearsal, titled "Wrong from the Start—Still Running."

In the same year another dinner celebrated John S. Phillips, a member for more than thirty years, who had been the friend and partner of S. S. McClure, the magazine and book publishing magnate, who was never a Player himself, but whose brother Robert Bruce had been elected. John was presented with a copy of his *Occasional Pieces,* articles he had written for and about The Players, autographed by many members. There was also another large volume of testimonial letters. The novelist Charles Norris was among those who paid tribute; he and his more famous brother, Frank, and sister-in-law Kathleen were all published by Phillips at *McClure's.*

While it was not exactly a social event, John Barrymore's last evening at the Club in 1934 became one of the enduring legends at No. 16, a tale far more credible than other stories circulated about him. In the months preceding this historic appearance, he had been much in the news. His alcoholism was already publicly acknowledged, and his friends grieved as they read of his hopeless slide downward, particularly since his brilliant performance in *Twentieth Century.* That had been followed by his departure for India to seek spiritual communion with Krishnamurti, the eminent Indian guru. Unfortunately, as Ben Hecht wrote later, he had made a short detour through a House of Joy, buying it out for an entire week, and never managed to see his guru.

As John Griggs, the Club's noted film historian, told the story, Barrymore's last night at The Players also involved his friend, James Kirkwood, the Clark Gable of the Teens and Twenties. Kirkwood had joined the Club in 1908, Barrymore the following year. In those days both had worked, along with other Players, at the old Biograph Studios on 14th Street, where D. W. Griffith was making pictures, paying $5 a day to his actors.

On the hot summer night that John appeared for the last time in Gramercy Park, Kirkwood was already there. His career was coming to an end, and he spent a good deal of time at the Club, where he was known as a ribald, gallant, funny man who had never lost his perspective. He was living in an apartment at 74 Irving Place, where Griggs also lived then, a place known as "Irving Chambers."

Kirkland was drinking a beer that night when, as he recalled, "I was embraced from behind, kissed on the back of the neck, and heard an unforgettable voice say, 'You beautiful bastard.' It was John Barrymore." After their fifth Scotch, Barrymore inquired what his friend had been doing.

"I'm broke," Kirkwood said. "One play—$60."

"Jim, I'm splitting up the bankroll," Barrymore said. "I'm going to write you a check for $2,500."

Kirkwood protested. "Not tonight, Jack. Don't spoil it."

"Why not?" his friend insisted. "The girls will get it anyway."

Then, or later in the evening, Kirkwood got his check. Barrymore played pool, and kept his temper when someone called him "The Great Profile," but he had endured too much when some unfortunate bores began freeloading on him, and he left with Kirkwood. They circled the park a while before returning.

Peering down the staircase, Barrymore whispered, "Are they gone?" They had, and the two friends resumed their reunion at the bar until it closed at 2 A.M., after which they departed for Barrymore's suite at the New Yorker Hotel, bringing two imperial quarts of Scotch with them. Since they had stayed in the Club for a time to finish the Scotch, it was now 5 A.M. Ordering two dozen Scotch-and-sodas from room service, John turned to his other primary interest in life and got out his little black book of interesting ladies. They were on their way to one of these addresses when, about 6:30, a taxi ran over Kirkwood's leg, breaking his ankle in two places. As a crowd gathered, Kirkwood said, "Beat it, Jack," and Jack prudently did so.

Later that morning Griggs got the news that Kirkwood was in the charity ward at Bellevue. He left at once with his wife, whom he had married only two months before, and hurried to the hospital, stopping off at the Club to get a pint of Scotch he could smuggle in to his friend. "He'll be needing it about now," Charlie Connolly reckoned.

At the hospital Griggs found Kirkwood in a ward flanked by two men suffering from razor cuts. A blonde actress who was in the play Kirkwood had been about to act in for a brief run sat holding his hand. "His rhetoric seared the ward," Griggs wrote later. The Scotch was eased into his hand, and after a quick swallow, he produced the dirty, rumpled check for $2,500 which Barrymore had given him, and asked Griggs to cash it for him.

By the time Griggs got to the bank, however, payment had been stopped. Barrymore's alert manager, a Mr. Hotchener, had been waiting for Jack when he returned and asked him at once, "Have you written any checks?" Barrymore admitted he had written one for an old friend, and Hotchener had used his power of attorney to stop it.

Five years later Kirkwood saw his friend for the last time in Chicago, where Jack was making an agonizing farewell appearance in that travesty of a play *My Dear Children*. "Barrymore's mind was cloudy, his wit bright," Griggs wrote later of that meeting. Sadly, he was never seen again at the Club.

In the mid-Thirties, when the worst of the Depression was over, social life at the Club had revived to such an extent that something of the old chafing-dish era prevailed. Alleyne Ireland was one of the leaders of this revival. A scholar who was an authority on Conrad, Ireland's somewhat imperious manner did not win him numerous friends but he could hardly be ignored. He wore a beard that made him look remarkably like Joseph Pulitzer, whose secretary he had once been. Ireland always appeared to be broke but he never lacked for dinner companions because of his celebrated salad dressing. It was so remarkable that anyone who had ever tasted it was prepared to stake Alleyne to dinner if he would make the dressing.

In the dining room a ceremonial hush fell whenever Ireland began his mystic ritual. Forks were suspended and often a small crowd gathered round to watch him as he took the ingredients from two waiters who were known as "Lysander" and "Demetrius." It was a small spectacle to see Ireland demand, imperiously, "First, the drys," as he mashed sugar, salt, and dry mustard in a bowl. "Now—the wets," he continued, introducing chives, garlic, and other ingredients in the order of their degree of wetness. Like an alchemist, he poured in vinegar and olive oil, finally tossing the whole salad with the expertise of a master chef.

There were trenchermen in the Club who could match the exploits of those turn-of-the-century eaters whose feats were still recounted. Samuel Merwin, the noted magazine writer, easily won all awards for sheer quantities consumed. When he died at the Club in 1936 many members believed it was the result of overeating, a verdict apparently shared by his son, who called Sam (not without sorrowful affection) "A food drunkard."

Some of the old culinary amenities, however, were beginning to disappear. A hardy survivor until the early Sixties was what members called "the Club Cheese"—not the covered plate on the bar, Brian Hooker's delight, but a jar of spreadable cheese, accompanied by sea biscuits, on every table in the dining room. The only such staples surviving today are the Club's Welsh rarebit and chipped beef on toast, and they are menu items. The cheese was free.

Even in the Depression it was still possible to eat virtually around the clock at The Players. At breakfast there were an à la carte menu and five "combinations." Actors and retired members were inclined to drift in just before the breakfast menu went off at noon, Sundays at 1 P.M. If these late risers could get into their seats before the clock began to strike, it was possible to order a combination breakfast for 60 cents. After the last chime, however, the same food would cost double, as an à la carte lunch. From noon until 2 P.M. the dining room Round Table was in session and literati appeared at the other tables. Dinner was offered from 5:30 to 8 P.M., with the actors arriving first, followed by the others. After 8, it was still possible for the elegant haute monde, arriving late, to dine à la carte until midnight or later.

Such noted gourmets as Lucius Beebe were not above dining at the Club. Beebe reported in his New York *Herald Tribune* column that he had the courage (or the simple chutzpah) to take H. T. Parker, noted drama critic of the Boston *Transcript*, to No. 16, where he could expect to find an actor who, as Beebe put it, had "at one time or another felt the adroit bludgeonings of H.T.P.'s reviews about his ear." Drama critics were still not admitted as members, and were not even encouraged as guests, but no bloodbath occurred after Beebe entered with Parker. Instead, as Beebe wrote, "His presence precipitated a minor festival that approached flag-raising proportions." He had entered at lunch time but the visit ran on through teatime, and then to a six o'clock dinner, after which the no-doubt-bemused critic left for a European vacation in the vineyards along the Rhine. Parker described his visit, said Beebe, "as the most agreeable preview of his experience" in the wine country.

A visitor of another sort was Joe DiMaggio, who was brought in for lunch by the *World-Telegram*'s superb sportswriter, Joe Williams. He was shown the rooms, the playbills, the portraits, and was told about Booth, Jefferson, and Drew. To all this, the *Bulletin* reported, Joe responded with an appreciative "Gosh!" He was introduced to various eminent members, and there were further "Goshes!" All this was duly narrated by Williams in his column.

All the visitors, celebrated or not, saw a Club that had been refurbished until it shone with something of its original glow. The renovations of the Twenties had been a splendid start, but the assault on decaying conditions that Bill Tachau led through the Thirties was an even greater physical rejuvenation. New construction outside the clubhouse had forewarned of necessary changes as early as 1930, when the view from the back porch to 19th Street was closed for good by the construction of a new building that rose to about the same height as the rear portion of the National Arts Club, leaving only a draught of air through a narrow slit. Some light was cut off and the ailanthus tree in the garden barely survived the blasting.

In 1937 Tachau began a new round of cleaning and modernizing by renovating the card room, installing an efficient ventilating system, contemporary lighting, and redesigning the fireplace. The niches were rebuilt to match and bookshelves were installed, along with card tables and chairs, the latter reproductions of the originals. All these furnishings were gifts of Mrs. Sydney Booth, in memory of her husband.

A more radical move that generated some controversy was the removal of the librarian from his desk at the rear of the library to the small room next door known as the conversation room, but also called the Booth Library because it contained the Founder's private volumes. Both researchers in the main library and those members who were merely sleeping there, it turned out, had found the presence of the librarian disturbing, although it was not explained why. The librarian had been disturbed, too, particularly by the sleepers. Now, in a major move protested by some members, the Booth books were moved to his bedroom on the third floor and installed in two cases built behind his bed, while the librarian moved into the conversation room.

An even more drastic and far more welcome move was the rehabilitation of the bar and billiard room downstairs, where complaints about crowded conditions were regularly made to the board. The board wavered for some time on this issue, as it had on the Booth Library removal, but Tachau prevailed with logic and the kind of detailed planning only an architect of his stature could provide. A new ventilating system was installed and the mailboxes, which had been scattered about, were gathered in one place. The bar itself was given a new dress, and Charles B. Falls painted a portrait above it—not the one we see today but a composite of Players who had leaned against it. Tachau also added a sound-deadening ceiling of acoustic tiles.

In the Great Hall, as it was now called, the original couches were replaced by a new set in vivid orange-red leather, which led some critical members to inquire, "Where are the girls?" Much later they were replaced by more sober maroon resting places.

In the rear of the property, having earlier excavated to make room below the garden, Tachau and his committee finished restoring the surface. What was left of Edward Simmons's murals were preserved, decorative panels of trellises were erected, the porches were given new railings, the courtyard was paved, and a new fountain built for the benefit of Myrtle the Turtle and a new colony of goldfish. Myrtle herself disappeared in the summer of 1938 and there was some grieving on the back porch until it was learned that she herself had been a replacement. Two members tossed a coin to see who would buy a third Myrtle. The winner also provided her with a sort of escalator so that she could slide into the water, but this convenience was disdained by the ungrateful Myrtle.

With the increase in wall space gained by the renovation downstairs, some of the Club's pictorial treasures reappeared in a setting where more members could admire them. These included the photograph taken on the *Oneida*, when the historic meeting that gave birth to The Players took place; a choice drawing by Oliver Herford; and a group of sketches made in the Club by John Wolcott Adams.

All of Tachau's modernization program was greeted with howls of protest as it went along, just as the rehabilitation process in the Twenties had been, and as all subsequent efforts to preserve and enhance the Club's physical property would be. These protests ranged all the way from the customary resistance to any change at all, to Clarence Budington Kelland's cry of outrage when he first viewed the restored library: "Now it will take another fifty years to get this place looking natural again."

Most Players, however, welcomed the changes and applauded the work of Tachau and his committee when it was completed. This appreciative audience included a number of new members, many of who had joined during a period between February 1 to December 31, 1935, when fees were suspended in an effort to bring in more qualified members and bolster Club funds depleted by the Depression. This influx was considered nothing less than a rejuvenation, since it brought in a solid core of enthusiastic not-so-famous newcomers as well as a galaxy of the well known. It was now easier than ever to drop names or pick them up at The Players, with recruits such as Philip Barry, Lionel Barrymore, Richard Barthelmess, A. A. Berle, Jr., James Cagney, Dixon Ryan Fox, Paul Gallico, Walter Huston, John Holm, John Huston, Guy Kibbee, Josh Logan, Pare Lorentz, Frederic March, Ogden Nash, and Whitney North Seymour. In the following year Jean Hersholt, Arthur Kober, William Allen White, and Laurence Olivier could be added to the list.

In addition to the need for dues-payers, the drive for new members in the Thirties resulted from an unusually large number of deaths in the Club's roster as the initial generation began to disappear from the scene. In 1930 there were more than 600 ex-Players but in 1936 a list of members showed only 53 still living who had been members before or during 1900. The only original living member at that time was William Gillette.

Memories of earlier times were fading, as they always do. Helen Ormsbee, writing in the *Herald Tribune*, told of a veteran first-nighter (no doubt a Player) who took his nephew Ronald to the Booth Theatre to see

You Can't Take It with You and on the way in pointed out the large bronze bust of Booth in the entrance, remarking, "That's Edwin Booth."

"Edwin who?" Ronald inquired.

The shocked uncle tried to explain and Ronald did his best to show interest, but the most he could manage was, "He built this theater?"

The Club made efforts to preserve what it could of the past that seemed worth preserving. In April 1934 at the Cornish Arms Hotel the Employees Ball was revived, the fourteenth of these annual dances. More than 200 attended and Melvyn Douglas invited the entire cast of the play he was currently appearing in, *Moor Born*. A year later there was an encore at the Hotel Delano but then the custom was allowed to die out for no particular reason, or so it appeared. Cordial relations between employees and members continued in the traditional way as they still do after a century.

In 1938 the Club could look back on its first half-century with more than a little satisfaction. There had been few deviations from Booth's original purposes, and none of any significance. Financial independence, thanks to the Founder's original gift, had been preserved even in the face of national financial disaster when other clubs had been driven to the wall, with some casualties. It had remained on Gramercy Park in spite of strong agitation to move uptown in the Twenties, leaving it the oldest club in terms of continuous residence in one place.

Survival had been made possible not only by good management but also through the tremendous effort of its actor members in producing the long string of revivals. Membership had not only recovered from its sharp Depression losses but had actually increased. Many of these were former members who had come back for reinstatement. And as the *Bulletin* observed, "Young men are joining the Club nowadays who scarcely know the names of some of the distinguished men who comprised its early membership. But they all know about Booth."

No wonder The Players found much to celebrate when they held their grand anniversary dinner at the Waldorf-Astoria in November, the unique event described before. Earlier that year, in April, there had been another celebration in Hollywood for West Coast members, attended by a list of actors reading like the cast of an all-star movie, as they gathered in the grill room of the Bel-Air Country Club: Walter Abel, Sidney Blackmer, Humphrey Bogart, James Cagney, Louis Calhern, Charles Coburn, Walter Connolly, Russel Crouse, Melvyn Douglas, James Gleason, Nunnally Johnson, Guy Kibbee, Howard Lindsay, Gene Lockhart, Montague Love, Herbert Marshall, Frank McHugh, Robert Montgomery (who was toastmaster), Frank Morgan, Ralph Morgan, Ogden Nash, Elliott Nugent, Pat O'Brien, Tyrone Power, and Basil Rathbone—among others.

As the final year of the Thirties ended, the Club was preparing for even more remarkable progress—a hope that would soon be interrupted by the third war in its brief lifetime. A special meeting of the board in November approved a revised constitution and elected a new and enlarged Board of Directors, including George M. Cohan, Arthur Goodrich, Clarence Budington Kelland, John Charles Thomas, Gene Buck, Frank Craven, and Philip Merivale—again, among others.

At the annual meeting a few weeks later the new board dealt with a question that still remains somewhat vexed, the definition of that vague term: patrons of the arts. The resolution unanimously adopted declared that these members would be defined as "those gentlemen associated remotely with or sincerely interested in the Arts, who shall be, by their personal distinction or qualities, congenial with the other members. This classification will include such doctors, lawyers, Army and Navy officers, bankers and men of general business as qualify in the judgment of the Board, under the definition above. This Patron group shall be limited to 125 and shall be elected only by the Board, not by the Executive Committee."

With this step taken, the Club moved into the war years.

CHAPTER 8

The Forties

FOR SOME PLAYERS THE MOMENTOUS DECADE OF THE FORTIES BEGAN with a shocking event quite unrelated to the storm that had broken over Europe—the election of a drama critic to membership. Burns Mantle was the first to be admitted, in 1940. He had been drama critic of the New York *Daily News* since 1922 and, more notably, the editor of the annual *Best Plays* record book since 1920. Mantle was able to enjoy life at the Club only eight years, until his death in 1948, but he was made as welcome as though he had never written anything that was less than flattering about his fellow Players.

Lucius Beebe, who had in some measure paved the way by bringing the Boston *Transcript*'s critic to lunch a few years earlier, an event preciously recounted, could now turn his undivided attention to the Club's culinary accomplishments, which remained at their customary high level on the eve of Pearl Harbor. It was a kitchen that could even produce a creditable baked Alaska for private parties. As co-host for one of these affairs, Beebe wrote in his column that "the food was as fine and the service as gracious as I have ever known anywhere. Never in the Drovers' Inn in Chicago [the great stockyards restaurant], or in Kansas City, have I encountered a more splendid cut of beef, and the sturgeon will, with me anyway, enjoy an immortality in memory."

Members were encouraged to have these private dinners for other members, often in foursomes, on a weekly, fortnightly, or monthly basis. It was an activity promoted largely by word-of-mouth and through the *Bulletin*. One of the more unusual of these events was a dinner organized by the Players Club Class of '81, which held its first meeting on December 29, 1941, an affair whose hilarity and optimism had not been appreciably dimmed by Pearl Harbor. Members were told to come in the costume of the period, which prompted F.P.A. to appear in a diaper, held together with period fastenings. Later, he reappeared in an '81 college sweater.

All was far from hilarious at the Club, of course, in those early days of the war. A service flag was soon hung on the west wall of the main entrance, and by 1944 the star that hung in its center recorded 84 members in the service. Another star numbered at 14 the number of employees.

Talk in the Club centered on the war, as one would expect, but as always there was room enough left over to discuss (and complain about) the third renovation in Club history, which began in 1941 and continued through 1942. It was not on the scale of those in the Twenties and Thirties, but it was enough to renew hot debate while the work went on. A new hand was now at the helm of the house committee. Bill Tachau had done his job and departed; his successor was Ray Vir Den, whose somewhat spectacular career will be noted in this volume's last chapter.

Vir Den began somewhat modestly in late 1941 by renaming the reading room the living room, leaving magazines and papers within reach in its precincts, but removing to the library any more serious reading that might be lying about. There was new carpeting on the living room floor and the furniture was rearranged. Overhead and out of sight, a new roof on the clubhouse had been completed.

Immediately controversial in early 1942 was the removal of the card players from the grill room to the card room upstairs. This move was generated by protest letters from Rollin Kirby and Roland Winters, among others, who complained that the card and backgammon players had usurped the tables and made it impossible for late lunchers or drinkers who liked to gather in the afternoon to find places for food and conversation. Anyone who brought guests, they pointed out, would be forcing them to stand up. The board agreed and moved the card players amid cries of persecution.

Such indignities, however, were trivial compared with the outrage of those older members who liked to seek the seclusion of the reading room. Approaching it one spring morning in 1942, they found the great doors closed for the first time in more than fifty years. Opening them and peering inside, they were further shocked to see the paintings gone, the tattered furniture missing, and the floor bare. Four painters in white uniforms were perched on high scaffolding, filling in cracks in the old brown paint that had never been disturbed since Stanford White had it applied.

Criticism and suggestions poured into the house committee and the board. Someone said that if all of them had been adopted, the room would look as though Rube Goldberg had designed it. At least one critic carried his advice direct to the source. Albert Sterner, a noted portrait painter, was discovered one day kneeling on the floor of the room in his shirtsleeves, giving one of the house painters a lecture on raw colors and how to mix them.

When the room began to emerge from its renovation, with the dust of a half-century removed, some members were surprised to see that it was pure Georgian. When the doors were opened again after three weeks, the walls of the room were a warm Georgian gray-green, with the furniture reupholstered in brown, rust, and gold. The three Sargent portraits of Booth, Jefferson, and Barrett were back on the walls, looking much brighter.

Vir Den then went to work on the top floor, and as the *Bulletin* observed, "You wouldn't know the old place." Again there was a generous application of fresh paint. Three of the rooms were completely done over, with new furniture, hangings, and pictures. Two modern showers were installed, and in the medicine closets the house committee had thoughtfully decreed a first-aid kit for morning shavers with unsteady fingers. An extra sleeping room was also added on this floor, made out of what had been a storeroom. Freshly painted, papered, and furnished, it was named the John Cummings Hunt Room. Sleeping rooms had been in great demand at the Club, the rentals adding considerably to revenue.

In the renovation of 1942, long tables were added at the bar, one on each side as they appear today, but they too evoked loud complaints from some members because, it was said, the gatherings there were too large for social comfort and too complicated for private drinking.

"A man wants a single quickie at lunch," one indignant member wrote to the committee, "or maybe a couple at cocktail time; he runs into a charming group and finds himself compelled, by the laws of custom and hospitality, to take four or five before he can successfully tear himself away. Can't something be done to curb this growing menace? Why can't we have either a tacit understanding among members that buying drinks is as prized an expression of independence as any of the other customs endearing us to club life? If it is a good rule at other clubs, why shouldn't it be a good rule at The Players?"

The house committee asked for guidance in this matter, and got an abundance of it. Nothing was changed in the end; time and custom overwhelmed the complaints. Nor did anything come immediately of the campaign begun by Charles Hanson Towne and Carl Crow to have a brass rail at the bar. This campaign's slogan was, "A bar without a rail is like blindness without Braille," and fifty-cent contributions were invited for a Brass Rail Fund. There was no opposition but it took some time for this modest improvement to become reality.

When Vir Den's committee had finished its work, the clubhouse boasted not only the renovations described, but redecorated walls in grill room, card room, library, and bar; polishing of the oak paneling everywhere; new curtains; and old chairs recovered in red leather. By popular demand, nothing was changed in the dining room: breakfast, luncheon, dinner, and supper were still available.

One alteration occurred in spite of the committee. The ailanthus tree that had so long charmed members in the garden was cut down in mid-1943, a victim of the apartment house that had been built on 19th Street. Roots had been cut away, and for a time the trunk and branches stood like a skeleton. Desperate efforts were made to cover its nakedness with ivy, but in the end it was considered too unsightly and no longer useful. Diners on the piazza, particularly, mourned its passing.

By the end of December 1942, with so many other changes in the Club that year, it was hardly considered upsetting to have Booth Day celebrated for the first time on the anniversary of his birth, November 13. This was intended as an experiment, but it was so successful that it proved to be an all-day affair. About one hundred members gathered for lunch, after which George Odell, a Player since 1898, stood beneath the newly restored painting of Junius Booth and spoke warmly of his son. Then, following tradition, Charlie Connolly laid a wreath at the foot of the statue in the park. More was planned, but the weather was so threatening that members moved back inside for the rest of the program.

But then they lingered on through dinner, merging a November Pipe Night with a newly planned rededication ceremony. John Erskine was Pipemaster, and Frank Crowninshield and Judge James Garrett Wallace the speakers. A remarkable program followed, including music by Mishel Piastro, concertmaster of the Philharmonic, and Joseph Schuster, its first-chair cellist, accompanied by Arpad Sandor; Lanny Ross, singing Shakespearean songs; and several other delights.

The rededication coincided with an extension of the Club to the West Coast, where many of its members now lived and worked. The origin of what was called Players West came in 1941 when Charles Coburn sought to find a place where these California exiles could gather and pretend they were at No. 16. It would not only be such a rendezvous but also a place to entertain prospective new members.

Finding a home for Players West was not easy, however. Hollywood was not equipped for it. There were few places with "rooms," and apparently none with a stage, which the movie people thought was a bizarre request. It was suggested by Coburn that a house be purchased and remodeled, but none that the agents showed his committee seemed right for the purpose. One was a mansion on a hilltop with a view of Catalina, an Italian palace with a swimming pool surrounded by an artificial sand beach. There were sunken baths inside and sunken gardens outside. Somewhere, said the *Bulletin,* reporting on the search, there must be sunken owners. The original cost had been $750,000; Players West could have it for a mere $50,000, including $5,000 worth of gold leaf in the projection room. Coburn pointed out to the agent that the mansions's location was hazardous. It could be reached only by a long, winding, private road with hairpin turns, and on a foggy day these turns could reduce the membership.

But the agent was resourceful. He took the committee to see an athletic club in Beverly Hills, complete with auditorium, stage, bar, restaurant, pool, locker room, and two squash courts. Unfortunately, it was a rainy day and the roof was leaking badly. Bath towels had been spread out to absorb the flow. There was another small problem. The owners said that the only way the West Coast Players could gain possession was to admit all the athletic club's members.

Coburn and the committee were seeing parts of Hollywood seldom viewed by tourists. The agent took them to the old Trocadero, where they found this famous nightclub in ruins, left idle for a long time, and only the remnants of its restaurant, fancy taproom, and powder room to remind the visitors of its past glories. The agent optimistically believed the owner might lease it, and might even provide a clubhouse and theater at his own expense. But when the committee's bid was received, the owner, just recovering from pneumonia, said no. He did not want a "one-purpose" building.

Adjourning to Coburn's apartment, the committee realized that there was no way out. If they wanted a clubhouse and theater, they would have to build one. The answer seemed immediately at hand. There was a vacant lot directly across the street from Coburn's apartment, with a view of Los Angeles and the ocean beyond. The prospect for an outdoor dining terrace for summer evenings was enticingly plain. The price was $50,000, but the elderly lady who owned it wanted an income for life, which meant $300 a month, plus taxes, until she died—an event that seemed not too distant, since she had heart trouble. One of the committee members knew her relatives, however, and he reported that they were all centenarians or better. It would be cheaper to buy the lot outright.

An architect was engaged and he presented the committee with a plan for a Georgian clubhouse, with an adjoining playhouse to be named the Edwin Booth Theater. It would cost nearly $400,000, completely equipped, and everyone agreed on a money-raising campaign. Coburn began the fund with a $5,000 contribution. A bond issue returning 2 percent, open only to Players, was set up, and it appeared that the campaign would succeed. But just as it was about to be launched, Pearl Harbor intervened. Coburn and the others could only count themselves lucky that it had not gone further; they would have been burdened with a project they could probably not have completed.

Eventually, much more modest quarters were found and an appeal was made to No. 16, where members had been following this saga with exceptional interest. At the annual meeting in 1942 it was voted to give Players West every possible assistance, which meant the blessing of the Club and its board, and the transfer of whatever programs, photographs, and other theater memorabilia could be spared for decoration. The younger generation of Players on the coast supported Coburn's committee and on July 17, Players West held its first Pipe Night, with Walter Hampden as guest of honor, Pat O'Brien as Pipemaster, and Gene Lockhart as chairman for the event.

Reports continued to trickle in from Hollywood about the progress of Players West. There had been a Players Day, it was said, with more than 120 members and their guests present. A Ladies Day had been held on April 25, 1943, with Harry Davenport as the official host. Eventually the West Room, as it came to be called, published its own *Bulletin*, edited by Eric Kalkhurst. In 1944 this publication had a list of 220 members and wrote of a Pipe Night honoring Frank Craven for his sixty years and three weeks in the theater. It had been billed, Hollywood style, as "A Super Colossal Show—eight Big Acts and a Galaxy of Stars."

Players West proved to be a good idea that could not survive the long haul because of constant changes in the entertainment industry and the often transitory character of those who worked in it. Nevertheless, it held on for some time and produced several notable events.

In 1942, however, whatever was happening either at No. 16 or on the coast had to take second place to the overwhelming reality of war. This time there were no vigilante groups organizing secretly at the Club, as there had been in 1917, but simply a policy of doing whatever could be done. Immediately, any member who was unable to pay his dues because he was in service had only to say so and the dues would be remitted.

By 1943 the income lost from the remission of dues was nearly balanced by voluntary contributions from those who were not in the armed forces. Many of these members increased their own quarterly payments. Even so, the onset of war meant another long financial crisis for the Club as inflationary costs of supplies and services began to make themselves felt.

It was particularly frustrating because other revenues were so good that if times had been normal the books at No. 16 would have balanced.

Players and the Club itself were active in war work of all kinds, contributing not only manpower but money to the American Theater Wing War Service.

If there was one way in which wartime shortages were felt most at the Club, it was embodied in Charlie Connolly's 1943 announcement that the rationing of cheese had compelled the discontinuance of the bar cheese so beloved of Brian Hooker and others, leaving only pretzels and crackers for the disconsolate. This amenity was not resumed until the war ended.

Another kind of crisis arose at a special meeting of the board in August 1943, when Secretary John Knight opened the session by reading a letter from Dave McKinlay, one of the Club's most loved members, who had served as treasurer for years. McKinlay wrote: "I have told Mr. Whitney Darrow a dozen times he could have my resignation as a member of the Board whenever expedient. This is due to two facts: (1) I am old and no good and have enough of the humbleness of wisdom to realize it. (2) I am away from New York more than half of the time, and therefore would be no good to the Club half the time, even if I was any good any of the time. I love the club, and the management of it, more than tongue can tell, and feel honored to have served it for so many years. But—in resigning, I wish it distinctly understood that I reserve the right to bawl out the management whether I am in the right or in the wrong. Here goes a great deal of affection to all of you."

A respectful silence greeted Knight's reading of the letter, then Darrow moved acceptance of McKinlay's resignation, with words of great regret and profound thanks. In his report of the meeting, Knight wrote: "With amazing lack of delicacy, this motion was seconded by Mr. McKinlay. Other members declined to vote, and the motion was carried by the unanimous vote of Mr. McKinlay. It was then proposed that Mr. McKinlay also compose his own epitaph as a universally beloved member of the Board—a suggestion that was greeted with loud interruptions and numerous counter proposals from the petitioner."

As the war moved toward its climax, further restrictions were imposed on Club activities. After the disappearance of the cheese, the house committee began to curtail services in the dining room, since many of its staff were in the armed forces or had gone to better jobs. Sunday meals and breakfast were discontinued, there was no afternoon tea in the lounge, and no meals were served between 3 and 5:30 P.M. The office was closed on Sundays. Breakfast was resumed in the fall of 1943, however, and tea was then available at the bar, where it failed to win much applause.

On Booth Day in 1943 Margaret Webster became the first woman to give the annual address, beginning a custom that has continued to the present. Other guests included Paul Robeson, then starring in *Othello*, with José Ferrer as Iago and Uta Hagen as Desdemona. Miss Webster presented the Club with an autographed letter of Edmund Kean's from the collection of her great-grandfather Benjamin Webster, who had been one of London's foremost actors and managers in 1862 when Booth was playing there.

As Howard Lindsay, then vice-president, accepted the letter and began to speak, he was struck by dizziness and fell back into the arms of those standing behind him. Taken to a couch in the library, he was examined by Dr. Richard Hoffman, the Player who had been with Don Marquis at the pool table when a stroke temporarily blinded him. Hoffman diagnosed Lindsay's problem as indigestion, complicated by an attack of intestinal poisoning. A. H. Van Buren, Lindsay's understudy, played his role in *Life with Father* that night and also for several performances. Lindsay recovered and served as Club president after Walter Hampden's retirement, but the incident, as in Marquis's case, was a first warning.

The wreath was duly laid after Howard's collapse and in the excitement no one thought to read Kean's letter, addressed to Edward Crooke, Theatrical Agency Office. It concerned a debt to "Little Breeches," as Kean called Charlotte Cox, his "significant other," as she would be known today. Charlotte was the wife of a London alderman who later sued Kean for two thousand pounds, charging him with the theft of his wife's affections. In the letter Kean wrote: "I owe Little Breeches 20 pounds, which I cannot send her till I get to Newry, but if she particularly wants it before then I have told her to ask you and you may draw it in my name from Holt. I will remit it to him—instead of her—but perhaps this may not be the case." Evidently a man of at least some honor.

By the end of 1943 the two-man crusade of Carl Crow and Charles Hanson Towne to equip the bar with a brass rail had begun to show signs of success. Their plea for funds had been answered with a substantial collection and the two made an expedition to the old shops on the Bowery in search of an authentic piece. They fond one and it was installed, as we can see today. Its source was appropriate. The new brass rail had once been in the bar of the National Theater at Bowery and Chatham Square, where Booth made his first stage appearance—or at least his first "announced" appearance on any stage, supporting his father Junius in *The Iron Chest*.

Adding a footnote to the story of their acquisition, Crow and Towne wrote to the *Bulletin:* "The initials J.B.B. of the man whose foot so often rested on this rail are scratched on it, but unfortunately can only be seen from the floor."

With the war nearly over, the Club began to reassess its membership in late 1944 and plan for the future. The board entertained the discussion of certain perennial problems. A question was raised as to whether there were as many actor members as there had been, and if not, should there be an effort to recruit them. A census was taken, disclosing that there were presently 278 out of a total of more than 800 who were affiliated with the professional theater, including directors, writers, and stage managers, as well as actors. No action was needed, the Board concluded.

Indeed, the annual meeting that year on June 4 was described as the most harmonious within living memory. Several changes in the constitution were proposed by the board and brought no objections. Only a month before there had been a lively controversy about a proposal to change the dues and reclassify membership ratings, but all these reforms were now accepted with enthusiasm. The reports of officers were uniformly optimistic.

There was reason for optimism. In spite of difficult conditions during the war years—and they were by no means over—the financial condition of the Club was sound, and it was possible to contemplate a substantial postwar future. Parts of that future remained conjectural. No one could forecast what the proposed (and accepted) rise of 15 percent in dues for all classes would mean to future membership figures. For two years when, in 1946, associate members would be reclassified as nonresident members, there would be no increase in dues for this portion of the membership, since they had been granted two years' grace. Still another unknown quantity was the effect of a new ruling that all members who wanted to make contributions to the Club for its welfare and maintenance would have to make them payable to the John Drew Fund, all to be earmarked for charitable purposes, not to be applied to any other Club program. That meant an end to the kind of individual and group fund-raising for specific purposes that had been traditional from the beginning.

This change was not likely to create difficulties, most members agreed, but there was still controversy about the status of resident and nonresident actor members. At the 1944 meeting, Secretary John Knight made an effort to put this problem in a historical perspective. In the first Club constitution, adopted January 7, 1888, he pointed out, the pertinent article read: "No actor or Manager can be elected or become a nonresident member within a year from the time when he has acted or produced a play or musical performance upon any stage within 20 miles of the City of New York." This was modified almost immediately in a provision that prevailed until 1918, to read: "Actors not engaged for the whole dramatic season within 20 miles of the City Hall may become resident or non-resident members in the discretion of the Board of Directors."

In 1908 a qualification was added: "Actors admitted as non-resident members shall have all the rights of resident members." An amendment in 1924 made another change: "Actors may become resident or non-resident members in the discretion of the Board of Directors. Actors admitted as non-resident members shall have all the rights of resident members." During the same year, the associate member classification was adopted, declaring: "Any person eligible to resident membership of this club, who has neither a residence or a place of business within one thousand miles from the City Hall, New York City, shall be eligible to Associate Membership and shall be entitled to all the privileges of the Club, except the right of holding office." Dues were then established at $25 for the classification. It was this membership that the board, by its action of 1944, merged with the nonresident Players, whose dues were then $57.50.

Knight also provided statistics on what percentage of the Club membership was legitimately associated with the theater and its allied arts. In 1890, he disclosed, the actor members had numbered 20 percent of the total; in 1900, 24 percent; in 1910, 29 percent; in 1920, 27 percent; in 1944, 34 percent. By including "managers and dramatists" with the actors, the percentages were only slightly higher: in 1890, 26 percent; in 1900, 27 percent; in 1910, 35½ percent; in 1920, 39 percent. In 1944, when the classification read "stage, screen, and radio representatives," they constituted 40 percent. Total membership figures had risen from 326 in 1899 to a peak of 1,100 in 1915, a figure not surpassed up to 1944, when it had declined to a wartime low of 810, with a loss of 159 members since the beginning of the conflict.

Cheered by these and other reports, the Board began to plan for postwar progress, beginning with the inevitable renovations that appeared to be always needed to keep the old house from deteriorating. The most welcome repair work that began in 1946 was the restoration of the airconditioning system in the grill room, which had collapsed shortly after Pearl Harbor, causing the inhabitants to sweat out the remainder of the war. The house committee noted that it had cost $3,000 when Bill Tachau had it installed in 1936, while a new one in 1946 would have cost more than $6,000. The repair bill was about $725.

The kitchen was scrubbed and painted and the splendid inlay floor of the dining room, worn too thin for further scraping, was given a protective coating of varnish. New radiators were installed on the dining porch, and the lattice at the far south end of the garden was mortised and screwed together to avoid further collapse. One change unconnected with the decay of the war years occurred after a severe August storm had blown off a large iron outdoor flue that had connected the furnace heating The Players with another chimney running up the side of the Parkside Hotel. The house committee had always considered this device a monstrosity and they were not sorry to see it go, although its exit was spectacular and potentially dangerous since it weighed a ton and fell on the roof about 3 o'clock in the morning outside the quarters of John Martin, who claimed next day that he went right back to sleep.

Next to the return of air-conditioning, no restoration was more welcomed than the return on a historic day, August 7, 1946, of the bar cheese—cheddar, at 75 cents per pound. Harold Pulsifer quickly added to the stock, bringing in quantities of cured brick, cured Swiss, and aged cheddar. Pulsifer explained that he had been stricken by the memory of all the cheese he had eaten during twenty-seven years of membership—perhaps even more than Hooker's consumption—and had decided he must repay in some measure.

The Club was now functioning on a more or less completely reorganized basis. It had a manager as well as a steward. Herbert F. Erb, the new manager, had been keeper of the books and accounts. Charlie Connolly, who had been called superintendent of the help and of the bar and grill, remained as steward, with personal attention to the bar and liquor privileges, under Erb's direct supervision. These privileges, by law, now reverted to the Club's exclusive control.

One thing that remained more or less out of control was the Club elevator, which had balked from time to time since Bernhardt's unforgettable entrapment. On a February night in 1945 it struck once more, this time at the president himself. Apparently it preferred distinguished passengers. The hour was late. Most of the transients had departed, a few members were having a last drink, and Hampden, who at that time was living upstairs, announced that he was going up to bed.

Somewhere between the second and third floors the uncertain elevator stopped and refused to go further. Hampden rattled the door, stamped on the floor, and yelled, but no one heard for a half-hour, although he could hear laughter from the bar below. One shout, however, succeeded in arousing a sleeping resident upstairs, the gentle John Martin (his real name was Morgan Shephard), who roused himself and padded down to see what was wrong. Having discovered Hampden, he went in search of the nightwatchman but failed to find him. It was now 3 A.M. and everyone else had gone home. It took another few minutes for John to find the watchman asleep in the bowels of the Club and another half-hour after that before Hampden was released—all told, an hour and ten minutes of captivity. The elevator was a prime candidate at that moment for inclusion on the list of renovations in the Club, already begun.

Upstairs, a program to segregate and refurbish the Booth relics was begun, including the cases in the Great Hall. A librarian, Elizabeth Barrett of the New York Public Library, was appointed to assist the library committee in selecting books for binding and repair and to catalog the major works. May Davenport Seymour, curator of the Theatre Collection of the Museum of the City of New York, had agreed to take over the streamlining of the Booth costumes and the artifacts displayed in the safes between the main hall and the grill room. Those that were considered impossible to display properly went to the Museum of the City of New York, while the Players Club Collection at the Public Library would provide a home for such additional playbills and printed curios as could be salvaged from the renovation.

In all the sweetness and light of postwar revival, however, there were warning signs of problems to come. On Founder's Night in 1946, attendance was so low that its existence seemed to be threatened. Wives were blamed by those who attended. After decades of sacrificing their husbands' company on New Year's Eve, the war had generated revolt and in its aftermath there was a general reluctance to part with them on one of the year's most festive nights. Obviously, changes would have to be made.

More immediately threatening in 1947 was the red ink produced in the restaurant's accounts. With wartime ceilings removed, prices of food had risen sharply so that the average cost that year had climbed to 70 cents per meal, as against 43 cents only the year before. The direct loss was $800 in this department alone, while wages were also rising—10 percent that year. Prices had to be raised, but the famous luncheon special remained intact at 85 cents, with a daily special dinner added, an improvement often discussed but never made.

On the bright side, a new chef had arrived, the steaks were back to their prewar size, and the wine cellar was in the process of renovation, having been depleted during the war. New storage facilities were constructed for the wine and a special committee produced a smaller but well-balanced wine list, with markups held down to 50 percent. "Every bottle a buy," the committee promised. The list was designed by Bill Plante and decorated with drawings by John Falter.

Having been short of controversies for some time, the members found a new one in the case of the telephone booth that had long stood between two columns at the entrance. It was not exactly a new cause célèbre, having simmered beneath the surface for years, but now it emerged in full battle array. Called "the outhouse" by some ribald members, the booth had originally been the property of the Gramercy Park Taxi Cab Association, an institution now extinct. It had been supported by the members of the Club most likely to need its services at night. Frank Murphy, whose career has been previously noted, was Club taxi-caller. He had been succeeded after his death by a man who sat on one of the flower urns from 8 A.M. until late at night, lending a certain distinction to the Club's facade, in the opinion of some members.

When he became a member of the house committee, Charles Kinsolving disagreed, and tried to abolish the "outhouse" but discovered that it had become an icon, fiercely treasured by older members, particularly Dave McKinlay, who had often in earlier times been shepherded into a cab in the helping arms of Murphy. Kinsolving charged that as a result of the controversy over the telephone booth, McKinlay had succeeded in getting him removed from the committee. But in 1947 Dave had gone to live in Tucson, and as the argument came to a boiling point once more, Kinsolving again urged removal but generously insisted that McKinlay must be consulted. That was done, and elicited a typical, and endearing, response from Tucson: ". . . All I do know to my way of thinking anything that is very useful is beautiful and that Chic Sales edifice in front of the Club was good and very useful and will be again when economics get settled. Imagine Pipe Nights or any night for that matter when the Club gets really going again, as it will, without taxicabs! When Bill Tachau and Charlie Kinsolving were on the house committee and conspired to throw out the lovely privy in front, I started to fight them tooth and fang and claw, because I used taxicabs. But I didn't have to use many teeth or fangs or claws because I found most of the members I talked to were as selfish as I was and liked to use taxicabs too. May I state I found when scrapping with them that neither Bill Tachau nor Kinsolving ever used taxicabs. Q.E.D. If you see Charlie, please give him my love and tell him my idea of a happy time would be to bounce him up and down on a barrel cactus, then take him to the hospital in a taxi."

Nevertheless, the "outhouse" was removed, and taxis became progressively harder to find.

At the annual meeting of 1948 it was reported that the Club lost money for the first time in many years. The Players was now confronting head-on the great postwar inflation that eventually transformed the country and launched the greatest boom it had ever seen. Its first symptoms were the increased price of food and liquor, and of labor costs, already a problem in 1946. The board estimated that the loss in the coming year, 1949, would approach $5,000. The loss on every meal served in the dining room was 90 cents, and there had been a net loss of five members that year, an ominous sign.

Plainly, something had to be done, and the board called on its various committees to suggest ways and means of meeting the deficits. The house committee had already made several proposals, but these were found wanting. There were indications that a financial gridlock was developing. The more food bought, the deeper the deficit hole. It was suggested that voluntary contributions be called for in the traditional way, but that was now forbidden by the changes in the constitution. In any case, there was the danger that it would become an annual necessity. But whenever a small increase in quarterly dues, no more than two or three dollars, was suggested, any such proposal was voted down.

It was clear to the board, however, that raising dues was the only realistic option, and that was done in 1949. About $10 a year was added, so that with taxes the quarterly charges would not exceed $37.50—about the equivalent of two dinners at the Club, it was pointed out to doubtful members. But even this would not be enough, and it was voted to put lunch and dinner menus on an a la carte basis in the dining room, which was losing about $2,000 a month in early 1949.

So the decade ended, with repairs both physical and financial. The only member not objecting to anything was a new house cat, the last of a long line, named La Cucuracha, who liked to sleep on the writing table blotter.

PART THREE

Modern Times

CHAPTER 9

The Fifties

HAVING SUCCESSFULLY SURVIVED BOTH A GREAT DEPRESSION AND A great war, the Club moved into the Fifties in a hopeful mood, buoyed by the optimism of the late Forties. The good cheer did not last long. A chill blast from the Winter 1950 issue of the *Bulletin,* unprecedented in its bluntness, precipitated a wave of apprehension among the more realistic members.

Written by Charles Kinsolving, not by Bill Plante, who had become editor with that issue, the *Bulletin's* editorial outlined the Club's condition in uncompromising terms never seen before in this house organ. The Club, Kinsolving wrote, had "a reserve fund which could be wiped out with five successive years of current deficits, practically no waiting list and the spectre of a possible loss of considerable supporting membership on the West Coast if the West Room is compelled to close at the end of this year," as seemed likely.

Were the members inclined to do anything about their situation? No, Kinsolving said, and elaborated: "Every time proposals are put forth designed to save the Club's financial integrity and, in fine, its very existence, great bellows of reaction come from the longhorns around the bar, and dignified programs are howled out of existence by the very members who should take the responsibility of refreshing the organization with acceptable and congenial new members. If the Club's trend in memberships continues along its present charted curve, you will see your organization gradually disintegrate, through inadequate funds to hire help, insufficient dues to sustain the traditional comforts which the Club has offered since its foundation. . . . It would be devastating if The Players reverted to the type of membership campaign undertaken by the Advertising Club, the Lotus, the Lambs, or even the Metropolitan. . . . If the whole membership would subject itself to the proper concern with this problem, the Club would soon find itself with an upward trend in membership and stability."

This analysis was greeted with divided opinions, as usual, and nothing was done about attacking the Club's problems seriously for the next five years. At board meetings in 1951 the major question was what to do about Founder's Night, which was rapidly disappearing through a continued drop in attendance. An initial compromise was made in 1951 by having it on the same evening but at an earlier hour, beginning with a special dinner for members only in the grill room at 8 o'clock. Then, at 9:30, everyone would gather in the main lounge for the address and the remainder of the ritual. After that, members with other commitments were free to leave.

On the night of this innovation, Players began to gather for the first time in Club history at 7 o'clock. Charlie had already brought up a half-dozen bottles of Perrier Jouet, 1937, last of the stock, in preparation for the event. It was a measure of how much the reform had been needed when only 55 members appeared for dinner, with eleven others showing up later for the ceremony. Messmore Kendall, the publisher, was speaker that evening, and besides the customary obeisance to Booth, offered a reminiscence of his career as an actor in Buffalo Bill's Wild West Show, when he was a small boy in the early Eighties. His assignment was to ride ahead of Cody on a buckskin pony and toss glass balls in the air for the great marksman to shoot down. Kendall's acting career was cut short when Cody beat him with a banana stalk for some minor offense, and fired him.

This beginning of Founder's Night reform was instigated by Vice-President Howard Lindsay, who presided more often at board meetings now because of Walter Hampden's failing health. Earlier in 1951, he had argued that social pressures were making it awkward for even the most loyal members to spend New Year's Eve at the Club. He suggested, first, that it be held as usual for those few devoted Players who could manage it, but that it then be repeated a few nights later for the others.

Counter proposals were made. Kinsolving suggested that the ceremony be moved to the night of January 1, thus preserving the day if not the hour. That motion was carried but Donald Geddes proposed another motion, to have it on the morning of January 1, calling it "The morning after the year before Founder's Day breakfast." Charles Coburn reported that the West Room was celebrating Founder's Night as soon as possible after New Year's Eve, simply turning back the clock for it.

Obviously, the problem was far from settled and the early dinner compromise was eventually worked out for that year. For three years members tried to make that plan work but it was never popular. Wives were far from placated. In 1955 the board issued a new ruling: Founder's Night would be held on the Sunday closest to December 31. With a slight stretch, that meant January 8. Traditionalists still objected to this further flouting of custom and heads were shaken, but the rise in attendance justified the move—87 that year, the largest for some time, augmented by the further innovation of permitting male guests to attend. This move represented a major breaking away from the past.

But the past refused to retreat. It was celebrated, in fact, on November 13, 1953, when CBS Radio, on its program titled "Stage Struck," devoted the whole hour to telling the story of The Players. The broadcast was carried by a hundred stations from coast-to-coast, with an estimated Hooper rating in the millions, most of whom had probably never heard of No. 16.

Booth himself appeared on the broadcast, with the bit from Othello he had recorded in 1890; it was the first time his voice had ever been heard on the air. Dennis King brought Shakespearean playing down to the present with the soliloquy from *Hamlet,* "The Play's the Thing." The hour opened with the announcer setting the scene of Gramercy Park on New Year's Eve, 1889, with Walter Hampden, playing Booth, reenacting the gift of No. 16 to The Players. The story went on from there, down to the present, with Booth Day 1953 reenacted, including Dorothy Stickney's speech and the wreath-laying itself described.

As the program unfolded it was quite properly an all-star cast that related the Club's history in song and story. Marc Connolly described No. 16. Alec Templeton played and sang tributes to various Players; Sir Cedric Hardwicke read Thomas Bailey Aldrich's poem about the Sargent portrait; Dennis King read Booth's handwritten appraisal of the character of Hamlet as it had appeared in his own scrapbook; and Charles Coburn eulogized Booth, proposing a toast to him. From London, Clark Gable read a declaration honoring the art of acting; Maurice Evans, playing Hamlet, gave the address to the players; and Rex Harrison did Marquis's "A Certain Club."

There was still more. Elliott Nugent read a message from Frank Sullivan in which, to the shock of many Club listeners, a mythical member's wife deplored the Club's financial condition. Deems Taylor read Mark Twain's "The Awful German Language," while Bobby Clark did a scene from *The Rivals*, with Lon Clark, and Maurice Evans read the "What must a King do now?" speech from *Richard III*. The announcers describing the scene in the park were Mike Wallace and Dan Seymour.

Surely enough stars to light up any sky. But it would not have been a Players' event without some kind of objection, even one done with a deft tongue-in-cheek, in the Club's tradition. It came in the form of a letter from Witter Bynner, in Hollywood, expressing general approval of the program, but protesting against the omission of so many Players who should have been on the show. There were less than thirty on the air, Bynner said. Where were Thomas Chalmers, Jimmy Cagney, Pat O'Brien, George M. Cohan, Robert E. Sherwood, John Mulholland, and Percy MacKaye? Bynner demanded an explanation from the house committee, and called for an investigation.

When this celebration was over, reality set in. It was plain that even with all the renovations of the Forties accomplished, more needed to be done, and still another overhaul began in 1954. New springs, mattresses, and carpets were installed in every bedroom, and during the summer there was a complete overhaul of the toilets adjacent to the pool room and the private dining room upstairs, which was assigned to the ladies, for the first time. They were "now often our guests," the *Bulletin* reported, without further comment.

There was resistance to changing the male counterpart below stairs. Some members did not want to lose the old-fashioned stalls, with their pull-chains and cigar rests, but Bill Tachau, who was in charge of this operation, beat back the resistance, pointing out that he had been there since 1906 and was not sorry to see the advent of modern plumbing.

One reform was short-lived. To save money, breakfast had been discontinued the previous year just as the season for eating it on the back porch began. Business had fallen off since it had been decided to close the dining room from 10 to 11:30 A.M. Now, in response to pressure from members, breakfast was restored, but it was already a doomed institution.

On the surface, Club affairs appeared tranquil in 1954. The annual meeting that year was a rare occasion: no complaints were heard. The books were reported as in the black by $1,700, as against a deficit of $8,000 the previous year, and there had been a net gain of ten new members. In 1955 there appeared to be an equally rosy outlook. In the fall all previous records were broken for attendance at Club events. The Pipe Night of November 13 had an attendance of 184, which was twice the average for these affairs for the preceding two years.

The major event of 1954, however, was the retirement of Walter Hampden as president, the first not to die in office. He departed reluctantly, but he had been in ill health for some time, and Howard Lindsay, next in line, was in effect already directing the affairs of the Club. On February 10, Lindsay was duly elected president, with Dennis King moving up to the vice-presidency, assuring that he would be next—much more of a certainty since Lindsay had agreed to take the presidency for only ten years. Hampden survived little more than a year after his retirement; he died June 11, 1955.

When Lindsay became president he made an assessment of the Club's condition and found that the current euphoria about its affairs was an illusion. Summarizing what he found ten years later, Donald Seawell, speaking at a Lindsay Pipe Night after his retirement, asserted that in 1955 the Club had a life expectancy of less than eight years. For a long time annual losses had been met by borrowing money from the Reserve Fund, the Club's only available asset. By 1963, at the current rate of borrowing, it would be exhausted.

Lindsay reversed the process. Over the next decade more money was poured into the Reserve Fund to pay for the loans than had been taken from it. By 1965 the Club was in the soundest financial condition it had ever been.

As soon as the first black ink began to appear, Lindsay took as much money as he dared and resumed the renovations begun in the early Fifties and temporarily suspended after the red ink had reached alarming proportions. In spite of all the cleaning that had gone on before, the clubhouse was once more losing its patina. Layers of dirt and cobwebs had accumulated; a thorough cleaning was long overdue. As it turned out, this renovation would take a decade.

A large portion of the cost would be borne by the library. In May 1957, a plan was first proposed to create the Walter Hampden Memorial Library as a separate institution, making it a part of the educational system of New York State, which would permit Players to make a greater contribution to the library, and for it to help the Club. On October 25, 1957, the New York State Board of Regents granted a charter to the library, and its first executive committee was named: Paul Hampden, Club secretary, as chairman; Donald Seawell, Club treasurer; and Newman Levy, chairman of the library committee.

In the language of the charter: "The Walter Hampden Memorial Library is chartered under the Education Law of New York as a non-profit, tax-exempt library, access to which is restricted to qualified scholars or writers who must make application to use it. Every Player is a qualified person. Gifts made to the Library are tax-deductible, but gifts made directly to the Club are not. The books, playbills and other material in the library are still the property of The Players."

At the beginning of its new life in 1958, the library had about 10,000 books, one of the finest collections on the American and English theater anywhere. There were also about 6,500 old playbills, all predating the modern form of theater programs, and about 10,000 photographs, not counting a separate collection of some 5,000 photos of silent screen actors and productions. Original prompt books, manuscripts, and scrapbooks numbered in the hundreds, not to mention thousands of letters.

The library would, in time, be of considerable help in keeping the Club solvent, but meanwhile, in the winter of 1957–58, a so-called Stimulating Committee began a campaign to acquire new, well-qualified members. With Peter Turgeon as chairman, the committee included Fielder Cook, Bill Duff, John Cecil Holm, and Al Bennett. During the next six months it succeeded in bringing 25 new members into the Club, calling its efforts not a membership drive but a process of aiding and abetting interest in joining.

For those already in, life went on as usual. The great caper of the Fifties, or at least the one best remembered, is what became known more specifically as the "Great Football Bet." It arose, as so many of those pseudo-events had done before, from a luncheon conversation. A few members had been discussing the imminent razing of New York's oldest apartment building on 18th Street, between Irving Place and Third Avenue, where Jack Shuttleworth, the diminutive pool player, former magazine editor, and Club favorite, had lived for years.

During the discussion there were those who thought it would be more profitable to make a large parking lot out of the site than build a new apartment house on it. There was already a parking lot at 18th Street and Irving Place, but Paul Hollister disdained it. "Oh, that's not so big," he said. "Why, I could kick a football the length of it."

Ordinarily that would have been an easily accepted opinion, since Hollister had played football at Harvard, in the Class of 1913. But he was in the presence of fellow Players, among whom nothing was ever taken for granted or considered unchallengeable.

"Bet you $100 you can't," Shuttleworth said, seizing the opportunity.

The bet was on. An inspection was made, and it was learned that the field was 70 yards long. The affair began to take on momentum as opinions and side bets proliferated. It was decided that in fairness Paul should have twelve tries with a regulation football, and be permitted to kick it any way he chose.

The kickout occurred on a Sunday morning early in June. Hollister and Shuttleworth appeared at the appointed time, surrounded by their respective backers. Paul was wearing pointed-toe Western boots, while Jack contributed the football and a kicking tee. Stanley Hughes had gone much further in his preparations. He arrived in an ambulance, with accompanying stretchers, oxygen, and first-aid kit. Peter Turgeon brought an interested and somewhat bemused guest from Australia.

When Hollister applied his boot to the ball for the first time it skittered off to one side, as did the second try. The third went straight enough but bounced back. After that attempt, Hollister began to limp, claiming a strain in the right thigh, but Roland Winters, acting as trainer, gave him a massage and he returned to the kicking tee. The massage appeared to give him renewed strength, as he kicked the ball 47 yards on the sixth try. The seventh, however, was a discouraging attempt. For his eighth blow, Paul decided to try placing the ball sideways on the ground, off the tee; it was a dismaying failure. Back on the tee again, the ball sailed high in the air, took a helpful forward bounce when it landed, and came to rest against the wheel of a car near the far right corner of the lot. It was Hollister's best kick, but still short; he gave up and paid off. There was a happy denouement, however. Shuttleworth invited everyone inside for a drink.

Those who were still drinking at the bar regretted the passing in 1958 of John Newman, who retired on the eve of his eightieth birthday as night bartender after fifteen years, on doctor's orders. He was succeeded by Juan Rodriguez, who soon became a fixture in the Club.

As the decade ended, the renovation begun by the Lindsay administration was at last in full swing. The managing committee placed a suggestion box in the Great Hall, announcing its presence there, and eliciting a large number of letters inquiring where the Great Hall was. Older members still called it the main hall, and younger ones usually referred to it as the lounge, if they called it anything at all beyond simply "upstairs." It was said that the Great Hall designation was used for the first time in the committee's announcement, the title credited to Lindsay, but in fact it had been in use for some time and its origins are obscure.

By any name, the Great Hall now had a new oyster-white paint job, and the same paint had been applied to reading room and grill. Members found the appearance of maroon walls on the stairwell and upper floors startling. The grill boasted new black-and-white flooring. Brass studs and other hardware on the front door seemed almost too brilliant, but the committee promised they would soften, as would the lacquer on the chandeliers.

The Booth room now bore a somewhat new look. Its chandelier had been polished, the rug cleaned, and the bed and table covers cleaned and mended. Deep red cotton material had replaced the old brown velvet window hangings, while the tattered upholstery on sofa and chairs had been replaced with a flowered pattern covering, much like the lovely old wallpaper above the wainscoting.

Outside the Booth room, a huge lighting fixture that had hung almost all the way down the stairwell, menacing traffic both up and down, had disappeared to a new home at the Museum of the City of New York.

For years the top bedroom floor had been badly in need of paint, and its lighting was regarded as deficient. Consequently, occupancy had fallen off. These rooms were completely renovated, with new wiring installed to make air-conditioning possible. The bedroom doors were repaneled and rehung so they would be airtight. With this accomplished, the occupancy price was raised to $5–$6 per night.

On the landing by the coatroom a new floor was installed, and a new parquet floor laid down in the grill room. During Christmas week in 1959, the kitchen was closed and stainless steel equipment installed, adding to the new refrigeration equipment put in during the summer. But there was still more to do in that department, as well as in other parts of the Club. Alfred B. Carb, who had succeeded Tachau as chairman of the building committee, promised that it would be done. Carb was the proper man for the job. A lawyer, he represented clients who let extremely large maintenance contracts annually.

There were staff changes, too, in 1959. Herbert Erb became business manager, and Andrew Amend was brought in from the Biltmore to be manager. The Club would also need a new steward. After 40 years, Adolph Delabar was ready to retire on his pension.

Argument accompanied all these changes, needless to say, even improvements in the bar and pool rooms, the most used portions of the Club, where a savings bank resembling a cash register was installed beside the pool table. Pool winners were asked to ring up their quarters, resulting in a sharp increase in revenue.

The cheese was moved from one end of the bar to the other, making room for a large cigar humidor. A bench dividing the pool and bar areas was shifted westward, helping to alleviate gridlock, a change accomplished in spite of the violent vocal—and, some said, physical—resistance of Roland Winters. No one, however, mourned the passing of the old brass cuspidors, removed by order of the City Health Department, although there were complaints about the removal of the Pear's soap and bay rum from the washroom.

In spite of all these improvements, the Lindsay administration still had a distance to go in its effort to pull the Club's finances into the black. In 1957 a net loss in membership had been reported for the first time in five years, and the operating deficit in the budget that year had been nearly $7,000, accounted for by a new union contract. While conditions had generally improved, progress was slow. In May 1959 a net gain of 35 members was recorded, but at the same time the operating loss was still nearly $3,400.

The new library did not have funds to reimburse the Club, and in fact was not obligated to do so beyond the extent to which it might have money available. There had been an appeal for contributions from members to support the library, but the response was negligible. The board reminded Players that if they had responded to the library appeal as they had to the John Drew Fund in the past, the Club would be in the black. Now there was no help for it. Dues were raised, to $150 for residents and $75 for nonresidents, the largest increase in No. 16's history.

If the state of the Club appeared still gloomy, the managers could at least see dim lights at the end of their particular tunnel, and believed it was not an onrushing locomotive. While the new library was not functioning in the way it would later, it promised to be an important source of financial help, higher dues would certainly produce more income, and the general movement of the Club appeared to be onward and upward. The Sixties, everyone said, would be a different story.

CHAPTER 10

The Sixties

WOULD THERE EVER BE ANY END TO RENOVATING NO. 16? A GOOD MANY members asked that question as the troubled Sixties began and the most radical change yet proposed came before the board and the membership. The short answer was no. The clubhouse had been a relatively old building when Booth bought it, and Stanford White's alteration had been chiefly designed to adapt it for Club purposes. By the early 1920s, as we have seen, it was badly in need of repairs, and natural aging had produced the same necessity to clean and renovate every decade since then.

But the proposal made in 1960 was more far-reaching than anything done previously, because it called for the elimination of a portion of the Club that had been part of its tradition almost from the beginning—the back porch dining area and the garden beyond it. The necessity, however, was clear. The dining room had to be enlarged, or Pipe Nights, open houses, and large gatherings of any kind would have to be either curtailed or dropped because constantly rising attendance had stretched the old dining room well beyond its capacity. There was only one direction to expand—southward over the porch and the garden.

There was an immediate outcry at this sacrilege, but by this time President Lindsay was in firm control and he prevailed. Not only would the extension be made, but there would be still another club-wide rehabilitation program. He entrusted the job to two of the Club's most devoted members, Porter Wylie and Alfred Carb. At the same time he pointed out to the opposition that taking care of the clubhouse was an ongoing job without end as the building continued to age. "Taking care" in this

165

instance meant not only the extension and badly needed structural strengthening, but the restoration of precious objects.

A case in point was Booth's dressing table, which stood under his portrait as Richelieu. Amazingly, it had never been cleaned. When it was restored at the beginning of the new campaign, and after three-quarters of a century's accumulation of dirt and dark varnish had been removed, it glowed like the jewel it was. Booth had carried that dressing table with him, heavy as it was, wherever he played.

Under Lindsay's leadership,the Club had recovered substantially from the financial crisis of the Fifties and could afford the alterations. For one thing, the $25,000 in bonds Booth had given the Club to establish a reserve fund that would guarantee continuity had increased so greatly that it was now, or soon would be in 1963, worth more than twelve times the original value. In 1960 the Club was in the black by $12,800.

Another vision of the Founder's had come to pass. When the membership was assessed statistically, the proper balance he had envisioned among actors, members of the allied arts, and patrons of the arts had been achieved, although some controversy lingered about the latter category.

The exact breakdown was as follows: men of the theatre (actors and all the related categories), 355, or 42.97 percent; artists, 37, or 4.47 percent; writers, 117, or 14.15 percent; musicians, 16, or 1.94 percent; artists' reps, 7, or .85 percent; journalists, 99, or 11.95 percent; publishers, 83, or 10.05 percent; and patrons of the arts, 113, or 13.67 percent.

With the opposition stilled if not entirely satisfied, reconstruction of the dining room began and the new room opened for lunch for the first time on October 17, 1961. It had been the only expansion of the main floor since Stanford White's original remodeling. All the other floors had been both remodeled and expanded, some of them several times, and it was surprising that the dining room had remained unaltered for so long. Built to accommodate a membership limited to 250, it had not changed for 73 years, and by law was restricted to 68 occupants. Now, with a membership of nearly 900, the new room could seat 183 legally.

This major alteration was first discussed officially at the May 28, 1961, annual meeting, with a record 113 members attending, held in the old dining room. Lindsay began by pointing out that the Club was in violation of the law that day, because the legal limit of the room was 68 people. Every Pipe Night, he added, dozens of people pleaded, usually in vain, for a seat within the room; one member complained that for twenty years he had never sat anywhere but on the porch for a Pipe Night. At open houses, people had to sit as far away as the Writing Room (now the Windsor Room), beneath Howard's portrait, after carrying their food all the way from the dining room. They had been discussing the problem for years, Lindsay told the members, and it was time to act. For those who didn't want to part with the backyard, he added, it should be remembered that it was already in ruins, the result of a hurricane.

Still, there was considerable protest at the meeting. Some members charged that the directors were plotting to mutilate the dining room Booth had loved. In fact, Booth had never seen it. As house committee chairman from 1925 to 1931, Harry Watson had changed the original Stanford White design to its 1961 form at a cost of $80,000. No one who had known him could fault Watson for this deed. He had been so devoted to the Club and spent so much time there that, when he died, his wife wrote a somewhat embittered note to the directors saying that she had lost Harry to The Players and they should bury him. They did.

When the vote was taken on the extension, twenty-one member directors approved and it was carried. In less than two weeks, 147 members had contributed more than $25,000 to the building fund. Work began on June 1.

Paneling the new dining room was feared to be expensive, but the architect, Lee Schoen, obtained it at a bargain price, $1,500, from a large fabric house. New it would have cost $25,000. Some of the panels had come from a Herfordshire mansion designed by Grinling Gibbons, and constructed before 1694. Members had insisted on saving the three murals by Charles Fall on the west wall of the old porch, so they were restored and stretched on wood panels to decorate the west wall. A state-of-the-art sound system was contributed by a distinguished Player, Avery Fisher, whose name would be perpetuated at Lincoln Center.

As had been the case before, the renovation disclosed several defects that might not have been discovered until further, and more expensive, damage had been done. The basement drainage system was discovered to be clogged; it was cleared and partly rebuilt. The building's electrical system proved to be out of balance and had to be corrected. There was a partial renewal of the ventilation system in the kitchen and basement. Several building violations and fire hazards were removed.

There might not have been an overrun on the estimated cost, $90,000, but the east and west walls turned out to be in a state of decay and had to be rebuilt from deep footings, raising the final bill to $113,000. Asked for contributions and pledges, the membership responded with amounts ranging from $10 to $2,500; the total was $29,873.91. The remainder was supplied from the Reserve Fund, to be paid back during the next fifteen years.

If there was one disturbing note after the new dining room opened in splendor, it was the discovery that someone had removed 65 pieces of the flat silver. They were never recovered.

As the members gathered in their new dining room, blazers could be seen displaying the Club's coat of arms for the first time. The patch was (and is) embroidered on black felt in gold, silver, red, and black. A scroll supports it, bearing the Booth family motto, *Quod Ero Spero,* "What I hope, I shall be." In the language of heraldry, the crest represents a lion passant and langued, embroidered in heavy gold. Mane and tail tip are made to stand out in lighter gold metallic thread. A wreath of red and silver supports the crest. A shield or escutcheon, colored solid gold and edged with a heavy gold thread, makes a frame for three wild boar heads. The heads—known in heraldry as Sinister, Erased, and Erect—are embroidered in heavy silver with red and black silk detail, and the scroll supporting the whole thing is in white silk, bearing the motto in red letters, edged in heavy gold thread, accentuating the traditional folds.

Why wild boars? some curious members asked. (The lion was taken for granted, but had there been a misspelling of the other animal?) Heraldry experts disclosed that the wild boar is one of the principals in this ancient art, often applied to a warrior's armorial bearing. There were further translations: "Erased" means torn off roughly; "langued" means tongued, used when the tongue is a different color than the animal's; "passant" is applied to animals in a walking position; "sinister," of course, is the left side; and "wreath" signifies two strands of silken rope supporting the crest.

A heavy load to carry, but The Players bore it well. The Lindsay administration soon introduced various innovations at the Club, beginning in 1960 with a brief series of pre-theater dinners, followed by evenings at such plays as *Irma La Douce* and *Camelot.* There were also two gourmet dinners, intended to be annual events but apparently not successful enough to continue. The final affair that year represented the long-delayed triumph of the ladies over Founder's Night—a New Year's Eve party to which wives and other female companions were invited. More than fifty bottles of champagne were consumed.

The open house on Sunday was already a tradition by 1961, with one or more distinguished members honored on these occasions, beginning with Sir Cedric Hardwicke and Dennis King. That year it was the turn of Ralph Bellamy and Vinton Freedley. Among those previously honored had been Marc Connolly, Elliot Nugent, James Cagney, Roland Winters, Frank McHugh, and Max Gordon.

In 1962 one of the more remarkable events was the first of two occasions when the restaurateur Sou Chan, whose House of Chan, palace of Chinese delights, then flourished on Seventh Avenue, brought his chefs and large quantities of food to No. 16 on a Sunday afternoon. The 367 members lucky enough to get reservations filed down into the pool room to find the green table roofed over and covered by a large scarlet table-cloth. On a silver platter lay a barbecued pig 42 inches long, still warm from the fire. Two sittings were held in the dining room upstairs as the guests filed up from below, carrying silver platters heaped with meat, testimonials to the chef's carving artistry below. Some of the materials for this feast had been flown in from the Gulf, Hong Kong, and California.

A singular amenity prevailed in the Club during the early Sixties—a barbershop in what is now the storeroom just off the Club office on the third floor. Ralph the barber presided there and exchanged pleasantries with the members, some of whom considered him the best in town. He worked Monday through Friday, from noon until 4 P.M. Unfortunately, Ralph died in April 1965, and his successor, Charles Salvia, did not operate much longer after that event. The barbershop eventually gave way to the inexorable need for more space.

On Founder's Night, January 7, 1962, the interior of the Club was photographed for the first time, with members present, for publication in the *Saturday Evening Post*, to illustrate member Corey Ford's affectionate article about The Players. Just a year later the National Park Service invited the Club to have No. 16 registered as a National Historic Land-mark, and on April 9, 1963, the Board voted to accept, with thanks.

A final touch was given to the exterior of the clubhouse in 1964 through the generosity of Randy Brownell, the treasurer, who donated the solid brass railing which encloses everything but the entrance. The top rail is supported by well-proportioned oval rods, ornamented with round medallions sculpted from three ancient Greek coins, the design repeated along the railing. Possibly the oldest of the medallions is the bee of Ephesus, the goddess Diana's symbol. There is also the owl of classical Athens, and a bull over a porpoise, representing a coin from Thurium, an Italian city of Magna Graccia on the Gulf of Tarentum. These three coins were reproduced from originals in the coin collection of the Chase Man-hattan Bank. The railing itself once enclosed executive offices of the Union Square Savings Bank.

A major event of the Sixties was the changing of the guard in 1965, when Howard Lindsay completed his promised decade, full of accom-plishments, and retired to become president emeritus. He left behind a salutary record. During his time in office the Club had been brought back to budgetary balance, with a surplus; membership had increased by about 150; and members were making twice as much use of the Club as they had before.

Some members believed that the main ingredient Howard had injected into the Club was discipline, his own, and to prove it they cited the crisis in 1961 when fire broke out in the bar during a Pipe Night. While the firemen were putting it out, Lindsay had set a splendid example by reclining on a couch upstairs with a drink in his hand, waiting for the firefighters to leave.

When he retired, Howard himself was given a Pipe Night, at which Donald Seawell, among others, recounted his accomplishments. By the time all the tributes were completed, it was so late that when the guest of honor rose to respond, he had no time to say anything he had planned. Later, he tried to get it all down for posterity, with this result, in part:

"During the 18 years I lived in the Village, I managed to get to the Club almost every day. I recalled how when I left my house to go to Gramercy Park my footsteps quickened and in my mind ran a line of poetry: 'And the need of a world of men for me.' [The reference was to the last line of Robert Browning's quatrain, "Parting at Morning"]. . . . One of the great changes in the last century has been the advance in the desegregation of the sexes. Before Prohibition, for example, the cocktail hour was entirely a masculine occasion. It is no longer so."

Then Howard went on to talk of other advances made by women, and of how at the Club they came now not only on Ladies' Day, but to open houses, the New Year's Eve party, and to Easter breakfasts. Soon (although Lindsay did not predict it) they would be welcome at lunch every day, dinner once a week, and even be given limited downstairs privileges at night. In a preview of the argument that would take place twenty years later, Lindsay said: "Women may make further inroads into our bastion, but it seems to me that if The Players ever loses its basic masculinity, it will lose its chief and most valuable element."

Robert Humphreys had once told him, he went on, that the wonderful thing to him about the Club was that when you entered its doors, you were nobody. "It didn't matter how wealthy you had become, what your achievements were, or your reputation in the outside world—you were simply a Player among other Players. Let me add that when you enter our house, you can be yourself. In truth you *have* to be yourself. Affectation and pretense can not live within our walls."

Lindsay summoned up expert testimony to support his beliefs about the Club, invoking the words of that consummate Player, John S. Phillips, who said: "We are chosen as men of good will . . . we do not try to change each other. We differ and are glad of it. The charm of this place is the bewildering variety of its untrammeled membership. . . . There is a common feeling for the sweet ease of freedom that brings understanding men close together. By the occasional use of intelligence and what tolerance we can command, we get on here in reasonable accord—peace without victory."

At the end of the retiring president's moving speech, the dining hall was formally designated as the Howard Lindsay Room.

After the dinner was over and the members had gathered in the bar, as usual, Charlie Connolly told a story illustrating aptly what Lindsay had been saying upstairs. About two years before, Charlie recalled, a recently elected member gave a party in the card room, an affair attended to by Charlie and Albert. When it was over, the host came over and said to Charlie,"I know this is against the rules, but you two boys have been wonderful to me tonight, and here's something for you. I know I'm breaking a rule."

"If it will put your mind at ease," Charlie said, "you're not breaking a rule. There *is* a rule in the Club against tipping employees, but there's no rule against tipping members. And I happen to be a member."

By custom, the Club's vice-president, Dennis King, now became the sixth president, the first Englishman to hold that office. In his acceptance speech, Dennis observed that he had heard of The Players as a young actor in Britain at the Birmingham Repertory Company. He thought of it as a rather special club for New York actors, and was aware that Booth's visit to the Garrick had been in part its inspiration, but when he became a member and saw what the Club was really like, and what Booth had given to it, he viewed it in a different light. What the Founder brought to The Players, he said, was "much more than a pattern for existence or a charming house in which Players could meet and roister and reflect. Booth bestowed love upon his dreams for The Players. He dwelt among Players with great warmth and affection. His regard for the men of his profession and for his countrymen who joined them in Gramercy Park was always based on a deep feeling for civilized human relationships and an abiding dedication to the highest aspirations of the mind and heart. It is this legacy of Booth's which pervades The Players."

There were still Players who had grown old with that legacy. On April 9, 1965, Bill Tachau celebrated his ninetieth birthday at the Club, and blew out nine candles, one for each decade; he had been a member since 1906. He was joined for the celebration by Jack King and George Middleton, both of whom had become members in 1903.

One of Tachau's disciples was honored the following year, when Herbert Erb was elected to honorary membership—along with Harry Truman. Tachau had recognized him as a possible asset in 1932, when Erb had come to the Club as a member of an auditing team to set up a bookkeeping system that would, everyone hoped, put the establishment on a businesslike basis at last. The team worked for a year, and when they were through, Tachau asked Erb to stay on, first as manager from 1945 to

1958, then as business manager. He was one of the hardest working Club employees, who often spent Saturdays and Sundays at his desk.

In 1966, the club inaugurated The Players trip to London, which became an annual event, still well patronized. On that first excursion, 154 members traveled on a chartered plane, at the rate of $180 each, ostensibly to spend a week seeing new plays and dining in the best places. (If they had been eating at the Club that year, they would have joined the general mystification at lunch on a June day when the menu offered the following puzzling dish: "Avocado stuffed with beef stew." For only $2.)

As soon as the first London excursionists landed, they scattered in all directions—the Continent, Ireland, other parts of England. Many spent at least part of the time in London, however, and John Mulholland attended a magicians' convention.

Since the birthday of the Founder fell on Sunday in 1966, the tradition of the luncheon was altered for the first time so that an open house could be held, as it would have been ordinarily on that day. Consequently it was the first time that ladies, other than a guest of honor, were present. Jessica Tandy was that year's lady of the theater to be honored. Her eloquent tribute to Booth was a small drama in itself, closing with Miss Tandy in tears as she quoted from *Julius Caesar,* "This was a man!" Then she smiled through the tears at her audience, and said, "Well, if Gielgud is entitled to tears, so am I."

The new president, Dennis King, began to be an even more familiar figure in the clubhouse as he spent more time there. It was pleasant to see him in the afternoon when he was often at the pool table during tea time, with a tea cart in tow. Surprisingly to some, he made an effort—there were members who called it a crusade—to bring some purity into the language heard in the grill room, a feat (if he had accomplished it) equivalent to reforming Chicago.

Dennis was at the Round Table one day when there was a particularly noisy crowd at the bar. As he glanced over in annoyance, it seemed odd to him that most of the raucous sounds appeared to be coming from the Reverend Richard Gilbert and a group of his guests. Suddenly one ejaculation, louder than the others, lingered in the air: "Jesus!"

At that, Dennis got up and moved toward Gilbert, intending to remonstrate. But as he got closer, he observed from the reversed collars that there were several other clergy in the group, and it occurred to him that someone might have used the word in a legitimate context. By that time, however, he was too close to Gilbert to retreat, and he felt obliged to say something.

"Dick," he remonstrated, "we just mustn't talk business in the Club."

On a quieter day, in November 1966, Dennis learned that the aged Tachau was now the only living Player to have seen Booth play. Details were provided. It had occurred in Louisville, when Tachau was eight or nine years old, and the play was *Julius Caesar,* performed in Maccabee's Theatre. But another claimant for this distinction had already appeared. In his Founder's Night address in 1957, George Middleton related that when he was eight years old in 1888 he had seen Booth play, a few years before Tachau. Ten years after Booth's death, Middleton became a Player.

But the more immediate past was slipping away too. Howard Lindsay, the first president emeritus, a designation created for him, died on February 11, 1967, at his home. The Club was closed for the service and he was truly mourned. Then, on Founder's Night on January 5, 1968, Charlie was unable to pass the cup for the first time in anyone's memory, and Herbert Erb took his place. By that time, Charlie was in the Actors' Home in Englewood, New Jersey, where he died on August 12, 1969.

In the spring of that year some of the Club's oldest institutions were also beginning to show signs of wear. On Ladies' Day, for example, there were only slightly more than a hundred guests, and the attendance was seen to be dwindling every year. Some believed it was the result of a gloom then prevailing on Broadway, but others pointed out more realistically that the day had once been on the house, and drinks were now more expensive.

Yet the spirit of the Club that Lindsay and King had spoken about so fervently persisted with no visible abatement. That was made apparent once more in the 1969 Pipe Night for James Cagney, with Robert Montgomery as Pipemaster. Among those present were Peter Lind Hayes, Max Morath, Al Simon, and Harland Dixon, who had taught Cagney to tap dance. A new version (or at least new to most of those present) of the famous grapefruit-in-the-face scene emerged. Originally, it was said, Bette Davis had been scheduled to play the Mae Clark role, but had to cancel after agreeing. In its first version the script had called for Davis, an old friend, to slam the grapefruit into Cagney's face, but the scene was reversed after Miss Clark got the part, and she was both struck and immortalized.

Montgomery, McHugh, and Hayes contributed stories about Cagney, but Morath was the hit of the evening with his ragtime songs—until Cagney came on and brought down the house with a song in Yiddish. Earlier on that Sunday afternoon he had come into the Club, quietly, as he liked it. He was in New York only once or twice a year, usually to be found at a corner of the bar, and had avoided a night in his honor for a long time, although the entertainment committee had been loaded down with requests.

Early that afternoon Judson Philips, an old friend who was then living at the Club, arrived there, went to his room and unpacked, then wandered down to the Great Hall. The Club seemed deserted, but from the empty dining room, Philips could hear a piano tinkling out "H-a double r-i, g-a-n spells Harrigan." Peering, he saw Al Simon at the piano, a familiar sight, and the stocky figure of Cagney, then a still limber 69, doing a tap routine.

At the dinner that night, Cagney didn't do his softshoe, as had been planned, but failed to perform it for a reason peculiar to him. At the head table with him was Harland Dixon, by this time in his nineties, who had not only taught Cagney to dance but had been one of the best himself. He had arrived with his battered felt hat, ready to do his old routine with Jimmy, but it was plain he would never be able to manage it. As Philips related, "I saw Jim whisper to him, a protective arm around him. The dance routine was never mentioned or attempted. Jimmy wouldn't have embarrassed him for anything in the world."

It was an emotional evening, all told. As Pipemaster, Montgomery appeared his usual cool and collected self, but when he began to talk about Cagney, affection overcame him, his voice broke, and his cheeks were wet. Embracing Jimmy, he kissed him on the cheek and sat down, unable to go on. When Cagney finally spoke at the end of the evening, he was given one of the greatest ovations ever heard in the Club.

And 1969 continued to be a festive year. In May, Sou Chan made a second appearance as the host of a Chinese feast, with two sittings for the 317 guests lucky enough to get reservations. Fortune cookies were specially prepared, containing sayings about the Club and its members. During dinner, Chinese musicians performed on the stage, playing rare instruments, and when they were not playing, John Mulholland, disguised as a Chinese conjuror, performed his celebrated tricks.

It was typical of Sou Chan's devotion to the Club and its members that a week or so later, on a visit to Dallas for a wedding, he flew on to Houston, where Paul Hollister, on his way to a permanent home in New Mexico, lay ill in a hospital. Sou Chan reported on his visit, and soon after came a letter from Hollister, in which he characteristically had a good Players story to tell.

It appeared, Hollister said, that Frederic Remington had come back to the Club after a visit in Europe, and lunched there on the first day with Childe Hassam, one of his best friends. Hassam reported that he had been doing some painting while Remington was away, and wondered if he wouldn't like to come back to the studio and have a look.

At the studio, while Remington relaxed with a drink, Hassam rustled through his work and at last picked out a canvas, put it on an easel, rolled it into a good light, stood back and asked Remington's opinion. From the far side of the room, Remington, who was by this time somewhat over his alcoholic capacity, swayed slightly as he assumed his most judicial attitude. Finally he delivered his verdict: "Hell, Muly! I got an aunt upstate can knit a better picture than that."

Muly was Hassam's affectionate nickname. His fellow artists, so it was said, called Hassam's painting style after this incident, "Muly's Stitch."

That story told of a Club and a nation far removed from the turbulent 1960s scene, when Hollister related it, but those older members who read it in the *Bulletin* recognized it at once as a true evocation of the spirit at No. 16.

CHAPTER 11

The Seventies— And Beyond

TO SOME OF THE OLDER MEMBERS IT APPEARED THAT THE CLUB HAD been undergoing a change in the Sixties, a change that became even more pronounced in the Seventies. Partially it was the inevitable result of changing times, but also it was the departure of some members who had been fixtures at No. 16 for a long time.

Paul Hollister's death in 1970 removed one of the Club's most devoted members, as did the demise of John Mulholland a short while later. Mulholland's friend, the agent Thomas Stix, recalled that at a birthday party for the magician's wife 35 years before, John had given her a large terrarium filled with plants, exotic and otherwise. It had never been refilled or replaced, Stix said, but it was still as healthy as ever. A florist named Trepel, about to open a new shop (he was also an amateur magician), was told of the miraculous terrarium and asked if he could borrow it and display it at his opening. Trepel told Stix a few days later, "Tom, that terrarium is the worst advertising I've ever done. Everyone looks at it and asks me if the ones I have for sale will last as long." When John heard that remark, he was delighted. "Best trick I ever did," he boasted.

Still another change in Club management occurred as the new decade began, when Clifford Davis was appointed manager of the Club. He had begun working at The Players as a lunch waiter in 1958, at the same time

177

holding down a job as night manager of the Jumble Shop, a Greenwich Village restaurant. His rise had been rapid. Lindsay had sent him a letter of commendation in 1965, and three years later he was presented with a scroll saying, "The Players salute you," signed by all the regulars. Now, in 1970, King sent him a letter expressing a unanimous vote of the board, commending all he had done for the Club. For Cliff Davis, however, all this was secondary to the honor conferred on him when he had been asked to pass the loving cup on Founder's Night, after Charlie Connolly's passing.

In a further rearrangement of the office, Herbert Erb retired as executive director in 1970 after 38 years of service. He had not only supervised routine activities in the business office, but took a personal interest in doing anything he could for members, most of whom he knew personally. It was Erb, too, who had the difficult task of handling the seating arrangements at Pipe Nights. An honorary member of the Club since 1965, he would continue on the rolls as Honorary Executive Director.

A change of more consequence came in 1970 when Dennis King, unable to finish his term as president, resigned because of increasing ill health, and was succeeded by Alfred Drake. Alfred had been as popular at the Club as he was on the stage, where his Broadway career had begun in 1937 with *Babes in Arms*. After that, of course, had come his historic roles in *Oklahoma, Kiss Me, Kate* and *Kismet*.

Drake was hardly more than installed before Dennis died on May 21, 1971. As always with the departure of an eminent Player, stories were recalled of his living presence at the Club. A favorite about Dennis was his boxing match with John Barrymore. He remembered that incident one night when he had been playing pool with Norton Mockridge, in his time a star of the *World-Telegram's* brilliant staff.

Having heard that Mockridge had been a professional club fighter, Dennis steered the talk around to boxing that night, and asked gently, "After we finish this, why don't we go a few rounds?" Norton declined politely. He was not deceived by Dennis's elegant mannerisms, having been told that he was an excellent boxer and a fine athlete. He was also president of the Club, and besides, as Norton said later, he was afraid Dennis might knock him out.

Norton conveyed the reasons for his refusal and Dennis smiled. "Lots of people have been deluded by my gentle manner," he said. "In fact, some people have been dreadfully mistaken." And then he told his Barrymore story.

Dennis related that he had come to America in 1921 to play a small part in *Claire de Lune,* a play written by John Barrymore's wife, Michael

Strange, starring John and his sister Ethel. "I was 24 at the time," he said, "and Mr. Barrymore was about 38. We were both in excellent shape. He worked out in a gym regularly, and I'd found an empty room at the top of the theater where I could do calisthenics and punch a bag.

"One night I got into costume for my role, as a magnificent fop of the period, and went to the wings to wait for my entrance cue. I was wearing a square-cut white wig, a small black heart patch on my upper left cheek, and a small black club patch on the side of my chin, with a flowered waistcoat, silken breeches, silken stockings, and black shoes with red heels and golden buckles. In my left hand I held a long, golden-headed cane, and in my right, a black sable muff.

"Mr. Barrymore came up beside me, looked me over, and gave me an elegant sneer. 'King,' he said, 'I hear you box.' Although I remembered that his father, Maurice, had been lightweight champion of the British Army in India, I admitted that I did box a little.

" 'Put 'em up,' Jack said, raising his fists.

" 'But sir,' I protested.

" 'Put 'em up and let's see how good you are," he insisted. Just then the orchestra began to play the overture, and while they were getting into Mozart, I took my hand from my muff, stripped the rings from my fingers, kicked off my high-heeled buckled shoes, and laid my long, golden-headed cane on the prop table.

"I had a good look at Barrymore, strong and trim, a well-balanced figure in tights, and of course one of the most beautiful faces I had ever seen. I put up my fists.

"We spent a few minutes feinting, then he led with his right—a great mistake. Instinctively, I shot out my left and I could feel it thud on his jaw. It was simply a reflex action, but there on the floor, out cold, lay the greatest Hamlet on the American stage since Edwin Booth. It took twenty minutes before they could bring him around and the show could go on."

Dennis was one of the Club's most talented raconteurs, and Peter Turgeon recalled that he liked to tell a story about his wife, who was living in their country place. Dennis was away on tour when she heard prowlers down by the garage one night. Leaping out of bed, she threw up the window and yelled, "Quick, George, get your gun and let out the dogs!" The intruders fled in terror. She told Dennis about it when he returned, and he asked, "Why did you call out for George?"

"Well, I could never have frightened anyone away by calling out for Dennis, could I?" she said.

Turgeon recalled that in 1969 he and Dennis had been in a picture written and directed by Garson Kanin. At a bachelor dinner at Jimmy Cagney's one night, someone asked Dennis what the part was like. After only a moment's thought, he answered, "You might compare it with the fart of a medium-sized mosquito."

It seemed to be the time for reminiscence in these early years of the Seventies—another indication of change. When Roland Winters gave the address on Founder's Night in 1971, he departed from the usual custom of eulogizing Edwin Booth yet again and gave the hilarious members a collection of stories confirming his ranking as another of the Club's best raconteurs.

"John McNulty," he began, "once referred to The Players as the 'Sand Box.' As I look around me, I see what he meant. A professional steward we once had referred to the Club as an asylum run by the inmates. Well, there are all sorts of things you can call the Club, but one thing you can't call it—you can't call it dull. . . ."

Winters, in his speech, evoked the memory of John McNulty, whose stories had so enlivened the pages of *The New Yorker* and the New York *Daily News*. McNulty had come to him one day, Rollie said, and remarked in a conspiratorial tone, referring to a fellow member, "I don't know about that feller. He's got a kindly eye—like an undertaker's night bell."

Another beloved Player of the past, Winters went on, was F.P.A., always a favorite subject of stories. He recalled that Rollin Kirby had once said of Frank, after beating him in a pool game: "I feel sorry for old Frank. After I took his dollar, he slunk away from the table with a hurt look in his eye like a collie who had just been kicked by Albert Payson Terhune."

Winters remembered that Russel Crouse had once gone to Canada on a moose hunt, and having actually shot a moose, with the help of an expert guide, rushed to the animal and gazed down at it. Apparently seeing some resemblance, he shouted, "My God! I've shot Frank Adams."

Frank and Roland had been frequent partners at the pool table, Winters said, and one day Frank remarked that they had always played very smoothly together. "Frank, old buddy," Winters replied, "we *are* great together. Never a harsh word. The Harmony Twins."

"That's right," Frank said, "Harmony and Grits."

Still another memorable Player, said Winters, was Norman Anthony, who had once been editor of the old humor magazines *Life* and *Judge,* as well as the founding editor of *Ballyhoo.* In his social life, Winters recalled, Anthony was a professional Good Time Charlie, to whom writing was only an avocation. He considered that wine, women and song were his life's work, and he was never idle. Naturally, he always seemed to be broke, even when he was making money.

A friend said to him, "I saw you on the street the other day, Norman. I was in a cab and I waved, but you didn't see me. You were in a sidewalk café with a lady."

"Wrong on both counts," Norman said. "That was no lady, that was my wife. And that was no sidewalk café. That was my furniture."

Perhaps it was this incident that led Norman to a pool table aphorism: "He's shooting like a man dispossessed."

Winters recalled another noted Player, Jack King, who was noted for saying whatever was on his mind. King watched with dismay as a new member, making his first appearance since election, alienated everyone by introducing himself profusely to all those at the bar, and then compounded the gaffe by noisily buying drinks all around. He himself was so drunk that he simply wandered off. But next night he returned, and seemed astounded when those at the bar obviously shunned him. He drank by himself for a time, then walked over to King, who was watching a bridge game.

"Fine club this is," he complained loudly. "Last night I bought drinks for everybody, and tonight nobody even knows my name. You . . . I bought you three drinks last night. What's my name?"

Jack gave him a penetrating stare. "None of your goddamn business," he said, and turned away.

In contrast, Winters shifted his reminiscence toward the nearly legendary figure of Jack Shuttleworth, noting that Jack described himself as, "A prince of good fellows, generous to a fault, and the possessor of a razor-sharp legal mind." None of these attributes were in evidence, said Roland, on a cold Christmas Eve when Jack stood at a street corner on Third Avenue in front of a supermarket, shivering in the falling sleet as he clutched two enormous bags of groceries in one arm, and held a wretched looking part-cocker spaniel on a lead with the other hand. He was waiting for his wife to come out of the supermarket.

Down Third Avenue came a down-at-heels prostitute, seedy and quite drunk. She stopped and stared at the pathetic figure of Shuttleworth, clutching his bags and his dog. With an almost fastidious gesture, she pulled her sleazy coat around her more tightly, and staggered past Jack up the Avenue. As she went by, Shuttleworth heard her mutter, "I'd rather be a whore and drunk. Merry Christmas."

Perhaps it was a forecast of things to come, or only a reflection of changing times, but ladies were appearing more often at the Club in the early Seventies, not only as guests but as the subject of tributes. An open house for Dorothy Stickney in the spring of 1970, for instance, soon after the death of her husband, Howard Lindsay, was illuminated by the showing of a full-length film of her reading of Edna St. Vincent Millay's poems in her one-woman show about the poet, *A Lovely Light*.

In 1971 Lillian Gish appeared at an open house in her honor, and saw one of her early pictures, *The Romance of Happy Valley*, traveling all the previous night from an engagement in New Hampshire to reach No. 16 on time. Later that year Bette Davis was the open-house guest and saw one of her earlier films, *The Catered Affair*. Present on that day was Sandford Dody, a Player who had worked with her on her autobiography, *The Lonely Life*, published in 1960.

Helen Hayes was the guest at the annual Booth birthday luncheon in November 1972. For her, it was only another incident in her long association with the Club. She had acted with John Drew in *The Prodigal Husband* at the Empire when she was only fourteen, although she played a mature woman. Later, she had lived with her mother just around the corner on East 19th Street, and had paid her first visit to the Club in 1922 at the play party following the Club's production of *She Stoops to Conquer*, in which she played Constance Neville. At the luncheon she recalled how, as a child in her native Washington, D.C., she had listened to her grandmother tell about visiting Baltimore to see Booth in *Hamlet*.

There were more movie stars in 1973: An open house for Myrna Loy, and another for Joan Crawford, who shed a few tears in the dark when she viewed one of her old movies, *A Woman's Face*. She was given a standing ovation by those present, and Alfred Drake read a loving telegram from George Cukor, who had directed the picture. Crawford was presented with an inscribed silver bowl. "What shall I do with it?" she inquired, holding it up. "You could use it for nuts," Drake suggested.

There were eight or ten open house events every year in these early days of the decade, although the special guests were not always ladies. A series of mixed buffet dinners was begun in 1972 and lasted for a time. At the Booth birthday luncheon, of course, a lady of the theater was always the speaker by tradition, and in these days the guests included Lauren Bacall, Julie Harris, Dorothy Stickney, Margaret Leighton, Jessica Tandy, Mary Martin, and Tallulah Bankhead.

There was an attempt to revive The Players as a theatrical producer in 1972, but it was a modest step and confined to the dining room rather than Broadway. The production was a play by Richard Harrity, *Hope Is the Thing with Feathers*, directed by Joseph Hamer, and produced by Richard T. Herd, with a cast including actors who were not stars but hoping to be. Since they were also making the rounds at the time, and some of them got jobs, fourteen cast changes had to be made during the course of a limited rehearsal time. Hamer not only acted in the play, but worked the light board, ran the tape recorder, and took tickets. Since the scene was Central Park, the production was done in the round, with a platform in the middle of the dining room.

For one Player, John Call, it was his last appearance on any stage. He was a comedian who mimed his entire role in *The Little King*, Otto

Soglow's failed musical, and later played in many of Joseph Papp's Shakespeare productions. At the Club he was notable for his willingness to lend money. Call himself borrowed small amounts often, but meticulously paid them back as soon as possible. St. John Terrell remembered that Call had borrowed from him just once, on the afternoon before he died—and returned it that same evening from his bridge winnings.

To the relief of many members, there were no further renovations of major consequence in the Club during the Seventies, but that did not preclude relatively minor adjustments. In 1972 the Walter Hampden Memorial Library assumed responsibility for maintaining the Booth room—that "nest among the treetops of Gramercy," as the Founder had called it. After The Players had become a Registered National Historic Landmark, the room and the clubhouse itself were a matter of interest to connoisseurs of all kinds. In 1963 the room was the subject of a lecture at the Winterthur Seminar on Museum Operation and Connoisseurship, by Robert H. P. Hendrick of Colonial Williamsburg. Later, the Smithsonian Institution's Division of Cultural History expressed a desire to learn more about the Club's history and traditions.

When the library took over responsibility, its first move was to repair and restore the Oriental carpet, a task undertaken by the associate librarian, Carl Willers. He consulted with Virgil Birch, curator of the Islamic Department at the Metropolitan Museum, and determined that the rug was a Caucasian floral, woven in the Kuba (or Shirvan) area in the early nineteenth century. A twin, Birch said, could be seen in the Oriental rug collection at the Metropolitan Museum.

The Club was still acquiring treasures. Ethel Barrymore Colt appeared at a Ladies' Night in May 1973 and presented the Players with a handsome bust of John Drew. Both she and Peggy Wood, who was a special guest of honor, told anecdotes about the Club's third and much-loved president. They recalled that it had been just a century ago when "a dreadful young man" appeared on the stage of his mother's Arch Street Theatre in Philadelphia, speaking his first lines in W. Blanchard Jerrold's one-act farce, *Cool as a Cucumber*. A half-century later, in 1923, he was honored at a testimonial dinner in the Biltmore Hotel, commemorating that first appearance.

The art committee was hard at work in the late Seventies with a redecoration of the lower floor, notably the bar, grill, and pool room areas. The work consisted mostly in matting, reframing, and rearranging the picture collection. Thirty theatrical drawings by Frueh were placed in the men's room. Some unique original art, recently given to the Club, was hung. Al Hirshfeld's distinctive representation of Booth was centered in the grill, beside drawings by Milt Caniff and of Lee Falk's "Phantom."

Some of Frederick Dorr Steele's theatrical impressions were installed, along with a rare pencil drawing by Charles Dana Gibson of Oliver Herford. John Falter contributed an oil, painted from his well-known pencil drawing of F.P.A. at the pool table. Falter wrote: "Once, when FPA was in that exact pose, his pants dropped to the floor like two sandbags. He made his shot and pulled up his drawers, with no comment."

In 1973 the new stereo control room and 16 mm. projection booth began to function in the dining room. To install it, two windows had to be punched into the north wall near the ceiling. Behind the new windows lay a well-lighted and freshly painted, air-conditioned control room that had once been known as the Black Hole of Calcutta, used for years as a dead storage room by the library; before that it had served as a dining room for waiters.

All Pipe Nights were now recorded on the new facility, as well as the remarks made on Founder's Day and the Christmas carol festivities. The new projection booth was in use for the first time at the Joan Crawford open house. Although Avery Fisher had been the chief donor of the new facilities, work on both the booth and stage had been donated by Bill Mason and an engineer friend, who was not a member. It took nine months of labor.

Early in 1978 members of the Club staged a full-scale production of Shakespeare's *The Tempest*—the first such revival of The Bard seen at 16 Gramercy Park in many years. Directed and produced by Michael Alexander, the play was cast with a variety of professional and amateur Players. Alexander Scourby was a commanding Prospero, with a celebrated voice to match his physical presence. Other professionals included Robert Andrew Bonnard as Caliban, Albert M. Ottenheimer, Maxton Latham, Blaine Courtney, Bernard Pollock, and Lucian Douglas as Ferdinand. Robert Carter and William Jenkins represented the amateur actors, of which the Club has always had a strong contingent. Three fine professional actresses—Maureen Alexander, Laurie Nicole Winn, and Marta Brennan, who played Ariel—completed the cast. After offering a dinner performance at the clubhouse on March 19, 1978, the company also performed the play next door at the National Arts Club, and, through the offices of Charles Maurice, gave a staged reading of *The Tempest* at the Lighthouse for the Blind.

At the end of 1979, with the last decade of the Players' first century just around the corner, Richard McBain, who had been manager of the Whitehall Club, became the Club's new manager on July 1, and remains so as this is written. He brought a devoted new direction to the Club's management in a period that was to see further changes.

The history of the Eighties remains to be written, when it can be viewed with some perspective and seen as a whole. We have witnessed the departure, through ill health, of two more presidents, Alfred Drake and Roland Winters, and the arrival of our present president, Jose Ferrer. He has presided over still another renovation of the Club, again badly needed. Edwin Booth's old house continues to struggle with the passage of time. As the century closes, the Clubhouse has been renovated for the sixth time and once more glows like the jewel it is. There has been some turmoil in this last decade of The Players' first century, but then, as we have seen, that has been true of every decade before it.

What remains inextinguishable is that peculiar spirit we have always celebrated. It is embodied in those institutions and icons that comprise life at No. 16—both its artifacts and the members themselves. They are the subject of the remainder of this volume.

PART FOUR

Icons and Institutions

CHAPTER 12

Arts and Letters

A STOREHOUSE OF THEATRICAL ART AND THE PRESENCE OF MANY FA-
mous names from the theater and Hollywood have combined to
overshadow the fact that the Club has always been literary as well as
theatrical, beginning with Twain and Aldrich. From the start, No. 16 has
been a literary gathering place, and its collection of art only emphasizes
that fact. Members see examples every day: Gordon Stevenson's portrait of
founding member Mark Twain, and not far away, Marshall Goodman's
portrayal of Ben Lucian Burman.

O. Henry was not a member, but he was a regular visitor. Three Nobel
Prize winners have been Players: Eugene O'Neill (honorary), Ernest
Hemingway, and John Steinbeck. And among those literary figures not
already mentioned in previous chapters, there are Thornton Wilder, John
O'Hara, Ford Madox Ford, Arnold Bennett, John Erskine, Francis Mar-
ion Crawford, Christopher Morley, Ring Lardner, Finley Peter Dunne,
Van Wyck Brooks, Bruce Catton, Hervey Allen, Owen Wister, John
Gunther, and Harrison Salisbury. A similar list of poets would include
Vachel Lindsay, James Russell Lowell, and Leonard Bacon.

Among the playwrights: Marc Connolly, Maxwell Anderson, Arthur
Miller, Arthur Wing Pinero, Philip Barry, Lawrence Stallings, and Alan
Jay Lerner. The humorists number James Thurber, Harry Leon Wilson,
Munro Leaf, Hugh Lofting, Ludwig Bemelmans, and Dick Cavett. There
have been such essayists as John Mason Brown, Lowell Thomas, John K.
Hutchens, John Fischer, Don Herold, Alistair Cooke, Westbrook Pegler,

189

William Lyon Phelps, Walter Lippman, Charles Dudley Warner, Irvin S. Cobb, James Boyd, and Bruce Barton.

This is name-dropping on a massive scale, true enough, but it is only a small sampling. True, too, that some were members for relatively short periods, although others were devoted Players until their deaths. Taken all in all, however, the literary membership of the Club has been extraordinary, unmatched by any other with the possible exception of The Century Association.

Some but by no means all of these writers are represented in the Club's equally extraordinary library, which is, of course, a theatrical collection. Beginning with the libraries of Booth and his friends, it has steadily expanded through the past century until it occupies every inch of available space and presents a continuing problem of storage. That has been a problem almost from the beginning. We can imagine the mingled pleasure and consternation in 1918 when Mrs. Elizabeth Shattuck Hayes presented the Club with the Shattuck Collection of theatrical photographs—about 4,000 photos in 80 albums, which had been buried in an attic storeroom for more than four years. That was typical of the kind of treasures which have poured into the constantly expanding shelf and storage space.

The Club has had many librarians, but one of the most remarkable is remembered now only by older Players. He was Patrick F. Carroll, who died on March 16, 1965. Officially the librarian, he was also the Club historian. No one had a greater knowledge of No. 16, or possessed a deeper understanding of the Club and personal involvement with it.

Pat came to the Club as a pool boy in 1932, when energetic young men were still hired to rack up the balls and keep score. It was a job without a future, and Carroll was ambitious. After a year or so he departed and for a time held various jobs, from waiter to a subway construction dynamiter, before he came back in 1936 to stay for the remainder of his life, except for a two-year hitch in the Air Force in World War II.

It was the omnipresent Bill Tachau, then chairman of the house committee, who brought Carroll back, hiring him as a handyman but sensing in him the possibilities that later made him virtually indispensable. As part of his chores Pat began working in the library, arranging, repairing, and taking care of the books, pictures, playbills, and hundreds of pieces of memorabilia that needed constant attention. There in the library he found his calling. During the next decade he became an expert librarian, with no professional training.

Pat Carroll would have been a model for one of Horatio Alger's heroes. While he worked all over the Club as a handyman, he spent long hours in the library after his other duties were completed, teaching himself the art of bookbinding, among other things, and it was not long before members realized he was their chief source for both theatrical and Club information. To anyone who raised a question in either area, the answer was, "Ask Pat." His progress was all the more remarkable considering that his limited education had been confined to a technical high school. But he had been given an appreciation of the classics by his father, and from that background he elevated himself to become a scholar.

In the Fifties, when Newman Levy became chairman of the library committee, he relieved Pat of his handyman duties and made him librarian. "I'm the luckiest man alive," Pat said. "I'm doing exactly what I want to do." He did it so well that when the extension to the library was completed in the mid-Sixties, it was designated as "The Pat Carroll Library Extension."

Staats Cotsworth, who headed the arts committee for years, recalled that Pat came to him one day in 1963 to tell him what had been discovered during the renovation of the card room. Workmen who had removed Truman Fassett's full-length portrait of Walter Hampden had found behind it a large black rectangle, a piece of canvas stuck to the wall with paperhanger's paste; it looked vaguely like a picture. Somewhere in the Club, Pat said, he knew there was a copy by William Merritt Chase of Velaquez's celebrated "Portrait of an Artist," listed in an old catalog of Players art as #114. No one, however, had been able to find it. Was this the missing painting? It was. Francis Moro, who had restored other paintings for the Club, was called in. He peeled the canvas off the wall with great care, restored it, and it was hung at the end of the dining room.

In the Pat Carroll Extension was placed John Mulholland's great collection of books, posters, playbills, and other ephemera about magic, which he gave to the Club. It was probably the best collection of its kind in America, and was supplemented further after the magician's death.

The collection contained material on the lives of magicians as well as their magic, the earliest items dating back four centuries to Reginald Scot's *Discourse of Witchcraft,* published in 1584, the first printed book disclosing the methods of magicians. Most of the books were in English, but European and Asian tongues were also represented. There were privately circulated books and periodicals, and files of letters, pictures, programs, publicity, and Mulholland's personal mementos. The extension was specially built to house the collection, but it proved to be impossible to care adequately for this magnificent storehouse, and it had to be sold, the sale coming at a time when the library badly needed the money.

The Booth section of the library contains thirty volumes of his prompt books, with texts, stage business, and directions of all the major plays in which he had acted. The volumes in his personal library carry marginal comments. Letters from Booth to scholars display his careful analysis of important characters in the plays, and demonstrate the profound study he gave to exact meanings, characters, and every other detail of the plays. Besides the books, his own collection includes playbills, casts, portraits, scenes, costumes, small properties, paintings, prints, pieces of sculpture, costumes, and noteworthy property bits.

There were 9,000 volumes in the Walter Hampden Library by 1938, and it has grown ever since. Its chief treasures are exceptional: second, third, and fourth Shakespeare folios, and first folios of Beaumont and Fletcher. Old quartos from such early dramatists as Colley Cibber and Ben Jonson are in the collection, as well as the texts of more than 5,000 plays. Nearly a thousand volumes deal with the lives of actors and managers, biography and memoirs. There are shelves of books about stage history and criticism, volumes on art and technique, costumes, and hundreds about the Bard.

Among the 50,000 playbills there is a rare complete series of plays at the Boston Museum, from its opening to its close, besides a set of forty-eight that chronicle the dramas at the famous old John Street Theatre in New York between 1791 and 1795. A comprehensive collection of programs relate to Edmund Kean, and there is an extremely rare program of Dryden's *Secret Love* at the Theatre Royal in 1667.

Between 1928 and 1938 the library began to collect materials for a history of the then-current stage, and the result is a profusion of individual folders containing cuts, programs, and notices of about 300 contemporary actors and actresses of that decade.

All this hardly begins to catalogue what is in the Hampden-Booth Theatre Library, and omits entirely the paintings that have looked down from its walls. These began with Booth's gift of fifteen portraits of early American and English actors, painted by John Neagle and bought by the Founder from the John E. Owens collections. Among them are canvases of Edmund Kean as Richard III, William B. Wood, and Joseph Cowell.

The first librarian at The Players was to have been Booth's close friend, William Winter, a temperamental but authoritative drama critic of his day. In his life of Booth, Winter wrote: "He asked me to join it [meaning the Club] and he proposed that we should join together in that club and with the aid of its library, compile and write a history of the theatre in America; and that design would have been accomplished had it not presently been resolved by the directors that professional reviewers of the stage were not eligible for membership."

Booth did not entirely regret this decision even if it affected his friend; he was often divided in his mind about the "crickets." An incident shortly after the Club began convinced him that the rule was a good one. He wrote: "I read a review by this critic friend of a play in which had appeared an actor whom I knew to be always intelligent and earnest and deserving of respectful consideration. But this review was more like a bitter personal attack upon my brother actor than a fair-minded estimate of his work, and when I saw him come into the club that afternoon and begin scanning the papers, I thought how painfully awkward it would be if after reading that column of abuse he should meet here the man who wrote it."

While the work of maintaining the library's vast collection goes on daily in our time, under the direction of Raymond Wemmlinger, librarian since 1986, the art at No. 16 has not increased appreciably since earlier days, and the task has been simply to preserve it, besides restoring those paintings that have turned up from time to time, tucked away and forgotten, like the Velasquez copy.

William A. Mackay, an artist himself, was the first of many subsequent chairmen of the art committee to carry out these objectives. In the late Twenties, when he took charge, his first task was to clean some of the older pictures; it happened to be his specialty, and he undertook the job himself.

One of his first efforts was to restore the portrait of an already forgotten actor, Thomas Abthorpe Cooper, whose family was otherwise noted because a daughter married President Tyler's son. This picture had been listed as a copy of a portrait by Gilbert Stuart, but as the layers of grime were removed, Mackay could see that no copyist would have been capable of such brushwork. Its stroke and sure touch signaled the presence of the master himself. Searching through the Club records, Mackay found the letter from the painting's donor to Booth, authenticating that it was a genuine Gilbert Stuart. Restored, it was hung in the same room with the Sargent portraits of Booth and Jefferson.

Those portraits, of course, are the prizes of the Club's art collection, particularly the magnificent depiction of Booth. In his biography of Sargent, Charles Merrill Mount discloses that shortly after White remodeled the Club, he heard that the art committee was about to give the Club a portrait of the Founder, and hastened to assure the members that his friend John Sargent was the only man who could do the job properly. Meanwhile, no doubt with White's connivance, Booth informed the committee that even though he disliked posing, he would do it for so distinguished an artist as Sargent.

All this was conveyed to the artist, and on the Saturday of Christmas week, 1889, he arrived at No. 16, an after-lunch cigar in his mouth as usual. Booth was anything but prepared for portraiture. He was dressed for travel, his luggage was on its way to the station, and he was about to depart. Unperturbed, Sargent suggested that they begin at once. There is no record of what was said, but Sargent must have been extraordinarily convincing because Booth changed his plans, agreed to pose next morning, and promised he would give all the time he could until the following Saturday, and even that morning, before he took a 3 o'clock afternoon train.

With this verbal contact made, the two men stood before the fire in Booth's grate and Sargent studied his subject for the first time at close range. As Mount unflatteringly puts it, he looked "down into the actor's pasty face, where he saw the same dull opacity that characterized Irving's," whom he had also painted. True, Booth was pallid without makeup, and his usual expression was one of quiet melancholy; he seemed perpetually exhausted emotionally. Sargent may have thought he didn't have much to work with.

That night, Booth's friend Thomas Bailey Aldrich called on him and gave him some gratuitous advice. If he was going to sit, Aldrich told him, according to Mount, he should first "lock himself in a dark room and sandpaper his soul. Otherwise, the pitiless painter would betray every secret sin. . . ." Booth was not really in danger; no one could have said he was heavy-laden with sin.

Booth arrived promptly next morning at Sargent's studio on 23rd Street. Regarding the actor as he turned from the large canvas he had prepared, the artist saw again what he had seen the day before—a man with personal tragedy written on his face, otherwise a limp and expressionless subject. Sargent tried to provoke a more animated expression in his model, but after a few more sittings, he gave it up and began painting Booth as he saw him, in Mount's words, "limp, dull, his thumbs thrust into his pockets in a gesture expressive of futility and morbid musings." Possibly because he was not confident about what he was producing, Sargent made a separate sketch and sent it to the committee for approval. The members were delighted; it was exactly Booth as they saw him. But Sargent didn't give up easily. During rest periods, he sat down at the piano in his studio and played the most inspirational music he could think of (he preferred Liszt), and that pleased Booth, who did not, however, change expression.

By the second week in February the portrait was finished, and all those involved were invited to come and see it. Portrait painters will not be surprised to learn that everyone was delighted with the picture except the subject. As Mount put it, "The pose spoke of causal informality, a raggedness of posture that he was not certain exactly expressed himself." Booth asked Sargent whether this was a pose he had struck, or whether the artist placed him in it, and the astute Sargent pointed out that Booth was standing in exactly that pose even as he asked the question. It was, in fact, the pose he often took as Hamlet.

A background was needed for the figure, so Sargent brought his canvas to the Club and painted in the Great Hall's mantel, with the paraphrase of Shakespeare's epitaph that Booth had ordered inscribed over the fireplace in bronze letters:

Goode frende for frendships sake forbeare
To utter what is gossipt here
In social chat lest unawares
The tonge offend thy fellow Plaiers.

When Booth at last saw the finished portrait, Sargent asked him, "How do you like it?"

"Frankly, I don't think it looks like me," Booth said.

"Can you spare me three-quarters of an hour?" the artist inquired.

Booth said he could, and Sargent scraped out the face, repainting it perfectly in less than an hour.

So goes the legend, part of the tradition that says Booth wrote, in a letter to Aldrich, that he didn't like "the long, thin legs and graceless trousers," and brought to the Club a huge clock, placing it before the portrait, where it stood for more than thirty years, until the art committee of that time decided the story was untrue and removed the clock.

What Booth actually wrote to Aldrich, however, was exactly the opposite. It was his verdict that "the whole thing, even the long thin legs and graceless trousers are me and mine." As for the tradition that Booth hid his legs with a clock, the best witness may be Walter Oettel, who reports in his *Sketch Book:* "Some years ago when The Players contained numerous artists of an 'older school,' so called, it was decided by a group sitting in judgment upon the Sargent portrait of Mr. Booth, that his feet had been made too large, and his legs too long. Thereupon Commodore Benedict gave a beautiful bronze clock and corresponding end pieces to be placed on the mantel so that they would unsuspectedly hide both regrettable defects.

"Now another class of art critics, being told that the real Edwin Booth did indeed have long feet, has decreed that the clock and endpieces be taken down, regardless of legs or feet. Unless they be, positively, serious obstacles to the quick removal of the canvas in case of fire, I humbly hope they will be restored to their places, at least on Ladies' Day, if not on all days. They are beautiful and essential things. So many members have remarked upon this, they have made me bold."

That was never done. The tall bronze clock came to rest atop the magazine rack opposite the Booth portrait. But there was one other salutary result of the original work: Sargent became a member of the Club in January 1890 and remained so until 1897. His portrait of Booth was given to The Players by Benedict on Founder's Night, 1890.

As a companion piece, Sargent's portrait of Jefferson shows him as Dr. Pangloss in *The Heir-at-Law,* catching the twinkling charm of the man who was then one of the best-loved actors of comedy in America. It is considered among the artist's finest works, and was a joint gift of Booth and Barrett to the Club in 1891. When he first saw it, Oliver Herford observed the somewhat vaporish air of the doctor's wig and remarked, "Jefferson is the only actor who can make smoke come out of his hair."

Sargent's father, a doctor, had crossed the Atlantic with Jefferson, and the artist himself was one of the actor's old friends. He was fascinated by Jefferson's flexible countenance, and made three whimsical oil sketches of his head, saving the smallest canvas for his own collection.

Jefferson liked to paint, between seasons, and took his work more seriously than his fellow Players did. Not long after he became president, he hung one of his canvases, depicting a watermill, on the west wall of the pool room, with a special light fixed over it. No one dared make an issue of it, but there was grumbling that serious painters of high reputation in the Club were not permitted to hang *their* pictures on the increasingly crowded walls of No. 16. As for Jefferson's watermill, it was dismissed as no more than "a neat piece of work."

It would require a volume as large as this one to describe the remainder of the Club's art collection. Scholars and interested Players will find its contents carefully catalogued in the library. But some are worth noting here, simply to indicate what treasures the Players possess.

There is, for example, Johann Zoffany's "David Garrick," whose death, as Dr. Johnson observed, "eclipsed the gayety of nations," and Henry Inman's "James H. Hackett as Rip Van Winkle," memorializing the actor who was the greatest Rip until Jefferson's arrival. Of special interest to The Players is Stebbins's bust of Charlotte Cushman, one of the first American players to appear in London. Her staff as Meg Merrilies and crown worn as Queen Katherine are in the Club's collection.

Mark Twain's inscribed photograph to Booth recalls the time he was writing *Joan of Arc* anonymously, and brought pages from the manuscript down to the Club, reading it to appreciative friends as the work of a young writer he had discovered, and commenting warmly on the author's style and ability.

A touching memory of Booth's life is the painting in his room of his first wife, the lovely Mary Devlin, copied by Carle J. Blenner after the original by Eastman Johnson. When he visited the Club, James M. Barrie regarded this picture thoughtfully before he delivered his opinion: "A verra byutiful face, a verra *byutiful* face."

One of the most striking pictures in the Great Hall is the large portrait of Jefferson painted by John W. Alexander, N.A., the gift of his wife, which shows the actor in the character of Bob Acres in *The Rivals*. Even more exceptional is the portrait of Booth as Richelieu, at the right of the Great Hall's fireplace mantel, painted by John Collier, R.A., in 1881, the gift of William Bispham.

In the grill room is the Thomas Nast drawing that created the symbolic Tammany tiger, and Rollin Kirby's cartoon establishing the symbol of Prohibition as a tall, cadaverous, pinched-face figure with a tall hat. From a later time is Gordon Stevenson's study of Mark Twain, hung on the west wall of the pool room at the end of 1943, after having made the rounds of various loan exhibits, including one at the Century, with several more scheduled later.

Twain's pool cue, as noted earlier, had hung on the wall for years, but a picture of someone else was hung beneath it. Several Players wanted to know why there wasn't a picture of Twain instead, and this plea was heard by Stevenson, a Player who had known Twain slightly. Seeking the help of those still alive who had known him well, he painted a portrait of the great man in his spare time, and presented it to the Club. It was duly hung beneath the cue. A photograph was taken and sent to his daughter, then Clara Clemens Gabrilowitsch (before her second marriage), who lived in Hollywood. She wrote to Stevenson: "How marvelous! Truly magnificent! I nearly kissed his cheek—a little tearfully." But, as all artists will understand, the compliment was accompanied by a complaint: "Is it to emphasize the thoughtfulness of the expression that you have Father draw in his under-lip? The only time I remember his doing that was when at the same moment he stroked his chin with thumb and first finger."

Hundreds of Players have walked by the glass cases containing the Club's collection of theatrical mementoes, but few know what is inside them. A brief sampling:

Foils used by Booth as Hamlet and Charles Fechter are there, and nearby is Launt Thompson's bust of Booth as Hamlet, whose reproduction is in the lobby of the Booth Theater.

A tomahawk used by Edwin Forrest as the Indian chief Metamora, also his Richard III sword, and the wig he wore as Lear, as well as copies of the magnificent coronation robes worn originally by Richard himself; the court costumer made these copies for Edmund Kean.

The costumes Booth wore are more familiar to members, but there is also his Hamlet dagger, and his Don Cezar de Bazan sword. There is the glove of Matilda Heron, the most famous Camille of her day, who threw it to Booth from her box at a benefit he gave on May 1, 1857. Since he was only 24 at the time, he always treasured this recognition of him as an actor from so distinguished a fellow artist.

A coat worn by Booth as Claude Malnotte in *The Lady of Lyon* is a testimonial to Booth's only relative failure. He seldom played Claude or that much more noted lovestruck youth, Romeo, because both he and the critics agreed that he was not a convincing stage lover.

Tucked in with all these are such disparate items as a life mask of Keats, and a check for $200,000 in payment for the book rights to a venture not yet undertaken when this check was written. It represents the single major success of Twain's excursion into book publishing, Charles L. Webster & Co., drawn by the firm to Julia Grant for rights to *General Grant's Personal Memoirs,* which the dying soldier dictated, and on which he made final proof corrections up to the day of his death. It was a huge seller. Twain presented the cancelled check to the Club. And almost unnoticed among all these items is The Players' own *ex libris,* drawn by that superb illustrator Howard Pyle.

There has been an astonishing assortment of curious mementoes and odd collections scattered through the clubhouse. One of the latter was the array of 102 pewter mugs that once decorated the shelf around the grill. They were in constant use for years, and as Walter once put it, "the older the mug, the prouder the owner." It was the custom to preserve each mug after the owner died, and many of these owners were friends of Booth or noted actors in their own right. Some bequeathed their mugs to a younger member. But at last the Club ran out of space and the collection ended abruptly.

More pewter could be found in the dining room, which in Walter's day boasted the finest collection of handmade pewter plates, silver services, and trophy punch bowls anywhere in the country. The plates were several centuries old, used by ancient Germanic tribes in religious ceremonies. There were huge round platters of Teutonic design, representing the best handiwork of monks in the Middle Ages. It was not difficult to imagine Saxon kings eating from deep plates of heavy pottery. There was also a solid silver punch bowl, given to Booth by the Club's architects, and a silver tray that had once belonged to Sarah Bernhardt, given to the Club by Rodman Wanamaker, who was not a member.

Several anonymous or semi-anonymous plates and inscriptions can be found in the grill, with mysterious inscriptions such as "to the bride." One of these is a small brass plate on the woodwork above the left end of the bar, which says simply "Egan." Standing by it one day, Storrs Haynes was intrigued by this particular artifact and was determined to discover its

JOSEPH JEFFERSON

JOHN DREW

WALTER HAMPDEN

HOWARD LINDSAY

DENNIS KING

ALFRED DRAKE

ROLAND WINTERS

JOSE FERRER

origin. There had been two Players named Egan, he found—Martin in 1914 and Maurice in 1920. The plate refers to neither one, however, but rather obscurely to Jacob "Jac" Wendell, Jr., mentioned earlier, whose "Egan story" was part of Club legend before either of the real Egans was a member. In telling it, according to one early Player, Jac gave "a superlative display of sheer virtuosity," but unfortunately no one remembers what the story was.

Tucked away in the card room for a time was Thomas Hicks's fine portrait of Booth as Iago, given to the club by the Century Association in the 60's, and the Club also possesses a small painting by the same artist of Booth in the same role: it hangs in the Reading Room.

Robert Sully's portrait of Booth's father, Junius, which is over the Great Hall fireplace, has an unusual history. Hanging in a mansion near Richmond during the Civil War, it was damaged during a raid on the house when a saber thrust put out one of the eyes in the picture. At Booth's request, Eastman Johnson repaired the damage.

Above the couch in the Great Hall there once was displayed a splendid portrait by J. Alden Weir (it is elsewhere now) of a forgotten actor, Edmond Sheppard Conner, who was not only one of Booth's best friends but a charter member of the Club. The picture represents two figures "bright youth and snow-crowned age," but they are both Conner, who was born (in a manner reminiscent of Booth's affinity for 3's) at 9 o'clock on the ninth day of the ninth month in the ninth year of the nineteenth century. On the stage at the age of five, as Laperouse in the play of that name, he made his professional debut at the Walnut Street Theater in Philadelphia in 1829, beginning a spectacular career which did not end until the spring of 1885, when he played Richelieu for the 1,113th time at the Opera House in Paterson, N.J. He died six years later in Rutherford, at 82.

Helena Smith Dayton's portrait of Walter Hampden, done in seven sittings, is well known to most Players. Those who knew him are struck by his youthful eyes, looking as Clayton Hamilton saw them when their lifelong friendship began in Brooklyn. Not as many members know that Hampden, like his brother Paul Dougherty, a well-known painter of land and seascapes in California, was a promising artist before he decided to become an actor.

One of the most remarkable single collections presented to the Club was Albert Palmer's delayed gift to the library of the records belonging to the Union Square Theatre which he managed with such success between 1872 and 1883. Palmer, as we saw earlier, was a founding member and a vice-president of The Players, but he had also been a librarian before he became a theater manager and he knew how to preserve the record of his life at Union Square in meticulous detail. His collection consisted of twenty-one large portfolios, containing every playbill and clipping. In his home workshop Pat Carroll built the folio-size boxes to house it, with a separate shelf for each portfolio. In addition to the clippings, photographs, lithographs, and playbills, Palmer's collection included the autobiographies that he had persuaded his leading players to set down in their own handwriting. Oddly, Palmer did not leave these treasures to the Club directly. Butler Davenport, a member sometime before 1916, bought them when Palmer's estate was disposed of in 1906, and gave them to the Club.

One of the more familiar paintings at The Players is Gordon Stevenson's portrait of Howard Lindsay, which was unveiled at the Pipe Night in his honor on October 30, 1960, described earlier. At the unveiling, Russel Crouse presented Lindsay with the board's resolution that had started this project on its way, contained in a hand-inscribed and colorfully illuminated parchment. Stevenson's portrait shows Howard at his most relaxed and convivial, in a casually informal pose. The background is one of the Victorian rooms in his own house, but he is seated on a chair from the Club bar. The picture hangs in what is now known as the Windsor Room, once the writing room.

One of the most unusual treasures in the Club is in the dining room named for Lindsay—the two stained glass windows depicting the figures of Richard Mansfield and David Garrick, both dressed as Richard III. They were acquired by Staats Cotsworth, a well-known actor who was also a painter and photographer and a devoted member who did as much for the art committee as any chairman has ever done.

The acquisition of the Garrick-Mansfield Windows, as they are known today, began when Cotsworth was playing in Philadelphia in October 1962. On a stroll through the city he walked by a small junk shop at Locust and Quince Streets. He stopped to admire a backlighted six-foot-high stained glass panel, the Mansfield window. As a man who had just been made chairman of the art committee, he realized that he was looking at a prize the Club must have. Cotsworth went in to talk with the proprietor, and found the Garrick window as well. The shopkeeper told him the windows had come from the old Garrick Theatre at Chestnut and Juniper streets, and had been brought to him as a consignment by an owner who wanted $3,500 for the pair.

As it turned out, Staats was not the first Player to discover this prize. Ben Edwards, an actor member, had seen them the week before and thought the Club must have them. They had also been spotted by the master of properties in a new play called *Banderol*, trying out in Philadelphia, and he had described them to Robert Downing, still another member acting in the play, who declared, "These belong at The Players." Four other members of the cast, all Players, agreed.

Returning to New York, Cotsworth found a letter to the art committee from Eugene Connelly of Philadelphia, providing more information about the windows. They were the work of Nicola D'Ascenzo, an Italian artist in 1898–99, and had been installed in the lobby of the Garrick in 1900. After the theater was torn down in 1936 they had made their way through a number of warehouses before falling into the hands of an unknown person. Connelly identified himself as simply an interested party, reporting that the panels had recently been offered to Vincent Sardi, who suggested that The Players would be interested. Connelly said he agreed the panels belonged there.

Now began a bargaining game, with the mysterious Mr. Connelly in the middle. Having obtained approval from the executive committee to buy the panels, Cotsworth wrote to Connelly that the Club was ready to buy, but the middleman replied that the unknown owner had taken the panels back from the junk shop and was holding them for an expected offer from a restaurant owner. Connelly added that a certain well-known actor was also interested in buying, and he advised haste.

Cotsworth hastened, greatly aided by a sudden, anonymous gift to the library of $2,600, with $2,000 specifically designated to buy the windows. Staats conveyed a firm offer of $2,000 to Connelly, who accepted but said the owner wanted "to see the color of their money." More phone calls followed. It appeared that the owner wanted cash, and to get a check through the usual process would take more time. The owner indicated that he was about to accept a $1,500 cash offer from the well-known actor. At that point, Connelly proved to be a friend as well as a negotiator, and floated a personal loan to pay the owner and obtain the windows himself.

On November 8, Louis Rachow, then the Club's librarian and now its curator, went to Philadelphia to close the deal, carrying in his pocket a check which Herbert Erb had made negotiable after much telephoning. Rachow arranged for transportation and insurance, and the windows arrived at the Club on November 11. Lee Schoen, the architect, arranged the place in the dining room which they now occupy. An authority on stained glass has evaluated them for insurance purposes at $3,500, a figure which has since increased.

By some law of nature, perhaps, what has been given to The Players has, in a few regrettable instances, been taken away. There were small thefts at the Club in the Twenties and Thirties, but not until 1970 did anything major disappear. In that year a person or persons unknown (perpetrators, as the police would call them) stole the miniature of Junius Brutus Booth from the writing room wall, and two other pictures as well, a portrait of the actor Joe Evans by Abbott Thayer, and one of Dudley Digges by Gordon Stevenson, from the wall of the stairs to the Great Hall. The robberies occurred within days of each other and were never solved.

Fortunately, that year was also one of acquisitions, particularly work by Everett Raymond Kinstler. His charcoal drawings of John and Lionel Barrymore were hung in the pool room, flanking Twain's portrait, and his portrait of Dennis King was hung in the Great Hall, in a prominent place.

A death that year produced still another acquisition. Marie Apel, the British sculptor, had died in London, and her daughter, Marynia, formerly with the *London Telegraph* but now living in Washington, had written to Sir John Gielgud, inquiring about a life-size bust her mother had done of him as Richard II in *Richard of Bordeaux,* a London success in 1932. Gielgud suggested The Players might like to have it because "they have always been so generous to me when I have been in America." A small group gathered at the Club when the formal presentation of the Gielgud bust was made in 1972. Those present reported that Sir John looked "handsome and youthful," and would henceforth be "in good company."

The Kinstler works brought renewed interest in this artist, who had been a member since 1970, and Robert Carter was sent by the *Bulletin* to find out more about him. Carter did not have far to go. Kinstler lived next door at the National Arts Club, and the interview took place in his studio there, a room large enough to hold a fountain and a collection of his work ranging from early Western comic strips to a poster of John Wayne that was painted for the Cowboy Hall of Fame. An easel used by James Montgomery Flagg, another Player, was a silent reminder that he had been Kinstler's friend and mentor. Flagg never knew John Drew, but his portrait of Uncle Jack is among the Club's art treasures.

After his eyesight failed and he was unable to draw, Flagg was compelled to direct commissions elsewhere. He recommended Kinstler for a portrait of Lionel Barrymore, and it was duly hung at the Club. Staats Cotsworth, who had been a friend of the artist long before he became a Player, remarked that there ought to be a picture of Jack to accompany his brother, and Kinstler obliged. In his studio at the Arts Club, Ray also did two drawings of Percy MacKaye, whose own studio was just below, and a sketch of Robert Edmond Jones, as well as a pencil head of John Carradine. His watercolor of Bert Lahr still graces the Club's men's room.

Kinstler continued his painting of Club presidents in 1976 with Alfred Drake, a project that began with an almost casual invitation one night to come to the studio. "I'd like to do a head of you," Kinstler said. He planned to do a charcoal sketch, as he had done of the Barrymores, one that could be used for the announcement of a Pipe Night. But when

Alfred was seated, Ray discovered that he had no paper and resorted to a canvas board, upon which he began to sketch in oils—a head and shoulders, which he shortly presented to Drake.

"Alfred, where do you think you'll hang this?" Kinstler inquired.

"Are you giving it to me?" Drake wanted to know.

Surprised, Ray said, "You mean you thought you were just posing as a model?"

"Well, I assumed so," Drake said.

"No," Kinstler told him, "I'd like you to have this."

It was the beginning of a friendship, but at that point there was no thought of giving a Drake picture to the Club. That assignmnent came early in 1978, when Ray learned that the board wanted to commission a portrait, to be ready in October. Alfred was then seventy, but Kinstler thought he had scarcely changed in appearance since his great success in *Kismet*, fifteen years before, so he painted him in the costume he wore in that show, as we see him today.

The earlier portrait of Dennis King was another matter. Kinstler was not a member in 1969, although he had been a frequent visitor since 1950, when Harold Hendee, an actor, had first introduced him to the pleasures of No. 16. Later, the Club's informal resident painter, Joseph Cummings Chase, invited him to several programs. Chase had done the sketch of Don Marquis over the bar. Ray had also been the guest from time to time of Percy MacKaye, the Good Gray Poet of Gramercy Park, as his friends called him—a man more than six feet tall with a shock of white hair, who usually wore a velvet jacket.

Perhaps because he had already painted Howard Lindsay as well as the Mark Twain portrait, Gordon Stevenson would have been the logical choice to paint Dennis, but Kinstler was chosen instead. It was typical of the spirit that has always pervaded the Club that Stevenson called Kinstler when he heard the news and said, "Raymond, I'm very pleased they picked the right man to do the portrait. I'm delighted you're doing it."

When the picture was finished and acclaimed by everyone, some of the Players who saw it realized with astonishment that even though Kinstler was a familiar figure at the Club, he was not a member. "No one ever asked me," Ray said simply. He was at once proposed by Bill Plante and elected, soon becoming chairman of the art committee. Kinstler was following a long Club tradition of electing artists as members, beginning with such giants as Hassam and Remington, and coming on down to more recent painters such as Stevenson, John Falter, Norman Rockwell, James Montgomery Flagg, Milton Caniff, and Ralston Crawford.

One of the more recent art acquisitions at the Club was the 1982 gift of two original watercolors by John Barrymore, both scenes from *Hamlet*, painted in 1937 and given by Spencer Berger. Hung in the library, they were an accompaniment to Barrymore's Hamlet chair, a gift of Robert Andrew Bonnard, and Booth's *Hamlet* prompt book.

So we come at last to the artifacts of the Booth room. They are relatively intact since the death scene described earlier, but we have learned more about them. The mystery of the Hamlet skull, for example, is at least partly explained, although cloaked in another garment of legend by the discovery of something that had been there all the time—Thomas Bailey Aldrich's description of it in a book of essays, *Ponkapog Papers,* published in 1903 but long since obscured by time.

Aldrich confirms that the skull was, indeed, used by both Booth and his father in Hamlet, and he tells its story: "There is extant in the city of New York an odd piece of bric-a-brac which I am sometimes tempted to wish was in my own possession. On a bracket in Edwin Booth's bedroom at The Players . . . stands a sadly dilapidated skull which the elder Booth, and afterward his son Edwin, used to soliloquize over in the graveyard of Elsinore in the fifth act of *Hamlet.* It appears that a vagabond, rogue and horse thief—the sort of man who might appeal to Junius Brutus Booth— was befriended by him. The horse thief was ultimately brought low by the law and executed. To his horror and amazement the fellow had his head delivered to Booth, having taken all the necessary legal steps to make the bequest valid—and with the request that Junius Brutus use the skull in the fifth act of *Hamlet.* He did, as did our founder—and now the horse thief's skull—a fellow of infinite jest—like other members—occupies its place in our club."

This does not explain the other skull that was extant for a time, and the story asks us to believe a tale without any other verification, from a storyteller who liked to tell them, but it hardly matters. We accept the skull today, and everything that it recalls.

When we look at Booth's room, we are not now surveying splendid works by great and near-great artists that dominate the walls in other parts of the Club. We are seeing the spirit of another time, another way of living and feeling and thinking, a world that Booth infused with his own personality. It is a spirit that, wholly outdated as it may seem in the contemporary world, is the one that generations of Players have kept alive.

"Simple but refined taste," Walter Oettel called it. There is the brass bed, with its canopy of yellow satin, an ebony lounge and handsome Chippendale bureau. A low seat has been made by crossing four swords, and there are two upholstered chairs. Mary Devlin, Booth's lost love, looks down from the adjacent happy company of five of her husband's most intimate friends. A bust of Shakespeare is above the desk, and under it a copy of the legend on his tomb at Stratford. Several small swords and daggers Booth used on the stage are hung near the fireplace.

He loved cigars. The humidor with his name engraved on it lies on the table, and beside it in a case with a glass cover is a volume of William Winter's poetry, opened to pages 98 and 99, the last lines Booth ever read. It is hardly surprising to see Shakespeare's picture on one wall, near a copy of the family coat of arms. On the opposite wall is a framed testimonial from the Edwin Forrest Lodge of the Actors Order of Friendship, signed by Louis Aldrich, President.

In the sitting room is a large table around which stand four chairs. There are two highbacked chairs on either side of the fireplace, and a Chippendale desk flanked by two bookcases between the front windows. Against the opposite wall is the embroidered lounge where Booth's friends so often sat and talked with him.

It is all there—art, literature, the theater, and friends—the fabric of Booth's life, and of the Club he created.

CHAPTER 13

Ladies at the Club

WHEN THE PLAYERS WAS FOUNDED A CENTURY AGO, THE CONCEPT OF A gentleman's club was an accepted fact, unchallenged even by those militant suffragettes who were demanding the vote, a privilege it took them thirty-two years more to acquire. The all-male club was an idea imported from England, where it had been an upper-class institution, and it existed almost from the beginning in America.

There was one important difference, however. In England, if a man's home was his wife's castle as well, his club was sacredly male, not to be profaned by a female presence under any circumstances. It took years of pressure to permit women inside the doors even as visitors.

At The Players, British custom was adhered to where membership was concerned, but women were permitted entry within less than four months of the Club's founding, although under the most limited circumstances. These circumstances gradually relaxed over the next century, but every relaxation was resisted and it took radically changed social and legal patterns to break down the last barrier as the Club's first century ended.

Even in late nineteenth-century New York, the capital of a still patriarchal society, it would have been incongruous for the Club to ignore women. All of its members worked in the arts with women on a more or less equal basis, and that was particularly true of the theater. It was hardly surprising then, that the first declared institution at The Players was Ladies' Day, inaugurated on Shakespeare's birthday, April 23, 1889.

Three guest invitation cards were allotted to each member, but within two years, the response was so great that this number had to be reduced to a pair, and that figure prevailed for some time. Other amenities also had to be scaled down because of the overwhelming popularity of Ladies' Day. For the first two or three years, an American Beauty rose was exchanged with each guest for her invitation card, but roses were as relatively expensive then as they are today, and they had to be abandoned in a few years, when the crowds grew to 660 in 1907 and 638 in 1911.

Ground rules were laid down at the start. Ladies were not permitted to go below into the grill room or pool room, and in fact were welcome only in the Great Hall and its adjoining rooms, and in the library. Considerable anxiety was expressed about the staircase leading to the library floor, and a sign was posted warning, "Don't Stand on the Stairs!" As time went on, however, attendance began to fall off and danger was averted without further closures.

The durability of the rules is surprising, considering how rapidly America changed after the Great War. Until 1943 only six exceptions had ever been made to the decree barring ladies from the Club except on Ladies' Day. They were made for Sarah Bernhardt (twice), Madame Modjeska, Lady Forbes-Robertson, Madame Clara Louise Kellogg-Strakosch, Mrs. Pedro de Cordoba, and Edwina Booth Grossmann, who had open access to her father's rooms as long as she lived.

What broke down the rules over a long period of time was the fact that many wives did not share their husbands' devotion to the Club. That was particularly evident on Founder's Night when it was held on New Year's Eve, as we have seen, but it was increasingly plain as time went on, and in fact became a part of Club folklore.

An inveterate card player who lived only a few doors away, it was said, spent so much time at the Club that he scarcely saw his family. One night a fire broke out in the neighborhood, and his small son ran to the apartment window, shouting, "Mommy, mommy, I think it's The Players."

"Come on, dear," his mother said, with a glance at her alarmed husband, "let's go fight the firemen."

An eloquent testimonial to this feeling occurred during one of the most unusual Founder's Days, November 13, 1953, which was Booth's 120th birthday and John Drew's hundredth. Dorothy Stickney was chosen to be the Lady of the Theater that day, giving the customary Booth tribute after the luncheon to a large assemblage of Players and another guest of honor, Mrs. John C. Devereux, Drew's daughter, who did not speak.

Stickney, an actress as well known as her husband, Howard Lindsay, departed from custom as she stood before the fireplace in the Great Hall. In part, she said: "Perhaps Mr. Booth could foresee what this club would someday come to mean to a certain group of men. I doubt if it ever occurred to him what it might mean to one woman—me. I wish I could thank him; perhaps I can by saying 'thank you' to all of you to whom he somehow still lives. If I were a man, this is the only club I'd want to belong to—but in a curious way, I feel I do almost belong—not a real blood relative, of course, but a sort of 'Player-in-law.' The glimpses I have had of the Club have made me understand Howard's great affection for it and why he likes to spend so much time here. I could never blame him—I could only envy him.

"It is quite an experience—perhaps I should say profession—to be a 'Player's wife.' Some people call it 'Player's widows,' but these are really only the ones of us who are married to card-playing and pool-playing Players. When Walter Connolly was alive, his wife Nedda Harrigan summed that up neatly for all of us when she said, 'When they win, they win; when they lose, they break even.'

"There has never been any misunderstanding in our household as to the place The Players occupied in Howard's life. He made sure that was understood before we were married. He told me we would never be able to spend New Year's Eve together—and for 23 years we never did. I've had mixed feelings about all those New Year's Eves. I think it's been about one-third annoyance at not being with him, and two-thirds envy of him for being here. Anyway, in behalf of all Players' wives, I'd like to say a special 'thank you' for the change in custom."

No such graceful complaints were heard at the beginning, however, and Ladies' Day quickly assumed the aspect of an important event at the Club. It was suspended in 1893 because of Booth's illness, and it was cancelled again on April 23, 1905, because of Jefferson's death, and a third time in 1928 because of alterations to the clubhouse. It was not always observed on the same day, for various reasons. If Shakespeare's birthday happened to fall on a matinee day, for example, it was moved to a more convenient time, or when it fell on Easter Sunday, as it did for the first time in Club history in 1916.

There have been landmarks along the way. Joe Jefferson, as president, addressed the gathering in 1901, but that was the only time such a thing occurred. In 1903 Annie Russell was the star of the day and dedicated the new fountain just installed in the garden. An innovation was introduced in 1910, with a string orchestra installed behind a screen of potted palms in a corner of the veranda. In 1914 attendance reached an all-time high, with 683 ladies in attendance.

Ladies' Day in 1937 was notable for two reasons. President Walter Hampden could not be present to head the receiving line because he had not recovered from a leg injury, and for the first time the ladies invaded the lower regions. Palms placed strategically on the stairs leading down, and discreet warnings, had deterred them from investigating the hallowed precincts of the bar until then, but someone had made the mistake of calling the bar a café, and that proved to be irresistible. To the horror of older members, the barriers fell and the initial invaders became a flood.

The *Bulletin* conveyed a delicate sense of outrage at this occurrence: "It was demonstrated that palm fronds are not effective barriers against the progressive woman. A good many went down, and some stayed until 7 o'clock, somewhat to the embarrassment of the house committee. On the general topic of woman's place in the Club there is no constitutional provision against women visitors, or even against women members. Exclusion is a matter of tradition, not of law, and the time of visits is determined by the board."

Even the most traditional member, however, would not have wanted to discourage Ladies' Day. Nowhere else in town could such a charming all-star cast of women have been assembled every year. What better company could Players have had in April 1927, for instance, when the guest list included Julia Marlowe, Jane Cowl, Eva La Gallienne, Blanche Yurka, Louise Closser Hale, Francine Larrimore, Sara Teasdale, and Aline Mac-Mahon, with David Warfield and Edward H. Sothern standing at the head of the stairs to receive them? Or in 1933, to take another year at random, when the guests included Selena Royle, Anita Loos, Enid Markey, Kathleen Norris, Ida Tarbell, and Carolyn Wells?

There were a few Ladies' Days considered historic in Club history. In 1946 invitations were sent to friends of Players who had been celebrities in the theater, and the result was what could only be called Old-Timer's Day. May Davenport Seymour, the queen of tragedy in another era, was chosen as the guest of honor and was presented with a gold cigarette case as a souvenir. She was no stranger to the Club, having been of exceptional help in restoring the relics, wardrobe articles, and similar items among the art treasures.

One of the most amusing days was that of 1947, when Ingrid Bergman was the guest of honor, and the house committee did its best to isolate her from the eager throng. The committee had warned everyone in advance that any offers of assistance from members would be refused. A determined assault was made, however, and it flushed out Miss Bergman, who proved to be as charming as everyone had expected. Recent guests of honor have included Geraldine Page in 1986, Lynn Redgrave in 1987, and Marian Seldes in 1988.

The records show that attendance at Ladies' Day fell off steadily after 1948, when 500 ladies and members attended. In 1957 there were only 47 ladies who came as guests of the board, and 101 others who were guests of members, with 77 other members attending ladyless, for a total of 225, a record low.

The enduring popularity of the day for at least one lady was evident in 1958, when an always welcome guest was Bijou Fernandez, who had been a guest at every Ladies' Day since she was old enough to stand. A daughter of the family that for years owned the most powerful theatrical agency in New York, she had been a child actress and a perpetual friend of The Players almost from its earliest days. During the years of the Club's annual revivals, she had been in charge of the sale of souvenir programs and contributed to the financial success of all these productions. Now in her eighties, she had appeared the previous year at the Booth birthday ceremony, where she was a special guest but was not called upon to speak. Tyrone Guthrie did the honors that day.

Of the six exceptions made for admitting women, beyond Ladies' Day, by far the most memorable was Sarah Bernhardt's visit in 1911. The occasion was a reception and dinner for her at the conclusion of an extraordinary eight-month, coast-to-coast "farewell" tour. She arrived limping badly, which she did her best to conceal. On the long tour she had kept this disability from her audiences by deftly using the backs of furniture or the arms of fellow actors to support herself, and yet, when the action called for it, had thrown herself down on the injured knee time after time. In less than four years her leg would have to be amputated.

At the reception in No. 16 she insisted on standing and serving tea herself during the reception, unable to sit down until it was time for dinner. Obviously, she was exhausted from the tour; heavy makeup concealed the lines of fatigue as well as age in her face. She was, after all, 62 years old when she had opened the tour in Chicago, and after that had either played in or directed no less than ten different plays during the first week, and later gave six or seven night performances and at least four matinees every seven days. Small wonder that when she tried to read a telegram from John Drew at the dinner she discovered after a few fumbles that it was upside down, and when it was set straight, found that she would have to have it translated. Through it all, she was smiling and generous with those whom she called her fellow artists.

After dinner she expressed a desire to see the library, and particularly Booth's room, but by this time she doubted her ability to climb the stairs and so was taken to the tiny elevator we know today as the "Sarah Bernhardt Room." This elevator had been installed early in the Club's life at the request of older members who lived there and found it difficult to climb the stairs from grill room to the fourth floor. They had raised a fund through private subscription to buy it, and many who saw Bernhardt approaching it could recall the historic day when it was given its first trial run. A member named Horace Dinwiddie (a patron of the arts) had been first to open the door and draw back the latticed gate, step inside, and push button #3. The occasion was celebrated with champagne for dinner that night. Booth had used the elevator often, particularly when his health began to fail.

At this point the facts cease and the legend begins. Its most popular version, as one Player reported it, perpetuated in a hundred retellings, was as follows: "She entered. The door was closed and the wire pulled, but . . . the elevator refused to budge. It was dark, and but room for two, Madame and Francis Wilson, the actor. The divine Sarah became alarmed. Repeated yankings of the starting wire produced no result, except to increase Madame's alarm. She became voluble in her appeals to be *'laissez sortir.'* The door was at last flung open and Madame, after a mighty sigh of relief, came out, smiling."

Another witness was Elie Edson, a Player who was also Bernhardt's press agent, and had accompanied her on the tour. Here is his version: "On this night . . . I was seated in the rear parlor where tea is now served, when suddenly I saw Madame Bernhardt coming from the main stairway. According to Charlie, she had come up in the elevator with Francis Wilson. They had been stuck in the elevator, as was customary in those days. When I caught sight of her, she was leaning heavily on the right arm of Otis Skinner, holding himself very erect, and smiling with that endearing, amused smile so characteristic of him. After they had advanced a few steps, diminutive Francis Wilson, with a majestic bow and broad smile, offered his left arm to this lady of international dramatic renown, and seemed to bow his already bowed legs in order to lower his height to hers. . . ." A true press agent's account.

As the story grew in scope, later versions had La Bernhardt trapped in the elevator for an hour, emitting terrified cries in French, and there were other ornamentations of an even more fanciful nature. Fortunately, there was another and more reliable witness present that night, Walter Oettel, whose devotion to Booth apparently led him to accept the legend that the lights went out at the moment the Founder died, but who balked at embracing a tale in which his idol was not involved. Here is the account he wrote in his *Sketch Book,* and it has the ring of truth:

"I was asked to operate the car. This pleasant task gave me the opportunity of coming to close contact with the distinguished guest. I respectfully followed her into the elevator. As it measures only three by four feet, we were obliged to stand very close to each other. In such delightful juxtaposition, one of Madame's beautiful roses fell from her corsage. I slowly pulled the rope, but the car would not move; our combined weight was too great. I stepped out—but not without the rose—which I picked up from the floor of the elevator. Its recent wearer told me I might keep it . . . Francis Wilson had been standing by to watch the success of our ascent, and he now stepped forward to offer his assistance. He tried his luck with the rope, it actually rose about three feet, Sarah was getting nervous, so Wilson allowed the car to descend gently. They both turned, smiling, and climbed the stairs."

After numerous other failures less spectacular over the years, there was a movement in 1946 to rip out this recalcitrant and outmoded apparatus, and install a more modern version. But Rollin Kirby mounted a campaign to prevent the change, and he was successful. If it was ever removed, Kirby said, it should be given to the Smithsonian. But it remains, a historic icon, forever known as the Sarah Bernhardt Room. Besides the legend, it also inspired Gelett Burgess to his memorable quatrain:

The Elevator's in the wall,
And no one uses it at all;
Bernhardt was stuck in it, they say,
For all I know, she's there today.

Even if the legend had been highly exaggerated, however, it could have hardly exceeded the excitement at the Club three years earlier, when a dray drawn by a span of Percherons drew up to the Club on a fragrant spring morning. Two Spanish-American war veterans who were riding on it got off and unloaded a large slab of stone, leaned it against the door, and departed. An arriving member summoned the doorman, who was already on his way, and together they read a chiseled inscription on the rock, which looked more like a marker to commemorate a battle, as indeed it did. The inscription read: "Mrs. Sally Genung's card conveying compliments to the one who initiated the series of breakfasts at The Players at noontime on Sundays." Those breakfasts had deprived Mrs. Genung of the Sunday morning company of her husband, Charles. It was, perhaps, the first gun fired in the ladies' revolt.

The War Between Men and Women (to borrow James Thurber's phrase) did not begin to break out seriously at the Club until the Thirties. It could never have been called a real war, but more a series of skirmishes, after each one of which the Club drew back to previously prepared positions. Serious discussion of the issue in 1935, most of it at the Round Table downstairs, led to a revival of Scudder Middleton's earlier proposal that if Ladies' Day were to be continued, there should also be a Gentleman's Day. This was not taken seriously by anyone. But in 1948 the house committee initiated what some termed a treasonous act, which the *Bulletin* characterized as "one of the most controversial experiments yet undertaken in this oasis of masculinity." It voted to set aside one Monday every month when members could bring lady guests for dinner, although they would not be permitted to bring them below stairs to the grill room.

To quote the *Bulletin* again, this proposal set off a "spontaneous revulsion" that left the idea dead in the dining room. The "wailing wall at the east end of the bar" started a petition, and before the experiment could begin on October 24, a hardy band of members led by Henry Lanier and Edwin Corle literally stormed the board of directors meeting. They presented the board with their petition, nailed to the club bar "like Luther's theses," as the *Bulletin* aptly described it, and soon had dozens of signatures. Faced with revolt, the executive committee went into session hastily and voted to postpone the plan indefinitely.

The Committee protested that this scuttling of their idea did nothing to relieve the deficit, which they said the plan had been intended to do. The protesters countered with suggestions: Why not a grand lottery? Or a championship bridge match in Madison Square Garden? Or, even more outrageously, removing members from the bedrooms upstairs and turning them into a bordello, with double rates charged for the Booth room. Quite evidently, the members were not yet prepared to take the question of what to do about the ladies, if anything, very seriously.

The issue simmered below the surface for three more years, until the annual meeting in May 1951, when the subject of women being allowed in the dining room on Saturday or Sunday night came up for the second time. "The crackling of hackles was audible as far away as Fourth Avenue," the *Bulletin* reported. Robert Winternitz, then chairman of the house committee, defended the idea. It would produce money for fresh paint in the Club, badly needed, he said, not to mention the air-conditioning, which was constantly breaking down. If no revenue could be raised immediately, Winternitz warned, the Club would be compelled to dip into capital. In any case, he added, the place was practically deserted on Saturdays and Sundays, so the threat of contamination would be minimal. As a clincher, he pointed out that if members took wives to the Club now and then, subjecting them to its charms, it might lower resistance at home to the hours spent away from the hearth.

Much argument followed, but nothing resulted from it. The following year, at the annual meeting on May 25, 1952, the discussion was renewed. A motion was made to permit women in the dining room one night a month, but members temporarily avoided a decision by referring the proposal to the house committee, where it had originated in the first place.

It took still another year to accomplish, but after further heated debates it was decided in 1953 to institute a Ladies' Night as well as a Ladies' Day, and in two years the plan was pronounced a success, even by the opposition. In the first two seasons, Ladies' Night had an average attendance of

145, and on October 9, 1955, the attendance was a record 206. By that time the occasion was designated as an open house. All this coincided with a sharp decrease in the number of those attending on Ladies' Day.

Another milestone was passed on Booth's birthday in 1966, when the tradition of a luncheon was changed to permit an open house instead, at which, for the first time, women other than a guest of honor were invited. They heard one of their number, Jessica Tandy, give an address that moved those present.

Since then, as all members know, the presence of women has gradually increased, always welcomed at lunch and on any night when dinner is served, as well as appearing at most Club functions with the exception of some Pipe Nights. In 1988, the final barrier fell when the board voted to admit women as members, to take effect the following year. There had been pressure from the City of New York to enforce its local law requiring all private male clubs to admit women. The Century Association had taken its case to the Supreme Court, but The Players concluded not to wait for that decision and to accept the inevitable. What that might mean for the Club's second century, no one could be certain.

CHAPTER 14

The Pool Table: Folk Tales and Real Tales

AT NO. 16 THE POOL TABLE HAS ALWAYS OCCUPIED A SPECIAL PLACE, even among those members who have never played the game. It commands attention and demands to be heard. From Twain's cue on the wall to the shifting galaxy of players who have bent over it, the green table has generated its own folklore as well as more legitimate memories.

Card playing has always been popular, too, and might have preceded the pool table as an institution but it got a slow start because Booth believed that cards led to gambling, and therefore it was not permitted at the Club as long as he lived. It was not the gambling as such that he objected to, but he feared it would lead to bad feelings. That was a little naive on the Founder's part. Wagering quickly became a way of life at the pool table, too, as it would have anywhere. There is no record that it ever created any real trouble.

In historical time, card playing at the Club actually began on the first week of the Club's existence, with gentlemanly games of whist, the standard fare; but with the arrival of a pool table in 1904, an institution was created that the pasteboards could never match. There were, in fact, two tables at the beginning, pool and billiards, with the second squeezed in at the room's waist, requiring singular dexterity with the cues at both. When this obviously impossible situation was corrected, the second table was removed. It left cuts about three inches deep in the wall projections at the middle of the room, which proved to be exactly right for holding a glass.

The remaining table was made of sturdy stuff. It lasted for thirty-two years until, in 1936, it became obvious that it would have to undergo extensive repairs or be replaced. There were a few avant-garde players who wanted a modern table, with pipestem legs and a purple cloth. The pool committee came down solidly for a traditional table and a green cloth. It was supplied by an unexpected donor, Sam Forrest, a man who never played pool himself and wanted only to do something for the Club. He declined an offer to play Kelly on the table for the remainder of his life, with no payment exacted for scratches.

There was another loss and gain that summer of 1936. Someone made off with the Bill Cup, a silver trophy bought by subscription in 1919, and played for in sixteen annual conquests, with the winner's name inscribed on it every year. Henry Hering, a respected pool player himself, came forward with the gift of a silver bowl to replace the cup.

After the pool table was solidly established as an institution in the early years of the century, legends (with a factual basis) were soon created. One of the most remarkable was the rise of a club within the Club, called "The Royal Order of Loyal Owls." There were strict qualifications for membership. First, an applicant had to be a Kelly pool player. Second, he had to be able to hold his liquor over a sustained period of time. Finally, he had to play Kelly three nights in succession until daylight, or at the least, dawn.

Among the original members were Frank Byrne, Walter Connolly, and Frederic Steele. Three other original Owls—Harold Gould, John C. King, and Ivan Simpson—were still alive in 1951. The Club's night clerk, Arthur Sherman, was made an honorary member because he had to work until 4 A.M., the Club's closing hour in those days. After being elected, new members were renamed Elmer. The winner of every pot had to buy a drink for everyone else, and these lucky players could be counted on to order the most expensive drink in the place at the time, gin and ginger beer, which cost forty cents. This happy tribe also had a mascot—a small owl that sat for many years on the southwest bracket in the pool room. It was stolen in 1960.

Members of the Owls were noted for their extraordinary endurance, as one would expect. Harold Gould, for example, played until six or seven in the morning on occasion, after which he went to work at his job as salesman for a large woolen concern, arriving as usual at nine. Gould once played a tournament game in the Club with another member, with the condition that each one should wear white tie and tails, gloves, and silk hat during the entire game. The Owls flourished for a few years until, as Frederic Steele observed, they "passed into history, disrupted by war, matrimony, and other hazards."

By 1938 nearly 150 tournaments had been played on the pool table, besides a long series of team matches with the Lambs, alternating between clubhouses. During the Great War the pool players helped the cause by subscribing three Liberty Bonds and making them tournament prizes. The first tournament attracted 72 players, including John Drew. Matches were contested, as Dorr wrote later, "at all times of day or night and under all conceivable conditions—some in silence and decorum, some with incredible din, some dry, some wet, some in correct evening dress. . . ."

Stories began to spring up about the pool table and a folklore was created, made up of real and fanciful tales. One of the earliest related that Owen Meech, a character actor, was absorbed in a telephone book one day, standing near the pool table. Still turning the pages and utterly oblivious of the game in progress, he moved closer to the table and spread the book out on the green cloth. The players were so struck by this act of sheer sacrilege that they were unable to speak. Meech paid them no attention. He found his number and moved away again to the telephone, never realizing that he had become an instant anecdotal hero.

One member alleged that he had seen the ghost of Thomas Gray at the Club in 1928, watching the pool players and leaving behind him this "Elegy Written in a Downstairs High Chair," which began:

> The curfew tolls the knell at four each day
>   High-living herds wind slowly o'er the lea,
> The poolman homeward plods his weary way
>   And leaves the club to Kelly and to me.

By all odds, Kelly was, for many years, the favorite game. It never pretended to be a quiet pastime and, one particular summer during the Great War, when a long period of hot weather prevailed and windows were up all about Gramercy Park, the habitual commotion around the Kelly table grew to such proportions that complaints poured in not only from staid members resting in the upstairs bedrooms, but from the National Arts Club, other neighbors, and so it was said, from the other side of the Park. Although John Blair, head of the house committee, was a Kelly devotee himself, he understood that drastic action was required, considering the quantity and quality of the complaints, so he decreed the abolition of Kelly. Only "straight pool" would be permitted, he said, speaking for the committee.

A strike ensued. The Kelly players declared that if they could not play their game, no one else would use the table. Since pool was at that time a profitable source of revenue for the Club (fees for the use of the table were charged until sometime in the Twenties), revenues were seriously cut.

Obviously, the strikers would have to win, but meanwhile a melancholy gloom settled on the pool room. Will Bradley, who had not heard of the strike, came in and began to play his usual morning game until he was informed and removed. One night during the strike John Barrymore came in with a friend after a late supper. He stopped dead at the foot of the stairs. Cues had been wound with bows of black crepe, and on a black-draped high chair stood the Kelly pill bottle, flanked by two mortuary candles.

It could mean only one thing. "My God!" Barrymore exclaimed. "Uncle Jack is dead."

Order was restored within a week of the strike's beginning, the decibel level soon reached its customary peaks, and the players displayed their usual absorption in the game. So absorbed were Eddie Donnelly and Dick Malchen one evening that they failed to notice Jack King, quietly slipping past the table from time to time. With every trip he brought another ball from the extra set and slipped it on the table unobtrusively. Unaware, the players continued to shoot until they were weary and someone noticed that the scoreboard registered twice the correct total.

One of the most faithful Kelly players was Royal Cortissoz, whose elegant critical prose was always on display in the art columns of the *Herald Tribune*. He played in a pink waistcoat bulging with cigars, his cuffs turned up. He carried his precise English to the table, making an exception only for the times he missed a critical shot, or made some other error. For these occasions he had an entire vocabulary of phrases expressing frustration—"Holy tackhammers," or "Suffering catfish," "Great Caesar's Aunt Hattie," or *in extremis,* "Dirty dishes, *quelle shot.*"

The pool table was always a center of hilarity, and it became a center of Club life in the days before air-conditioning, when prolonged hot periods drove members downstairs, where they were permitted to shed their jackets and eat all their meals there in relative comfort.

Mostly, however, they played pool, accompanied by a certain pool-table ribaldry, which was traditional and permitted. It was silenced only once. A sudden thundershower broke one night, and two ladies passing by took shelter in the doorway. They could not actually be admitted, members agreed, but two chairs were brought just inside the door for them to wait out the storm. At that moment, a burst of sound erupted from below.

It was the Kelly players. Informed of the ladies' situation, however, conventions were observed, and until the storm passed, only Cortissoz-like remarks were heard. It was further proof that a code of civility did exist at the table. The players also exhibited a tender regard for each other. When Jac Wendell, one of the Club's most inveterate players, died, the table was draped in black and not used again until after the funeral.

In action, however, the attitude of the pool players toward each other was jocularly critical, sometimes with a slight knife-edge showing. Mark Twain did not play pool ordinarily, but liked an occasional billiard game, although he was no more than a fair player. He came in on a Saturday afternoon one day, when the Club was sunk in its usual weekend quiet. Looking around, Twain saw that John Malone was the only available billiard partner and invited him for a game. While they played, a mutual friend of both watched for a time. Mark was playing badly, and when he missed what seemed like a simple shot, the member said mildly, "I've seen you play better than that, Mark."

"Yes," Twain said, "I'm like a chameleon; I take my color from the man I play with, and Malone never makes a damn shot."

For those who did not play, the pool devotees were sometimes the object of elaborate satire. At the annual meeting in 1924, John S. Phillips introduced what he said was a quaint manuscript he had just found in a Club storeroom, titled "Rollo's Visit to the Club," in which an ancient member of the house committee relates the story of a trip to No. 16 by his 18-year-old nephew. An excerpt illustrates the kind of nineteenth-century humor that still survived in 1926, when it was written:

As they are going upstairs from the billiard room, Rollo says to his Uncle John: "I didn't know grown men used those nasty words, uncle—you know—ending in K and T." When they are seated at a table upstairs, Uncle John explains: "You will learn, my dear nephew, that as years pass men return to the primitive and infantile. They find, by experience, that they can never really grow up or become civilized. And in certain places, such as clubs, the illusion is freely abandoned. At times they toss off the pretense of maturity, which the outer world compels them to uphold. That is what keeps them young, Rollo. You do not see on the forehead of even the oldest the black spot of the Struldbrugs, those horribly and perpetually aged creatures of the Island of Luggnagg, as reported, you remember, by Captain Lemuel Gulliver. But these childish phenomena of speech and conduct are secrets of the male cult. The day will come when female suffrage and equality of the sexes will furnish other places where such throwbacks will not only be proper, but almost demanded. This may lead to a decline in club life, for the monopoly of indecent conversation will be broken up and its prerogatives scattered in exclusive restaurants, hotels, cabarets, and the smarter homes.

"A club, Rollo, is the natural domain of gaiety, laughter, fun, of genuine mirth and jollity. And these do not need much infusion of vulgarity for full blossoming. . . ."

At about the same time, Brian Hooker, the "Connecticut Cheese Hound," composed a poem directed to the Kelly players, cast in the same form as the cheese poem:

> Ye Kellye-shooter ys a Bum
> He risketh more hys Income
> On Hye & Lowe & Jacke & Jill
> & who shall hold ye Luckye Phyll.
> & if he doe a lousie Shot,
> Or if another wynn ye Pot,
> He speketh Language ruff & rude
> Involving Moral Turpitude.

The pool and billiard players took themselves seriously, however, when the occasion demanded. They not only organized tournaments, but on one occasion were the beneficiaries (with the whole Club) of a prize from another contest. In 1905, when the Union League Club sponsored a handicap billiard tournament, the winner, James R. Morse, was presented with a handsome copper chafing dish which passed, somehow, in later years to Rea Irvin, one of the pool table's most devoted artists, who donated it to the house committee, which in turn gave it to Adolph at the bar.

Adolph suggested that if only he could have the proper cheese, he would exercise his celebrated ability to mix superior rarebits for weary pool players any time after 9 o'clock on any night except Sunday, his day off. Jack Shuttleworth brought back a large wheel of Wisconsin cheddar from the Washington Market, enough to soothe the pool players for a long time.

Artifacts on and near the pool table were simply accepted as part of tradition, or as no better than the players deserved, as in the case of the ivory pool balls themselves, said to be the finest in New York. But those waiting to play often speculated on the brass-lined cutouts directly opposite each other in the supporting beams of the room. Various explanations were offered for these ledges, about three feet from the floor and approximately sixteen inches long and nine inches wide. Some believed they were constructed to support Reginald Birch's arms while he watched a game. Others asserted they were meant to be rests for F.P.A.'s cigars.

Charlie, the fountainhead of Club wisdom, provided a more accurate explanation.

In the Club's early days, he said, when the bar was in what later became the waiters' pantry and there were two tables, one for billiards and one for pool, one of these was directly between the two beams. Players at this table found that often when they swung a cue, they encountered one of the beams. They complained to Stanford White, who simply had the offending sections of the beams removed, creating the brass-lined niches.

When the billiard table was removed, however, it meant that nine hundred members were forced to use one pool table. The increased wear and tear made a recovering essential in 1927, and in order to keep it in a better state, the pool committee came down from its mountain with Ten Commandments to Respect the Cloth, duly posted on the wall. As the *Bulletin* observed jocularly, "The seventh legalizes free-for-all companionate Kelly between 4 and 6:30 P.M."

It was the pool players themselves, however, who mattered most, and they were an extraordinary lot. In the Twenties the painter George Bellows was considered one of the best Kelly players. An energetic and versatile man, then in his early twenties, he sang in a church choir on Sunday mornings and played semi-pro baseball in the afternoon so that he could earn enough money to paint for the remainder of the week. It was a short trip from his studio on 19th Street to the table at No. 16.

Serious players regarded Kelly with disdain, but they acknowledged its existence by establishing the custom, extant for more than twenty years, of leaving the table in the late afternoon so that the Kelly players might frolic. John Wolcott Adams called this period the Children's Hour. Later, it was known as the Masterwork Hour, self-advertised as "a program of the world's finest pool shooters and artists."

Of all those artists, the most eminent was John Adams, who was for years considered the best player in the Club, as well as one of its best-loved members. Before he died in June 1925 at 51, he was the unofficial Club champion, and chairman of the pool committee, which he ruled as a benevolent despot. Adams was a Downeaster, full of tart New England sayings, a joyous singer of Puritan hymns, and ready to denounce anyone who profaned the sacred green cloth. He was affectionately known as the autocrat of the billiard table. A noted illustrator in his life outside the Club, he had been a member since 1914. No. 16 became his home to an unusual degree.

When he was not actively using his cue, Adams liked to draw on the pool-room blackboard, creating images enchanting onlookers and casually erasing what he had done, with his endearing grin. But others of his little sketches, done on Club notepaper or lunch cards, were carefully preserved.

He never withheld one from a friend who wanted it, and the friends cherished them.

Adams' time at the Club was overlapped by Frank Sullivan, one of the best American humorists, who was brought in by Rollin Kirby in 1925. Sullivan announced that he was an inveterate nonpool player, consequently he joined the Putites, who heckled the pool game from their adjacent round table. Sullivan described the Putites as "the boys who play the match game around the Put-Thyself-Into-The-Trick-of-Singularity table." It was this proximity that inspired one of the most durable pool table legends.

As Sullivan described it, "I recall the night we Putites discovered that Rea Irvin was a sucker for a Sousa march; was, in fact, the only man alive who could whistle the March King's entire repertory. The others had all been shot. There was a pool game of great moment that night and Rea was one of the pivot men, but he was putty in the hands of us Putites. No sooner would he lift a cue than we would start singing a Sousa march. Mr. Irvin, fascinated as though by a nest of cobras, would *have* to drop his cue and join us. We formed a procession finally, and with Mr. Irvin and his cue as drum major and baton, in the order named, marched seven times around the table singing "Stars and Stripes Forever," in an attempt to bring down the pool table, like Jericho's walls.

"Probably never before has the old Booth mansion been called on to cope with so many decibels at one time. The startled tea drinkers upstairs saw their cups jump in the saucers. After numerous circuits of the table, Rea and his followers grew exhausted and developed sore throats. Everyone retired to the bar to toast Rea and John Philip Sousa."

Affectionate titles were bestowed on some pool players, or on their deeds. F.P.A. recalled the day Frederic Steele hit the object ball so gently that thereafter such a shot was called a Shirley Temple. He remembered, too, the daily noon game between Rea Irvin and Charley Falls, and Kirby's appearances at the table, where he created what his fellow players called a Kirby, that is, hitting the cue ball a blind wallop. An Anthony (named for Norman) was made by knocking a ball off the table. A Chalmers (for Thomas) was being unable to hit the object ball three inches away from the cue ball. In later years, a "Guy Repp" was a shot in which the cue ball traversed the entire table without hitting anything. (Chalmers was also known as the One Man Mob because of his overpowering voice.) And as for F.P.A., he ran 81 on a memorable evening, and was thereafter known as 81A.

Sometimes real players visited the Club and demonstrated how it should be done. On a December night in 1932, Ralph Greenleaf, twelve times world champion, had dinner at The Players and later gave an exhibition, besides playing a game with Henry Hering, then the Club champion. The score: Greenleaf, 125; Hering, 16. Greenleaf had a high run of 61. On the following night Greenleaf defended his title against a former champion, Benny Allen.

The pool table had become such an institution that even in the worst of the Depression, 1932, the pool committee persuaded the house committee to do something about the conditions of the pool room. The unsightly lockers in the space around the table in the men's room were removed, and the mailboxes placed where they are today. A fine old settle was restored to its former position, and the whole place repainted. In 1943, however, when a new cloth was needed, it was bought with proceeds from Gertrude the Pig, in which players who scratched dropped nickels. In the first ten days she collected $47.78.

As time went on and new players slowly replaced the old, fresh unbelievers appeared too, and one, Gelett Burgess, produced this poem:

> I never watch a game of pool
>   I never care to watch one.
> But still at pool I'm such a fool,
>   I'd rather watch than botch one.

It did not replace its model, the famous Purple Cow.

One of the noted players of the Sixties was Arthur Arent, who died in 1972. Rollie Winters called him "a good citizen, a good conversationalist, a fine writer, and a good companion, but a *great* pool player." The game was important to him, although he was a gracious winner and a good loser. Arthur deplored lucky shots, calling them "lucky bastard shots." On an afternoon when he was missing relatively easy shots, he observed, "When I miss shots like that, it's like DiMaggio going 0 for 9 in a double header." He played the game with intensity, integrity, and skill, and quite naturally became chairman of the pool committee, organized pool nights and the annual tournament, and did whatever else was needed (if it was) to make the green table an integral part of Club life.

Much of the humor at the table, and elsewhere in the Club, depended on the sophisticated pun, at which there were several masters in the Club. One of the best was Bill Plante, who was also known as one of the most accomplished raconteurs, a man who would rather tell a story than listen to one. Bill was watching one day as the Reverend Jesse William Stitt leaned across the table, cue poised, studying the shot he hoped to make. There was little hope he would make it, since he was regarded as the worst player in the Club.

As he hesitated, contradictory advice came from all sides, but he ignored it, hit the fourteen ball as he had planned, and watched as it kissed the seven, which ricocheted off two banks, neatly nicked the eight, and disappeared in the middle pocket as the eight slid in too. There was an outburst of appreciative and unbelieving applause.

Sidney Slon, who had been watching, turned to Plante, who had exhibited no emotion whatever as he witnessed the miracle. "The good father's pool has certainly improved," Slon remarked.

"Why shouldn't it?" Bill replied. "God is his cue-pilot."

Puns survive today at The Players—another miracle.

As a letter from Pauline, John Mulholland's widow, disclosed after his death, the magician who graced the Club for so many years did not play pool but he made it his business to preserve the table's surface for those who did. John was particularly worried about Sunday evenings, when the downstairs rooms were crowded and the pool table often became a convenient place to set down glasses. Inevitably, there was frequent spillage and consequent damage. To prevent these near disasters, John enlisted the help of Louis Rachow, then the librarian, on Sunday afternoons and set up magic displays on the table. He theorized that members would not want to desecrate these obviously valuable memorabilila, and would find other places to set their glasses. He was right.

In the early Seventies the acknowledged best player in the Club at eight-ball pool was Russell (Rusty) Miller, regarded as equaling John Adams, the redoubtable champion of earlier years. On December 15, 1972, Steve Miserak, pocket billiards world champion for the past two years, came to the Club and took on Miller, who was then a new member, in a one-hundred-point straight pool match. The audience included such current sharks as Martin Gabel, Arent, Mort Marshall, George Wieser, Winters, and about forty other people. Miserak won without difficulty, 100 to 48, but Jack Shuttleworth asserted, "He'd have no chance with me at 8-ball, if only my handicap was put at 4, where it belongs."

One of the traditions at The Players, cherished in its own peculiar way, has been the longstanding feud between bridge and pool players. When the two games were in proximity, the distance between green table and round table was so short that each side could easily encourage the other. Thus the bridge player would be heard remarking, "He couldn't make that shot with a clam rake," and conversely, the pool player, observing that a bridge player might be in the way of a cue extended backward, would remark, "Don't ask him to move, stick your cue in his ear."

A truce was customarily declared in the late afternoon, when both sides gathered at the bar to exchange true stories and other lies, greatly enriching the lore of both games. Often, as one Player observed, these stories were set pieces, heard at rehearsals or at Sardi's. On occasion, the venerable figure of Charlie Connolly joined in; he had heard them all, and knew a few no one else had heard. He was also a master of the delayed punchline, as the following incident discloses.

At the bar one afternoon Charlie placed a hand on the shoulder of an avid pool player and said, "I see you got a new cloth on the pool table." He paused, plainly in a reminiscent mood. "In the old days," he went on, "we had a member who was a textile importer. He supplied us with the finest grade of imported Belgian cloth, for free." Charlie paused again, and looked down modestly. "For some reason the feller took a shine to me and sent me to his tailor to have a suit made. It was a beautiful suit, a beautiful suit. One day I got caught in the rain. I took the suit to the little tailor around the corner from where I live. His name was Levy, or something. He looked at me and said, 'Charlie, this is a beautiful suit, a beautiful suit.' He paused, and his listener waited for the snapper, but Charlie turned and walked away. A moment later, he was back and his hand resumed its position on the member's shoulder. "By the way," he said, "that little tailor I mentioned. He had a daughter. Maybe you've heard of her. Her name is Paulette Goddard."

Another favorite tale of the early Seventies concerns Henry Fisk Carlton, whose fellow pool players decided to present him with a cuestick when he resigned as chairman of the pool committee. Two of the players consituted themselves as a committee and set out to find the finest stick money could buy. They were so proud of it that, before it was presented, they passed it around to be admired by the others. When it was Bart Spicer's turn, he turned the cue over in his hand admiringly, studying its inlaid mother-of-pearl, the elaborate woodcarving and scrollwork, then handed it back.

"Beautiful," he said, "positively nostalgic. Reminds me of a bedpost in a Mexican whorehouse."

The great days of the pool table are gone. There are still earnest players and good ones, but the popularity of the sport has diminished, for no discernible reason. All that remains of the old days is the folklore, of which this chapter has offered only a small sampling. For that alone, the pool table has a deserved place in Club history.

CHAPTER 15

Memorable Pipe Nights

BUT WEREN'T THEY *ALL* MEMORABLE? THAT WOULD BE HARD TO DENY IF we take a generous view, but to borrow from George Orwell, some were more memorable than others. Certainly, in sum, they qualify as the Club's most distinctive institution, one that has given exceptional pleasure to generations of Players.

When the first Pipe Night was held cannot be established from Club records, but it was sometime during 1905 and although these meetings were always irregular, they have flourished ever since. The early affairs were quite different from those we know today, however. They began at midnight, for those who were either on the stage or in the audience of New York theaters. The smoking of churchwarden pipes gave the occasions their name and the designations of a Pipemaster to lead the festivities. Presidents and vice-presidents of the Club were the traditional pipemasters at first but after a decade or two, others took over from time to time and there has been no firm pattern in recent years.

One of the attractions at the beginning was the free distribution of tobacco, along with a keg of beer. Both the tobacco and the beer disappeared soon after the turn of the century, but there was no diminution of cigarettes, or ordinary pipes, and no decrease in the consumption of spirits. The entertainment at first was informal and unplanned. But eventually there was a sense that some structure was needed, and a chairman was appointed for the occasions, succeeded at last by a Pipemaster. The black tie did not arrive until the Twenties.

There is not much doubt about the most memorable of these early Pipe Nights. Several later versions exist, but Walter Oettel, who was there, describes it best in his *Sketch Book:* "Mr. Arnold Daly was chairman. An hour after midnight Daly stepped into the clouds of tobacco smoke and called out someone from behind the heavy curtains of the big bay window; a trim little figure in a dazzling Pierrot suit. Daly introduced the figure with a little speech as a young actor whose services were greatly in demand." It was, in reality, Bessie Abbott, a soprano from the Metropolitan Opera, who sang several songs, to great applause. She was instantly recognized by most members.

Bessie sat down at the long table, toasts were offered, and jokes made. It was an innocent enough prank, but the story of how Daly brought a woman into the Club through the kitchen and up a ladder to the grill room was too good to be kept within the Club, in spite of Booth's admonishing words over the mantel above the fireplace. The newspapers carried accounts of what had happened, and the board felt compelled to act. Daly was expelled next day.

One of the most moving of these early Pipe Nights was for Harry Lauder. He told those present how he had entertained soldiers going into the trenches during the Great War, and again as they were coming out, a grim contrast. Because he was a short man, Lauder had to get up on a chair in the grill room so that everyone could see him. Once there, he related how he had gone to the battlefields with a small piano strapped to his car and an accompanist inside. He wanted only, if he could, to divert these men, so many of whom were about to die. He spoke with a choked voice about his son, his only child, who died at the front, and as someone wrote later of Harry, "How we loved him that evening at The Players."

On another occasion Charlie Chaplin appeared at a Pipe Night, with none of the trappings that made him the beloved Little Fellow. As one of those who were present described it: "He stood among us as himself. . . .We rose and cheered him."

In the Twenties, President John Drew officiated at Pipe Nights whenever he was in town. The evenings had still not quite taken the form they would assume later, as a description of the occasion on December 8, 1923, attests, when J. M. Kerrigan was Pipemaster, with 130 members present and many guests. Several of the members sang and played the piano. The favorites were now such encore numbers as "Sylvia," and "Mandalay." But mostly, as the *Bulletin* observed, "The evening was given over to stunts and nonsense."

Gene Lockhart, for instance, gave voice and piano impressions of a Spanish dancer and an afternoon tea party. Bobbie Edwards played his ukelele and sang slightly risqué songs. Gitz Rice, the composer, sang his "Dear Old Pal of Mine," in the styles of Beethoven, Strauss, Rachmaninoff, Grieg, Sinding, Irving Berlin, Liszt, and Sousa. Pipemaster Kerrigan also sang and told stories. The period quality of these stories can be gathered from just one of them: an Irishman learned from the new preacher that Sodom and Gomorrah were ancient cities; until then, he had always thought they were man and wife.

There was a stir in the Club when it was announced that a Virgins' Pipe Night would take place on May 1, 1926, but inquiries produced the explanation that the evening would be for new members, "new stars who have arisen in our midst." Walter constructed a handsome Maypole decoration for the grill room table, and extravagant offers were made for the poster Oliver Herford drew to advertise the event. That night's virgins were William Slavens McNutt (a popular writer of the day), Laurence Stallings, Howard Lindsay, Alleyne Ireland, and Joe Cook. This occasion was so successful that a second Virgins' Pipe Night was held the following year, at which Frederic Dorr Steele was Pipemaster.

The idea of a Pipe Night for newly elected members had begun as early as 1924, *sans* virgins in the announcement of the night. It was notable for a man who wasn't there, John S. Phillips—no newcomer but one of the Club's most cherished members. He had been invited to be the speaker but circumstances prevented it and he wrote a letter instead. It remains the best statement of the spirit which has held The Players together for a century, that "high and beneficent spirit," as he called it, "that abounds within the old walls of our Club." Addressed to "Dean Don" (Marquis, who was Pipemaster), his letter reads, in part:

"This spirit was born and continues because The Players are a race of gentle anarchists. . . . There is no constraint. We are chosen as men of good will, accepting each other so fully that no other code is needed for us to live happily together. We do not try to change each other. We differ and are glad of it. The charm of this place is the bewildering variety of its untrammeled membership. Each one is unembarrassed because he knows that there is at least one bigger fool than himself in the club; and if he is in doubt, his nearest tablemate will, in all good feeling, testify for him to the same purport."

One of the most memorable Pipe Nights of the Twenties occurred in 1927, with Edwin T. Emery as Pipemaster and an all-star cast, including William Gustafson, basso of the Metropolitan Opera; Eddie Dowling, star of the current "Honeymoon Lane"; J. C. Nugent, who offered a few words about Hamlet and other characters; Gene Lockhart, who mimed a speech in which he did everything but talk; and Charlie Chaplin, offering his idea of a Spaniard explaining in his native Spanish his impression of a bullfight, a characterization not in the least handicapped by the fact that Chaplin could not speak Spanish.

There were a good many other all-star nights in the Twenties, as one could expect from casts that included John Barrymore, Robert Benchley, Donald Ogden Stewart, Frank Craven, Eddie Cantor, Ernest Truex, Ed Wynn, Frank Crummit, and Harry Houdini.

In the Thirties, George Middleton became the first chairman of a duly constituted entertainment committee, designed to organize Pipe Nights. So many Players went to Hollywood during the decade that The Players' West Room, noted earlier, was able to have its own Hollywood Pipe Night in 1939, but there is no record that it was ever repeated.

An innovation occurred in December 1936 when, for the first time, Pipe Night evenings were made a testimonial of a guest of honor. John Gielgud was first to be selected, and drew an unprecedented 292 members, one of who declared that there had been "no such night since the old days." At the head table with Gielgud were Hampden, Otis Skinner, Arthur Bryon, Sir Gerald Campbell, George Middleton, John Charles Thomas, John Barbirolli, and Ruggiero Ricci. At nearby tables were Maurice Evans and Sir Cedric Hardwicke. Thomas sang for the first time since becoming a member, and Ricci, then one of the most noted violinists of the day, played for this distinguished audience.

The Forties produced some of the most remarkable Pipe Nights yet seen. At the height of the Big Band era in 1942, and in spite of the war, Swing Night was declared, with Jack Smart as Pipemaster. Smart played drums in a group that included such Dixieland immortals as Peewee Russell, Max Kaminsky, Louis Prima, Eddie Condon, J. C. Higginbotham, and John Kirby. Later, with Art Hodes on drums, Carmen Cavallaro played piano in a quite different style, and still later, the great black jazz violinist, Eddie South, appeared. At the end of the evening the Club introduced its own swing group: Harry Hohm on the accordion; the two Starretts, Cliff and Paul, on bass fiddle and guitar respectively, with Smart again on drums.

A few months later came another memorable musical evening, this time an operatic Pipe Night, with Wilfrid Pelletier of the Met (a member), and several stars of that grand old house: Charles Kullman, Frederick Jagel, John Brownlee, Leonard Warren, and Salvatore Baccaloni. Edward Johnson, the Met's manager, spoke, as did Deems Taylor and Roland Young.

Alfred Lunt was honored in June 1947, anticipating that most extraordinary of all Pipe Nights (in the opinion of many) that occurred later when he was joined by his wife. Howard Lindsay was Pipemaster for the first Lunt Pipe Night, and appearing on the bill were Bobby Clark, John Mulholland, Dudly Digges, James Barton, Paul Robeson, and John Gielgud. Richard Dyer-Bennett, then at the peak of his folk-singing fame, sang both at the dinner and later in the reading room. Jimmy Durante and Lawrence Olivier sent messages of regret.

Another unusual Pipe Night, in 1947, was a Report on the World, a format never repeated although it was highly successful. With A. A. Berle as Pipemaster, the speakers included Joseph Barnes, then foreign editor of the *Herald Tribune;* Russell Hill, then an editorial writer for the same paper and formerly its European correspondent; General George Kenny, Chief of Strategic Air Forces; and William Laurence, science editor of the New York *Times.* Afterward members gathered at the bar for another historic occasion. It was Adolph's last night as bartender; next day he became steward.

By far the most unusual Pipe Night of the Forties, and certainly one of the most memorable in the history of this institution, was Burlesque Night in May 1944, which was organized by John Chapman, *Daily News* drama critic, as chairman of the entertainment committee. The highlight of the evening was Ernest Truex and Walter Hampden in a riotous reprise of an old Weber and Fields routine. A real burlesque comedian, Joey Faye, also performed. It was the only Pipe Night ever to be reviewed in the press by a drama critic. John Chapman wrote next day in the *Daily News:*

"It had not been difficult to imagine Truex, who has spent his lifetime being funny, as Joe Weber. But when it became known that Hampden, noted tragedian, respected gentleman, president of The Players, and the finest Cyrano de Bergerac I ever saw, was to play Lew Fields in the old 'hypnotism' sketch, doubts were expressed by the members. There must be a catch in it, they said. He wasn't really going to do it, was he?

"He was, indeed, for he had been put on a spot; his club had asked him to do something and he wasn't the man to refuse. 'Certainly, I'll do it,' he said on the phone from his Ridgefield, Connecticut, home. 'I'm no comedian and I never saw Weber and Fields and I'll be terrible, but I'll do it.'

"The sketch was memorably amusing. . . . First off, they had a conference with a couple of hardened burlesquers, Joey Faye and Mandy Kaye, about what they should do. Joey and Mandy then dictated the script to the Club's astonished secretary. Then the stars had a couple of rehearsals under the . . . direction of Faye and Kaye. The performance was perfect. . . . This was no thing to clown through, even though it was just a bit to be played once for a few friends. Their timing, their Dutch comic accents, were splendid, for they had worked just as hard and intelligently as if they were preparing highly paid roles that might last them a season or more."

These pseudo burlesquers were so hilarious that they upstaged the real veterans of the baggy-pants era who came on—Sidney Fields, Sidney Stone, and Jack Mann. Nevertheless, these reminders of another day performed some oldtime burlesque skits that, as the *Bulletin* reviewer put it, "had everyone in stitches for the better part of two hours."

As a fitting climax to the Forties, Charlie Connolly was honored at the Pipe Night of March 20, 1949, for his fifty years of service to the Club, an event reported in the *Times,* the *Herald Tribune,* and *Newsweek.* A near-record crowd turned out, occupying all the space between the back porch and the reading room. Howard Lindsay asked the club secretary to read the resolution of the board making Charlie an honorary member, and Pipemaster Lodewick Vroom, an old member who had known the honoree longer than anyone else at the Club, read telegrams from various parts of the country. Charlie was celebrated in verse by a sonnet from Percy Mackaye, and verses by Wallace Irwin, read by Leo Carroll. Among the entertainers were Peter Donald, whose character, Ajax Cassidy, on the Fred Allen Show, was by that time familiar to most Americans. Henry Lanier presented Charlie with a gold watch and a purse, while Ray Vir Den gave him a gift from the Dutch Treat Club. There were other tributes as well, to which Charlie responded with a simple, moving speech. Everyone sang "Auld Lang Syne" and repaired below.

A surprise of the evening was the appearance of Norman Anthony, who had never before attended a Pipe Night.

For 1958 the entertainment committee produced both more innovations and an encore. Most memorable was the first Ladies' Pipe Night, of 1958, an historic occasion not repeated. For the first time, Howard Lindsay opened the evening with, "Ladies, fellow Players. . . ." After that, both Cornelia Otis Skinner and her literary partner, Emily Kimbrough, spoke and Martha Wright sang, Dorothy Stickney read from the poems and letters of Edna St. Vincent Millay, and Charlotte Rae, who had recently starred in *Li'l Abner,* also entertained.

Another innovation in 1954 was a Baseball Night on a Sunday evening just before the opening of the season, with Red Smith as Pipemaster. The Yankees were represented by George Weiss and Casey Stengal; Walter Alston, for the Dodgers; and Chub (Charles) Feeney, the Giants. (Dear, dead days!) Al Schact, the clown prince of baseball, represented himself and he was followed by the eminent sportswriter, John Lardner.

An encore, in 1958, was another Jazz Pipe Night, this time with Stan Freeman, Mitch Miller, and for most of the evening, the Errol Garner Trio.

Perhaps the most memorable Pipe Night of this decade came on March 28, 1954, when the honored guest was the celebrated Mary Garden, one of the great sopranos of her day. It was the second time a woman had been so honored; Sarah Bernhardt had been the first. Vincent Sheehan reminded Mary that the Divine Sarah had preceded her, and she answered, "That's all right. Sarah was a friend of mine."

There was much reminiscence on the Mary Garden Night. With Francis Robinson of the Metropolitan as Pipemaster, Hiram Sherman was introduced and recalled the days when he was a spear-carrier at the Chicago Civic Opera, at a time when Miss Garden's *Salome* was closed down by the authorities as an indecent performance through the efforts of the League of Law and Order, whose president said, "I wish Miss Garden would come to see me; I should like to reform her." Olin Downes, music critic of the *Times,* remembered how Mary had enchanted Boston with the exception of its noted critic, Herman Krehbiel. Later, informed of his death, Miss Garden had responded fervently, "One less!"

The forthright singer's response at Pipe Night was a little in the same vein. She told of her musical career, especially her close relationship with Debussy, speaking from notes at first but interrupting herself with so many ad libs that she threw away the notes and continued with an uninhibited recital. "I began at the top, I stayed at the top, and I quit at the top," she concluded triumphantly.

Another musical evening occurred on March 23, 1952, when Caruso was honored posthumously, again with Francis Robinson as Pipemaster. Recordings by the great tenor were played, after which Sol Hurok and Fritz Reiner were asked to take bows. Walter Abel spoke, recalling that he had worked on the same bill with Caruso as a super, for 75 cents a night, while the star was earning $2,500 for every appearance. As a former secretary and close friend of Caruso, Bruno Zirato, manager of the Philharmonic, also spoke.

There were also two posthumous nights for playwrights in the Fifties. Robert E. Sherwood was celebrated by John Mason Brown, Maxwell Anderson, Alfred Lunt, and Raymond Massey, while Eugene O'Neill was honored by Frederic March, Jason Robards, Jr., Frank McHugh, Alan Bunce, William Laurence, Max Wylie, Lanny Ross, and José Quintero.

In the long history of Pipe Nights the premier vintage crop was harvested during the otherwise turbulent Sixties. It was remarkable that this should be so, because by that time the Entertainment Committee had seemingly exhausted every possibility in its efforts to provide at least four such nights every year. There had been nights for sports personalities, newscasters, foreign correspondents, lawyers, musicians, magicians, circus performers, special holidays, and the Irish. Only former child stars and animal actors had been purposefully overlooked.

Yet the Sixties opened with something of a bang during the winter-spring season of 1960–61. At an evening honoring Sean O'Casey, Robert Moses as Pipemaster surprised some members by delivering what could only be described as an intellectual address. O'Casey himself sent a word of grateful appreciation from his home in Torquay, Devon. That was followed by a Shakespeare Pipe Night, with Herbert Ransom as Pipemaster, starring Maurice Evans and Dennis King. Then came a real novelty, a War-Between-the-States Pipe Night, designed to offend no one. Bruce Catton was, quite naturally, the Pipemaster, and he introduced Hamilton Basso, Oscar Brand, and others. A Sports Pipe Night soon after, with Red Barber as Pipemaster, brought Frank Graham, Yankee executives, Toots Shor, Gene Tunney, Kyle Rote, and Howard Cosell, among others—a truly extraordinary mixed bag.

But the highlight of the decade, and for that matter of all Pipe Night history, came on February 10, 1963, when Alfred Lunt and Lynne Fontanne were honored. It was a historic occasion, Lunt had been a Player since 1920; in 1963 he and his acting partner were celebrating their fortieth anniversary, and Miss Fontanne became the third woman in Club history to be honored. With Howard Lindsay as Pipemaster, the guests heard from Sir John Gielgud, Sir Ralph Richardson, and Peter Ustinov, with Marc Connelly and George Burns representing the United States. More than 300 members had applied for admission that night, but only 240 could be accommodated. The others had to be satisfied with a recording of the occasion, an album made especially (and only) for The Players.

In her response, Miss Fontanne disclosed that she had brought The Players a present, Sarah Siddons's reading desk, which is now in the corridor just outside the library.

Not much could have exceeded that evening for sheer excitement at the Club, but a precedent had been set two years before, on November 12, 1961, when a Mark Twain Pipe Night played to a full house. It was the first night to be held in the new dining room, and for the first time the Great Hall and the adjoining rooms were not filled, although they would be for Lunt and Fontanne. Hal Holbrook was scheduled to give his impersonation of "Mark Twain Tonight," which he had been playing across the country but, before he could begin, clouds of acrid smoke billowed out of the bar, where a smoldering chunk of insulation had ignited in the ventilation system. Those who had been having a pre-dinner celebration fled; the firemen arrived and quickly put out the blaze without undue damage. Those who had argued and won, against much opposition, the case for glass doors at the foot of the stairs leading into the grill room were vindicated that night.

When the initial excitement had diminished, Holbrook was coming down from upstairs, where he had been putting on his elaborate makeup and costume, and encountered a fireman on the stairway, on his way to check the vents. The fireman came stumbling back into the grill room. "I just saw where they keep the old ones," he reported to his mates. "They'll never believe me at the station, but I could swear this one looked just like Mark Twain."

Brooks Atkinson, who presided as Pipemaster when order was restored, reported the event two nights later in his *Times* column, "Critic at Large," which carried the headline: "The First Virtue of a Gentleman's Club/Decorum Survives an Ordeal by Fire."

Memorable musical evenings continued in the Sixties and one that no one could forget was Sol Hurok Night, on March 27, 1966, with David Wayne as Pipemaster. Artur Rubinstein was there to honor the impressario, as was Martyn Green, who sang for the guests, with Al Simon at the piano. One of the greatest performances ever heard on a Pipe Night was Gina Bachauer's "The Great Gates of Kiev," greeted by a rising ovation, with Rubinstein first to rise. The climax of the night, however, was Marian Anderson's brief tribute to Hurok, in which she said: "He had difficulty in putting us in places where we knew we would like to go. He never flinched. He used every power in the hands of an impresario. In my hometown he said, 'If you do not take this season, you cannot have the ballet.'" It was an extraordinary Pipe Night, conceived by Avery Fisher and produced by Hal James.

Another packed house greeted Maurice Chevalier on a spring night in 1965. At 77, this ageless singer and actor was near the end of his career (he had been born in the year the Club began), and during the previous season he had been honored at The Dutch Treat Club, where he bowed, sat down, and did not sing. It was to be different at The Players. Introduced by Dennis King, in French, he talked informally about his life, sang in the voice that Paul Hollister joked had "the quality of an elderly but loveable sheep," and even danced. Robert Preston, as Pipemaster, also introduced Alexander Cohen, Chevalier's producer, who spoke briefly, and Al Simon, who played a medley of Chevalier hits. It was, everyone agreed, one of the best Pipe Nights in living memory.

Still another exceptional musical evening occurred on October 6, 1963, as another capacity crowd honored George Gershwin in a most unusual tribute, with Howard Lindsay as Pipemaster. He introduced Deems Taylor, and then Carl Van Vechten, who had been one of Gershwin's earliest professional friends in New York and had written the first article about him. Al Simon, who had been one of the composer's rehearsal pianists, performed a Gershwin overture, followed by Mitch Miller, who had played oboe in the pit orchestra when *Porgy and Bess* opened in Boston.

After Stan Freeman had offered more Gershwin music, Lindsay explained that Vinton Freedley would have given the address of the evening, but was in the hospital with a leg injury. Howard read the speech Freedley would have given, after which Peter Turgeon spoke briefly and sang an obscure Gershwin song, "We're Pals." Mario Braggioti rose and told about visiting Gershwin when he was working on *An American in Paris,* and had a large assortment of French taxi horns on the piano. The composer asked Mario to accompany him on the horns while he played the score. This scene was reenacted with Simon on the horns. Braggioti then sat down at the piano and played his version of "Rhapsody in Blue." Skitch Henderson spoke and introduced Irving Barnes, who had recently sung Porgy in the Soviet Union. Barnes did two of the numbers from the show, with Skitch at the piano.

The regret letter of the evening came from Paul Whiteman, who wrote from his home in New Hope, Pennsylvania, that he could not be present because, ten years previously, he had founded the Duck Shooting Championship of America, an annual event in New Jersey, and was compelled to be present at this. "We shoot all day and have a dinner afterwards," he wrote, and went on: "You can imagine how sorry I feel, for I owe George Gershwin a great debt. It seems kind of funny that I was the famous guy when he wrote "Rhapsody in Blue," and now I kind of bask in its glory. I have been so pleased that I contributed a bit to George's career, for he is the only composer we have ever had in America who successfully transposed jazz into the symphonic medium. As you know, the "Rhapsody" is played by every symphony orchestra in the world at least once a year, including Russia. . . . It is a real disappointment that I can't be with you to honor the man I consider the greatest."

Among the memories of the Sixties no one who was there can forget the night Ringling Brothers Circus came to the Club, on April 26, 1965, with Bill Ballantine as Pipemaster. John Ringling North, a Player himself, could not be present, but he sent his brother Henry as a stand-in, along with other members of his staff. The attractions, of course, included jugglers, acrobats, tales told by the tiger trainer Charley Baumann, and by Manfred Fritsch, a highwire artist. Even the clowns were there. These performers joined members downstairs afterward at the bar, and after a considerable amount of alcohol had been consumed by everyone, a midget broke into tears and bellied up to a member standing near, arriving just above his belt buckle, and began to pound on him, complaining, "The trouble is, nobody understands us." At that some acrobats, erroneously believing their comrade was being ill-used, joined in and it took some time to restore order.

The regret telegram of the decade came from Walter Kerr, who found himself unable to attend a Critics Pipe Night in the autumn of 1962. "Extremely sorry I cannot join you in the beehive tonight," he wrote. "Have been reading Randall Jarrell and he says that critics are like bees, one sting lasts longer than a dozen jars of honey. Please tell my colleagues to watch what they say, and The Players to believe nobody but Brooks Atkinson, who is entirely trustworthy due to his retirement. Have a good time and save me a piece of critic."

Certainly the most unusual Pipemaster (in this case, pipemasters) of the Sixties or any other period presided in 1965 at the Rodgers and Hart Pipe Night, when Kukla, Fran, and Ollie (the puppet voices of Burr Tillstrom, plus Fran Allison) played that role, to everyone's delight. No one who was present can forget how moved Dick Rodgers was that night when the tributes to him seemed to overflow the room.

Perhaps the most unusual Pipe Night of the Sixties, however, was the one given on October 4, 1964, for Rea Irvin, a legendary figure at the Club, as he was at the *New Yorker*, where he had created its first cover, the ineffable Eustace Tilley, and served as its art director. Among the 179 guests that night, there were many, most of them newer members, who had never actually seen Irvin, but it was also true that at the *New Yorker* itself, where mysterious tribal customs prevailed, there were also staff members who had never seen him either. Ogden Nash, one of the evening's speakers, admitted that he had never met Rea until that night. In either case, it was hard to believe. Rea was then celebrating his fiftieth anniversary as a Player.

Mark Connolly, as Pipemaster, read messages of regret from such *New Yorker* stalwarts as Garrett Price, Whitney Darrow, Jr., Peter Arno, and Gluyas Williams, but the magazine's president, Raoul Fleishmann, was present. Ogden Nash spoke of Irvin, as did Ralph Ingersoll, the *New Yorker*'s first managing editor. They were followed by Rube Goldberg, who recalled that he and Rea had been struggling young artists together in San Francisco, before they came East together in the customary search for fame and fortune.

When he rose to acknowledge the tributes, Irvin told one anecdote as memorable as the evening itself. There was a member who had been borrowing small amounts from his fellow Players for a long time, never repaying them. The debtors, consulting among themselves, concluded that someone ought to speak to him. The elected member approached the delinquent and said, "George, don't you think this borrowing has gone rather far?"

"It's a disgrace," George agreed. "But how did I know I was going to live this long?"

On April 12, 1962, an all-star cast saluted the memory of Don Marquis, with Ed Anthony presiding. The saluters included five Johns—Griggs, Alexander, Seymour, Holm, and Call—besides Lindsay, Dennis King, Elliott Nugent, James Rennie, Luis Van Rooten, Homer Croy, Staats Cotsworth, and Charlie Connolly.

The era of the Seventies began briskly with a Pipe Night for Fredric March and his wife, Florence Eldridge, with Arthur Cantor as Pipemaster, on December 6, 1970. John McPherrin, an old school friend, and George Schaefer flew in from the West for the occasion. With the aid of a projector and screen, Bosley Crowther, movie critic of the *Times,* gave the guests a montage of the two honorees in some of their famous past films.

This was followed soon after, on January 31, 1971, with a night for the revival of *No, No, Nanette.* Present from the cast were Ruby Keeler, Jack Gilford, Helen Gallagher, and Patsy Kelly, along with Donald Saddler, who did the choreography, and Vincent Youmans's twin son and daughter, Vincent, Jr., and Ceciley Youmans Collins. Lee Jordan introduced the always-welcome Al Simon, who played an overture of Youmans's songs and accompanied Lanny Ross as he sang more of them. Irving Caesar, the only living member of the team that created the musical, sang the immortal "Tea for Two" with Patsy Kelly, and the evening ended as everyone joined in with "I Want to Be Happy."

There was an aborted attempt to have a Noel Coward Pipe Night in 1971, but the honored guest had to cancel because of a phlebitis attack he was suffering in Montreal. When he recovered, he said, he promised to "get the hell direct to Jamaica and the sun." Meanwhile, he sent The Players a present—a first edition of "Nothing is Lost," No. 34 of an edition of 85 copies printed on a handpress in Harvard Yard by the Lowell-Adams House Printers, and inscribed, "To The Players, with my affectionate best wishes, Noel." This little-known poem of Coward's, issued in 1966, reads:

Deep in our sub-conscious, we are told
Lie all our memories, lie all the notes
Of all the music we have ever heard
And all the phrases those we loved have spoken,
Sorrows and losses time has since consoled,
Family jokes, out-moded anecdotes
Each sentimental souvenir and token
Everything seen, experienced, each word

Addressed to us in infancy, before . . .
Before we could even know or understand
The implications of our wonderland.
There they all are, the legendary lies
The birthday treats, the sights, the sounds, the tears
Forgotten debris of forgotten years
Waiting to be recalled, waiting to rise
Before our world dissolves before our eyes
Waiting for some small, intimate reminder,
A word, a tune, a known familiar scent
An echo from the past when, innocent
We looked upon the present with delight
And doubted not the future would be kinder
And never knew the loneliness of night.

Two years after his 1971 cancellation Coward was finally honored with a Pipe Night in February 1973, but it was an evening overshadowed by sadness. Noel by this time lay gravely ill; he died in April. He knew about the evening, however, and was touched by it. He sent a tape saluting the cast of "Oh! Coward!" a revue then playing uptown, whose three-member cast came down that night on their day off and did the show for The Players. Coward's taped tribute to them said: "Here's to this cast, may they find happiness and a reasonable pride and may their touch on life be as light as a seabird's feather, and may each sorrow politely step aside."

With Donald Seawell as Pipemaster, the Pipe Night without its honoree went ahead, as Max Gordon, who was quite ill himself, spoke of Coward. He had produced *Design For Living*, with the Lunts, who had sent a recording to be played at the occasion. In it, Lynn Fontanne told of giving Coward a bath at a time when he was ill and had asked to have his back rubbed. She went into his bedroom without looking and performed her errand of mercy—"I didn't peek," she said—and it wasn't until she had left the room that she realized she had been wearing nothing under her apron, and was completely nude from the rear.

A few weeks later, having been told about the success of his Pipe Night, Coward sent a grateful message to the Club, the last they would ever hear from him. "Dear Alfred [Drake] . . . dear Don [Seawell] . . . and all dear Players: I do want to thank you, every man jack, for honoring old Coward and his cast of thousands in this way. As one of the 'Pipes,' which Don assures me I am, I feel greatly flattered and I wish with all my heart I could be spending a warm, cozy evening with you. Here in Jamaica it is at the moment raining heavily and is much, much colder than Alaska. I haven't seen my clever and attractive cast since that never-to-be-forgotten night of January 14, so I would like to take this opportunity of telling them that I

A CERTAIN CLUB

think they have made a brilliant job of the cast album. I send them all my congratulations and my fervent hope that it'll make a great deal of money! Once more my thanks to The Players for their hospitality tonight and my affectionate best wishes to you all."

Coward, it should be added, had been made an Honorary Member.

There were other, less spectacular pleasures in 1971—the Danny Kaye Pipe Night, at which Joseph L. Mankiewicz would have been the hit of the evening if Kaye himself had not dazzled everyone by putting on an inimitable show of his own. And there was Pare Lorentz, the film maker and a Player for some time, who spoke about his career before screening his two masterpieces, *The Plough That Broke the Plains* and *The River*.

Still another highlight of the year came on December 17, with the Jack Benny Pipe Night. As the *Bulletin* put it, "From the moment he walked up the nine steps to the Great Hall, he was a smiling player among Players. At President Alfred Drake's reception in the Walter Hampden Memorial Library, Jack Benny sat in friendly converse with, as he said in a later note, 'our own people.' A man near him asked, 'Have you been here before?' Jack replied, 'Never. But this (he waved a hand around the gracious room) is the way I knew it would be.'"

Never a spontaneous comedian, Benny told no jokes that night. Introduced by Isaac Stern, another violinist, as Pipemaster, he recalled experiences from his long career. He remembered how, as a young actor, he admired a monologist named Julius Tannen and followed him around for months, watching his act whenever he played. It was a devoted study with mixed results. When he made his first appearance at a small theater in New York, *Variety's* critic wrote, "Out walked a guy by the name of Jack Benny. Evidently he has seen Julius Tannen. But not often enough."

Before Benny spoke, Joanna Simon, Al Simon's niece and Carly's sister, sang songs from Benny pictures, with her uncle at the piano, and Jesse Block, half of the famous comedy team of Block and Sully, added his tribute. It was an unexpectedly quiet night, but a deeply felt one. Benny was made an honorary member in May 1973. He died a year later.

By contrast, the Milton Berle Pipe Night on November 10, 1974, was as hilarious as anyone could have expected from the master of spontaneous comedy. Introduced by Ben Grauer as Pipemaster, Berle told The Players that he had been made Abbott Emeritus of The Friars, "a position which has the same cachet as being choreographer on the Walter Cronkite News Program." Berle was at his best that night. Everyone present was awash with laughter, and Mrs. Berle, who was present, said later that she hadn't seen her husband so happy in twenty years.

It would have been impossible to top the events of the Sixties and Seventies, so it is not surprising that nothing has occurred to surpass them. But there have been a few memorable occasions, nonetheless, beginning with the Max Gordon Pipe Night in 1970, at which Dennis King announced his retirement as president, and Pipemaster Brooks Atkinson introduced Alfred Drake as his successor. Gordon was saluted with a barrage of hits from his productions, sung by Nancy Dussault, Melissa Hart, Hal Linden, and Stanley Grover, with Harold Rome and Al Simon at the pianos. But it was Melville Cooper who stopped the show with "Me and Marie," a song he had sung in one of Max's productions 35 years before.

There was, too, the Kurt Weill Pipe Night of 1973, at which Josh Logan was Pipemaster, and Alfred Drake disclosed that Josh, who had been a member since 1935, was attending his first Pipe Night. Logan responded that being Pipemaster was the best way to start. He sang "September Song" himself, and introduced the other stars of the evening—Jack Gilford, Will Holt, Dolly Jonah, Robert Rounseville, and the cast of *From Berlin to Broadway*, along with the conductors Jay Blackton and Lehman Engel. Lotte Lenya closed the evening with a perceptive and moving tribute to Weill.

Rex Harrison's Pipe Night in May 1975 drew one of the largest audiences in the history of the Club, with Martin Gabel as Pipemaster, and another capacity audience greeted Alfred Drake in January 1979, when he was honored with Walter Kerr as Pipemaster. On this occasion, Everett Raymond Kinstler's portrait of Drake was unveiled. Of it, Alfred said: "To ask an artist to reach back nearly a quarter of a century and recreate a character as then played by an actor whose only relationship with Dorian Gray is the presently predominating color of his hair, is a most unreasonable request. Yet it is not beyond the imagination and powers of Ray Kinstler."

The final decade of The Players' first century is still too new to be memorable, but at the beginning, it had already produced one occasion sure to be on the list of remembered Pipe Nights, when the next one is compiled. In September 1981, Al Simon was given an honoring which many thought had been too long delayed. Michael Price, director of the Goodspeed Opera House, was Pipemaster, and among those paying tribute were Arthur Schwartz, Frances Gershwin Godowsky, and Al's niece, Joanna.

Whatever Pipe Nights have followed, Players will not only remember the splendid entertainments in the dining room, but the long and pleasant evenings that have always followed them below stairs, where the traditional fellowship of the Club is forever celebrated.

CHAPTER 16

They Were All Players

IN HIS FOUNDER'S NIGHT ADDRESS OF 1980, ROGER BRYANT HUNTING observed that the history of The Players is anecdotes and reminiscences, and as the preceding pages have amply demonstrated, he was right. At the same time, however, that history is not merely a record of idle remembrance. It is the story of how more than four thousand men have remained faithful to an ideal for a century.

What kind of men are capable of such a rare thing? We have met many of them in previous chapters, but there is a need to explore further, to find a better definition of what Players have meant to their Club, and even more important, what the Club has meant to them. From time to time, one member or another has been cited by admirers as "the greatest Player of them all," meaning those who have contributed most to the Club, and to whom the Club has been a way of life. Oddly enough, none of these candidates has been a celebrity.

That fact doesn't denigrate the famous, but rather underlines what The Players has meant to those most devoted to its spirit, and emphasizes how truly democratic the Club has always been, as Booth intended.

Let us walk now through a gallery of Players, representative of all the others, and see what kind of people we have been these past hundred years. A good place to begin might be John S. Phillips, one of Sam

McClure's most noted editors, who has been quoted before and will be again—a prime candidate by many previous members for "greatest Player." It was Phillips who made that Founder's Night address in 1931 which is still considered the best of a distinguished lot. At that moment the oldest member was Freeman Tilden, who joined in 1916, but there were also such relatively new ones as Frank McHugh, who came in 1927, and John Davenport Seymour, a 1924 arrival. McHugh had already acquired the happy reputation he held for years as a man who could be guaranteed, whenever he appeared in the grill, to regale everyone with stories about his family troupe, and about the Hollywood, New York, and London stages.

Among the "old crowd" of earlier days, one of those who exemplified Phillips' definition of Club spirit was Ed McNamara, a former Paterson, New Jersey, cop who had been Caruso's only pupil, and who often filled the grill room with his rich Irish baritone. He joined the Club in 1928. The handsome mahogany counter on the bar was the gift of his friends, given in his memory. There is no inscription; for years it was known simply as "Mac's Bar." McNamara and three of his friends—Jimmy Cagney, Clarence Budington Kelland, and Ray Vir Den—kept a summer place at Martha's Vineyard which they called "The Crab's Nest," well known on the Island for its superb cuisine and loud conversations. When McNamara died he was buried in the cemetery at West Tisbury, near his summer place.

Another great entertainer in the bar was Charles Hanson Towne, who had enjoyed a remarkable career as both actor and writer. Whenever he entered the grill, everyone present would greet him with a shout of "Charrrrlles Hannnnnsssoon Townnnnnnnn," followed by a round of applause. Peter Turgeon, a pillar of the Club for years, recalled meeting Towne when, as a very young actor, he was appearing in the third company of *Life With Father,* in which Towne played the Reverend Dr. Lloyd. At the first rehearsal Peter thought Towne must be the real thing— an old character actor, who must have appeared with the greats of his time. Towne disillusioned him; it was his professional debut, he said, although he had once played Ben Franklin in a Dutch Treat Club show.

In his other life as editor, poet, and author, Charlie Towne had come to know more celebrities than the young Turgeon had even read about, and as the tour progressed, he demonstrated that fact with every stop. He introduced Peter and other cast members to Booth Tarkington, Mary Roberts Rinehart, Fritzi Scheff, and Governor Saltonstall of Massachusetts, all with equal aplomb. In Richmond he had tea with Ellen Glasgow. In Asheville he called on Thomas Wolfe's mother. In Emporia, Kansas, his old friend William Allen White welcomed him and the cast. While the

THE GREAT HALL, sometimes called
The Lounge or just "Upstairs" by members,
shows the latest renovations.

THE DINING ROOM,
known also as The
Howard Lindsay
Room.

YOU SHALL NOT BUDGE YOU GO NOT TILL I SET YOU UP A GLAS

THE GRILL ROOM, with
words of caution
behind the bar.

CARD ROOM TABLE, attributed to Mark Twain. The Card Room is where new members are interviewed by the Admissions Committee; sometimes the scene of private parties.

THE POOL TABLE in the Grill Room, with members' personal cues hanging in racks on the wall.

THE LIBRARY today. Photographs under glass on the table are of celebrated actresses of the past.

show ran in Hollywood, Charlie Chaplin came for tea and crumpets. Everywhere there was scarcely a performance at which some celebrated personage failed to come around to see Towne.

As an actor, Charlie almost failed to survive at the beginning of the tour. On opening night in Baltimore he went sky high in his lines, shocking his friends Dorothy Gish and Louis Calhern, who were present. Afterward, Howard Lindsay assured him that two members of the second company had done the same thing, and in the same theater. Charlie promised to do better, and in fact never blew another line while the tour lasted. It ended when the Second World War broke up the cast. It was Towne and Calhern who later brought Turgeon into the Club.

An early member of the Club who probably knew even more celebrities than Charlie Towne was Isaac Marcosson, who traveled the globe for the *Saturday Evening Post*, interviewing the famous and near-famous. If it was Horace Greeley who invented the interview, Marcosson perfected it. In 1906 he was the first reporter to interview the Standard Oil Company's hitherto inaccessible president, John Archbold.

Writing of Ike in his *Sketch Book*, Walter Oettel observed: "In his habits of dress, he reminds me of John Drew. His gay striped and figured shirts, with matching ties, have become a mark of individuality that never escaped interviewers. Employees of the Club have learned to recognize the staccato tap of his bell in the dining room." (By "interviewers," Walter meant that Marcosson had become such a notable figure himself that *he* was the subject of interviews.) Ike's life at the Club was a long one. Joining in 1907, he was a regular member of the Round Table for nearly sixty years, when he wasn't somewhere else in the world.

Marcosson recalled the day he entered the grill room for the first time and looked around. At the Round Table were Grover Cleveland, Mark Twain, Saint-Gaudens, Aldrich, and Sargent. At an adjoining table sat John Drew, George Arliss, and E. H. Sothern. Not far away was Childe Hassam, and in a few moments Augustus Thomas arrived with his guest, David Belasco, in tow. But in time it was Marcosson who occupied a high place at the table, bringing with him as guests such people as Lord Northcliffe, General Goethals, and others. By then he was a celebrity among celebrities. Drew and Otis Skinner were particular friends, and when Skinner's wife had a daughter, Ike proposed to her at once and was accepted. Thus, in a way, he was still engaged to Cornelia Otis Skinner for a large part of his life.

Marcosson created his own persona, so that in November of 1952 he could tell the Round Table grandly (with tongue firmly in cheek), "Just for today, gentlemen, you may call me Ike." Even more, he liked to be called Marco, for that other great world traveler. When he wasn't at the Club or traveling, Ike worked at his trade, writing, and turned out thirty books in addition to his numerous articles for the *Post*. He thought of himself as a reporter, and he was one of the best.

Since he did not marry until late in life, he was a habitué of the Club whenever he was in town, both at lunch and when it was crowded after dark. As the autocrat of the Round Table, he sat in the armchair inherited from William A. Mackay, and if he got carried away, pounding the table, he was likely to be restrained gently by Bill Tachau or his publisher, Frank Dodd. Always elegantly tailored in his Savile Row suits, Ike eventually abandoned the eye-stopping Charvet shirts that prompted Lord Northcliffe to call him *le Roi de Chemise*. At home the walls of his Gracie Square study were lined with autographed pictures, mostly of friends: Theodore Roosevelt, J. M. Barrie, General Christian Smuts, Herbert Hoover, Frank Norris, Walter Hines Page, Kemal Ataturk, Lloyd George, and a galaxy of other famous names. The world was his village.

Marcosson frequented the Club for so many years, bridging several generations, that he became a legendary figure. One writer who had discussed his exploits in a biography of George Horace Lorimer (it was, in fact, the author of this volume) had assumed in the late forties that Ike was dead, and had been assured of it by some former associates. But one day a dapper, sprightly figure appeared at his table in the dining room and introduced himself: "I'm Ike Marcosson," he said. "You thought I was dead." Not only was he still alive, but had only recently served as a lieutenant-commander in the Navy during the war, during which he also worked for the British in M1.5.

The impact of such celebrities as Ike and his friends on less well-known members was often devastating to new members, both in the early days and later. Henry Hering, a young sculptor who joined in 1908 and remained a member for forty years until he died at 75, remembered well his first visit to the Club as a guest. Escorted out to the porch, he saw Twain, White, and other notable figures sitting at the Round Table. To his astonishment, he was invited to sit with them. "If anyone had suggested then that I would one day be a Player myself, I'd have said they were nuts," he wrote later. But he became notable in his own right, executing (among other commissions) the statue of Parnell in Dublin, done from a drawing in *Punch*. Of Hering, one of his fellow Players said: "He has the roughest exterior and the gentlest interior of any man in the club."

The camaraderie of Players could survive even those who appeared least likely to succeed as members. That was the case with Richard Harding Davis, apotheosis of foreign correspondents in his time, who became a member in 1891. Davis was not only burdened with an oversized ego, but he was a man of formidable insensitivity. He committed what could have been the gaffe of the century when, after his election, he proudly presented a gift to Booth for the Club. It was a collector's item: A handbill from Ford's Theater on the night Lincoln was shot. Booth stared down at it, recognizing it at once, turned away and said nothing. The gift was never accepted.

Nevertheless, Davis was a member in good standing and in time became a part of Club folklore. In his ever fruitful *Sketch Book,* Walter tells of the time Davis reserved the private dining room for the fifteenth of a certain month, explaining that he would be out of town for ten or fifteen days and wanted to be sure that a dinner he had planned would be ready on that date. As usual, he left the arrangements to Walter.

At 7 p.m. on the fifteenth, the guests arrived and gathered in the library, then serving as a reception room for private dinner parties, as it would be later for honored guests at Pipe Nights. Time passed and the host did not appear. After a half-hour Walter went ahead and served the customary preliminaries, after which he called Davis's house and was told that he had left early in the evening. Calls to other clubs produced no trace of him, however, and at 8 Walter quietly urged the guests to sit down and have dinner. The guests didn't seem to mind. They were already making bets as to whether their host would show up at all.

It was 11 o'clock and the party was nearly over when Walter got a call from Davis, who admitted he had forgotten all about the affair and promised to come right down and explain. Greeted with cheers when he arrived, he apologized and offered an excuse too original to have been manufactured.

He had entered an elevated train at Franklin Square, he said, finding it so crowded he had to stand. After the train left the station, Davis noticed that the man sitting directly below him was a friend, one of the Harper brothers, William, reading a newspaper intently, with the pages spread wide, close to his face. Turning his head away a little, Davis stepped gently on one of his feet. William responded with a firm push at Davis's leg as he kept reading, but when the pressure was applied again, he emitted a low rumble of abuse.

At that, Davis pulled down the paper and returned the compliment. William took in the situation at once, but decided to go along with the joke. Further words were exchanged, and soon the car was in an uproar as people took sides in the presumed quarrel. The two challenged each other to fight, and began to get out at 28th Street. As Davis told it: "I shouted to the guard to make room for us. Everybody moved aside without being requested. When the train finally stopped, I offered my arm to Billy Harper. We walked out, arm in arm, and on reaching the platform, we raised our hats and bowed to the crowd. Amid clapping and cheering, we left the platform, but instead of going home I went with Billy to his club."

On another evening Davis again ordered a private dinner for friends on a certain date, but this time he told Walter it would be completely informal, "no flowers, menu, or cards, just a good dinner." Before the guests were called in that night, Davis slipped into the dining room to see if everything was ready. "The table looks empty," he said to Walter, "let's get something for the center." Walter reminded him that he had requested informality. "Well, that's so," Davis said, "but why don't we have the large silver punch bowl? It'll be just right." By the time Walter brought it, the host had lettered a sign to stand against it: "This is the identical bowl for the American Beauty roses I didn't get."

Arthur Brisbane was one of Davis's most intimate friends and they often sat together with other cronies until late at night, telling stories. Sitting in the bay window one evening, they began to talk about the guard mount at the entrance of St. James's Palace. These guards were mounted at all times, Brisbane insisted, while Davis argued just as insistently that they were not. As they went on quarreling about it, the others at the table drifted away until they were the only two remaining in the room. Their voices rose and the argument became so heated that one challenged the other to a duel—or so Walter, who heard it all, remembered later, although he found it hard to believe they meant it. In any case, he decided it would be best to cast himself as mediator to preserve the Club's dignity. Walter himself had lived in London, and knew that both men were right; guards were sometimes on horseback but dismounted at other times.

There was no violence that night. Walter wrote an unsigned letter to both, offering his information, and believing it would carry more weight if they did not know who sent it. The matter was not raised again, and in his memoirs Walter wrote that he believed he might have saved one of their lives, but tactfully refrained from saying which one he thought worth saving.

There are numerous stories about Players' devotion to their Club, but one of the most touching must certainly be the tale of William H. Bliss's luncheon. Bliss, a distinguished lawyer, had been ill for a long time, but although family and friends did their best to keep him in bed he was determined to go to the Club, where he had been one of the earliest Round Table members.

One afternoon Bliss told his wife that he must have lunch at the Club next day, even though his doctors had strictly forbidden him to leave his upstairs bedroom. Humoring him, his wife said nothing, but she called Walter and invited him to come to the house that night without her husband's knowledge. When he arrived, they planned a surprise luncheon for Bliss next day. Hurriedly inviting eleven members of the Round Table next morning, Walter hired a truck to bring the table itself, complete with chairs, linens, silverware, crockery, and glassware, to Bliss's house.

At 1 o'clock, Walter knocked on the stricken man's bedroom door. Seeing him, Bliss said, smiling, "You've come for me? How thoughtful of you. I was hoping I'd feel strong enough to make it alone." With the aid of a secretary, Walter helped Bliss to the elevator of his large house. They descended to the first floor and stepped into the dining room. Bliss could scarcely believe what he saw, as eleven men rose and greeted him. With tears on his cheeks, he walked around the table, shaking hands, and then sat down to the familiar menu cards, the food he had wanted to eat for so long, his favorite champagne—and above everything else, the conversation of his friends.

On the list of "greatest Players," the man most often cited by his fellow members was Bill Tachau, whose renovation exploits have been recounted earlier. Tachau became a member in 1906, the year Harry Thaw shot Stanford White, and when he died on December 28, 1968, he had established a record as the Player who had been a member longer than anyone else in Club history. He was the only one who had seen both worlds, past and present, and all that lay between. When he joined, the Club was almost in the center of the theatrical district; the farthest uptown theaters were on 30th Street. At No. 16, the peak hour of the week was Saturday after the final night curtain. In those days the Club had a large staff: two telephone boys, two at the desk, a doorman and two assistants, besides all the other necessary clerical personnel and kitchen staff.

Bill never married, apparently because no woman could really compete with his two great loves: Paris, where he lived for five years; and The Players. In this country he never lived beyond easy walking distance from the Club. In his chosen field, architecture, he made a considerable reputation, designing the Central Park band shell, later a landmark and the home of both the Naumberg concerts and the Goldman Band; and also synagogues, pavilions, hosptials, and armories. But The Players was his home, and in time his chief workplace as well.

A tall, spare, elegant man, always courteous and attentive, his voice quiet and his gaze dispassionate, Bill was the quintessential Player. He served on the board for twenty-eight years, with only a single brief interruption, and from 1932 to 1941 he was chairman of the house committee, a longer time than anyone had ever borne that particular burden, and his service on it was spectacular, as we've seen.

When he assumed that position, the staff was overloaded, the house falling apart, the budget in trouble, and the food was the worst in town, by general agreement. Calling in a professional advisory team, Tachau proceeded to shake up the place. He tried to fire the entire kitchen staff, but he was opposed by a long list of members who signed a petition insisting that a certain cook not be removed. Bill waited until he could insinuate the fact that all the dishes these same members were complaining about were the product of that chef. After this revelation, ejection was swift and the dining room was crowded every evening.

As for the budget, Tachau and his committee turned the tide by writing off bad debts and bringing back delinquent members in large numbers by putting them on a cash-paying basis. The renovations he made in the clubhouse added more to the Club's beauty and convenience than anyone except White himself had accomplished.

Tachau's work as an architect can still be seen in various parts of the New York landscape—besides the Central Park shell, first of its kind in America; three pavilions at the Central Islip Hospital for Mental Diseases; the Squadron C. Armory in Brooklyn; four other armories—but his masterpiece was the Club. Not only was it his real home, it became the most important part of his life.

A favorite Club story is how he left one freezing winter night with Charles Hanson Towne, and as they neared Fourth Avenue, Towne fell down in the snow and ice. Since he weighed nearly 275 pounds, Bill knew it would be impossible to raise him.

Charley announced he would scream for help, and did just that, so loudly it woke up the neighborhood and produced two policemen, who misunderstood and tried to arrest Bill for robbery. They took both men back to the Club to get matters straightened out and were greeted there by late pool and card players. A spontaneous celebration, including the officers, broke out. Much later, when the two started out again, Towne fell on the same ice patch. This time he was raised without further incident.

In the twilight of his life Bill looked back on a long career at No. 16, and said: "The greatest change I've seen in my day is the emancipation of women—taking the men away, wanting in themselves. It was more of a change than the ones caused by the Depression, Hollywood, the radio, and television all put together. They were even responsible for changing the paint on the walls; they didn't like it so dark."

When he died, Bill Tachau bequeathed $3,000 to the Club, and a head of himself done by Edmond T. Quinn, who had done Booth's statue in the Park, for which Tachau had designed the base.

While it could well be argued that Tachau was the greatest Player, Bill himself would have been inclined to nominate John Phillips, or perhaps Francis Wilson, who might have been president if it hadn't been for his naturally reserved manner. Wilson was responsible for starting the Club's long series of revivals, which did so much to insure its survival in the

Twenties and Thirties, and he also raised the money for the Booth statue. Another possible candidate, in Tachau's opinion, was Otis Skinner, another man who might have been president if he had not been identified with the producers when Actors' Equity was being formed.

Skinner's life with the Club was almost as long as Tachau's. When he died on January 6, 1942, he had been a member for fifty-two years and vice-president since 1927. In the days when John Drew was president and was often unable to attend on Founder's Night, Skinner had presided, and over the years had probably served on more committees than any other member. After his retirement he was able to spend more time than ever at No. 16, and seemed happiest when he was there.

A few weeks before he died, younger members listened in awe when he presided at the ceremony on Booth's birthday and recalled the man who had been his friend and early patron. Only a month before his death he had presided at the regular meeting of the board of directors in Hampden's absence. It was his last day at the Club. From there he went to the Plymouth Theatre, where he was scheduled to speak between acts of *The Wookey,* for an Actors' Fund benefit. He collapsed there and was taken home; he died a month later. After his death, Cornelia told the Club that her father, barely conscious, knew it was Founder's Night and regretted he had to miss it.

As a veteran committeeman, Skinner knew that to serve on the house committee required special qualities of willingness and tact, as well as knowledge. Those qualities were exemplified in Harry Watson, who served as chairman of that committee for three years in the Thirties. As an artist, Watson worked mostly in the outdoors, but he gave almost his entire time to the great refurbishing that he helped create during his tenure. His devotion was fanatical, rewarded with a dinner and a gold cigarette case. So well did he perform that not even the most seemingly outrageous act of his was enough to alienate his fellow committee members, or the board itself. Both a popular and a modest dictator, he had everything ready on time for Ladies' Day, but did not linger. "I'm no ladies' man," he said.

There were also those who served intellectually, particularly two eminent scholars, Brander Matthews and Clayton Hamilton. Matthews, last survivor of the sixteen incorporators, died on Easter Sunday, 1929, at 77, and his death marked the end of the Club's first era. When his funeral took place at St. Paul's Chapel, Columbia, the university he had served with such distinction, the pallbearers included three Players—Hampden, Hamilton, and Quinn, whose bust of Matthews had been unveiled at the university earlier. Matthews had been feeble in his later days, but managed to totter into the clubhouse once a week for lunch. His old friend, John

MacDonald, would whisper to arriving members on those occasions, "Mr. Matthews is here today." Everyone who could manage to sit or stand within listening distance would strain to hear those Matthews tales which might begin, "John Hay once told me," or "Have you heard what Colonel Roosevelt retorted when," or "When I said so-and-so to Coquelin, he laughed and answered," or "That's the one time I ever had a laugh on Walter Page."

Clayton Hamilton, noted as critic and writer, lived on after his friend until 1946. He had been a member since 1903. It was not only his intellect that made him so admired, but his extraordinary capacity for friendship; he gave of himself and what he had well beyond what anyone might expect. A. E. Thomas recalled meeting him at the Club entrance one day, looking distraught. Thomas asked him what was wrong, and Hamilton replied, "Nothing, but my friend Mike's going to have another baby, and I don't quite see how I can afford it." He was another Player who was at the Club almost until the hour of his death, playing bridge there only a few hours before he died.

Another early member who survived, noted for his devotion to the Club, was the artist Frederic Dorr Steele, who has appeared frequently in these pages. A member since 1905, he died in 1944, and it was as though a light had gone out in the Club. Like so many other Players, his life outside No. 16 had been highly successful. He was one of those artists who flourished in what has been called "The Golden Age of Illustration," when the best magazines carried his work. At the Club he was not only editor of the *Bulletin* for several years, but for a long time was wheelhorse of the pool committee, in which he boasted that he had served as "recorder, grand marshal, reminder, shock absorber, official defaulter, and handicapper for thirteen years." And yet, he added, "I escaped with a reasonably whole skin."

Rollin Kirby, whom Steele brought into the Club in 1912, wrote after Freddie's death of his friend's "noiseless entrance into the billiard room and the engaging little smile and almost apologetic 'hello' with which he responded to the greetings shouted at him. No one ever had fewer animosities than he. It is probable there were members who irked him, but I do not recall ever having heard any word of criticism fall from his lips. No one was ever less of an extrovert. But beneath this reticence lay a deep sympathy for and an understanding of the vagaries of that queer collection of fish known as The Players."

Not all the long-time members of the Club were as well known. Ben Roeder, for example, was the fifth oldest living member when he died in May 1943, having been a member since March 1892, more than 51 years. Roeder was so modest a man that when he first came in to pay his initiation fee and dues, he had to walk twice around the block before he dared to enter. He had been in the theater from the time he graduated from City College until his death, first with Daniel Frohman at the old Lyceum, then as assistant to Belasco for nearly a half-century. At his funeral, Channing Pollack recalled that he had been responsible for the theatrical and operatic career of *Madame Butterfly*.

Every year Roeder had gathered a group of his schoolmates for a private dinner at the Club, the last one of which was held only a month before his death, with seven survivors present. Like Tachau, he had only two loves in his life: the theater and The Players.

A living memory of the Founder was Sydney Barton Booth, Junius's son and Edwin's nephew, who had been on the stage for more than forty years, playing with such great names as Maude Adams, Lillian Russell, Jane Cowl, Grace George, and Alice Brady. Booth had been living in Connecticut for years when he died in 1937, but he was almost always present at the Club for Ladies' Day, knowing that the guests were charmed to be introduced to an actual Booth. At least twice on Founder's Night he read his uncle's presentation speech, and in 1934 he gave the memorial address.

Another reminder of the Founder was Edwin Booth Grossmann, Booth's only grandson, an artist who was elected in 1908 when he was only 21, and who died in February 1957. Grossmann was one of a remarkable group who came into the Club in the years just before and just after the turn of the century. There was, for example, Edward Hewitt, a grandson of Peter Cooper and the son of Mayor Abram Hewitt, who was elected in 1891. Ed Hewitt lived in his own house at 48 Gramercy Park North in 1900, and he was still living there in the late Fifties. Other notable New Yorkers who became Players in the 1890s were Nelson Macy (1895), Julius Steger (1898), and Burton Holmes (1899).

Hewitt himself had a most unusual career. At the time he joined the Club, he was working with Hiram Maxim on a design for a steam-powered flying machine, and later he developed an automobile which he manufactured in England. It was an engine of his design that powered the famous Mack truck, and in his home laboratory, Hewitt developed oils and varnishes that the Metropolitan Museum used for its art treasures. His active mind explored in every direction. Hewitt experimented with vitamins and other nutrients, and at seventy he was involved with fish-breeding experiments in his Catskills hideaway. When he died at 90 he was sure that he had just developed a new process of fertilization that would so greatly increase the protein value of forage crops that it would revolutionize the agricultural world. His autobiography was called, audaciously, *Days from Seventy-five to Ninety*.

In 1943 Hewitt delivered the Founder's Night address, and came to the Club whenever he could. In the summer of the year before he died, he arrived in New York for the centennial celebration of Cooper Union and had breakfast at the Club. Of that occasion, the *Bulletin* reported: "He had a kinetic quality about him, a rambunctiousness, even irascibility. At breakfast that day, he didn't want cereal, or eggs, but a lamb chop. It was unprecedented, but he got it, and ate it."

An all but forgotten early member of the Club is Thuré de Thulstrup, known to everyone as Thully, who joined in 1897 and died in 1930. He was one of the best American illustrators of the nineteenth century's last quarter; his work in *Harper's* alone demonstrated his remarkable versatility. He was best at news events and military illustrations, having been a soldier in his native Sweden. Thully's life had been more adventurous than most of his fellow Players. He had been an art student in Paris, and fought with the Foreign Legion in 1870, but in his last year his home, as it was for so many others of his generation, was The Players.

The devotion of these early members can be measured in a bizarre way by the number of them who either died in the Club (four) or were in it almost until the last hour. One of these was the writer Samuel Merwin, who died in October 1936. Four years earlier, at the depth of the Depression, Sam had been in deep trouble, even though he was accustomed to getting as much as $2,500 for one of his *Saturday Evening Post* stories. A fellow Player, hearing of his plight, offered him a small amount for a short history of the Club. Merwin accepted, and produced not a history but a charming word picture which he called "My Favorite Club." His love for it was evident on every page. Sam survived his troubles, and by 1935 had succeeded in getting a contract for a motion picture script. To celebrate, he came with a friend to the Club for dinner, and died suddenly, sitting in his chair at the table—happy in his favorite place, as he would have wished.

Rea Irvin survived his celebrated Pipe Night in 1964 for eight more happy years. When he died on May 28, 1972, at 90, he had been a member since 1914, and was nearly the last of that witty crew which had so illuminated No. 16 in the Twenties and Thirties. That was evident when James Nelson prepared a tribute for the *Bulletin,* and looked about for other crew members as contributors. E. B. White, S. J. Perelman, and Frank Sullivan were the only ones he could find. All of them agreed that Rea was "the essence and spirit of what a great Player should be."

Nelson recalled that when he was organizing the Pipe Night for Rea, he drove up to Irvin's house in Newtown, Connecticut, and sat talking with his old friend while he and his wife finished packing for a trip to their place in Frederikstad, St. Croix, where he eventually died. Rea was in a reminiscent mood. He remembered that after Harold Ross's death, he and his wife considered buying the editor's house, but instead discussed it with friends, who eventually bought the place. After they moved in they found a small iron safe tucked away in the attic. Opening it, they discovered a large envelope with a substantial amount of cash in it. Ross had written on the outside: "Get-away money."

Two Rea Irvin originals hang in the bar today as reminders of his presence: "Tomato Surprise," and "The Gentlemen of the Harem Entertain the Sultana."

Howard Lindsay's candidate for "most beloved" if not "best" Player was Charles Coburn, who joined the Club in 1910 and died in 1961. He might even have been its president if his acting career had not taken him to Hollywood. When Otis Skinner's death left the vice-presidency open, the constitution was changed to provide for two vice-presidents. Lindsay was elected first vice-president, Coburn second, but many in the Club believed that if Coburn had lived in the East he would have succeeded Skinner, and when Walter Hampden resigned later, would have been the unanimous choice for fifth president.

Having made his debut in New York in 1901, Coburn lived there until his wife died, except for touring across the country with her in Shakespeare plays. After her death he moved to Hollywood and began a second, even more successful career, but for him it was always exile. His heart was in the New York theater—and at The Players—which led him to establish the West Room.

At the Club, Coburn could, and did, indulge his passion for games of chance, whatever they might be—backgammon, pool, bridge, or poker. He was so addicted that on trips East, in his seventies, he demonstrated his well-known ability to play all night. Coburn could do that because he had the ability to take quick catnaps, particularly when he was dummy, but sometimes even when the cards were being dealt. When he took a quick look at a poker hand and saw that there was no hope, he threw it in and slept until someone woke him up to deal, or to pick up the next hand. "He was such fun to play with," Lindsay said, remembering those games.

Often in Players' self-portraits there are remembrances of how they were overawed by the Club and its prestigious members at first, until they understood its special camaraderie. For some it took longer than others. The writer Martin Flavin recalled that it was years before he felt at home, a non-actor stranger among people of the theater. He often came for lunch or dinner and sat alone in those years, seeing men around him whom he knew by name or sight, but he could not bring himself to intrude. There would be nothing more than a nod or a smile of greeting. But then one night the beginnings of a transformation occurred, as Flavin later related:

"I remember one such summer night when I sat alone at a table on the porch and two men were sitting at a table near me talking of the theater and having a good time. One of them stood up at last and came over to me. I think it was George Middleton. It would be like George to do it; and I think that his companion was John Emerson, of Equity. Anyway, George introduced himself, chatting for a moment, suggesting finally that if I were alone perhaps I'd care to join them. I did so gratefully, flattered and elated.

"John Drew was president then. I remember seeing him at the big round table in the window which was out of bounds for me. I don't remember that I ever met him or that I could then dream that I would come one day to occupy a seat at that table myself. But bit by bit, The Players came to be my home and its people to be my people."

One of those who could have given Flavin more self-confidence, and no doubt did, was Dave McKinlay, celebrated earlier in these pages. Not only was he a major help in getting the Club through a major financial crisis, and had much to do with the continuing renovation process, but he was a master at breaking down stiffness and self-consciousness. A big, husky man, he hated pretense and humbug of every variety.

When he died in 1949, at 80, it took the *Bulletin* six pages to recount the story of his life and works, the longest of these tributes it had ever printed. Dave had worked on the business side of *McClure's* as business manager until his fellow Player, John S. Phillips, invited him to take the same position in a new company that would publish the *American Magazine*. When this publication was sold to Crowell-Collier, Dave started his own mail-order bookselling business, D. A. McKinlay & Co. Later he was vice-president of William Morrow, and also held a partnership in a grain and lumber business in Lincoln, Illinois, before he retired in 1938. An extremely active Player for 33 years, Dave spent his last years in Tucson, where he missed the Club dreadfully and wrote long characteristic letters to his friends at No. 16.

We have seen earlier the energetic figure of Jacob "Jac" Wendell, Jr., and heard his quick repartee and the story behind that mysterious silver plaque affixed to a panel over the bar, bearing the single word, "Egan," commemorating Jac's famous story which no one can remember. He is yet another Player considered "best loved" at the Club in his time. His memory was still green forty years after his death in 1911, and the reaction to that event by his fellow members was extraordinary.

On the April morning when the black-bordered white card appeared on the bulletin board virtually no one sat down to lunch in the Club that day, by unspoken consent, and for two days afterward the pool table remained covered in silent tribute. On the day of his funeral, for the first time in its history the Club stood open but completely deserted for an hour and a half. Even the staff attended services in Calvary Church, where Jac had sung in the choir since he was a boy. The mourners numbered everyone from John Drew to Jac's brother Everett, also an old member of the Club. The church had reserved 62 seats for Club employees, and not one was empty.

During the next four decades a gradually diminishing group of Jac's friends met every year on the Sunday nearest to the anniversary of his death, and made a pilgrimage to his grave.

Another Player long remembered was Francis Byrne, whom John King described as "one of the finest, kindest, most liberal and best-loved men who ever graced our membership." He left two artifacts behind him—a silver water pitcher on the bar, bearing the inscription "To Frank," and the Byrne-Adams Bedroom, better known in its day as The Penthouse, and even earlier as the Club laundry. This bedroom was built and furnished by the friends of Byrne and John Wolcott Adams, most of them actors and artists.

Byrne was one of the four who died at the Club, but it was an accidental death. Tripping on the stairs leading down to the cloakroom, he fell head first and fractured his skull on the marble floor at the entrance. Taken upstairs to a bedroom, he died there next day without regaining consciousness. Other members regarded him as the Club's softest touch. If he didn't have the money in his pocket, he would find a way to get it. And as the *Bulletin* said of him, "His love of The Players amounted to a passion."

A familiar figure in the Club for years was Ray Vir Den, another Player who contributed a great deal of time, effort, and even his own money to making No. 16 both solvent and beautiful. His life outside the Club was spectacular. Growing up in Indian territory, in what was to be Oklahoma, he came to New York in the 1890s and began an operatic career, during which he married the noted soprano, Madame Frances Alda. Then, in an abrupt reversal, he quit the opera and went first to a job in Wall Street, then to the advertising firm of Lennen and Mitchell, where he became president in 1947.

Leaving the agency in 1952 when he was 56, he married again a year later, for the second time. His new wife was a Roman lady, Lucille Mara de Vescovi, a close friend of his late first wife, who is now known to wearers of fine ties as Countess Mara. For a time, Vir Den shuttled between America and Italy, making fourteen trips in the space of a few months, but in the summer of 1955 he bought a villa in Florence, meanwhile starting an entire new career as publisher of the Rome *Daily American*. He planned to come to rest at last in his Florentine villa, but died only a few months after he had moved into it.

A contemporary of Vir Den was Henry Lanier, a brilliant man of letters who was, like Ray and so many others, actively concerned with the Club. Joining in 1909, he became Club secretary for years and was editor of The Players Book of 1938, meanwhile helping extensively with the work of the library. Later, however, he underwent some sort of change and became a recluse on the fringe of his convivial fellow members. He lived at the Club in those years, and could be found every day in the wing chair just inside the entrance of the reading room, where he occupied his time with whodunits and generally meretricious literature. He seldom spoke to anyone, even when Ike Marcosson, arriving for lunch, greeted him with a cheerful, "Good morning, Henry." Still silent, he died in 1956.

John C. King was once called "the one remaining human fixture in The Players." Elected in 1903 and a charter member of the Golden Age crowd, he joined the Club with Witter Bynner, Cyril Nast, and George Middleton, and in time came to rival Tachau as the oldest club bachelor. At age 80 in 1960, he was also the oldest living member. In his lengthy lifetime he had known the giants of stage, screen, art, and literature. Born in Griffin, Georgia, in 1880, he meant to be an actor from his earliest days, declaiming Shakespeare in the family parlor. It was necessary, however, to spend time working in the family store to save enough money to get to New York. Once there, he found his brother Emmet already playing in a Broadway hit, and already a Player. Emmet met him at the station and took him to the Club for dinner, his first meal in the big city.

Working his way up in the usual fashion, King made his first New York appearance in 1913, in *Seven Keys to Baldpate*. Later he acted with such stars as Ethel Merman, George M. Cohan, Al Jolson, Hampden, W. C. Fields, and Lindsay. At the Club, he served on the board in the Thirties, read the dedication address on Founder's Night in 1928, and at one point was considered the Club's best pool player. Jack King liked to joke that he wanted to be remembered as the best friend of the Club cat, but plainly he was one of those not to be forgotten for many reasons.

From time to time, prominent men in New York and elsewhere were elected to honorary and perpetual membership in The Players, including Toscanini, General Eisenhower, General Bedell Smith, and many others. The only one known to refuse the honor, for reasons never explained, was Mayor Jimmy Walker. Few Players today know that Charles Townsend Copeland, the renowned "Copey of Harvard," was also one of these honorary members. At the time of his election in 1950, Copey was Professor Emeritus and Boylston Professor of Rhetoric. From the beginning, he had been stagestruck, adoring the Barrymores, Minnie Maddern Fiske, and most of all, Edwin Booth. Indeed, as a young Harvard instructor, he first came to public notice for his *Life of Edwin Booth* in 1901, which was edited by M. A. De Wolfe Howe, class of '87.

It was understandable that Copey should become an honorary member but some Players today still find it hard to believe that General Sherman was not only a member but an incorporator, theater buff that he was. A Player of our time, Henry Lee, reported in 1975 that when he became a member he told his young son, "General Sherman was a member of daddy's club," and the boy asked the logical question, "Why?" Discussing this incident with his wife, she remarked, "I didn't want to say anything in front of the boy, but I suppose the General liked to drink."

"Damn it," Henry protested, "You make it sound like a bottle club."

"Well, isn't it?" she asked in surprise.

But of course, as this history has demonstrated, it was (and is) much more than that, in spite of all the conviviality. A story told by Larry Gates at Founder's Night in 1978 makes the point in a revealing way.

"A year or so ago," Gates said, "a young colleague of mine, playing with me in *Hamlet,* asked me to invite him to the Club. I, of course, arranged for him to come for a visit as soon as we were both free. Asking him why he was interested in coming to The Players, he said, 'It may sound funny to you, Larry, but I'm trying to find out what I should value—to find out where my values lie.' He sensed that the place of the torch for the kindling of fresh fires is here."

Gates recalled that as a young unemployed actor, just back from the Second World War, he was in much the same position when he first entered No. 16. And he found friends who showed him the way. As he recalled for the Founder's Night guests: "I remember the perennial graciousness of Charlie Connolly, his continual kindness to me, the nutty guest actor. Franklin P. Adams always had a warm and understanding greeting, as did Tom Chalmers, Roland Winters, even Jack Shuttleworth. [He did not explain the "even."]

"My sponsoring members were hopeful and tolerant, indeed, for I continued on a guest card for nearly eight years. Still searching for those values I thought I understood, I decided against joining when invited to do so in 1947. In 1951, Rex Harrison, with whom I was playing at the time, said, 'Come on, cock, you should be a Player.' I agreed, feeling somewhat ashamed of myself for having been a freeloader as far as dues and initiation fees were concerned, and was proposed. At that time I became quite accidentally involved in Equity and union politics, and was thereupon turned down because a few members thought I was a fellow traveler. I wasn't. In Booth's compassionate tradition, which is The Players, the doubting members insisted upon apologizing a year or so later, which I felt was not necessary. . . . In a way they did me a favor, for I still enjoyed the privileges of the Club without any obligations except my house charges. I finally did become a member, but not before one last fling. . . .

"One evening, as a guest, I entertained not only two Player friends of mine but another guest in the grill. In fact, I recall trying to buy out the entire supply behind the bar for all present in the grill. As the evening drew to a close, I asked Juan, then father confessor, guide and friend, for a rough total of what I had spent. It was a mighty sum! So overwhelming in fact, that I dipped the addition slip into the water pitcher and pasted it over the first two letters of the last word of Hamlet's adjuration to his mother, Act III, Scene 4. It then read, "You budge not 'til I set you up a ass." For this sophomoric, but gleeful witlessness, a member eating his milk toast across the room summarily invited me to quit the premises. And quite properly, too. To this day, I don't recall paying the bill, but subsequently was much honored with membership. . . . I think I was beginning to learn something of what are real values to an actor and, if you will, a Player. . . ."

At the opposite end of the scale in understanding Club values and meanings was a man known to the world and most Players as John Martin. His real name was Morgan Shepard. He tried many vocations—miner, sailor, rancher, newspaper reporter, streetcar conductor—before he found his true calling, editing and writing books for children. The turning point in his life was the San Francisco earthquake of 1906, which not only ruined his designing business but injured him seriously. Recovered, he turned to what he had always wanted to do—be of service to children. For the next quarter century he edited *John Martin's Book*, a handsome illustrated magazine for children, and wrote his own books for them as well.

John was a small man and in his old age he had only 95 pounds on his frail body. Sometime in the Thirties he began to live at the Club, where he was universally loved. Numerous stories were told about him and he became something of a legendary figure. In the September hurricane of 1944 he was caught far uptown, although ordinarily he never ventured far from the Club. Without a raincoat or umbrella, he tried vainly to get a cab and then started downtown toward the Park. He wanted only to get home.

Arriving there by some kind of miracle, having walked all the way, he was soaked and thoroughly spent. Staggering downstairs to the bar, he was taken in hand by Adolph, who began his ministrations with a stiff hooker of Charlie's Best, after which he simply swung John up across his shoulders, and over his burden's protests carried him upstairs to his room. There he took off Martin's clothes and gave him a two-minute scientific massage, at which Adolph was adept. The next day, John was fully recovered without even the suggestion of a cold.

Near tragedies always seemed to be about to overtake John. On his way to the Club one night, a heavy manhole cover blew up in the street and landed within a few feet of him. Flames burst up and all the lights in the neighborhood went out, but John pursued his path to No. 16. He could have reached it blindfolded.

It was a Sunday evening in 1946 when John, returning home from dinner, paused to settle down in his customary chair in the shadow of Booth's portrait, reading and at peace. A charry odor smote his nose, and supposing there was something wrong with his cigarette, he snuffed it out. The odor grew worse, however, and John began to feel both dizzy and nauseated. It dawned on him that the room was getting foggy; looking around, he saw clouds of acrid smoke drifting out from the old register grating at the right of the mantel.

John hurried to the stairs and called for Charlie, who was down below, reading. But the summons was not a call for firemen. "Charlie!" John yelled. "Get me to the toilet quick." By this time he was not able to move around easily by himself. Charlie deposited him in the toilet before he called the fire department. The firemen found that insulation in the air-conditioner motor in the cellar was burning, emitting monoxide gas. When members heard the story, one of them said, "Johnny's smeller saved the Club."

Two years before he died at the Club on May 16, 1947, at 82, John Martin wrote a poem for The Players which he called "My Home":

This is my home, a calm retreat for me;
A happy place for weary heart and mind;
Here I may rest and never fail to find
Where I may set my wanton fancies free.
In retrospect, I always plainly see
My golden hopes fulfilled and all entwined
With certainties that never check, or bind;
So, I am given strength and will to be.
Here there are friends with kindly hearts and hands,
Then, much of beauty calm and dignified,
Where wraiths of vital genius gently roam.
Here, time has stopped and makes no dull demands,
For every binding fetter is untied.
Safe in my spirit in this goodly home.

John also left something more tangible to the Club besides his "all-embracing friendship, game but faltering steps, and his smile," as the

Bulletin put it. After various bequests, his will left everything else in his estate to The Players. He wrote: "In making the foregoing bequest to The Players, I have in mind my relatives to whom I make no bequests. I have been a member of The Players for many years whose facilities and activities in the world of art have given me much pleasure. After the decease of my beloved wife, The Players generously provided me with a place to live in their building where I was treated with kindness and consideration. In making my bequest to them, I do so as a token of appreciation and expression of sincere gratitude."

In the Founder's Night address of 1972, Arthur Arent told of his first appearance as a member, in which he at once discovered what he came to consider the true flavor of the Club. "I was seated in one of the tall chairs overlooking the pool table, when I noticed a gentleman at the top of the stairs doffing his hat and coat. He had been healthfully employed on the Coast making pictures, and this was his first visit to his club in a very long time. Those two doors weren't there then and I could see his face quite distinctly. He was happy. There was a glint of anticipation in his eyes and the secret ecstasy of a homing pigeon in heat.

"He tripped down the stairs into the grill and looked around, taking in the familiar scene—when he abruptly stiffened. The veins in his neck began to stand out like hawsers and his jowls took on the purple of a Tahitian sunset. Ignoring the outstretched hands and welcoming smiles of old friends, he pointed imperiously across the room, and in a voice that shattered the bifocals of elder statesmen at the bar, he thundered, 'What son-of-a-bitch moved that bench *over there?*'"

How successfully Arthur had absorbed this brand of Club spirit was evident in the story told by his doctor in a letter to Roland Winters, written shortly after Arent died in December 1972. While he lay dying, his doctor related, a young physician was also in attendance, referred to with professional courtesy as "Dr. Smith." Arthur had been in a coma, but a few days before his death he was conscious again and said to his nurse, "I want to speak to Dr. Smith." When Smith arrived in the room, he found Arthur slipping back into unconsciousness, but he shook the patient a little, saying, "Mr. Arent, this is Dr. Smith. You wanted to speak to me?" With a final effort, Arthur managed to raise himself on one elbow and pronounced distinctly, "Dr. Smith, you are a horse's ass." They were his last words.

A final statement of a far different but equally characteristic nature came from Bill Plante, a member from 1944 until he died in 1979, and known to everyone in the Club as a wit with an endless fund of stories, most of them censorable. A member (this one) leaving the Club with him one night and walking up Fourth Avenue had their conversation interrupted by the passage in the street of a huge crane being pulled along, its giant extension bobbing and weaving overhead. Bill regarded it thoughtfully. "I wonder what that thing looked like when it had feathers," he said.

Bill kept up the wit that had so often filled the grill room with laughter until the end. About a week before his death he was in intensive care at the hospital, seeming to be in a coma. His wife, Dilly, was sent for. Leaning over his bed, she said, "Bill, Bill, how are you feeling?" Opening one eye, Bill could see what seemed to him an assemblage of doctors, nurses, interns, and aides. "Hell," he said, "if I felt any better, I'd sell tickets."

Plante was an acknowledged master of that Club staple, the sophisticated pun, if indeed such an animal exists. One day he was greeted by a member who had in tow a distinguished guest he was bringing to lunch and whom he intended to propose for membership. The candidate was an extremely serious man who was known (but not to Bill) as a sworn enemy of puns. The guest launched on a story of how in India he had come upon two Bengal tigers mating. They were no more than ten yards away, he said, and he had only one bullet in his gun.

"Have you ever heard of anything more astonishing?" the guest demanded.

That was a direct challenge to Bill. Leaning forward, he said: "I once heard of a cat that ate cheese and waited over a mouse's hole with baited breath."

Ordinarily, however, new and intended members were greeted at the Club with the particular consideration from old members that had been prevalent from the beginning. When Sidney Blackmer, a Player for 53 years, died in October 1973, Eric Lloyd told how he had met Blackmer on his first Pipe Night—a meeting of one of the oldest and one of the newest members. Blackmer, said Lloyd, extended "a welcome and companionship that embodied all that being a Player means. I may have given him my arm to lean upon but it was he who led the way. He introduced me to other members and entertained and enlightened me with stories of the past. When I bid him goodnight for the last time earlier this year, he jokingly said, 'If you meet my doctor, don't tell him you saw me.'"

One Player has been especially honored, not only with an Open House but a *thé dansant,* the first in Club history. That was Jack Shuttleworth, forever immortalized by Buck Crouse's remark, "Shuttleworth, if you were half a man, which you are. . . ." At the open house honoring him, Roland Winters noted that Shuttleworth was also known at various times as "Scrabblethwaite, Shuttlecock, Scooter, and Schikelgruber." James O'Neill, then the oldest member, called him "the drummer boy from Shiloh."

The diminutive Shuttleworth was the youngest man ever to be editor of a major humor magazine, *Judge*. At the Club, he became one of its most constant members, involved in virtually everything that went on, and, in Winters's words, "the only man in the club who, when he descends the stairs into the bar, by his mere presence causes the lights to burn more brightly."

In the Twenties Frank Sullivan had held something of the same position for a time, but the Club saw less and less of him in later years as he spent more of his days in his Saratoga home. Whenever he came to New York, however, he always appeared at the Club until at last the agoraphobia from which he suffered prevented him from going anywhere. After that, the Club came to *him* as much as possible. His friends went upstate to visit him whenever they could, bringing news of No. 16. Of Frank's earlier days, Jack Iams, one of those friends, said: "You could always tell he was in residence the moment you entered 16 Gramercy Park. There was something about his presence—his gentleness, his kindness, and of course, his wit, that made itself felt throughout the Club whenever he was there. I can see him now, sitting in one of the lofty chairs besides the pool table—which made him look even taller than he was. In later days he was no more than a name to newer members." Sullivan died in February 1976 at 83; he had been a member since 1925.

Among the devoted Players who were not noted in the arts or even well known outside their own circle, was Joseph D. Massoletti, who died in 1973. Joe had some of the characteristics of the best Players of the past: that is, he was modest, gentle, courteous, and a lover of food and wine—indeed a gourmet and connoisseur. But in another respect he was unique—more of a listener than a talker. He did a great deal for the club he loved, much of it known only to the Board.

For a quarter century, Massoletti entertained some of his Player friends every summer at his fishing lodge on the Outer Banks, near Cape Hatteras. It was an eagerly awaited event for those friends, among whom were Sidney Blackmer, Porter Wylie, F. P. A., Jack Iams, Ralph Bellamy, Asa Bordages, Marc Connolly, John Falter, Sou Chan, Dennis King, Rea Irvin, Jason Robards, Donald Seawell, and John McNulty, who described their host as "quietly elegant."

When these and other guests from the Club first made their way to the lodge it took two days, traveling by car, ferry, and finally across fifty miles of loose sand, beach grass, and scrub pine, where no road had ever been laid down. Later on the vacationers flew to Norfolk, where Joe's chartered plane brought them to the beach directly in front of the lodge. Once there, they could use Joe's sport-fishing boat, with a captain in charge, and inside the lodge they enjoyed the work of Joe's chef, who produced the kind of excellent food to be found at a restaurant that Joe and his son Everett (also a member) owned at 70 Pine Street, called simply "Massoletti's." In spite of the name, it was not an Italian restaurant. Massoletti was a first-family name in Virginia, and one of his ancestors had been a pallbearer at George Washington's funeral.

Sometimes Joe had parties for his Player friends at 70 Pine, where he liked to serve what he called a "simple Southern dinner," consisting of Chesapeake Bay oysters, broiled pompano, roast quail, collard greens, spoonbread, hearts of palm salad, and key lime pie, washed down with corn whiskey bottled in 1868 at Charleston.

As the Outer Banks began to develop into the sprawling summer place it is today, Joe watched the encroachment with dismay. When he saw a house being built about a half-mile down the beach, he sold out and bought a ranch in Cuernavaca, about an hour from Mexico City in the mountains. The Players' summer soirees were transfered to this remote spot and continued for years until Joe died there.

Among the regular Massoletti guests was that other renowned restaurateur, Sou Chan, whose superb Chinese cuisine had twice been transferred from uptown to No. 16, as described earlier. Sou, who died in 1978, had come to America from Canton when he was only nineteen. He began his career in New York without money, friends, or a knowledge of the English language. By the time of his death at 69, he possessed farms and apartments in New York and Florida, owned both a Porsche and a Mercedes, and was sole owner of his famous Seventh Avenue restaurant, the House of Chan. Not many of those who ate there knew that he also had written three books and contributed to national magazines. He was active in the Overseas Press Club, but his real love was The Players, where his friends were numerous but had to be appended to a long outside list that included waiters and bus boys, as well as Harry Truman and Dwight Eisenhower.

Sou Chan was very far from being the stereotypical inscrutable Oriental. He had a lively and often unorthodox wit. Once, when his restaurant was being picketed, he sent out tea and fortune cookies to the pickets, who opened the little shells and found their fortune: "You ain't got a Chinaman's chance."

Marc Connolly once described Sou Chan's debut as a card player at the Club. "We didn't know him well then," Marc wrote, "and we watched his poker-playing style with some apprehension. I can still recall that night . . . recall the mask-like expression as with sinister Oriental inscrutability he quietly arranged the cards that had been dealt him into a neat pile, slowly brought them to within two inches of his nose, and carefully spread them open fanwise until he could see, and as his eyes flew open in completely phony astonishment, Mr. Sou Chan exclaimed, 'Mama Mia!' "

One night Sou challenged no less a renowned cardsharp than Howard Lindsay, and, as Connolly told it: "Sou and Howard both showed nerves of steel. We knew Howard well; we knew he had some of the elements of the good poker player—the courtesy of a gentleman, the heart of a lion, the rapacity of a hyena—and it was interesting to watch these two magnificent players. After each rise the challenged party would pause only for a brief slur on his opponent's character and a slight reference to his idiocy in underestimating the superiority of the speaker's hand.

"The tension mounted until the 37th counter-raise. Then a curious change could be seen on the stony features of Mr. Chan. The reptilian smile faded. A look of plaintive concern supplanted it. Was Mr. Chan's devilish cunning about to manifest itself in an even more horrible form? Not at all. What we were witnessing was a gaping wound under the armor of a Chinese warlord. Almost wistfully, almost pleadingly, he gazed at our beloved President's unaltered deadpan. 'Wha' you want, Howard? Blood?' "

Sometimes those who did much for the Club labored in relative obscurity, their work known only to a few. Such was Ezra Shine, whose death in 1977 disclosed to those who didn't know it that as Club treasurer he had been a prime factor in saving it from bankruptcy. He had done the same thing for a variety of stars, including Tallulah Bankhead, the Lunts, Howard Lindsay, and other actors, acting as manager of their financial affairs. They relied on him, too, for all kinds of assistance, and in consequence became his close personal friends. His death, as the *Bulletin* observed, "brought feelings of grief mixed with helplessness" on the part of his clients.

At the Club it brought grief too, but also gratitude for what Shine had done to bring The Players back from the edge of bankruptcy. He was treasurer of the Club and a valuable member of the board until he resigned in 1970. One of his little-known accomplishments was to draw up, at the instigation of President Dennis King, a code of conduct and dress within the Club, incorporated in the house rules and observed today. If there were a Hall of Fame for those who had contributed most to the Club, it was generally agreed Shine would have been a member.

Yet in the half-dozen or so years between his resignation as treasurer and his death, he did not often come to the Club. He took a dim view of the fiscal policies that followed his departure, and he was unhappy about enforcement of the code of conduct, believing that dress standards were lax, the cries of anguish from the bridge players too noisy, and the presence of women too frequent. He disapproved of all these things and said so, but his devotion to the Club never wavered.

So often in walking through this gallery of Players, there is repeated evidence of such devotion, sometimes exhibited in extraordinary ways. There was, for example, William Edgar Fisher, an eminent bookplate designer and typographer. Three years before he died in October 1956, Fisher had a premonition that it would not be long and wrote to the board: "It looks as though that soon there would be a little black-bordered card on the bulletin board with my name inscribed thereon and I'd like to do something pleasant about it. I would wish to have some farewell drinks with all my fellow Players and I am asking for your approval of my plan. I want to 'buy the bar' for a day, 12 noon to midnight, when all drinks would be on me and free." It was done, on January 21, 1957, and Fisher would have been happy to know that bar patronage was three times more than normal.

Still another candidate for "most beloved" Player was George Melville Cooper, who lived at the Club in Room #7 for five years, going out only occasionally for a visit to Sardi's on Saturday, or to do just a little more work in the theater. His last appearance was in *Charley's Aunt* at the Paper Mill Playhouse in the summer of 1970. He had to give up golf because of his health, but he continued to pursue his other hobby, the Club—and pursuit was the proper word. Apparently nothing could keep him from it, but eventually, on a trip to the Coast, he was lured by the sunshine and went to live there in the early Seventies in the Motion Picture Country House, where he died.

Hollywood, or simply California sunshine, claimed many Players, but that seldom appeared to diminish their feelings for No. 16. They wrote frequent letters and visited whenever they came to New York. Jerome Kern, who died in November 1945, spent most of his time in Hollywood, but in 1943 he proposed his newborn grandson, Steven Kern Shaw (born to his daughter, one of Artie Shaw's several wives) for membership. Kern wrote to the membership committee that he had "known the candidate most intimately since his birth," and "barring profligate extravagance in the use of fresh linen, and a tendency to a slightly well-mannered gluttony, the candidate, young Shaw, seems to give every promise of becoming, at the appropriate date, a credit not only to his sponsors but to The Players as well." Charles Coburn seconded the nomination.

Robert Benchley was also a Hollywood exile, a member since 1939; he died in the same month as Kern. When he joined the Club, according to F. P. A., Benchley remarked that he could scarcely wait until his obituary appeared, citing him as "a prominent clubman." It was not a long wait.

Anyone encountering John Cecil Holm at the Club in the Seventies would have thought him as much a part of the scenery as the furniture, but this accomplished actor confessed in his 1974 Founder's Night address that "one has to find his own way to be a Player." John recalled his first Pipe Night in 1936, when Hampden was speaking seriously to the assemblage, and suddenly a member about to come down the stairs from the second floor stumbled, fell, and landed in a heap on the floor of the Great Hall. Heads and chairs turned, Hampden took off his glasses and turned to see who was interrupting him. Someone helped the fallen member to his feet, and he was asked to leave immediately, since he was unhurt. The doorman, shocked more by the sacrilege than the possible injury, hurried him out as rapidly as possible.

The incident made John so tense that he decided on the spot to abstain from any refreshment, assuming that it was an excess of alcohol that had led to the fall. Two hours later in the grill room, still trying to behave in the most circumspect way, Holm backed into a small end table and sent it crashing to the floor, and in trying to catch it, he fell too. The proverbial hush fell on the room, and Holm had an awful vision of Hampden confronting him sternly, and the hall man hurrying down to bring him his hat and coat.

"I'm cold sober," he protested to the member standing nearest him.

"Perhaps that's your trouble," the man said, and they bought each other drinks.

Sometimes, however, there were members whose personalities somehow never quite fitted in, or they believed that was the case. John Malone, as Mark Twain disclosed in his story related earlier, was one. Lewis Thompson, who died in 1972, was another. In Thompson's case it was self-imposed. Thompson liked to characterize himself somewhat melodramatically as "a lone and tragic figure." But that was not exactly true. Members were divided in their feelings about him. Some thought of him as a splendid companion. Others considered him taciturn and sarcastic, or at least grouchy, and they avoided him. It was true that Thompson did not suffer fools or bores gladly, or, as Harry Walker said, "He refused to suffer them at all."

Thompson had an admirable command of invective. To a bridge partner who had made a series of bad plays, he growled, "Your only problem is that you have delusions of adequacy." Of another, who had just aided him in losing $65, he argued that this man should be subject to a law, for which he cited constitutional grounds, that would forbid him from ever picking up a card again.

Yet he had a kind and considerate side that he made strenuous efforts to hide. To older members he was always courteous and friendly and seemed to enjoy their company even when they bored others. Children quickly accepted him. A friend with fiscal or matrimonial problems could always count on a temporary bedroom at his place. He could be thoughtful, even sentimental, and then savage a few moments later. Outside the Club, he was an award-winning author who was also in corporate public relations.

On his last night at the Club, Thompson spent an amiable half hour with his friend, Harry Walker, talking about many things, until he said he must leave. As Walker remembered, "Matt [the bartender] and I watched him stomp down the long, empty room, eyeing the world balefully through his new contact lenses. He seemed to have become what he always said he was—a lone and tragic figure." An hour later he was dead, at 57.

On the other hand, Heywood Broun might have seemed an even more unlikely candidate for the Club than Thompson, and in fact he protested, just before his name was proposed, "You know, I'm not much of a club man." It was not so. F. P. A., in his tribute to Broun when the columnist died in 1940, believed his friend made that remark simply to explain possible future long absences, perhaps occasioned by the imminent poverty he always feared. To Frank, he *was* a Club man—"260 pounds of excellent club man. Offhand, I don't know anybody who was more of a club man, quantitatively and qualitatively. Whenever he came to The Players and sat at a table alone, in about three minutes there would be five or six other members sitting there with him. . . . He seemed to me more like Don Marquis than like anybody else in the Club. . . . Like most other good writers, he hated work. The Players was his dish, for he was a Player, upper-and-lower-case."

Someone definitely not a club man, at The Players or elsewhere, was Fred Allen. He visited occasionally, and Jack Shuttleworth remembers that once they talked about advertising, for which Allen gave a definition: "An imaginary activity carried on in a vacuum." But when a friend at the Club proposed to put him up for membership, he replied on April 27, 1943, in his customary lower-case style: " . . . at assorted times during the past fifteen years, various members of this organization have expressed a desire to put me up for membership. i have never encouraged these gentlemen in their collective folly. i seldom have time to go places and it seems a waste of time to belong to a club of this sort if one is not able to add his fraternal bit to the venture. i have never joined the lambs, friars, elks, masons, woodmen of the world, or the knights of pythias for the same reason. i have never really joined the human race which has been running longer than any of the organizations above listed. i am going through life on a guest card and the more i see of the human race the more i feel like turning in my skin and requesting that membership be cancelled."

Robert Moses appreciated Allen's attitude. That master manipulator of public works wrote in 1980: "The Players is no place for sycophants. It is not a mutual adoration society of sardonic, snide wisenheimers and phrasemakers. This Club maintains spontaneity. It is the home of offbeat candor, not premeditated guff. . . . The Players is no Algonquin Round Table where humor is as spontaneous as a sock in the jaw or a kick in the rump. Don Marquis once said that at the Algonquin, 'They stroke a platitude until it purrs like an epigram.' I prefer the unrehearsed wisecracks of the pool sharks at The Players to the bitter, mordant Dorothy Parker humor broadcast from the Algonquin. I deprecate contrived brilliance and recall with glee memories of Don Marquis and his pool sharks exchanging pleasantries in the basement of The Players, with Archie the Cockroach, who couldn't punctuate on a typewriter, safe in the cuff of his boss's pants and Mehitabel the Cat under the table licking her chops."

The atmosphere of The Players was what most impressed a visiting writer from the midwest, Frederick Manfred, who wrote excellent regional novels as Vardis Fisher. About 1955 in Minneapolis his friend Waring Jones suggested that he stay as his guest at the Club on his trips East to see his publishers, and Manfred accepted. His first visit, he said later, was an eye-opener.

"I was made to feel at home instantly," Manfred said. "Nobody stared at my height. Nobody wondered if I had a right to be there. And after a while I fell into good conversations with a half-dozen congenial souls. We were all in the arts and a man could let his mind run in any direction and be appreciated if not understood. Some of the best dialogues I've ever been in occurred down in the grill: about Black Holes, the Big Bang Theory, comparisons of Bach and Beethoven, Faulkner, why a man's second marriage will work better than his first, the Vietnam War, etc. Presently it was suggested that I become a member. Waring Jones proposed me and Richard Herd seconded me. Soon I received notice that I was a member. And from that time on, I always felt my second home in America was at The Players."

It is the human relationships, as Manfred and all the others have understood, that have made The Players the special club it is. Nowhere has it been more evident than in the numerous stories about that ubiquitous Player, F. P. A. A tale recalled by Roland Winters will stand for the others.

Sometime in the early Forties, Winters entered the Club one night and encountered Frank just leaving. "Where away?" he asked, and Frank answered, "Uptown poker game." Winters knew that meant the private dining room at the Barberry Room, on 52nd Street, where George Kaufman, Howard Lindsay, Marc Connolly, and other members of the Thanatopsis and Inside Straight Poker Club were likely to gather. They were excellent players, well able to handle stakes of five, ten, and twenty dollars, buying in at $500.

But, as Winters observed, Frank was quite drunk as he left the Club, and obviously not in condition to play in such company. "Frank," he said, detaining his friend, "you're too drunk to play poker with that bunch of sharpies. They'll murder you." Frank gave him a drunken leer and suggested where he could dispose of his advice, but then he insisted that Roland go with him, and the invitation was accepted—not, as Winters said later, because he had any intention of playing, but in a comradely Player-like effort to save Frank, if possible, from something disastrous.

When they arrived the game was on and there was one chair open. The others saw Frank's condition, and protested at once, "You're too drunk to play." But F. P. A. ignored them and sat down in the vacant chair. Winters pulled up another chair behind him, in a position to see his hand.

Lindsay, always conscientious, made a final attempt to keep Frank out. "Believe me, Frank," he said, "you're too drunk to play," but the *World's* pride replied simply, "Deal the cards." Shrugging resignedly, Howard dealt, and Winters saw that Frank had a pair of threes. Someone opened, and soon the bid got around to F. P. A.. "Get out with your rotten pair of threes," Winters whispered. But Frank stayed, and cards were called for. Frank took three, and drew another pair of threes. The betting went on, and when the limit was reached, Frank called and took the pot.

Crying and moaning was heard around the table as Frank stuffed money in his pockets, first into the trousers, always sagging, then his vest, and at last his coat pockets—in all, about $900. As he did so, new cries arose: "Deal the cards, deal the cards, it's your deal, Frank."

Frank smiled on them as he turned to leave. "Sorry, gentlemen," he said, "I'm too drunk to play."

But yet, with all the genuine fellowship that characterizes the Club, Players are inclined to view themselves with a wry skepticism, perhaps in this more cynical day to avoid the impression of sentimentality. Roger Bryant Hunting, recounting the story of his first Founder's Night in 1958, said, "All I remember of that evening was the glow of good fellowship and my own pride in being a member. I was seated at a table with five or six older members. I listened entranced as they talked at length about various versions of Hamlet they had seen over the generations. I thought, 'How fascinating—what a home of culture, scholarship, and wit.'" Then he hastened to add: "It's also about the last time I heard such culture and scholarship here."

To this could be added the tale Jack Shuttleworth told on Founder's Night, 1978. On a quiet summer evening, he recalled, the club was nearly deserted except for Jack King, playing solitaire at the Round Table.

Charlie Connolly was at the bar, and Shuttleworth stood nearby with a small glass. At this point Gordon Stevenson came in, feeling exuberant about a portrait he had just completed, and ordered a bottle of ale to be poured in a pewter mug, as in the old days. Obtaining it, he went to join King. Watching this scene, said Jack, "I thought, there is what The Players is all about. Two of the oldest members of the Club—a Shakespearean actor and distinguished portrait painter—socializing just as Mr. Booth had hoped, and dreamed."

But the dream of Booth, via Shuttleworth, was rudely interrupted. King gathered up his cards, walked over to another table, and told Gordon, "Come over here—and I'll move again."

Yet such incidents, or more lively ones, in the end have been only mild ripples on the surface of life at No. 16 for these past hundred years. The rooms are full of more amiable ghosts, some of whose lives have been seen in these pages. Peter Turgeon in 1975 spoke of those he had seen in his own long years at the Club:

"J. Scott Smart rehearsing at the dinner table for his role as the 'Fat Man,' Harry Gilbert putting a light to his pipe filled with Hershey-bar shavings, and Arthur Arent racking the balls and licking his chops in anticipation of 'soup's on.' Charley Towne singing phony opera with Percy MacKaye looking as if someone had knitted him. There by the bar are Tony Brown and Tom Wenning, still trying to fathom the success of *Tobacco Road*. . . . Louis Jean Heydt brushes cigar ashes from the vest of a nodding F. P. A. as John McNulty whispers, 'Say nothing to alarm the ladies, but rejoin your regiment immediately'. Henry Carlton orders his 'once a year' drink, George Cooper shuffles in at an angle and Bernie Hart greets him with 'Fenimore doth approach!'

"Jack King pours himself some ice water from a silver pitcher engraved simply 'Frank.' Buck Crouse relates his one performance in a one-night stand as the one-line doctor in *Life with Father*, and how he blew it. Over at the round table, Ed McNamara argues voice technique with Ray Vir Den, while Johnny Call describes the vicissitudes of doing a commercial for Levi's bread. . . ."

Those were the ghosts Turgeon saw. Every Player who has known the Club well can summon up his own ghosts from the vasty deep of the century past, and each vision would be different. For the dream of Edwin Booth has been realized. The best of the actors and the best of all the arts and professions have lived together for a hundred years in as much harmony as human beings can endure, coming together as equals and brothers. To quote the words of that much-quoted consummate Player John S. Phillips once again: "Here hundreds of high-spirited men met, talked, laughed, ate and drank together in friendly converse—and passed on. Within these walls they have left something of themselves, each adding his mote to the perpetuating essence infused by the founder."

What of the next century? As it begins, the Club is in good hands. It has a new president in Jose Ferrer, a veteran Player who had already done much for the Club before he took the post from a retiring Roland Winters. A member since 1936, Ferrer had always been active in Club life even though, as was the case with so many other actor members, his profession requires him to be out of New York frequently.

With his election to the presidency, however, he brought a new resolve to restore the Club, physically and spiritually (so to speak) to its best days. Many members had perceived that reform was needed. Not only had the physical condition of the Club deteriorated again, as it had in previous depressed years, but the quality of the membership had been in a slow decline for some time, in the opinion of those older members who recalled better days.

Clearly reform was necessary and Ferrer went about it as soon as he took office. He injected new life into the management and other committees, inspiring them to make major changes. The result has been one of the most extensive and rewarding physical renovations in Club history. It was opposed by some members, as all half-dozen of those that preceded it were, but Ferrer, his board, and the committees forged ahead and produced, on the eve of the hundredth anniversary, a handsome new Club interior, along with other badly needed changes. A revitalized membership will take more time, but Ferrer was already pushing in that direction at the end of 1988. With the help of an able and devoted manager, Richard McBain, and an excellent staff, the Club is ready to enter a new era in its long history.

As the new century begins, no one can forecast what effect the advent of women members will have when it occurs. The Club voted their admission in 1988, anticipating the Supreme Court's decision upholding a New York law forbidding discrimination against them in private clubs. While no man (or woman, either) knows the future, we can be certain of one thing—that the spirit Edwin Booth infused in The Players will survive for yet another hundred years, if the members so choose. They have, one and all, made the Club what it is.

Officers of The Players

President

Edwin Booth	1888 to 1893
Joseph Jefferson	1893 to 1905
John Drew	1905 to 1927
Walter Hampden	1927 to 1955
Howard Lindsay	1955 to 1965
Dennis King	1965 to 1970
Alfred Drake	1970 to 1978
Roland Winters	1978 to 1983
José Ferrer	1983

President Emeritus

Walter Hampden	1954 to 1955
Howard Lindsay	1965 to 1968
Dennis King	1970 to 1971
Alfred Drake	1978
Roland Winters	1983

Vice President

Augustin Daly	1888 to 1895
Albert M. Palmer	1895 to 1905
William Bispham	1905 to 1909
Joseph F. Daly	1909 to 1916
Evert Jansen Wendell	1916 to 1917
Francis Wilson	1918 to 1918
Otis Skinner	1918 to 1920
Francis Wilson	1920 to 1924
Walter Hampden	1924 to 1927
Otis Skinner	1927 to 1942
Howard Lindsay 1st	1942 to 1955
Dennis King 1st	1955 to 1965
Charles D. Coburn 2nd	1942 to 1961
Donald Seawell 2nd	1961 to 1965
Donald Seawell 1st	1965 to 1970
David Wayne 2nd	1965 to 1970
Peter Turgeon 1st	1970 to 1973

Roland Winters 2nd	1970 to 1973
Roland Winters 1st	1973 to 1978
Peter Turgeon 2nd	1973 to 1978
José Ferrer 1st	1978 to 1983
Mortimer Marshall 2nd	1978 to 1979
Car Low 2nd	1979 to 1986
Garson Kanin 1st	1983
John B. Tucker 2nd	1986

Secretary

Laurence Hutton	1868 to 1892
Brander Matthews	1892 to 1893
Laurence Hutton	1893 to 1896
Charles E. Carryl	1896 to 1903
Harrison Blake Hodges	1903 to 1912
Hamilton Bell	1912 to 1913
Harry Rowe Shelly	1913 to 1916
Humphrey Turner Nichols	1916 to 1917
Hamilton Bell	1917 to 1918
John C. Travis	1918 to 1920
Humphrey Turner Nichols	1920 to 1921
Louis Evan Shipman	1921 to 1924
Clayton Hamilton	1924 to 1925
Will Irwin	1925 to 1925
Frank L. Warrin, Jr.	1925 to 1926
Clayton Hamilton	1926 to 1929
Henry W. Lanier	1929 to 1935
Robert Winsmore	1935 to 1937
Whitney Darrow	1937 to 1942
John Knight	1942 to 1955
Gordon Hamilton	1955 to 1957
Paul Hampden	1957 to 1960
Robert Downing	1960 to 1968
Jack Iams	1968 to 1971
Richard T. Herd	1971 to 1973
Ralph Camargo	1973 to 1978
Joseph Rhodes	1978 to 1980
Roger Bryant Hunting	1980

Treasurer

William Bispham	1888 to 1891
Albert M. Palmer	1891 to 1892
William Bispham	1892 to 1905
Wm. Cushing Bamburgh	1905 to 1906
Arnold W. Brunner	1906 to 1909
James Lees Laidlaw	1909 to 1915

Nicholas Biddle	1915 to 1917
James Lees Laidlaw	1917 to 1920
Nicholas Biddle	1920 to 1921
George P. Brett	1921 to 1924
David A. McKinlay	1924 to 1927
Frederic C. Mills	1927 to 1933
David A. McKinlay	1933 to 1939
Howard C. Lewis	1939 to 1944
Paul Kieffer	1944 to 1953
Eugene R. Spaulding	1953 to 1957
Donald Seawell	1957 to 1962
R. H. Brownell	1962 to 1967
Ezra Shine	1967 to 1970
Wilfred J. Halpern	1970 to 1978
Herman Singerman	1978 to 1981
Wilfred J. Halpern	1981

Assistant Secretary

George Christie	1935 to 1937
Charles D. Coburn	1937 to 1937
Harold McGee	1937 to 1939
John Cummings Hunt	1939 to 1941
Burns Mantle	1941 to 1944
Paul Parks corr. secy.	1941 to 1944
Paul Parks	1944 to 1945
Eugene R. Spaulding	1945 to 1953
Gordon Hamilton	1953 to 1955
Ben Lackland	1955 to 1957
Thomas Wenning	1957 to 1959
Robert Downing	1959 to 1960
John D. Seymour	1960 to 1961
Jack Iams	1961 to 1968
Franklin Cover	1968 to 1969
Richard T. Herd	1969 to 1971
Ralph Camargo	1971 to 1973
Ira Wolff	1973 to 1977
Joseph Rhodes	1977 to 1978
Roger Bryant Hunting	1978 to 1980
Joseph Rhodes	1980 to 1982
Robert Carter	1982 to 1988

Assistant Treasurer

John Carrington Yates	1929 to 1931
Harold W. Gould	1931 to 1933
Lodewick Uroom	1933 to 1935
Wm. Morris Houghton	1935 to 1936

Whitney Darrow	1936 to 1937
Howard C. Lewis	1937 to 1939
Harold McGee	1939 to 1941
John Cummings Hunt	1941 to 1947
Charles M. Kinsolving	1947 to 1953
Eugene R. Spaulding	1953 to 1953
Walter Wilds	1954 to 1957
George W. Jones	1957 to 1962
Herbert A. Dingwall	1962 to 1970
Girard Spencer	1970 to 1974
Harold S. Gelb	1974 to 1976
Herman Singerman	1976 to 1978
Wilfred J. Halpern	1978 to 1981
Willard Swire	1981

Chairman, Managing Committee

C. Edmonds Allen	1966 to 1970
J. J. Beaufoy-Lane	1970 to 1973
Richard T. Herd	1972 to 1976
Storrs Haynes	1973 to 1979
Charles Hohman	1979 to 1983
Charles Reynolds	1983 to 1986
Roy Doliner	1986
Robert L. Bien	1988

Board of Directors of The Players

Edwin Booth	1888 to 1893	Harrison Blake Hodges	1903 to 1912
Augustin Daly	1888 to 1895	Wm. Cushing Bamburgh	1905 to 1906
Lawrence Barrett	1888 to 1891	John W. Albaugh	1905 to 1909
Albert M. Palmer	1888 to 1905	Arnold W. Brunner	1906 to 1909
Laurence Hutton	1888 to 1900	James Lees Laidlaw	1909 to 1915
Joseph F. Daly	1888 to 1895		1917 to 1920
	1900 to 1916	Edwin Milton Royle	1909 to 1912
Henry Edwards	1888 to 1888	Otis Skinner	1909 to 1920
Joseph Jefferson	1888 to 1905		1926 to 1942
William Bispham	1888 to 1909	John H. Finley	1909 to 1910
Stephen S. Olin	1888 to 1896	Duff G. Maynard	1910 to 1911
William J. Florence	1891 to 1891	William E. Graham	1911 to 1915
Brander Matthews	1891 to 1897	Oliver Doud Byron	1912 to 1915
Francis Wilson	1893 to 1918	Hamilton Bell	1912 to 1913
	1919 to 1924		1917 to 1918
Charles E. Carryl	1895 to 1906	Harry Rowe Shelley	1913 to 1916
John Drew	1895 to 1927	Nicholas Biddle	1915 to 1917
Frank W. Sanger	1896 to 1903		1920 to 1921
Daniel Frohman	1897 to 1909	Henry Bacon	1915 to 1916
Howland Davis	1903 to 1903		1920 to 1923

John Blair	1915 to 1918	William G. Tachau	1931 to 1943
James Barnes	1916 to 1917		1954 to 1959
Humphrey Turner	1916 to 1917	Lodewick Uroom	1931 to 1935
Nichols	1920 to 1921	Wm. Morris Houghton	1933 to 1936
Evert Jansen Wendell	1916 to 1917	John C. King	1934 to 1937
John Wolcott Adams	1917 to 1918	George Christie	1935 to 1937
	1918 to 1920	Robert Winsmore	1935 to 1937
Shelley Hull	1918 to 1919	Whitney Darrow	1936 to 1945
George C. Riggs	1917 to 1920		1945 to 1946
David Glassford	1918 to 1918	Charles D. Coburn	1937 to 1938
	1919 to 1921		1941 to 1961
William Harcourt	1918 to 1919	Jay Fassett	1937 to 1944
John C. Travis	1918 to 1920	Harold McGee	1937 to 1944
George K. Denny	1919 to 1921		1945 to 1955
Bruce McRae	1920 to 1923	Kenneth MacKenna	1937 to 1939
John S. Phillips	1920 to 1924	Howard Lewis	1937 to 1944
Louis Evan Shipman	1921 to 1924	Samuel M. Forrest	1937 to 1941
Arthur Goodrich	1921 to 1924		1943 to 1944
	1926 to 1929	John Cummings Hunt	1939 to 1947
	1936 to 1937	Dudley Digges	1939 to 1945
	1939 to 1941	George M. Cohan	1939 to 1943
George P. Brett	1921 to 1924	Clarence B. Kelland	1939 to 1943
Malcolm Duncan	1921 to 1924	John Charles Thomas	1939 to 1949
A. E. Thomas	1923 to 1926	Henry Bruere	1939 to 1941
John Daly Murphy	1923 to 1926	Gene Buck	1939 to 1941
Clayton Hamilton	1924 to 1925	Frank Craven	1939 to 1941
	1926 to 1929	Thomas Shaw Hale	1939 to 1944
Don Marquis	1924 to 1925	Philip Merivale	1939 to 1942
David A. McKinlay	1924 to 1927	Wallace Morgan	1939 to 1941
	1933 to 1939	Rowland Stebbins	1939 to 1942
	1939 to 1943	Ben Lackland	1941 to 1944
Thomas H. Willard	1924 to 1925		1951 to 1957
Walter Hampden	1924 to 1927	Ray Vir Den	1941 to 1945
	1927 to 1954	Harry Staton	1941 to 1944
Ernest Glendinning	1924 to 1925	Burns Mantle	1941 to 1948
Will Irwin	1925 to 1925	Paul Parks	1941 to 1946
A. G. Andrews	1925 to 1928	John Knight	1942 to 1957
Henry S. Watson	1925 to 1931	Percy Moore	1942 to 1945
Frank L. Warrin, Jr.	1925 to 1926	Bobby Clark	1943 to 1949
William Courtleigh	1927 to 1930		1955 to 1960
George Middleton	1927 to 1929	Russel Crouse	1943 to 1948
Frederic C. Mills	1927 to 1933	Paul Kieffer	1943 to 1953
John Carrington Yates	1928 to 1931	Rollin Kirby	1944 to 1947
Walter Connolly	1929 to 1933	Richard J. Madden	1944 to 1946
Howard Lindsay	1929 to 1931	Elliott Nugent	1944 to 1947
	1933 to 1936	Edward H. Wever	1944 to 1950
	1942 to 1966	Gilbert Loveland	1944 to 1945
Henry W. Lanier	1929 to 1935		1946 to 1947
Harold W. Gould	1930 to 1933	James Cagney	1944 to 1948
Brian Hooker	1931 to 1934		1958 to 1964

John Chapman	1945 to 1946	Porter Wylie	1958 to 1962
John Falter	1945 to 1948	George Freedley	1959 to 1965
	1950 to 1952	George Kennan Hourwich	1959 to 1960
	1959 to 1960	C. Edmonds Allen	1960 to 1986
Eugene R. Spaulding	1945 to 1957	Alfred Carb	1960 to 1961
Richard S. Aldrich	1946 to 1957	Edmund Duffy	1960 to 1962
Robert Winternitz	1946 to 1953	John Effrat	1960 to 1963
Wm. Brown Meloney II	1947 to 1947	John Cecil Holm	1961 to 1964
Edward M. Crane	1947 to 1956	Henry B. Jones	1961 to 1962
Charles M. Kinsolving	1947 to 1953	George W. Stewart	1961 to 1970
Pare Lorentz	1947 to 1950	R. H. Brownell	1962 to 1967
Stuart Hawkins	1947 to 1948	Herbert A. Dingwall	1962 to 1970
Henry R. Hayes	1947 to 1955	Vinton Freedley	1962 to 1965
Henry Fisk Carlton	1948 to 1973	Peter Turgeon	1962
Leo G. Carroll	1948 to 1951	Luis D'Antin Van Rooten	1963 to 1970
Corey Ford	1948 to 1951	St. John Terrell	1962 to 1965
James Garrett Wallace	1948 to 1956	Staats Cotsworth	1963 to 1967
Thomas H. Chalmers	1949 to 1952	Hal James	1963 to 1969
	1957 to 1959	Sam J. Slate	1963 to 1968
Robert Montgomery	1949 to 1952	James Nelson	1964 to 1967
Frank Sullivan	1949 to 1952	David Wayne	1964 to 1970
Dennis King	1950 to 1971	James Cagney	1965 to 1968
Nelson Way	1951 to 1953	Herbert Brodkin	1965 to 1968
Sidney Blackmer	1952 to 1958	Hal Holbrook	1965 to 1968
	1960 to 1963	Esra Shine	1966 to 1971
John Herman Merivale	1952 to 1953	Franklin Cover	1967 to 1969
Julio F. Sorzano	1952 to 1955	Norton Mockridge	1967 to 1970
Alan C. Bunce	1953 to 1962	Rhomas L. Stix	1967 to 1970
Albert R. LeFoucheur	1953 to 1954	George Britt	1968 to 1972
	1957 to 1958	Richard L. Grossman	1968 to 1971
Joseph D. Massoletti	1953 to 1962	Mortimer Marshall	1968 to 1971
Francis S. Dixon	1953 to 1958	Morris Rittenberg	1968 to 1971
Gordon C. Hamilton	1953 to 1957	Alfred Drake	1968
Walter Wilds	1954 to 1957	Richard T. Herd	1969 to 1976
William P. Adams	1955 to 1958	Staats Cotsworth	1969 to 1970
John Mulholland	1955 to 1958	Max Gordon	1969 to 1978
William C. Plante	1955 to 1957	Roland Winters	1969
Donald Seawell	1955 to 1970	H. J. Beaufoy-Lane	1970 to 1974
George W. Jones	1956 to 1962	Alfred C. Bennett	1970 to 1984
Stanley Young	1956 to 1958	Ralph Camargo	1970 to 1985
Paul Hampden	1957 to 1960	John Drew Devereaux	1970 to 1970
Jack Iams	1957 to 1959	David Doyle	1980 to 1972
	1960 to 1972	Wilfred J. Halpern	1970
Thomas Wenning	1957 to 1960	Girard Spencer	1970 to 1974
John D. Seymour	1957 to 1961	Avery Fisher	1970 to 1970
	1964 to 1967	John D. Seymour	1970 to 1970
Ralph Bellamy	1958 to 1964	Leonard Patrick	1970 to 1974
Van Cartmell	1958 to 1960	George Wieser	1970 to 1974
Robert Downing	1958 to 1970	Donald C. Hays	1971 to 1980
James Rennie	1958 to 1961	Lee Hays	1971 to 1974

Walter Klavun	1971 to 1974	Theodore E. Kalem	1979 to 1985
Edwin Zimmermann	1971 to 1972	Garson Kanin	1979
Ira Wolff	1971 to 1977	Alexander Scourby	1979 to 1985
Alfred E. Simon	1972 to 1977	Robert A. Carter	1980 to 1988
Richard A. Mascott	1972 to 1978	Walter Cronkite	1980 to 1983
Kenneth H. Roberts	1972 to 1976	Robert Essman	1980 to 1983
Storrs Haynes	1972 to 1979		1985 to 1988
Avery Fisher	1972 to 1976	Sidney Slon	1980 to 1983
William Mason	1973 to 1976	Richard Hamilton	1981 to 1984
Harold Rome	1973 to 1976	Russell Miller	1981 to 1984
Harold S. Gelb	1974 to 1977	William Shust	1982 to 1985
Martin Gabel	1974 to 1986	Paul Franken	1983
Herman Levin	1974 to 1977	John Bartholomew Tucker	1983
Arlen Dean Snyder	1974 to 1976	Michael Bray	1983 to 1986
Paul Myers	1974 to 1978	Robert Burke	1983 to 1984
Richard Hamilton	1976 to 1979	Roy Doliner	1984
Carl Low	1976 to 1988	Larry Gates	1984
Joseph Rhodes	1976 to 1985	David Huddleston	1984 to 1987
Morris Rittenberg	1976 to 1977	Harding Lemay	1984 to 1987
John Otis	1976 to 1977	Victor Frankel	1985
Mortimer Marshall	1976 to 1979	Gerald F. Meyers	1986
Rosser Reeves	1976 to 1981	Eugene Smith	1986 to 1988
Herman Singerman	1976 to 1981	Sean Dillon	1985 to 1988
Charles Reynolds	1977 to 1987	Robert Giroux	1985
Ralph Schulz	1977 to 1980	Robert A. Bien	1987
Willard Swire	1977	Roger Hatch	1987
Lucien Douglas	1988	Tony Triolo	1987
Charles Hohman	1977 to 1984	Lee Falk	1988
T. Edward Hambleton	1977 to 1981	Richard Greenwald	1988
José Ferrer	1978	Werner Klemperer	1988
Roger Bryant Hunting	1978	Robert Lansing	1988
A. J. Pocock	1978 to 1984	Ben Sprecher	1988
Kenneth Roberts	1978 to 1981	Arnold Stang	1988
John Robert McCarthy	1979 to 1979	Max Weitzenhoffer	1988

Abbreviations

Acct. for Accountant
Act. for Actor
AdX. for Advertising Executive
A.F. for Actors Fund
Agt. for Agent
Amb. for Ambassador
Ann. for Announcer
Arch. for Architect
Art. for Artist
Auth. for Author

Bibl. for Bibliophile
Bish. for Bishop
Bnkr. for Banker
Brkr. for Broker
Bro. for Broadcaster

Cart. for Cartoonist
Chem. for Chemist
Cir. for Circus
Cler. for Clergy
Coll. for Collector
Comp. for Composer
Cond. for Conductor
Cons. for Consul
C.P. for College President

Dec. for Decorator
Den. for Dentist
Des. for Designer
Dipl. for Diplomat
Dir. for Director
Dl. for Dealer
Dram. for Dramatist

Edit. for Editor
Edu. for Educator
Eng. for Engineer
Engr. for Engraver
Exec. for Executive
Exp. for Expert
Expl. for Explorer

Farm. for Farmer

Ho. for Hotel

Ins. for Insurance
Inv. for Inventor

Jour. for Journalist

Law. for Lawyer
Lec. for Lecturer
Lib. for Librarian
Lit. for Literary
Lyr. for Lyricist

Mag. for Magician
Mer. for Merchant
Mgr. for Manager
Min. for Mining
Mnfr. for Manufacturer
M.O.T. for Man of the Theatre
Mus. for Musician

News. for Newspaperman

Orn. for Ornithologist

Phot. for Photographer
Phys. for Physician
Pian. for Pianist
Plant. for Planter
P.O.A. for Patron of the Arts
PrR. for Press Representative
Prin. for Printer
Prod. for Producer
Prof. for Professor
Pty. for Publicity
Pub. for Publisher

RAn. for Radio Announcer
RaX. for Radio Executive
R.E. for Real Estate
R.N. for Royal Navy
R.R. for Railroad

S.A. for Scenic Artist
Sci. for Scientist
Sclp. for Sculptor
Sing. for Singer
SMg. for Stage Manager
Surg. for Surgeon
Surr. for Surrogate

TvD. for TV Director
TvX. for TV Executive

Writ. for Writer

List of Members

The following pages list the entire band of Players from the founding of the Club in 1888 to the present day. Because of space limitations, it is not possible to include individual dates of membership.

Aarons, Alfred E.	*Mgr.*	Adkins, Jess	*Act.*
Abbate, Paul	*P.O.A.*	Adler, Bruce	*Act.*
Abbe, Charles S.	*Act.*	Adler, Jacob	*Act.*
Abbey, Edwin A.	*Art.*	Adler, Norman A.	*P.O.A.*
Abbey, Henry E.	*Mgr.*	Agar, John G.	*Law.*
Abbott, Charles	*Mgr.*	Aherne, Brian	*Act.*
Abbott, S.A.B.	*Law.*	Ahrendt, Carl	*Act.*
Abbott, Samuel Nelson	*Art.*	Ahrens, Edward H.	*Pub.*
Abbott (H.M.), George	*M.O.T.*	Aiken, Frank E.	*Act.*
Abel, Walter	*Act.*	Ainley, Henry	*Act.*
Abell, Howard	*Mus.*	Aitken, John W.	*Mer.*
Abendroth, Arthur Howard	*Pub.*	Aitken, Robert	*Sclp.*
Abingdon, W. L.	*Act.*	Albaugh, John W.	*Mgr.*
Abramson, William	*Law.*	Albaugh, John W., Jr.	*Act.*
Acheson, Barclay	*Pub.*	Albert, Allan	*Prod.*
Acovone, Jay	*Act.*	Albert, Ernest	*Art.*
Adamowski, Joseph	*Mus.*	Alberti, A. Degli	*Cons.*
Adamowski, Timothy	*Mus.*	Albertson, Jack	*Act.*
Adams, B. P.	*Edit.*	Albright, Hardie	*Act.*
Adams, Charles Leslie	*Act.*	Alden, Frank E.	*Arch.*
Adams, Edward D.	*Bnkr.*	Alden, Jerome	*Writ.*
Adams, Edward M.	*Eng.*	Alden, R. Percy	*P.O.A.*
Adams, Franklin P.	*Jour.*	Aldrich, David Beals	*Writ.*
Adams, George Matthew	*Writ.*	Aldrich, Louis	*Act.*
Adams, H. Mat	*P.O.A.*	Aldrich, Richard S.	*Mgr.*
Adams, Herbert	*Sclp.*	Aldrich, Talbot	*P.O.A.*
Adams, Jess	*Dir.*	Aldrich, Thomas Bailey	*Auth.*
Adams, John Cranford	*C.P.*	Aleinehoff, Eugene A.	*M.O.T.*
Adams, John D.	*Writ.*	Aleshire, Morris	*Art.*
Adams, John Wolcott	*Art.*	Alexander, Angelo	*P.O.A.*
Adams, Lee	*Lyr.*	Alexander, Arthur	*Mus.*
Adams, Mason	*Act.*	Alexander, Frank	*Writ.*
Adams, Robert C.	*Bnkr.*	Alexander, Herbert M.	*Edit.*
Adams, Robert K.	*Prod.*	Alexander, Jack	*Edit.*
Adams, Samuel Hopkins	*Auth.*	Alexander, John	*Act.*
Adams, W.I. Lincoln	*Writ.*	Alexander, Lawrence D.	*Brkr.*
Adams, William Herbert	*Law.*	Alexander, Michael	*Prod.*
Adams, William P.	*Act.*	Alford, Robertson	*P.O.A.*
Addison, Charles L.	*R.R.*	Alford Jr., Newell	*Law.*
Ade, George (H.M.)	*Dram.*	Alison, George	*Act.*
Adelman, Joseph	*Act.*	Allan-Allen, Baldwin	*Sing.*

Allaway, Howard	*Edit.*	Anderson, Robert G.	*Auth.*
Allegretti, Theodore	*Prod.*	Anderson, Thomas Darley	*Pub.*
Allen, Jr., A. J.	*Writ.*	Anderson, Warner	*Act.*
Allen, Alfred	*Mgr.*	Andrews, Albert G.	*Act.*
Allen, Alvoni	*Mnfr.*	Andrews, Charles E.	*Writ.*
Allen, Arthur B.	*Act.*	Andrews, Clarence	*P.O.A.*
Allen, Arthur S.	*Art.*	Andrews, Dana	*Act.*
Allen, C. Edmonds III	*Law.*	Andrews, Edwards	*Act.*
Allen, C. Edmonds	*Jour.*	Andrews, Kenneth	*Edit.*
Allen, Casey	*Phot.*	Andrews, Peter	*Writ.*
Allen, Charles L.	*Act.*	Andrews, Stephen P.	*Act.*
Allen, Francis R.	*Arch.*	Andrews, William L.	*Bibl.*
Allen, Henry	*Brkr.*	Andrews, William S.	*Act.*
Allen, Hervey	*Auth.*	Andriola, Alfred	*Cart.*
Allen, Jerome R.	*Arch.*	Andrus, John R.	*Pub.*
Allen, John M.	*Act.*	Anglund, Robert	*Dram.*
Allen, Malcolm	*M.O.T.*	Angly, J	*Jour.*
Allen, Mel	*Bro.*	Anhalt, Julian	*Mgr.*
Allen, Ralph G.	*Edu.*	Anhalt, Lawrence J.	*Mgr.*
Allen, Walter	*Act.*	Ankrum, Morris	*Act.*
Allen, William S.	*Art.*	Anselmo, Andy Thomas	*Edu.*
Allien, Laurent H.	*Mer.*	Anson, A.	*Act.*
Allinson, Michael	*Act.*	Anspach, Andrew A.	*P.O.A.*
Almirall, Lloyd V.	*Law.*	Anspacher, Louis K.	*Dram.*
Almirall, Raymond F.	*Arch.*	Antell, Bertel	*P.O.A.*
Almquist, Gregg	*Act.*	Anthony, David	*Prod.*
Alson, Peter	*Jour.*	Anthony, Edward	*Writ.*
Alsop, John	*Edit.*	Anthony, Eugene	*Act.*
Aman-Jean, Armand	*Art.*	Anthony, Joseph	*Edit.*
Amdur, Harry	*Art.*	Anthony, Norman	*Edit.*
Ameche, Don	*Act.*	Anthony, Richard W.	*Jour.*
Ament, Robert	*Edit.*	Anthony, Robert	*Act.*
Amerman, Lockhart	*Cler.*	Anthony, Robert	*Des.*
Ames, Albert	*M.O.T.*	Apfel, Oscar	*Dir.*
Ames, Leon	*Act.*	Appleton, Daniel F.	*Pub.*
Ames, Paul V. Jr.	*Act.*	Appleton, Henry C.	*Pub.*
Ames, Robert	*Act.*	Appleton, William H.	*Pub.*
Ames, Winthrop	*Dir.*	Arbuckle, Maclyn	*Act.*
Ammirati, Frank A.	*Act.*	Arbury, Donald	*Act.*
Amory, John	*Bnkr.*	Archer, Stephen M.	*Edu.*
Amussen, Robert	*Edit.*	Arden, Edwin	*Act.*
Andersen, Christopher	*Jour.*	Arent, Arthur	*Dram.*
Anderson, Dallas	*Act.*	Arents Jr., George	*P.O.A.*
Anderson, Edmund	*P.O.A.*	Arey, Wayne	*Act.*
Anderson, Harold M.	*Edit.*	Arliss, George	*Act.*
Anderson, John	*Act.*	Armbruster, Robert	*Mus.*
Anderson, Joseph	*Act.*	Armour, Allison V.	*Mnfr.*
Anderson, Maxwell	*Dram.*	Armour, George	*P.O.A.*
Anderson, Robert	*Dram.*	Armstorng, J.	*Pub.*
		Armstrong, Dale	*Jour.*

Armstrong, Robert	*Act.*	Bacon, Edward R.	*Law.*
Arnold, Dan	*Mer.*	Bacon, Francis H.	*Arch.*
Arnold, Edward	*Act.*	Bacon, Francis M.	*Mer.*
Arnold, Elliot	*Writ.*	Bacon, Frank	*Act.*
Arnold, Henry H.	*Force*	Bacon, Henry	*Arch.*
Arnold, J.H.V.	*P.O.A.*	Bacon, John H.	*Mgr.*
Arnold, Wade	*Writ.*	Bacon, Leonard	*Auth.*
Aronson, John	*Act.*	Bacon, Roswell	*Art.*
Arthur, Daniel V.	*Mgr.*	Baehr, George	*Phys.*
Arthur, E. J.	*Art.*	Bafficio, James A.	*Act.*
Arthur, Joseph	*Act.*	Bagster-Collins, Jeremy	*Prof.*
Arthur, Paul	*Act.*	Bailey, Charles C.	*Prod.*
Arthur, Phil	*Act.*	Bailey, George	*Edit.*
Arvold, Alfred G.	*Dir.*	Bailey, Isaac H.	*Mer.*
Arvold, Mason	*Art.*	Bailey, Vernon Howe	*Art.*
Ash, David	*Writ.*	Bain, Conrad	*Act.*
Ash, Lee	*Edu.*	Bain, George Grantham	*Jour.*
Ashcraft, Leon	*Phys.*	Bair, Thomas C.	*Act.*
Ashe, Edmund M.	*Art.*	Bairnsfather, Bruce	*Auth.*
Ashley, Ira	*M.O.T.*	Baker, A. Prescott	*R. E.*
Ashmore, Harry S.	*Jour.*	Baker, Benjamin A.	*A.F.*
Ashwell, Thomas W.	*Pub.*	Baker, Frederick Sherman	*Edit.*
Ashworth, Tucker	*Act.*	Baker, George Barr	*Jour.*
Astor, Vincent	*P.O.A.*	Baker, George D.	*Act.*
Atkinson, Brooks	*Writ.*	Baker, George F.	*Bnkr.*
Atkinson, Ted	*P.O.A.*	Baker, George Pierce	*Prof.*
Atterbury, C. L.	*Law.*	Baker, James Alan	*Writ.*
Atterbury, J. T.	*Brkr.*	Baker, Lewis	*Act.*
Atterbury, Malcolm	*Act.*	Baker, Melville P.	*Dram.*
Attwater, Allan	*Mgr.*	Baker, Ray Stannard	*Writ.*
Atwell, Roy	*Act.*	Baker, Robert M.	*Dram.*
Atwood, Albert W.	*Auth.*	Bakewell, Allen C.	*Mnfr.*
August, Tony	*M.O.T.*	Balderston, John L.	*Jour.*
Austen, Peter Townsend	*Prof.*	Baldwin, H. Gardiner	*Brkr.*
Austin, J. W.	*Act.*	Baldwin, H. W.	*R.R.*
Austin, Jr., Warren R.	*Writ.*	Baldwin, Robert M.	*Bnkr.*
Avery, Ira L.	*M.O.T.*	Balfour, William	*Act.*
Avery, Paul	*Act.*	Ballantine, Ian	*Pub.*
Avery, Samuel P.	*Art.*	Balmer, Edwin	*Edit.*
Avery, Val	*Act.*	Balsam, Martin	*Act.*
Axinn, Donald	*Edu.*	Bamburgh, Charles	*Ins.*
Ayers, Jack E.	*M.O.T.*	Bamburgh, William Cushing	*Ins.*
Ayres, Frank O.	*Ins.*	Bancroft, Joseph	*Chem.*
Babcock, Theodore	*Act.*	Bancroft, Samuel, Jr.	*Mer.*
Bach, George	*Phys.*	Bangs, Flecher H.	*Books*
Bach, Julian Sebastian, Jr	*Edit.*	Bangs, John K.	*Auth.*
Bacheller, Irving	*Auth.*	Banks, Sam A.	*M.O.T.*
Bachrach, David J.	*Phys.*	Banning, Kendall	*Edit.*
Backer, George	*Writ.*	Barandes, Robert	*Law.*
Backus, George	*Act.*	Barber, Donn	*Arch.*

Barber, Richard	*Agt.*	Barry, Philip	*Prod.*
Barbieri, Christopher A.	*Arch.*	Barry, Philip S. Jr	*M.O.T.*
Barbour, Thomas	*Act.*	Barry, Richard	*Writ.*
Barclay, Don	*Act.*	Barry, Robert	*Writ.*
Barclay, J. Searle	*P.O.A.*	Barry, William Edwin	*Act.*
Barclay, John	*Act.*	Barry, William F.	*Phys.*
Barclay, McClelland	*Art.*	Barrymore, John B.	*Act.*
Barclay, Sackett M.	*P.O.A.*	Barrymore, Lionel	*Act.*
Barclay, T. Harold	*Phys.*	Barrymore, Maurice	*Act.*
Barier, George	*Act.*	Barstow, Charles L.	*Edit.*
Baring, Cecil	*Bnkr.*	Barthelmess, Richard	*Act.*
Barirolli, John	*Cond.*	Bartlett, Arthur	*Writ.*
Barker, Henry Ames	*Arch.*	Bartlett, Francis	*Law.*
Barker, Reginald W.	*Act.*	Bartlett, Frederick Clay	*Art.*
Barkle, Richard N.	*Writ.*	Bartlett, Frederick Orin	*Writ.*
Barlett, Franklin	*Law.*	Bartlett, Philip G.	*Law.*
Barlett, Frederick	*Art.*	Bartol, Henry G.	*Brkr.*
Barlett, Frederick	*Writ.*	Barton, Bruce	*Auth.*
Barlett, Philip	*Law.*	Barton, Ralph	*Art.*
Barlow, Peter T.	*P.O.A.*	Barton, Willard	*Act.*
Barlow, Reginald	*Act.*	Baruch, H. N.	*Act.*
Barlow, S.M.L.	*Law.*	Basel, Amos S.	*Prod.*
Barnabee, Henry Clay	*Sing.*	Baskerville, Charles	*Art.*
Barnard, William Howard	*Mer.*	Bass, Robert	*P.O.A.*
Barnay, Ludwig	*Act.*	Bassett, Peter	*Act.*
Barnes, Courtlandt D.	*Pub.*	Basso, Hamilton	*Writ.*
Barnes, Edward Shippen	*Mus.*	Batchelder, John D.	*Coll*
Barnes, Eric Wollencott	*Act.*	Batchelor, C. D.	*Cart.*
Barnes, Frederick J.	*P.O.A.*	Bate, Don	*Writ.*
Barnes, Howard	*Writ.*	Bates, William O.	*Dram.*
Barnes, J. H.	*Act.*	Baum, Allyn Z.	*Jour.*
Barnes, James	*Writ.*	Baum, L. Frank	*Auth.*
Barnet, Sylvan	*Jour.*	Baum, Stanley A.	*Writ.*
Barnett, Michael	*Writ.*	Baume, Edgar	*Act.*
Barney, Charles T.	*Bnkr.*	Bayfield, St. Clair	*Act.*
Barney, Danford	*Auth.*	Baylies, Edmund	*Act.*
Barnhart, Robert K.	*Pub.*	Baylis, William	*Bnkr.*
Barnum, George	*Act.*	Baynes, Ernest Harold	*Auth.*
Baron, Maurice	*Comp.*	Beach, John H.	*P.O.A.*
Baron, Richard	*Pub.*	Beach, Rex E.	*Auth.*
Barr, Douglas	*Act.*	Beach, Stewart	*Edit.*
Barraclough, Sydney	*Act.*	Beach, Warren C.	*Army*
Barrett, Lawrence	*Act.*	Beach, Williams G.	*Act.*
Barrett, James S.	*Act.*	Beack, Jackson	*Act.*
Barrett, William E.	*Writ.*	Beahan, Charles	*Dram.*
Barrett, Wilson	*Act.*	Beal, John	*Act.*
Barrie, Leslie	*Act.*	Beals, Donald Marcy	*Pub.*
Barron, Charles	*Act.*	Beaman, Charles C.	*Law.*
Barron, Elwyn A.	*Dram.*	Beard, Daniel C.	*Art.*
Barry, Charles C.	*TvX.*	Beattie, Jr., Edward W.	*Jour.*

Beatty, A. Chester	*Eng.*	Benjamin, John	*Bnkr.*
Beatty, William H.	*Law.*	Benjamin, Park	*Law.*
Beaufort, John	*Jour.*	Benjamin, Paul	*Act.*
Beaufoy-Lane, H. J.	*M.O.T.*	Benner, Willard	*P.O.A.*
Beauley, William Jean	*Arch.*	Bennett, Alfred	*Law.*
Beaupre, Jon	*Act.*	Bennett, Arnold (H.M.)	*Auth.*
Beazell, William P.	*Edit.*	Bennett, Arthur	*Writ.*
Bechtold, John	*Art.*	Bennett, Jr., Harry W.	*P.O.A.*
Beck, Jr., Charles W.	*Engr.*	Bennett, Richard	*Act.*
Beck, George D.	*Art.*	Bennett, Robert	*M.O.T.*
Beck, Jackson	*Act.*	Bennetts, Leslie	*Prod.*
Beckerman, Bernard	*Edu.*	Bennis, Charles	*Exec.*
Beckwith, J. Carroll	*Art.*	Bennison, Louis	*Act.*
Bedlow, Henry	*P.O.A.*	Benrimo, J. H.	*Act.*
Beebe, Lucius	*Writ.*	Benson, George M.	*Prod.*
Beecroft, Chester	*Act.*	Benson, Mitchell	*Dir.*
Beecroft, Victor	*Act.*	Benson, Stuart	*Art.*
Beekman, James H.	*P.O.A.*	Bentley, Walter E.	*Cler.*
Beers, Nathan	*Mgr.*	Benton, Nicholas	*Prod.*
Beersman, Charles	*Arch.*	Benwell, Jack	*Act.*
Behrman, S. N.	*Dram.*	Berdan, John M.	*Prof.*
Beigelman, Mark	*Prod.*	Berenguer-Cesar, Jacome	
Bejan, Edward	*Writ.*	Baggie de	*Jour.*
Belasco, David	*Mgr.*	Beresford, Harry	*Act.*
Belden, Charles Denison	*Brkr.*	Berg, Carl	*Edu.*
Beldon, Sanford T.	*Pub.*	Berg, Charles I.	*Arch.*
Belknap, Henry W.	*P.O.A.*	Berger, Meyer	*Jour.*
Bell, Bernard Iddings	*C.P.*	Berger, Norman	*Art.*
Bell, Digby	*Act.*	Berger, Robert Armin	*Phys.*
Bell, E. Hamilton	*Art.*	Bergerman, Melbourne	*Law.*
Bell, Edward R.	*Bnkr.*	Berkowitz, Bernard	*P.O.A.*
Bell, James A.	*Jour.*	Berkowsky, Paul B.	*Prod.*
Bell, James H.	*Act.*	Berle, Jr., A. A.	*Law.*
Bell, Joseph S.	*Act.*	Berle, Rudolf P.	*Law.*
Bell, Ralph	*Act.*	Berlin, Irving (H.M.)	*Comp.*
Bell, Robert	*Prof.*	Bermingham, Arch	*P.O.A.*
Bellamy, Francis R.	*Edit.*	Berns, William	*Prod.*
Bellamy, Ralph	*Act.*	Benstein, Leonard (H.M.)	*Mus.*
Bellows, Gerorge	*Art.*	Bernstein, Nahum	*Law.*
Belmont, Oliver H. P.	*Bnkr.*	Berrien, Cornelius R.	*Writ.*
Bemelmans, Ludwig	*Wit*	Berry, Eric	*Act.*
Benchley, Nathaniel G.	*Writ.*	Bessell, Wesley S.	*Arch.*
Benchley, Robert	*Writ.*	Best, Herbert	*Auth.*
Bend, George H.	*Bnkr.*	Betcher, Albert M.	*Phys.*
Benda, Wladyslaw T.	*Art.*	Betelle, James O.	*Arch.*
Bendedict, Fred	*Bnkr.*	Bettini, Gianni	*P.O.A.*
Bender, Carl	*Art.*	Bettle, Samuel	*P.O.A.*
Benedict, Elias	*Bnkr.*	Betts, Edward R.	*P.O.A.*
Benedict, Robert	*Act.*	Betts, Samuel R.	*Law.*
Benham, James	*Art.*	Beyer, Kenneth	*P.O.A.*

Bickel, Karl A.	*Jour.*	Blanton, Alexander	*Pub.*
Biddle, Nicholas	*R.E.*	Blatter, Robert	*Art.*
Biemiller, Reynard	*M.O.T.*	Blauvelt, James H.	*Des.*
Bien, Robert L.	*Arch.*	Bleecker, John Van B.	*Navy*
Bigelow, Joe	*Writ.*	Blenner, Carle J.	*Art.*
Bigelow, John	*Lit.*	Blethen, Joseph	*Writ.*
Bigelow, Poultney	*Auth.*	Blind, Eric	*Act.*
Bigelow, William B.	*Arch.*	Bliss, Cornelius N.	*Mer.*
Biggers, Earle Derr	*Auth.*	Bliss, Mason	*M.O.T.*
Bill, Alfred Hoyt	*Auth.*	Bliss, William	*R.R.*
Billings, Henry B.	*Mer.*	Bliss, William H.	*Law.*
Bingham, Edfrid A.	*Auth.*	Block, Ralph	*Writ.*
Bingham, John	*Act.*	Blodget, Alden	*M.O.T.*
Binney, Harold	*Law.*	Blodget, Otis Skinner	*M.O.T.*
Birch, Reginald	*Art.*	Blodgett, Thomas H.	*Pub.*
Bird, Charles A.	*Mgr.*	Blood, William Findlater	*Act.*
Bird, John H.	*Law.*	Bloom, Philip	*M.O.T.*
Bird, William	*Writ.*	Blossom, Henry M.	*Auth.*
Birkett, Eastman	*Law.*	Blossom, Sumner N.	*Edit.*
Birmingham, Alan	*Act.*	Blum, Robert	*Art.*
Birmingham, Arch	*AdX.*	Blumberg, Alexander J.	*Mus.*
Birney, David	*Act.*	Blume, Robert R.	*M.O.T.*
Birnie, William A. H.	*Edit.*	Blyden, Larry	*Act.*
Birsh, Arthur	*Pub.*	Blythe, Samuel G.	*Writ.*
Bishop, A. Thornton	*Art.*	Boag, William	*Act.*
Bishop, Andre	*Dir.*	Boardman, Edward C.	*Law.*
Bishop, Charles B.	*Act.*	Bobbs, William C.	*Pub.*
Bisland, Thomas P.	*Eng.*	Bobowman, John	*Prof.*
Bispham, David	*Sing.*	Bobrow, Edwin Ezra	*Writ.*
Bispham, George T.	*Auth.*	Boehnel, William	*Jour.*
Bispham, William	*Mer.*	Bogart, Humphrey	*Act.*
Bitter, Karl	*Sclp.*	Bogert, William R. III	*Act.*
Bjorkman, Edwin	*Writ.*	Bohen, William F.	*Act.*
Black, Walter J.	*Pub.*	Bohorquez, Joseph	*Phys.*
Blackmer, Sidney	*Act.*	Bok, Edward W.	*Edit.*
Blackstone, F. Gordon	*P.O.A.*	Boker, Alfred L.	*Art.*
Blackton, Jay	*Mus.*	Boker, George H.	*Auth.*
Blacque, Valentine A.	*Brkr.*	Boles, James	*Act.*
Blagden, Samuel P.	*P.O.A.*	Bolger, Ray	*Act.*
Blaine, Emmons	*P.O.A.*	Bolte, Charles Guy	*Writ.*
Blair, John	*Act.*	Boltin, Lee	*Writ.*
Blair, Watson F.	*Bnkr.*	Bolton, Guy	*Auth.*
Blake, Arthur M.	*Mer.*	Bolton, Whitney	*Writ.*
Blake, Gerald II	*Writ.*	Boltwood, Edward	*Auth.*
Blake, Luther L.	*Pub.*	Bond, Frederick	*Act.*
Blake, Richard	*Writ.*	Bond, H. G.	*R.R.*
Blake, Richard	*Prod.*	Bond, Raleigh	*Act.*
Blakeley, Gene	*Act.*	Bond, Raymond T.	*Pub.*
Blanchard, Fred C.	*Dram.*	Bone, David William	*Auth.*
		Boniface, Jr., George C.	*Act.*

Bonn, Francis Autumn	*Act.*	Bradley, Will	*Art.*
Bonner, Charles W.	*Law.*	Bradley, William Aspinwall	*Writ.*
Bonner, Eugene McDonald	*Comp.*	Brady, Barrett	*Writ.*
Bonner, Paul Hyde	*Bibl.*	Brady, William A.	*Prod.*
Bonney, William E.	*Act.*	Brady, Jr., William A.	*Mgr.*
Booraem, Jr., Hendrik	*Exec.*	Bragdon, Claude	*Writ.*
Booth, Edwin W.	*P.O.A.*	Braham, Lionel	*Act.*
Booth, Edwin	*Act.*	Braley, Berton	*Writ.*
Booth, Franklin	*Act.*	Bramwell, William	*Act.*
Booth, John Hewlett	*P.O.A.*	Brandon, Peter	*Act.*
Booth, Junius Brutus	*Act.*	Brandt, Carl	*Lit. Agt.*
Booth, Sydney	*Act.*	Brandt, Carl D.	*Agt.*
Booth, William Stone	*Pub.*	Brandt, Joseph A.	*Pub.*
Boothe, Junius Brutus III	*Act.*	Brandt, Mel	*Bro.*
Boothe, Earle	*Act.*	Bransford, Bradley	*Act.*
Bordages, Asa	*Writ.*	Bray, Joseph E.	*Pub.*
Borden, Howard S.	*Mer.*	Bray, Michael	*Law.*
Borden, M.C.D.	*Mer.*	Braziller, George	*Pub.*
Borden, Marshall	*Act.*	Brean, Herbert Joseph	*Writ.*
Bordman, Gerald	*Writ.*	Brecher, Egon	*Act.*
Borglum, Gutzon	*Sclp.*	Breck, Edward	*Writ.*
Borie, Adolphe E.	*Mnfr.*	Breck, John Leslie	*Art.*
Borie, John	*Arch.*	Breeding, Earl B.	*Law.*
Boruff, John P.	*Act.*	Breese, James L.	*Bnkr.*
Borup, Doan	*Act.*	Breitbart, Douglas	*Prod.*
Bosworth, F. H.	*Phys.*	Breitenbruck, John	*Act.*
Bosworth, Hobart	*Act.*	Brennan, Joseph	*Act.*
Bosworth, William W.	*Arch.*	Brennan, Arthur "Buddy"	*Mus.*
Botsford, Stephen Blakeskee	*Pub.*	Brennecke, Jr., Ernest	*Lec.*
Bottomley, Roland	*Act.*	Brenner, Nyle	*Prod.*
Boudrot, Mel	*Act.*	Brent, George	*Act.*
Bourchier, Arthur	*Act.*	Brett, George P.	*Pub.*
Bourneuf, Philip	*Act.*	Brett, Jr., George P.	*Pub.*
Bournique, Lyman G.	*Mgr.*	Brett, Richard M.	*Pub.*
Bowdoin, George S.	*Bnkr.*	Brewer, Jr., George E.	*Dram.*
Bowley, Craig	*Act.*	Brewster, E. L.	*Bnkr.*
Bowman, Charles	*Mnfr.*	Brewster, Robert J.	*Exec.*
Bowman, John G.	*Prof.*	Brian, Donald	*Act.*
Bowser, Charles	*Act.*	Brice, W. Kirkpatrick	*Law.*
Boyd, James	*Auth.*	Brickelmaier, William J.	*Phys.*
Boyd, James	*Act.*	Bridgham, Clarence	*Lib.*
Boyd, Rutherford	*Art.*	Briesen, Hans Von	*Law.*
Boyden, Albert A.	*Pub.*	Briggs, Austin	*Art.*
Boyer, Charles	*Act.*	Briggs, M.J.G.	*Act.*
Boyle, John	*Jour.*	Briggs, William	*Edit.*
Brace, Donald C.	*Pub.*	Briggs, William Harlowe	*M.O.T.*
Bracken, Eddie	*Act.*	Brigham, Clarence L.	*Lib.*
Brackett, Charles	*Auth.*	Brilioth, Borje	*Edit.*
Brackett, Jeffrey R.	*P.O.A.*	Brink, William J.	*Jour.*
Bradford, Roark	*Writ.*	Brinton, Christian	*Act.*

Bristol, E. L. Macomb	*Phys.*	Brown, J. Appleton	*Art.*
Bristol, Edward N.	*Pub.*	Brown, John Mason	*Writ.*
Bristol, Herbert G.	*Pub.*	Brown, Julius L.	*Law.*
Britt, Albert	*Edit.*	Brown, Louis	*Arch.*
Britt, George	*Writ.*	Brown, Louis Francis	*Mgr.*
Britter, Eric	*Jour.*	Brown, R.	*M.O.T.*
Broad, Jay	*Edu.*	Brown, R. C. Jim	*Writ.*
Broadhurst, George H.	*Dram.*	Brown, Raymond J.	*Edit.*
Brock, Henry Irving	*Edit.*	Brown, Richard	*Writ.*
Brocklesby, William C.	*Arch.*	Brown, Reed, Jr.	*Act.*
Brodkin, Herbert	*Prod.*	Brown, Ritter	*Mus.*
Broglie, Thomas De Villiers	*Prod.*	Brown, Robert	*Act.*
Brokaw, Charles	*Act.*	Brown, Russ	*Act.*
Brokaw, Frederick C.	*Exec.*	Brown, Stephen A.	*SMg.*
Bromley, Theodore	*Mgr.*	Brown, Ted V.	*Pub.*
Bronfin, Arthur	*M.O.T.*	Brown, Thomas B.	*Mer.*
Brooke, Clifford	*Act.*	Brown, Thomas G.	*Mer.*
Brooke, Hugh	*Act.*	Brown, Vernon H.	*P.O.A.*
Brooke, Percy	*Act.*	Browne, Earle	*Act.*
Brooke, William	*Act.*	Browne, Michael	*Act.*
Brooker, Robert	*Act.*	Browne, Porter Emerson	*Writ.*
Brookfield, William	*Mnfr.*	Brownell, R. H.	*P.O.A.*
Brooks, Eric J. (Singerman)	*Act.*	Browning, Rod	*Act.*
Brooks, Frederick	*Mer.*	Broyles, Douglas	*Act.*
Brooks, Hewitt	*Act.*	Brubaker, Howard	*Edit.*
Brooks, John E.	*Mer.*	Bruce, H. Langdon	*Act.*
Brooks, Joseph	*Mgr.*	Bruce, Robert M.	*Art.*
Brooks, Van Wyck	*Writ.*	Bruenn, Laurie Philip	*Prod.*
Brooks, Walter	*Mer.*	Bruere, Henry	*Law.*
Broome, George Cochran	*Army*	Brundidge, Harry T.	*Writ.*
Brosokas, Charles	*Law.*	Bruning, Albert	*Act.*
Brotherson, Eric	*Act.*	Brunner, Arnold	*Arch.*
Broughton, Philip F.	*Comp.*	Brunton, Robert	*S.A.*
Broun, Heywood Hale	*M.O.T.*	Brust, Saul	*Pub.*
Broun, Heywood	*Writ.*	Bryan, Courtlandt D. B.	*Writ.*
Brower, Brock Hendrickson	*Writ.*	Bryan, Julien	*Writ.*
Brown, Albert O.	*Bnkr.*	Bryan-Brown, Adrian	*PrR.*
Brown, Alexander P.	*Law.*	Bryant, Charles	*Act.*
Brown, Anthony	*Act.*	Bryant, George E.	*Act.*
Brown, Arthur William	*Art.*	Brynner, Yul	*Act.*
Brown, David	*Edit.*	Buchanan, Arthur Falkland	*Act.*
Brown, David	*Prod.*	Buchanan, Barry	*Act.*
Brown, Edward M.	*Auct*	Buchanan, Thompson	*Dram.*
Brown, Ethelbert	*Art.*	Buchbinder, Norman	*P.O.A.*
Brown, Francis	*Writ.*	Buchner, Melvyn	*Act.*
Brown, Gilmor	*Act.*	Buck, Frank	*Exp.*
Brown, Harry Joe	*Prod.*	Buck, Gene	*Comp.*
Brown, Horace Manchester	*Phys.*	Buckler, Jr., Thomas H.	*Phys.*
Brown, Irving	*R.E.*	Buckley, Joseph J.	*Mgt*
Brown, Irving Swan	*Auth.*	Buckley, Robert	*Prod.*

Buckley, William T.	*Mer.*
Buckmaster, John	*Act.*
Buckstone, John C.	*Act.*
Buckstone, Rowland	*Act.*
Buckwalter, Brinton	*P.O.A.*
Bucquet, Harold	*Dir.*
Budd, Herbert	*Act.*
Budlong, John Post	*Pub.*
Buel, Clarence	*Edit.*
Buell, Ralph P.	*P.O.A.*
Buell, William	*P.O.A.*
Bugbee, George	*P.O.A.*
Bugg, Irving	*Writ.*
Bulkley, Henry W.	*P.O.A.*
Bull, W. Lanmun	*Bnkr.*
Bullard, Arthur	*Writ.*
Bullock, Walter F.	*Jour.*
Bumpus, Everett C.	*Law.*
Bunce, Alan C.	*Act.*
Bunce, Frank D.	*Mgr.*
Bunce, William Gedney	*Art.*
Bunker, Denis M.	*Art.*
Bunker, William	*Brkr.*
Burbeck, Frank M.	*Act.*
Burbridge, Charles	*Act.*
Burger, Knox	*Jour.*
Burgess, Gelett	*Writ.*
Burgess, Thornton W.	*Writ.*
Burkat, Howard	*M.O.T.*
Burke, C. Russell M.	*Dram.*
Burke, Edward F.	*P.O.A.*
Burke, Edwin	*Dram.*
Burke, John T.	*Act.*
Burke, John	*P.O.A.*
Burke, Melville	*Act.*
Burke, Robert J.	*Act.*
Burman, Ben Lucien	*Dram.*
Burnet, Dana	*Writ.*
Burnett, Harry	*P.O.A.*
Burnett, Vivian	*Pub.*
Burnett, W. R.	*Writ.*
Burnhome, Clement M.	*Bnkr.*
Burns, David	*Act.*
Burns, George	*Act.*
Burnside, R. H.	*Dir.*
Burr, Eugene	*Prod.*
Burr, Henry I.	*Pub.*
Burrell, Fred	*Act.*
Burrell, George	*Law.*
Burson, Harold	*P.O.A.*
Burt, Struthers	*Writ.*
Burton, Harry Payne	*Edit.*
Burton, J. C.	*Writ.*
Burton, Richard	*Prof.*
Bushmiller, Ernie	*Cart.*
Bushnell, Joseph	*Mer.*
Butler, Arthur W.	*Bnkr.*
Butler, Charles W.	*Act.*
Butler, Ellis Parker	*Auth.*
Butler, Frank Cecil	*Act.*
Butler, Geoffrey	*Lit.*
Butler, George B.	*Act.*
Butler, Henry Willis	*Dir.*
Butler, Howard Crosby	*Prof.*
Butler, Nicolas Murray	*Prof.*
Butler, Prescott Hall	*Law.*
Butler, Richard	*Mer.*
Butler, William	*Law.*
Butler, William J.	*Act.*
Butner, Lawrence	*Prod.*
Butt, Wilfred Lawson	*Act.*
Butterfield, Charles B.	*Act.*
Butterfield, Everett	*Act.*
Butterfield, Walton	*Prod.*
Butterworth, Charles	*Act.*
Bye, George T.	*Lit.*
Bye, Richard E.	*Pub.*
Byers, Ralph	*Act.*
Bynner, Witter	*Auth.*
Byram, John	*Edit.*
Byrd, Sam A.	*Act.*
Byrne, Donn	*Auth.*
Byrne, Francis	*Act.*
Byrnes, Gene	*Art.*
Byron, Arthur W.	*Act.*
Byron, Edward A.	*Writ.*
Byron, Oliver Doud	*Act.*
Byron, Ward	*Dir.*
Cable, Benjamin T.	*P.O.A.*
Cabot, Eliot	*Act.*
Cabot, Samuel	*Mnfr.*
Cagney, James	*Act.*
Cahoon, James Blake	*Prod.*
Caldara, Orme	*Act.*
Calder, A. Stirling	*Sclp.*
Calder, William	*Act.*
Caldwell, Charles H.	*Arch.*
Caldwell, Orville	*Act.*

Calhern, Louis	*Act.*
Calhoun, Chris	*Pub.*
Calhoun, Philo	*Writ.*
Calkins, Loring Gary	*Art.*
Call, John	*Act.*
Callahan, William F.	*Eng.*
Calleia, Joseph	*Act.*
Callen, Tarquin Miles	*M.O.T.*
Calmer, Ned	*Jour.*
Calvin, Frederick	*Writ.*
Camargo, Ralph	*Act.*
Cameron, Donald	*Act.*
Cameron, Rudolph	*Act.*
Cameron, Stewart	*Act.*
Camillucci, Gregory	*Act.*
Camp, Charles W.	*Jour.*
Camp, Frederick Edgar	*Mer.*
Campbell, Alan	*Act.*
Campbell, George T.	*Law.*
Campbell, Gerald	*Cons.*
Campbell, Jim	*Act.*
Campbell, Kane	*Dram.*
Campbell, Malcolm	*Brkr.*
Campbell, Maurice	*Mgr.*
Canby, A. H.	*Mgr.*
Canby, Henry	*Prof.*
Canfield, Cass	*Pub.*
Caniff, Milton A.	*Art.*
Cannon, Henry Le Grand	*Bnkr.*
Cannon, Henry W.	*Bnkr.*
Cannon, Norman	*Art.*
Cantor, Arthur	*M.O.T.*
Cantwell, Robert	*Edit.*
Cape, Jonathan	*Pub.*
Capen, Oliver B.	*Pub.*
Caples, John	*Writ.*
Capra, Frank	*Dir.*
Carb, Alfred B.	*Law.*
Carb, Stephen Ames	*Law.*
Carey, Arthur Astor	*P.O.A.*
Carere, John M.	*Arch.*
Carey, Leonard	*Act.*
Cargill, Jerome H.	*Prod.*
Carhart, James L.	*Act.*
Carleton, George M.	*Act.*
Carlin, Alexis	*M.O.T.*
Carlin, Joseph	*M.O.T.*
Carlson, Marvin	*Edu.*
Carlson, Robert O.	*Jour.*

Carlton, Henry Fisk	*Writ.*
Carlton, W. N. C.	*Lib.*
Carlton, Winslow	*P.O.A.*
Carlyle, Frank	*Act.*
Carmer, Carl	*Auth.*
Carnegie, Dale	*Auth.*
Carnes, Mason	*P.O.A.*
Carney, Art	*Act.*
Carniol, John J.	*Dram.*
Carpenter, Cliff	*Act.*
Carpenter, Edward Childs	*Dram.*
Carpenter, George R.	*Writ.*
Carpenter, Herbert S.	*Bnkr.*
Carpenter, Horace Thompson	*Pub.*
Carradine, David	*Act.*
Carradine, John	*Act.*
Carradine, Keith	*Act.*
Carrigan, Andrew	*Mer.*
Carrigan, William L.	*Mer.*
Carrington, Frank	*Dir.*
Carrington, Reginald	*Act.*
Carroll, Adam	*Prod.*
Carroll, Carroll	*Writ.*
Carroll, Edward L.	*Prof.*
Carroll, Howard	*Jour.*
Carroll, Latrobe	*Writ.*
Carroll, Leo G.	*Act.*
Carrter, John	*Writ.*
Carruth, Hayden	*Writ.*
Carryl, Charles E.	*Writ.*
Carryl, Guy Wetmore	*Auth.*
Carson, J. H.	*Mnfr.*
Carson, John B.	*R.R.*
Carter, Ernest T.	*Mus.*
Carter, Harrison G.	*Act.*
Carter, John Franklin	*Writ.*
Carter, M. Lloyd	*Act.*
Carter, Randall Ayres	*Law.*
Carter, Robert Peyton	*Act.*
Carter, Robert Ayres	*Pub.*
Cartmell, Tenney	*P.O.A.*
Cartmell, Van H.	*Pub.*
Cartwright, Charles	*Act.*
Carvill, Henry J.	*Act.*
Casamajor, George H.	*Edit.*
Case, Henry Jay	*P.O.A.*
Casey, Frank DeSales	*Art.*
Cashin, William	*Jour.*

Casselman, William A.	*Jour.*
Cathcart, George	*Pub.*
Catir, Norman J. Jr	*Cler.*
Catledge, Turner	*Edit.*
Catton, Bruce	*Writ.*
Cavett, Dick	*Act.*
Cavett, Frank Morgan	*Auth.*
Ccoolidge, Paul	*P.O.A.*
Cecil, Lawrence H.	*Act.*
Center, Robert Innes	*Pub.*
Chace, Edward G.	*Mnfr.*
Chalfen, Leo	*P.O.A.*
Chalfen, Lucian	*Jour.*
Chalfin, Paul	*Art.*
Chalmers, Thomas Hardie	*Sing.*
Chalzel, Leo	*Act.*
Chamberlin, Emerson	*Bnkr.*
Chamberlin, J. Frederick	*Bnkr.*
Chambers, David Laurance	*Pub.*
Chambers, Lyster	*Act.*
Chambers, Robert A.	*Mus.*
Chamlee, Mario	*Sing.*
Champlain, Robert	*Dir.*
Champney, J. Wells	*Art.*
Chan, Donald W.	*Edu.*
Chan, Sou	*P.O.A.*
Chanler, John Armstrong	*P.O.A.*
Chanler, Robert W.	*Art.*
Chanler, William Astor	*Exp.*
Chanler, Winthrop	*P.O.A.*
Chapin, Henry	*Writ.*
Chapin, Howard M.	*Writ.*
Chapin, Joseph H.	*Edit.*
Chapin, Josiah L.	*P.O.A.*
Chapin, William V.	*Brkr.*
Chapman, Carlton	*Art.*
Chapman, Frank	*Edit.*
Chapman, John	*Writ.*
Chappell, A. H.	*Mer.*
Chappell, Delos	*Prod.*
Charise, Andre	*Act.*
Charles, Richard L.	*Pub.*
Charlton, Loudon	*Mgr.*
Chase, Alden	*Act.*
Chase, Arthur	*Mgr.*
Chase, Arthur B.	*Pub.*
Chase, Burr L.	*Pub.*
Chase, C. Ward	*P.O.A.*
Chase, F. E.	*Pub.*
Chase, Joseph Cummings	*Art.*
Chase, Walter	*P.O.A.*
Chase, William B.	*Writ.*
Chase, William M.	*Art.*
Chater, Harry D.	*P.O.A.*
Chatfield-Taylor, Hobart	*Auth.*
Cheew, Beverly	*P.O.A.*
Chellas, Allen	*Writ.*
Cheney, Jr., Benjamin	*P.O.A.*
Chenery, Leonard	*P.O.A.*
Chenery, William L.	*Auth.*
Cheney, Harry	*Mer.*
Cheney, L. R.	*Mer.*
Cheney, Robert	*Mer.*
Cheney, Sheldon	*Auth.*
Chennels, Roy D.	*Pub.*
Chernuchin, Michael S.	*Law.*
Cherry, Charles	*Act.*
Chester, Willam S.	*Mus.*
Chevalier, Albert	*Act.*
Chew, Alexander D.	*P.O.A.*
Chichester, Charles F.	*Pub.*
Chilton, Carroll Brent	*Lec.*
Chipp, Howard	*Law.*
Chisolm, Andre	*Brkr.*
Chlapowski, Charles	*Mgr.*
Choate, Edward	*Prod.*
Chotzinoff, Samuel	*Jour.*
Christian, George	*Cler.*
Christie, George	*Act.*
Christie, Lindsay	*Jour.*
Christopher, Milbourne	*Act.*
Christopher, Thomas McKean	*Art.*
Christy, Howard	*Art.*
Church, Willam	*Eng.*
Church, Jr., John	*Eng.*
Churchill, Winston	*Auth.*
Churvh, Benjamin	*Sing.*
Churvhill, Berton	*Act.*
Chwast, Seymour	*Des.*
Ciccone, Sam	*Act.*
Cioffe, Charles	*Act.*
Citron, Cecil A.	*Law.*
Claiborne, Ross	*Pub.*
Claney, Howard	*Act.*
Clapp, John	*Edit.*
Clare, James	*P.O.A.*
Clarence, O.	*Act.*
Clarges, Verner	*Act.*

Clark, Alden	*Pub.*	Coe, Richard L.	*Jour.*
Clark, Alexander	*Act.*	Coffin, Dean	*Dir.*
Clark, Barrett	*Auth.*	Coffin, William A.	*Art.*
Clark, Barrett	*Act.*	Coggeshall, Henry	*Phys.*
Clark, Bobby	*Act.*	Coghlan, Charles	*Act.*
Clark, Edward F. Jr	*Law.*	Cohan, George M.	*Act.*
Clark, Jr., Frederic	*P.O.A.*	Cohen, Alexander H.	*Prod.*
Clark, George	*P.O.A.*	Cohen, Barry Lee	*Law.*
Clark, Hanna	*Act.*	Cohen, William Court	*M.O.T.*
Clark, John	*Prod.*	Colahan, Roger	*Pub.*
Clark, Lon	*Act.*	Colby, Michael E.	*Dram.*
Clark, Matt	*Jour.*	Colby, Stuart F.	*Act.*
Clark, Oliver	*Act.*	Colcord, Lincoln	*Writ.*
Clark, Thomas F.	*P.O.A.*	Coleman, Caryl	*Act.*
Clark, Wallis	*Act.*	Coleman, Charles C.	*Art.*
Clark, Walter A.	*Art.*	Coleman, M. Graham	
Clarke, Arthur C.	*Edit.*	(Gray) III	*Law.*
Clarke, Arthur L.	*Edit.*	Coleman, Philip C.	*Pub.*
Clarke, Caspar P.	*Dir.*	Collamore, Gilman	*Mer.*
Clarke, Creston	*Act.*	Collamore, Jerome	*Act.*
Clarke, Gage	*Act.*	Collier, Robert J.	*Pub.*
Clarke, George C.	*Mer.*	Collier, Walter	*Mgr.*
Clarke, John S.	*Act.*	Collier, William	*Act.*
Clarke, Leslie P.	*P.O.A.*	Collina, Alfred Q.	*Art.*
Clarke, Thomas S.	*Art.*	Collingwood, Charles	*Jour.*
Clarke, Wilfred	*Act.*	Collins, Alan C.	*Agt.*
Clarke, William F.	*Edit.*	Collins, Fred C.	*Act.*
Clarke, William K.	*Writ.*	Collins, Seward	*Pub.*
Clarke-Smith, Douglas	*Act.*	Collins Jr., Sewell T.	*Art.*
Claxton, Oliver	*Writ.*	Colt, Samuel	*Mgr.*
Clay, John C.	*Art.*	Colton, Arthur W.	*Auth.*
Cleary, Malachy	*Act.*	Colton, John	*Dram.*
Cleather, Gordon	*Mer.*	Colwell, Robert T.	*Writ.*
Cleland, Thomas M.	*Art.*	Colyer, Austin	*Act.*
Clemens, Samuel L.	*Auth.*	Colyer, Carlton	*Act.*
Clemons, Walter Jr.	*Jour.*	Comiskey, Charles W.	*Writ.*
Clemson, Walter J.	*Comp.*	Comstock, Alexander	*Mgr.*
Cleveland, Clement	*Phys.*	Compton, Forrest	*M.O.T.*
Cleveland, Francis	*Act.*	Cone, William C.	*Brkr.*
Cleveland, Grover	*Pres.*	Conklin, William B.	*Pub.*
Clift, Mongomery	*Act.*	Conkling, P. B.	*Art.*
Clisbee, George	*Art.*	Conlan, Frank	*Act.*
Cloudman, Harry	*Edit.*	Conley, Gordon	*Jour.*
Clough, Reginald	*Edit.*	Connell, Gordon	*Act.*
Clurman, Harold	*Dir.*	Connell, John	*Act.*
Cobb, Irvin	*Auth.*	Connelly, Marc	*Auth.*
Coburn, Charles	*Act.*	Conner, Edmon S.	*Act.*
Cochran, Charles B.	*Act.*	Conner, McCauley	*Art.*
Cockaday, Lawrence M.	*Edit.*	Connery, John	*Act.*
Cody, Philip C.	*Writ.*	Conness, Robert	*Act.*

Connett, Eugene V.	*Pub.*	Cordes, James J.	*Act.*
Connolly, Charles	*M.O.T.*	Corle, Edwin	*Writ.*
Connolly, Michael	*Act.*	Cormack, Bartlett	*Dram.*
Connolly, Walter	*Act.*	Cornell, Charles G.	*Mer.*
Connor, William F.	*Mgr.*	Cornwell, Dean	*Art.*
Conover, Gordon	*Act.*	Corrigan, Emmet	*Act.*
Conried, Hans	*Act.*	Corrigan, Jack	*Edit.*
Conried, Heinrich	*Mgr.*	Corrigan, Lloyd	*Act.*
Conried, Richard	*P.O.A.*	Corrigan, Robert W.	*Prof.*
Conroy, Frank	*Act.*	Corthell, Herbert	*Act.*
Conroy, Larry	*Act.*	Cortissoz, Royal	*Jour.*
Converse, Frederick	*Comp.*	Cosgrave, J.	*Edit.*
Conway, John D.	*Prof.*	Cosnar, Robert B.	*Prod.*
Conway, Kevin	*Act.*	Cossart, Ernest	*Act.*
Conway, Robert	*Jour.*	Costain, Thomas B.	*Writ.*
Conyers, Joseph	*Act.*	Costello, Ward	*Act.*
Cook, Augustus	*Act.*	Cotsworth, Staats	*Act.*
Cook, Beach	*Act.*	Cotten, Joseph	*Act.*
Cook, Charles C.	*Arch.*	Cotter, Frank G.	*Act.*
Cook, Charles T.	*Mer.*	Cotton, Fred A.	*Act.*
Cook, Donald	*Act.*	Cottrell, Edwin	*Brkr.*
Cook, Elisha, Jr.	*Act.*	Couldock, Charles W.	*Act.*
Cook, Howard W.	*Pub.*	Coulter, Elmer D.	*Law.*
Cook, James Fielder	*M.O.T.*	Coulter, Frazer	*Act.*
Cook, Joe	*Act.*	Courtenay, William F.	*Act.*
Cook, Joseph C.	*Prod.*	Courtleigh, William	*Act.*
Cook, Lucius M.	*Dir.*	Courtney, Blaine	*M.O.T.*
Cook, William W.	*Edit.*	Cover, Franklin	*Act.*
Cooke, Alistair, (H.M.)	*Writ.*	Covington, Treadwell D.	*Prod.*
Cooke, Charles E.	*Mgr.*	Cowan, Jerome	*Act.*
Cooke, Martin W.	*Law.*	Cowan, Pascal	*Act.*
Coolidge, Paul	*P.O.A.*	Coward, Thomas R.	*Pub.*
Cooney Jr., Dennis T.	*Act.*	Cowden, John P.	*TvX.*
Cooper, Clayton S.	*Auth.*	Cowdin, John E.	*Mer.*
Cooper, Courtney R.	*Writ.*	Cowing, Charles O.	*M.O.T.*
Cooper, F. G.	*Art.*	Cowl, Donald H.	*Mer.*
Cooper, Frederic T.	*Edit.*	Cowles, Eugene	*Sing.*
Cooper, George M.	*Act.*	Cowles, Gardner	*Edit.*
Cooperman, Alvin	*Prod.*	Cowley, Charles C.	*Pub.*
Cooperman, Eugene J.	*P.O.A.*	Cowley, Earl	*Act.*
Coote, Charles	*Act.*	Cowper, Archibald	*Act.*
Coote, Robert	*Act.*	Cox, Denton S.	*Phys.*
Copeland, Charles T.	*Prof.*	Cox, Kenyon	*Art.*
Copp, T. B. F.	*Writ.*	Cox, Paul	*Edu.*
Corbett, Harvey W.	*Arch.*	Cox, Paul R.	*Edu.*
Corbett, Hugh	*Edit.*	Cox, Richard J.	*M.O.T.*
Corbett-Palmer, Hugh	*Pub.*	Cox, Wallace	*Mus.*
Corbin, Austin	*Bnkr.*	Coxe, Davies	*Phys.*
Corbin, John	*Prof.*	Coxe, Henry	*Mer.*
Corcoran, George E.	*P.O.A.*	Coyote, Peter	*Act.*

Crafton, Allen	*Prof.*	Crosby, Raymond Moreau	*Art.*
Crafts, Griffin	*M.O.T.*	Cross, George D.	*Mer.*
Crager, Joel	*Act.*	Crouse, Russel	*Writ.*
Craig, Charles	*Act.*	Crouse, Timothy	*Jour.*
Craig, Horace S.	*P.O.A.*	Crovello, William	*Art.*
Craig, John	*Act.*	Crow, Carl	*Auth.*
Craig, John II	*Prod.*	Crowe, Gordon	*Act.*
Craigie, A. W.	*Prof.*	Crowell, Chester	*Writ.*
Crain, W. H. "Deacon"	*M.O.T.*	Crowell, Robert L.	*Pub.*
Crandall, Edward, Jr.	*Act.*	Croy, Homer	*Writ.*
Crandall, Ernest L.	*Law.*	Crozier, William Armstrong	*Writ.*
Crane, Charles R.	*P.O.A.*	Cruger, James Pendelton	*P.O.A.*
Crane, Edward	*Pub.*	Crumit, Frank	*Act.*
Crane, Edward M.	*Pub.*	Crump, Irving	*Auth.*
Crane, James L.	*Act.*	Crump, Leslie	*Art.*
Crane, Jefferson P.	*Act.*	Cubbage, Robert S.	*Mus.*
Crane, William H.	*Act.*	Cuddihy, H. Lester	*Pub.*
Cranefield, Paul	*Edu.*	Culbertson, Owen	*Writ.*
Craven, Edward	*Act.*	Cullman, Howard	*Mgr.*
Craven, Frank	*Act.*	Cullman, Hugh	*P.O.A.*
Craven, John	*Act.*	Cullum, John	*Act.*
Craven, Robin	*Act.*	Culpepper, William	*Act.*
Crawford, Alfred R.	*Act.*	Cumberland, John	*Act.*
Crawford, Broderick	*Act.*	Cumming, Alistar P.	
Crawford, F. M.	*Auth.*	Gordon	*Farm.*
Crawford, F. S.	*Writ.*	Cummings, Williard H.	*Mgr.*
Crawford, Kenneth	*Edit.*	Cummings, Willard W.	*Art.*
Crawford, Robert	*M.O.T.*	Cunningham, Philip	*Act.*
Crawford, William III	*Mus.*	Curran, Philip Read	*Jour.*
Crawley, John S.	*Act.*	Currie, Barton W.	*Edit.*
Crawley, Tom	*Act.*	Currier, Frank	*Mgr.*
Creason, Donald P.	*Edu.*	Curry, D. C.	*Mar.*
Creel, George	*Writ.*	Curtin, D. Thomas	*Auth.*
Crimmins, Edward C.	*M.O.T.*	Curtin, Robert C.	*P.O.A.*
Crimmins, John D.	*P.O.A.*	Curtis, Benjamin	*Pub.*
Crisp, Arthur	*Art.*	Curtis, Edwin H.	*Act.*
Crissan, Michael	*Jour.*	Curtis, George William	*Edit.*
Crockett, Albert Stevens	*Edit.*	Curtis, H. Holbrook	*Phys.*
Crofts, Frederick S.	*Pub.*	Curtis, John Jay	*Pub.*
Croly, Herbert D.	*Edit.*	Curtis, Paul A.	*Writ.*
Cromarty, Peter	*PrR.*	Curtiss, Charles C.	*Dir.*
Crompton, William H.	*Act.*	Curtiss, Philip	*Writ.*
Cromwell, Elwood	*Act.*	Curtiss, Williard	*Act.*
Cronkite, Walter	*Jour.*	Cushing, Howard G.	*Art.*
Cronyn, Hume	*P.O.A.*	Cushing, Tom	*Dram.*
Crooks, Richard	*Sing.*	Cushman, Edwin	*Act.*
Crosby, Bing	*Act.*	Cutler, Joseph Warren	*Arch.*
Crosby, Ernest Howard	*Law.*	Cutting, F. B.	*P.O.A.*
Crosby, John C.	*Writ.*	Cutting, W. Bayard	*P.O.A.*
Crosby, Percy L.	*Art.*	Cutting, William Jr.	*P.O.A.*

Czvornyek, William P.	*M.O.T.*	Davies, Brian	*Act.*
D'Alleva, Dominick	*Law.*	Davies, Julien T.	*Law.*
D'Angelo, Joseph	*Jour.*	Davis, Allan	*Prof.*
D'Aubigny, Lloyd	*Act.*	Davis, Donald	*Dram.*
Daedy, John A.	*Law.*	Davis, Edward S.	*Pub.*
Dague, Roswell	*Writ.*	Davis, Emery	*Mus.*
Dailey, John Hammond	*Act.*	Davis, Frank Hamilton	*P.O.A.*
Dainard, Michael	*M.O.T.*	Davis, Glenmore	*Mgr.*
Dall, John	*Act.*	Davis, H. P.	*Writ.*
Dalrymple, Alfred	*Prod.*	Davis, Howland	*Bnkr.*
Dalton, Charles	*Act.*	Davis, John E.	*Writ.*
Daltry, Joseph S.	*Mus.*	Davis, Milton F.	*Army*
Daly, Arnold	*Act.*	Davis, Norman	*Bnkr.*
Daly, Arthur J.	*Bro.*	Davis, Ossie	*Act.*
Daly, Augustin	*Mgr.*	Davis, Owen	*Dram.*
Daly, Charles P.	*Law.*	Davis, Owen Jr.	*Act.*
Daly, Joseph F.	*Law.*	Davis, Peter	*Dir.*
Daly, T. A.	*Auth.*	Davis, Richard Harding	*Auth.*
Damon, Stuart	*Act.*	Davis, Robert H.	*Auth.*
Damon, Virgil	*Phys.*	Davis, Robert B.	*Pub.*
Damrosch, Walter	*Mus.*	Davis, Shelby Cullom	*P.O.A.*
Dana, Walter Tracy	*Plant.*	Davis, Tech	*Writ.*
Danforth, Henry G.	*Law.*	Davis, William W.	*Cler.*
Danforth, William	*Act.*	Davison, Gates	*Prod.*
Daniel, Hawthorne	*Edit.*	Dawson, Coningsby	*Writ.*
Daniels, Edgar F.	*Act.*	Dawson, Gregory	*M.O.T.*
Daniels, Marc	*TvD.*	Dawson, Samuel	*News.*
Daniels, William Cooke	*Mer.*	Day, Edmund	*Act.*
Daniels, William P.	*Mer.*	Day, F. H.	*Act.*
Danner, Harry	*Act.*	Day, John Franklin Jr.	*News.*
Dargusch, Carlton Spencer	*Writ.*	Day, William H.	*Arch.*
Dark, Stanley	*Act.*	Dayton, Charles W.	*Law.*
Darling, Jay N.	*Cart.*	Dayton, Fred E.	*Writ.*
Darrow, Whitney	*Pub.*	De Becker, Harold	*Act.*
Dart, Harry Grant	*Art.*	De Fazio, Samuel	*M.O.T.*
Darwin, Philip W.	*Acct.*	De Leo, Roy	*Cler.*
Dash, Ray	*Act.*	De Santis, Joseph	*Act.*
Davenport, Basil	*Writ.*	De Shields, Andre	*Act.*
Davenport, Butler	*R.E.*	Deal, Edgar	*Brkr.*
Davenport, Harry	*Act.*	Dean, James E.	*Mer.*
Davenport, McHaig	*Auth.*	Dean, Robert George	*Writ.*
Davenport, Russell W.	*Edit.*	Dean, Will J.	*Dir.*
Davenport, Walter	*Writ.*	Dearborn, George S.	*P.O.A.*
David, Henry	*Writ.*	Dearth, Henry G.	*Art.*
David, Jeff	*Act.*	Dearth, Robert A.	*P.O.A.*
David, William	*Act.*	DeBelleville, Frederic	*Act.*
Davidson, Gates	*Prod.*	DeCamp, Charles B.	*Edit.*
Davidson, Gordon	*Dir.*	DeCamp, Charles Joseph R.	*Art.*
Davidson, Jo	*Sclp.*	DeCordoba, Pedro	*Act.*
Davies, Blair	*Act.*		

DeCordova, Rudolph	*Act.*	Di Cori, Ferruccio	*P.O.A.*
Deering, Charles	*Mnfr.*	Dick, A. B.	*Mnfr.*
Deering, Henri	*Pian.*	Dick. H.	*Auth.*
Deering, Roger	*P.O.A.*	Dick, Harris B.	*Pub.*
DeForest, George B.	*P.O.A.*	Dick, Sheldon	*Agt.*
Dekker, Albert	*Act.*	Dickens, Stafford	*Act.*
Deland, Lorin F.	*Writ.*	Dickey, Robert L.	*Art.*
Delano, Allen	*Dir.*	Dickey, W. Laurence	*Pub.*
DeLima, Charles A.	*Dram.*	Dickinson, C. Roy	*Auth.*
Dell'Orifice, Luigi	*Mus.*	Dickinson, Thomas H.	*Auth.*
Dellapietra, Stephen J.	*Act.*	Dickson, Gregory	*Writ.*
Delmore, Ralph	*Act.*	Dickson, Harris	*Auth.*
Dembner, S. Arthur	*Pub.*	Dietz, Donald	*Writ.*
DeMilhau, Louis J.	*Writ.*	Digges, Dudley	*Act.*
DeMille, Henry C.	*Dram.*	Dillaway, George W.	*Law.*
Deming, Henry C.	*P.O.A.*	Dillman, Bradford	*Act.*
Deming, Horace E.	*Law.*	Dillon, David	*Act.*
Dempsey, Jerome	*Act.*	Dillon, Joseph H.	*Mgr.*
DeMuralt, Carl Leonard	*Eng.*	Dillon, Sean	*Act.*
Denham, Reginald	*Dir.*	Dingwall, H. Allan Jr.	*M.O.T.*
Denhard, Charles H.	*Pub.*	Dingwall, Herbert A.	*Pub.*
Denison, Lindsay	*Edit.*	Disney, Walt	*Prod.*
Denlinger, Sutherland	*Jour.*	Ditrichstein, Leo	*Act.*
Denman, Herbert	*Art.*	Ditson, Charles H.	*Pub.*
Dennett, Roger Herbert	*Auth.*	Dix, William P. Jr.	*Mgr.*
Dennis, Frederic S.	*Surg.*	Dixey, Henry	*Act.*
Dennis, Howard	*Phys.*	Dixon, Ephraim W.	*Mer.*
Denny, George K.	*Bnkr.*	Dixon, Francis Stilwell	*Art.*
DeNovellis, Antonio	*Mus.*	Dixon, Robert	*Bro.*
Depew, Chauncey M.	*R.R.*	Dixon, Thomas Jr.	*Auth.*
Derieux, James	*Edit.*	Doan, Thomas C.	*R.R.*
DeSegurola, Andreas	*Sing.*	Doane, S. E.	*Writ.*
Desmond, Thomas C.	*Eng.*	Dobbyn, William A. Jr.	*Mgr.*
Deutchman, Ralph F.	*Phys.*	Dobie, J. Frank	*Writ.*
Deutsch, Alvin	*P.O.A.*	Dodd, Frank C.	*Pub.*
Devane, William	*Act.*	Dodd, Lee Wilson	*Dram.*
Devereaux, Jack	*Act.*	Dodge, Edwin S.	*Dram.*
Devereaux, John Drew	*Act.*	Dodge, Walter Phelps	*Writ.*
Devereux, Clifford	*Act.*	Dodge, William de Leftwich	*Art.*
Devine, Jerry	*Dir.*	Dodson, J. E.	*Act.*
Devine, Michael	*M.O.T.*	Dodson, Richard S Jr.	*Edit.*
Devonshire, Easton	*Eng.*	Dody, Sandford	*Writ.*
Devree, Howard	*Writ.*	Doherty, Chet	*Act.*
DeWilde, Frederic	*Act.*	Dolbier, Maurice	*Jour.*
Dewing, Thomas Wilmer	*Art.*	Doliner, Roy	*Writ.*
DeWitt, William Perceval	*Mnfr.*	Dolley, Charles Sumner	*Bio*
DeWolfe, Billy	*Act.*	Dolman, Gerald	*Law.*
DeWolfe, John	*Arch.*	Dominick, Alexander	*Mnfr.*
Dexter, Arthur	*P.O.A.*	Dominick, H. Blanchard	*Mer.*
Dexter, Robert	*Mgr.*	Dominick, H. B. Jr.	*Mnfr.*

Dominick, Manyard A.	*Pub.*	Dreyfuss, Richard	*Act.*
Donaldson, Ross	*Edit.*	Driscoll, Charles B.	*Auth.*
Donlevy, Brian	*Act.*	Driscoll, John H.	*Writ.*
Donnell, Cushing	*Dram.*	Driver, Edward A.	*P.O.A.*
Donnell, William W.	*M.O.T.*	Drouet, Robert	*Act.*
Donnelly, Edward	*Act.*	Drury, Allen	*Auth.*
Donnelly, John J.	*Mgr.*	Dryden, Robert	*Act.*
Donnelly, Leo	*Act.*	Duane, Edward L.	*Act.*
Donoho, Ruger G.	*Art.*	Dubin, Charles S.	*Dir.*
Donovan, King	*Prod.*	DuBois, William	*Dram.*
Donovan, Tom	*Dir.*	DuBoy, Paul	*Arch.*
Dooley, Robert M.	*RaX.*	Dudley, John L., Jr.	*Ins.*
Doolittle, Thomas B.	*Eng.*	Dudley, Stuart	*Law.*
Doran, Donald A. Jr.	*Edit.*	Duell, Holland S.	*Law.*
Doran, George H.	*Pub.*	Duff, J. C.	*Mgr.*
Dorne, Albert	*Art.*	Duff, William	*Pub.*
Dorney, Richard	*Mgr.*	Duffield, Kenneth Graham	*Bnkr.*
Dorsey, George A.	*Auth.*	Duffield, Pitts	*Pub.*
Doty, Douglas Zabriskie	*Writ.*	Duffy, Albert J.	*Writ.*
Doubleday, Russell	*Pub.*	Duffy, Edmund	*Cart.*
Doucet, Paul	*Act.*	Dugmore, Arthur Radclyffe	*Art.*
Douglas, Byron	*Act.*	Dukas, James T.	*Act.*
Douglas, James F.	*Act.*	DuMond, Frank Vincent	*Art.*
Douglas, Joel	*Prod.*	Dunbar, C. W. Harold	*Mnfr.*
Douglas, Kirk	*Act.*	Dunbar, Erroll	*Act.*
Douglas, Lester	*Art.*	Duncan, A. Butler	*P.O.A.*
Douglas, Lucien	*Act.*	Duncan, Angus	*Act.*
Douglas, Melvyn	*Act.*	Duncan, Augustin	*Act.*
Douglas, Paul	*Act.*	Duncan, Henry E., Jr.	*Ins.*
Douglas, Robert C.	*Pub.*	Duncan, James	*Act.*
Dove, Arthur G.	*Art.*	Duncan, Malcolm	*Act.*
Dovell, Ray C.	*Edit.*	Duncan, Peter	*Act.*
Dow, Frederic G.	*Law.*	Duncan, William Butler	*Bnkr.*
Dow, Louis	*Prof.*	Dunckel, W. A.	*Phys.*
Dower, Walter	*Art.*	Dunham, Walter J.	*Brkr.*
Downing, Robert	*M.O.T.*	Dunlap, George C.	*P.O.A.*
Doyle, David	*Act.*	Dunn, Edward Delaney	*Dram.*
Doyle, Richard L.	*Edit.*	Dunn, Thomas G.	*M.O.T.*
Doyle, William	*P.O.A.*	Dunne, Finley Peter	*Auth.*
Doyle-Murray, Brian	*Act.*	Dunning, N. Max	*Arch.*
Drake, Alexander W.	*Art.*	Dunstan, R. Jaffrey	*Act.*
Drake, Alfred	*Act.*	Durand, Harvey	*Bnkr.*
Drake, Francis Vivian	*Writ.*	Durand, Henry S.	*Phys.*
Drake, Galen	*M.O.T.*	Durham, Charles H., Jr.	*P.O.A.*
Drake, Lawrence	*Art.*	Durrance, Thomas Drake	*Writ.*
Draper, Arthur S.	*Edit.*	Durrell, Oliver H.	*Pub.*
Draper, Arthur G.	*News.*	Durstine, Roy	*Writ.*
Draycott, Wilfred	*Act.*	Duryea, Pierrepont	*P.O.A.*
Drew, John	*Act.*	Duval, William H.	*Bnkr.*
Dreyfuss, Michael	*Act.*	Duvall, Rankin	*Act.*

Duveneck, Frank	*Act.*	Ellis, Sidney R.	*Mgr.*
Dwight, Theodore F.	*Writ.*	Ellis, William H.	*Act.*
Dwyer, Charles	*Edit.*	Ellsworth, James W.	*P.O.A.*
Dyer, George	*Auth.*	Ellsworth, W. W.	*Pub.*
Dyer, George Lewis	*Writ.*	Elmendorf, Dwight L.	*Lec.*
Dyke, Ken R.	*M.O.T.*	Elser, Frederick B.	*R.R.*
Dykehouse, David J.	*Law.*	Elser, Jr., Maximilian	*Edit.*
Dykeman, C. H.	*Edit.*	Elterman, Warren B.	*Law.*
Dyslin, George	*Auth.*	Elton, Edmund	*Act.*
Earle, Gordon	*Art.*	Elward, James J.	*Writ.*
Earley, Edward F.	*M.O.T.*	Embury, II, Aymar	*Arch.*
Eastman, Carl	*Agt.*	Emerson, Guy	*Auth.*
Easton, Charles Philip	*Law.*	Emerson, John	*Act.*
Eaton, Frank A.	*Edit.*	Emerson, Nathaniel W.	*Surg.*
Eaton, S. B.	*Law.*	Emery, Edwin T.	*Act.*
Eberle, Robert M.	*Mgr.*	Emery, Gilbert	*Edit.*
Ecker, Frederick H.	*Ins.*	Emery, Henry C.	*Auth.*
Eddinger, Wallace R.	*Act.*	Emery, John Edward	*Act.*
Eden, Sidney	*Act.*	Emhardt, Robert	*Act.*
Edeson, Robert	*Act.*	Emmet, Devereux	*Bot*
Edlich, Stephen P.	*Art.*	Emmet, Edward F.	*Min.*
Edmunds, Ralph	*Mgr.*	Emmet, J. Duncan	*Phys.*
Edson, Elie C.	*M.O.T.*	Emmet, William T.	*Law.*
Edwards, Allyn	*Bro.*	Emmons, J. Frank	*Bnkr.*
Edwards, Ben	*S.A.*	Emmons, Kintzing Post	*Mer.*
Edwards, Felix	*Act.*	England, Paul	*Act.*
Edwards, George Wharton	*Art.*	Englebach, Dee	*Prod.*
Edwards, Henry	*Act.*	English, Daniel B.	*Writ.*
Edwards, Julian	*Dir.*	Enright, Walter J.	*Art.*
Edwards, Robert	*Art.*	Enslow, Ridley	*Pub.*
Effrat, John	*Prod.*	Epstein, Alvin	*Act.*
Egan, Martin	*Jour.*	Epstein, Harvey L.	*Art.*
Egan, Maurice Francis	*Writ.*	Erb, Herbert F.	*M.O.T.*
Egan, Michael	*Act.*	Eric, Fred	*Act.*
Eggart, Harry R.	*Act.*	Erlynne, Royden	*Act.*
Eggleston, George T.	*Edit.*	Ernst, John	*Writ.*
Egner, Frank	*Pub.*	Errol, Leon	*Act.*
Eichheim, Henry	*Mus.*	Erskine, Howard	*M.O.T.*
Einstein, Arthur W. Jr	*Writ.*	Erskine, John	*P.O.A.*
Eisenhower, Dwight D.	*Pres.*	Erskine, John	*Auth.*
Elbaum, Steven	*P.O.A.*	Erskine, Wallace	*Act.*
Eldred, Arthur	*Act.*	Erwin, Stuart	*Act.*
Ellington, Richard	*Act.*	Esler, Frderick B.	*Act.*
Elliot, Stephen	*M.O.T.*	Esmelton, Frederick	*Act.*
Elliott, Duncan	*P.O.A.*	Esper, William J.	*Edu.*
Elliott, Lee	*P.O.A.*	Essman, Robert N.	*Art.*
Elliott, Samuel	*Pub.*	Estabrook, Henry D.	*Law.*
Elliott, Steven	*Act.*	Esty, Harold M., Jr.	*P.O.A.*
Elliott, William	*Act.*	Etherington, W. F.	*Mnfr.*
Ellis, Edward	*Act.*	Evans, Brandon	*Act.*

Evans, Edwin T.	*P.O.A.*
Evans, Evan	*Mus.*
Evans, Henry	*Ins.*
Evans, Joseph	*Art.*
Evans, Lee	*Writ.*
Evans, Maurice	*Act.*
Evans, Reynolds	*Act.*
Evans, Stevenson H.	*Writ.*
Evarts, Sherman	*Law.*
Evarts, William H.	*Act.*
Everhart, Rex	*Act.*
Everitt, John Thompson	*Writ.*
Everitt, Samuel A.	*Edit.*
Ewell, Tom	*Act.*
Eyck, Barent	*Law.*
Eyre, Lawrence Bevan	*Dram.*
Ezdorf, Robert Von	*Arch.*
Faber, Leslie	*Act.*
Faeth, Gilbert E.	*Writ.*
Fairbanks, Frank P.	*Art.*
Fairbanks, Henry P.	*Mer.*
Fairchild, Charles	*P.O.A.*
Fairchild, Willard	*Art.*
Fales, DeCoursey	*P.O.A.*
Falick, Paul	*Law.*
Falk, Lee	*Prod.*
Fallon, John N.	*Jour.*
Fallon, Joseph A.	*Law.*
Fallon, Richard G.	*M.O.T.*
Fallows, Edward Huntington	*Law.*
Falls, Charles B.	*Art.*
Falls, Gregory	*Dir.*
Falter, George	*P.O.A.*
Falter, John	*Art.*
Fangel, Henry Guy	*Art.*
Fanning, Joseph T.	*Edit.*
Fanning, Leland	*Writ.*
Faris, Barry	*Edit.*
Farley, Frank C.	*Arch.*
Farley, Morgan	*Act.*
Farley, Philip H.	*Brkr.*
Farlow, Robert E.	*Pub.*
Farmer, Laurence	*Writ.*
Farnam, Charles H.	*Law.*
Farnol, Lynn	*Writ.*
Farnsworth, William P.	*Prod.*
Farnum, William	*Act.*
Farone, Dominick	*Act.*
Farr, Finis	*Writ.*
Farragut, Loyall	*R.R.*
Farrar, Frederick Moreton	*Art.*
Farrar, John C.	*Edit.*
Farrell, Frank	*Edit.*
Farrell, Thomas R.	*Law.*
Farrow, Miles	*Mus.*
Farwell, Arthur	*Comp.*
Fasselle, Robert M. De	*Eng.*
Fassett, Jay	*Act.*
Faulk, John Henry	*Writ.*
Faulkner, Barry	*Art.*
Faulkner, Edward D.	*Mer.*
Faversham, Philip	*Act.*
Faversham, William	*Act.*
Fawcett, Edgar	*Auth.*
Fawcett, George	*Act.*
Fawcett, Owen	*Act.*
Faxon, William Bailey	*Art.*
Fay, Charles Norman	*P.O.A.*
Fay, Frank	*Act.*
Fay, Sigourney W.	*Mer.*
Fearing, C. F.	*P.O.A.*
Fearing, D. B.	*Bibl.*
Fearnley, John	*Prod.*
Fedris, J. M.	*Mgr.*
Feiffer, Jules	*Art.*
Feist, Gene	*Edu.*
Feland, F. R.	*Writ.*
Feleky, Charles	*Mus.*
Felker, Clay S.	*Jour.*
Fellows, J. W.	*Brkr.*
Felshman, Neil	*Writ.*
Fennelly, Parker	*Act.*
Ferguson, Fred S.	*Writ.*
Ferguson, Robert V.	*Act.*
Fernald, John B.	*Dir.*
Ferrer, Jose	*Act.*
Ferrer, Miguel J.	*Act.*
Ferris, Walter	*Auth.*
Ferriter, Thomas	*Act.*
Feustel, Robert M.	*Eng.*
Ficken, H. Edward	*Arch.*
Field, Charles K.	*Auth.*
Field, Davidy Dudley	*Eng.*
Field, Edward M.	*Brkr.*
Field, R. M.	*Mgr.*
Field, Robin Lee	*Mus.*
Field, Salisbury	*Auth.*
Field, William Osgood	*Eng.*
Field, William Hildreth	*Law.*

Fielding, Edward	*Act.*
Fife, George Buchanan	*Jour.*
Filsinger, Ernst	*Writ.*
Finck, Furman J.	*Art.*
Findlay, John	*Act.*
Fine, Donald I.	*Pub.*
Finkelstein, Jerry	*Pub.*
Finklehoffe, Fred F.	*Dram.*
Finletter, Thomas K.	*Pub.*
Finley, John H.	*Edit.*
Finn, James Wall	*Art.*
Finney, Edward F.	*Prod.*
Firzgerald, Frank T.	*Surg.*
Fischer, Frank	*Prod.*
Fischer, Howard H.	*Act.*
Fischer, John	*Auth.*
Fischer, Leo	*Mus.*
Fischer, Robert A.	*M.O.T.*
Fish, Nicholas	*Bnkr.*
Fish, Stuyvesant	*R.R.*
Fishel, Mark	*Mnfr.*
Fisher, Alfred C.	*Act.*
Fisher, Avery	*Mus.*
Fisher, Charles¹	*Act.*
Fisher, Harrison	*Art.*
Fisher, Irving	*Act.*
Fisher, William Edgar	*Art.*
Fisher, William R.	*Surg.*
Fiske, Haley	*Law.*
Fiske, Harrison Grey	*Mgr.*
Fiske, Willard	*Prof.*
Fitch, William Clyde	*Auth.*
Fitts, Eugene C.	*RaX.*
Fitzgerald, Edward	*Act.*
Fitzgerald, Frank T.	*Surg.*
Fitzgerald, Michael	*M.O.T.*
Fitzgerald, Neil	*Act.*
Fitzhenry, Robert I.	*Pub.*
Fitzhugh, Robert T.	*Prof.*
Fitzpatrick, Daniel	*Cart.*
Flagg, James Montgomery	*Art.*
Flagg, Montague	*Arch.*
Flagg, Thomas J.	*Mer.*
Flagg, Thomas K.	*Act.*
Flagler, Harry Harkness	*P.O.A.*
Flaherty, Robert J.	*Prod.*
Flanagan, John	*Sclp.*
Flannagan, William W.	*Bnkr.*
Flannery, Harry W.	*Writ.*
Flavin, Martin A.	*Writ.*
Fleischmann, Julius	*M.O.T.*
Fleischmann, Raoul H.	*Pub.*
Fleming, Charles	*Act.*
Fleming, Henry S.	*Eng.*
Fleming, John	*Act.*
Flesch, Rudolph	*Writ.*
Fletcher, Andrew Jr.	*P.O.A.*
Fletcher, Jefferson B.	*Writ.*
Fletcher, Peter	*Mer.*
Flint, Austin	*Phys.*
Floherty, John J., Jr.	*Art.*
Flood, John	*Act.*
Florence, William J.	*Act.*
Flynn, John T.	*Writ.*
Flynn, Thomas	*Jour.*
Fogarty, Thomas E.	*Art.*
Fogarty, Thomas J.	*Art.*
Foley, Patrick J.	*Law.*
Foley, Paul	*Writ.*
Folford, Robert	*Act.*
Folke, Ellis	*Edit.*
Folsom, Henry T.	*Mnfr.*
Folwell, Arthur Hamilton	*Edit.*
Foote, Charles B.	*Bnkr.*
Foote, E. V.	*P.O.A.*
Foote, Emerson	*Writ.*
Foote, Horton	*Dram.*
Footner, Hulbert	*Auth.*
Forbes-Robertson, Johnston	*Act.*
Ford, Corey	*Writ.*
Ford, David C.	*Act.*
Ford, Ford Madox	*Auth.*
Ford, Hugh J.	*Act.*
Ford, Marcus	*Act.*
Ford, Paul	*Act.*
Ford, Paul L.	*Auth.*
Forman, Milos	*Dir.*
Forrest, Arthur	*Act.*
Forrest, George Chet	*M.O.T.*
Forrest, Samuel M.	*Act.*
Forsman, Harry	*Act.*
Fort, William L.	*Jour.*
Fortescue, Granville	*Auth.*
Fortesque, Kenyon	*Law.*
Fortunato, Samuel J.	*P.O.A.*
Foss, Kendall	*Jour.*
Foss, Martin M.	*Pub.*
Foss, Martin M., Jr.	*Pub.*
Foster, Donald	*Act.*
Foster, George F.	*Pub.*

Foster, Jack	Edit.	Freeman, Paul	M.O.T.
Foster, Maximilian	Auth.	Freer, Charles L.	Mnfr.
Foster, Paul	M.O.T.	French, Amos T.	P.O.A.
Foster, William D.	Arch.	French, Frederick W.	Mer.
Foulke, Roy A.	Auth.	French, Herbert Moulton	Edit.
Fowkes, Conard	Act.	French, S. B.	Brkr.
Fox, Austen G.	Law.	French, T. Henry	Mgr.
Fox, Beauvais	Writ.	Freud, Ralph	Prof.
Fox, Dixon Ryan	C.P.	Freundlich, Laurence S.	Jour.
Fox, Fontaine	Art.	Frey, Charles Daniel	Writ.
Fox, James	Act.	Fried, Michael	Prod.
Fox, Jim	Jour.	Friedkin, David E.	Prod.
Fox, Paul Hervey	Dram.	Friedlander, Emil	P.O.A.
Fox, Rector K.	Pub.	Friedman, Joel	Act.
Fox, Roger P.	Act.	Friend, George	Act.
Francis, Charles	Act.	Frohman, Charles	Mgr.
Francis, Eugene	Act.	Frohman, Daniel	Mgr.
Franck, Edward A.	Prod.	Froment, Frank L.	Mer.
Francoeur, J. M.	Act.	Frost, A. B.	Art.
Frank, Alexander F.	Act.	Fry, Horace B.	P.O.A.
Frank, Allan Dodds	Jour.	Fulford, Robert	Act.
Frank, Carl	Act.	Fuller, Frank	P.O.A.
Frank, Eugene	M.O.T.	Fuller, William H.	P.O.A.
Frank, Glenn	Edit.	Fullerton, Hugh S.	Writ.
Frank, Morton	Jour.	Funk, Wilfred, J	Pub.
Frank, Murray	Acct.	Furlong, John	Act.
Frankel, Aaron	Edu.	Furness, George A.	Law.
Frankel, Victor Hirsch	Phys.	Furness, Horace Howard	Auth.
Franken, Merritt	TvX.	Furness, Howard, Jr	Auth.
Franken, Paul	Prod.	Fyfe, James MacKenzie	Writ.
Franklin, Dwight	Art.	Gable, Clark	Act.
Franklyn-Robbins, John	Act.	Gabel, Martin	Act.
Franz, Robert	Agt.	Gaffner, Haines	P.O.A.
Franzen, Augustus	Art.	Gaige, Roscoe, C.	Agt.
Fraser, Colin	Art.	Galazka, Jacek	Pub.
Fraser, Colin Jay Jr	M.O.T.	Gale, Burton, Jr.	Bnkr.
Fraser, Edgar Lovat	Act.	Gales, Weston Spies	Mus.
Fraser, James Earle	Sclp.	Gallagher, Peter	Act.
Fraser, W. Lewis	Art.	Gallaher, Donald	Act.
Frawley, T. D.	Act.	Gallaudet, John	Act.
Freda, Frank	Act.	Gallico, Paul W	Writ.
Free, E. E.	Sci.	Galton, James E.	Pub.
Freed, Frederick	Prod.	Gamble, Charles Warburton	Act.
Freedlander, Arthur R.	Art.	Gander, Gustav H	Pub.
Freedlander, J. H.	Arch.	Gandert, Slade Richard	Writ.
Freedley, George	Writ.	Gangelin, Paul	Writ.
Freedley, Vinton	Prod.	Ganter, Carl R	P.O.A.
Freedman, Zac	M.O.T.	Gardin, John E	Bnkr.
Freeman, Alden	Arch.	Gardiner, Reginald	Act.

Gardner, Edward W	*Act.*	Gibbons, Herbert Adams	*Writ.*
Gardner, George P	*P.O.A.*	Gibbons, Lloyd	*P.O.A.*
Garfein, Jack	*Edu.*	Gibbs, Donald	*Writ.*
Gargan, William	*Act.*	Gibbs, Edward N.	*Ins.*
Garland, David S	*Writ.*	Gibbs, Hamilton	*Writ.*
Garland, Hamlin	*Auth.*	Gibbs, Robert Paton	*Act.*
Garland, James A.	*Bnkr.*	Gibney, Charles Francis	*Act.*
Garland, James A.,Jr.	*P.O.A.*	Gibson, Charles Dana	*Art.*
Garnett, Bradford	*Act.*	Gibson, George Routledge	*Bnkr.*
Garrett, Oliver H. P.	*Dram.*	Gibson, George H	*Edit.*
Garrettson, Frederick Prime	*Mer.*	Gibson, Preston	*Auth.*
Garrison, Robert L.	*M.O.T.*	Gidaly, Walter	*Law.*
Garrison, Robert L.	*Writ.*	Giddens, George	*Act.*
Garrity, Henry	*Mer.*	Gielgud, John	*Act.*
Garside, Charles	*Law.*	Gierlach, Chet	*Prod.*
Gaston, George Houston	*Ins.*	Giffen, R. L.	*Mgr.*
Gates, Larry	*Act.*	Gifford, Edwin	*M.O.T.*
Gaul, George	*Act.*	Gifford, Hazen	*Act.*
Gaulke, Ramon George	*Pub.*	Gilbert, David B.	*Bnkr.*
Gaunt, James	*P.O.A.*	Gilbert, Douglas	*Writ.*
Gaver, Jack	*Edit.*	Gilbert, Harry	*Mus.*
Gawtry, Lewis	*Bnkr.*	Gilbert, John	*Act.*
Gay, Harry H	*Brkr.*	Gilbert, Richard R.	*Cler.*
Gebhart, John C	*Writ.*	Gilder, Richard Watson	*Edit.*
Geddes, Donald Porter	*Pbu*	Gile, Bill	*M.O.T.*
Geddes, Norman Bel	*Art.*	Gilfether, Daniel	*Act.*
Geer, Langdon	*Mnfr.*	Gilford, Jack	*Act.*
Geisinger, Elliot	*M.O.T.*	Gill, George H.b.	*P.O.A.*
Gelb, Harold S	*P.O.A.*	Gill, Robert Stowe	*Act.*
Gellatly, John	*Coll*	Gill, Theodore	*M.O.T.*
Gelman, Howard	*Act.*	Gillam, Albert Burns	*Act.*
Genet, Ira	*Writ.*	Gillette, Abram D.	*Ins.*
Genthe, Arnold	*Art.*	Gillette, Daniel Gano	*Law.*
Genung, Charles H.	*Writ.*	Gillette, William	*Act.*
Geoghegan, John J	*Pub.*	Gilligan, Edmund	*Auth.*
Geraghty, James	*Art.*	Gillingwater, Claude	*Act.*
Geraghty, Tom J.	*Writ.*	Gillmore, Frank	*Act.*
Gerard, James W	*Law.*	Gilman, Arthur C.	*Mer.*
Gernert, Alan	*Bnkr.*	Gilman, Henry K.	*Mer.*
Gerrard, Douglas	*Act.*	Gilmore, Edward	*Writ.*
Gerringer, Robert J	*Act.*	Gilmour, J.H.	*Act.*
Gerry, Elbridge T	*Law.*	Gilpin, Charles H.	*Mer.*
Gershel, Lawrence	*Pub.*	Gilsey, John	*P.O.A.*
Gerson, Noel	*Writ.*	Gilsey, Peter	*R.E.*
Gerstad, John Leif	*Act.*	Gilson, Warren E.	*P.O.A.*
Gertler, Menard M	*Phys.*	Gingras, Jules	*Arch.*
Gesner, Clark	*Dram.*	Giniger, Kenneth S.	*Pub.*
Gettell, Richard Glenn	*P.O.A.*	Ginn, Hayward	*Act.*
Giangiulio, Nick	*Act.*	Girard, Erskine	*P.O.A.*
Gibberson, William H	*Act.*		

Girardot, Etienne	*Act.*	Goodwin, N.C.	*Act.*
Giroux, Robert	*Pub.*	Goodyear, A. Conger	*Mer.*
Gitelle, Gene L.	*Phys.*	Goodyear, William H.	*Auth.*
Gitlin, Irving	*Prod.*	Goold, Paul	*Art.*
Gitlin, Paul	*Agt.*	Goosen, Lawrence	*M.O.T.*
Glackens, W.J.	*Art.*	Gordon, Alan F.	*Prod.*
Glaenzer, Georges A.	*Mer.*	Gordon, George N.	*Edu.*
Glaenzer, Richard Butler	*Dec.*	Gordon, Henry C.	*Act.*
Glaser, Vaughan	*Mgr.*	Gordon, James Steward	*Edit.*
Glass, Montague	*Writ.*	Gordon, Max	*Prod.*
Glasser, Ephraim	*Prod.*	Gordon, Richard H., Jr.	*Prod.*
Glassford, David	*Act.*	Gorham, Charles O.	*Writ.*
Gleason, James A.	*Act.*	Gorman, Herbert S.	*Auth.*
Gleason, Russell	*Act.*	Gorman, Walter	*Dir.*
Glendinning, Ernest	*Act.*	Gotthold, Charles F.	*Act.*
Glover, William	*Jour.*	Gottlieb, Morton	*Prod.*
Gluck, James F.	*Law.*	Gottschalk, Ferdinand	*Act.*
Goddard, Don	*Writ.*	Gould, Bruce	*Auth.*
Godfrey, Bertram	*Act.*	Gould, Charles W.	*Law.*
Godfrey, Charles H.	*Bnkr.*	Gould, Christopher	*Pub.*
Godfrey, Peter	*Act.*	Gould, Gordon	*Act.*
Godfrey, Samuel T.	*Dir.*	Gould, Harold W.	*Act.*
Godwin, Parke	*Edit.*	Gould, Herbert L.	*Phys.*
Goelet, Ogden	*P.O.A.*	Gould, Howard	*Act.*
Goelet, Robert	*Law.*	Gould, Maurice S.	*Pub.*
Golde, Walter	*Comp.*	Gould, Wilbur James	*Phys.*
Golden, Fred	*M.O.T.*	Gould, Willis E.	*Dir.*
Golden, Harry	*Writ.*	Goulding, Edmund	*Dir.*
Golden, Samuel	*Pub.*	Goulet, Robert	*Sing.*
Goldin, Elias	*Mgr.*	Graeve, Oscar	*Edit.*
Goldman, Eric F.	*Writ.*	Graff, Clarence L.	*P.O.A.*
Goldman, Robert Paul	*M.O.T.*	Graff, Herbert	*Edu.*
Goldsmith, Merwin	*Act.*	Graff, Robert D.	*Prod.*
Goldstein, Leonard	*P.O.A.*	Graff, Wilton	*Act.*
Goldstein, Nathan W.	*Jour.*	Grafton, Samuel	*Jour.*
Goldstein, Samuel	*P.O.A.*	Graham, Edward	*Art.*
Gollan, Campbell	*Act.*	Graham, Elliott	*Pub.*
Gomez, S. Thomas	*Act.*	Graham, Frank	*Jour.*
Goodkind, Howard L.	*Edit.*	Graham, George M.	*Act.*
Goodman, Jules Eckert	*Dram.*	Graham, Philip L.	*Pub.*
Goodman, Julian	*Jour.*	Graham, Stephen	*Prod.*
Goodman, Marshall	*Art.*	Graham, Whidden	*Writ.*
Goodman, Philip	*Writ.*	Graham, William A.	*Dir.*
Goodnow, Edward	*Act.*	Graham, William E.	*Auth.*
Goodrich, Arthur	*Edit.*	Grainger, Kyle Z.	*Law.*
Goodrich, Arthur G.	*Pub.*	Granger, Alfred H.	*Arch.*
Goodrich, Casper F.	*Navy*	Grant, Kirby	*Act.*
Goodrich, David Marvin	*P.O.A.*	Grant, Lawrence	*Art.*
Goodrich, Henry W.	*Law.*	Grant, Suydam	*Bnkr.*
Goodspeed, Morton	*P.O.A.*		

Grattan, Stephen	*Act.*	Grismer, Joseph R.	*Act.*
Graves, Ralph A.	*Writ.*	Grissom, Arthur	*Edit.*
Graves, Ralph H.	*Writ.*	Griswold, Daniel P.	*Bibl.*
Gray, Alan E.	*Law.*	Griswold, F. Gray	*Arch.*
Gray, Gerald Hull	*Law.*	Griswold, W.M.	*P.O.A.*
Gray, Herbert Willard	*Edit.*	Griswold, Wesley S.	*Edit.*
Gray, Sam	*Act.*	Grizzard, George	*Act.*
Gray, Simon	*Dram.*	Grody, Donald	*M.O.T.*
Grayson, Martin	*Pub.*	Groesbeck, Ernest	*Bnkr.*
Grebanier, Bernard	*Writ.*	Gross, Irving	*M.O.T.*
Green, Burton	*Act.*	Grosset, A. Donald	*Pub.*
Green, Martyn	*Act.*	Grossman, Bernard A.	*Writ.*
Green, Paul	*Dram.*	Grossman, Richard L.	*Pub.*
Green, Philip A.	*Prod.*	Grossmann, Edwin Booth	*Art.*
Green, Stanley	*Writ.*	Grossmann, Ignatius R.	*Brkr.*
Greenberg, Alfred	*P.O.A.*	Grosvenor, William M., Jr.	*P.O.A.*
Greenberg, Edward M.	*Dir.*	Grover, Stanley	*Act.*
Greenblatt, Nathaniel	*Prod.*	Grymes, C.A.	*P.O.A.*
Greene, Clay M.	*Dram.*	Gude, John G.	*Agt.*
Greene, Frank	*Act.*	Guerin, Jules	*Art.*
Greene, Frederick. S.	*Eng.*	Guild, Curtis	*Edit.*
Greene, Harold	*P.O.A.*	Guiteras, Ramon	*Phys.*
Greene, R. Kempton	*Prod.*	Gunter, Archibald C.	*Auth.*
Greene, Richard	*Act.*	Gunther, John	*Writ.*
Greene, Walter D.	*Act.*	Gurnee, Augustus C.	*Bnkr.*
Greene, Ward	*Writ.*	Gussow, Mel	*Jour.*
Greenfield, Edward L.	*Jour.*	Gustafson, William	*Sing.*
Greenleaf, Mace	*Act.*	Guthrie, William D.	*Law.*
Greenstreet, Sydney	*Act.*	Gutierrez, Gerald	*Dir.*
Greenwald, Richard	*P.O.A.*	Gutman, Walter	*M.O.T.*
Greer, David H.	*Cler.*	Guzzetta, John S.	*Law.*
Greer, Milan	*Writ.*	Gwenn, Edmund	*Act.*
Gregg, John R.	*P.O.A.*	Habirshaw, W.M.	*Eng.*
Gregorian, Vartan (H.M.)	*Edu.*	Hackett, Albert	*Act.*
Gregory, William H.	*Act.*	Hackett, Charles	*Sing.*
Grene, Frederick S.	*Eng.*	Hackett, E. Byrne	*Pub.*
Greppo, Francis	*Act.*	Hackett, Francis B.	*Writ.*
Gresham, Harry	*Act.*	Hackett, James K.	*Act.*
Gresham, Herbert	*Act.*	Hackett, Norman	*Act.*
Griffen, Benjamin	*Mer.*	Haddaway, Thomas H.	*Act.*
Griffin, Walter	*Art.*	Hadden, J.E. Smith	*Mer.*
Griffith, Charles E.	*Pub.*	Hadfield, Henry J.	*Act.*
Griffith, D.W.	*Prod.*	Hadley, Earl J.	*News.*
Griffith, Raymond	*Prod.*	Hadley, Henry K.	*Mus.*
Griffiths, David G.	*Prod.*	Haenigsen, Harry	*Cart.*
Griffiths, Farnum P.	*Law.*	Haff, Le Roy B.	*Mer.*
Griggs, John	*Act.*	Hagedorn, Charles G.	*Edit.*
Grimm, Paul H.	*Eng.*	Hagedorn, Christopher	*Pub.*
Grimwood, Herbert	*Act.*	Hagedorn, Herman, Jr.	*Auth.*
Grip, John	*P.O.A.*	Hager, Louis	*Prod.*

Haggard, Godfrey	*Cons.*		Hamilton, Hale	*Act.*
Haggard, Sewell	*Edit.*		Hamilton, James Shelley	*Writ.*
Haggin, Ben Ali	*Art.*		Hamilton, James	*Des.*
Hague, Albert	*Act.*		Hamilton, Richard	*Act.*
Hague, Andrew	*Act.*		Hamilton, William G.	*Eng.*
Hague, Robert L.	*P.O.A.*		Hamilton, William H.	*Pub.*
Haight, Charles C.	*Arch.*		Hammerstein, James	*Dir.*
Haines, Robert T.	*Act.*		Hammesfahr, George	*Pub.*
Hale, Alan	*Act.*		Hammond, Charles P.	*RAn.*
Hale, Arthur	*Writ.*		Hammond, John C.	*Writ.*
Hale, Edward Everett III	*Act.*		Hampden, Burford	*Act.*
Hale, Herbert D.	*Arch.*		Hampden, Paul	*Writ.*
Hale, Swinburne	*Law.*		Hampden, Walter	*Act.*
Hale, Thomas Shaw	*Law.*		Hampel, Alvin	*Prod.*
Hale, Walter S.	*Act.*		Hampton-Cain, Michael	*Act.*
Hale, William Bayard	*Jour.*		Handyside, Clarence	*Act.*
Hall, DeWitt C.	*Mer.*		Hanford, Charles B.	*Act.*
Hall, Edwin Trowbridge	*Mer.*		Hanley, Lawrence	*Act.*
Hall, Frederick Garrison	*Art.*		Hanley, William	*Writ.*
Hall, Gilman	*Edit.*		Hanlon, Brendon	*Act.*
Hall, H. Oakey	*Brkr.*		Hannagan, Steve	*Jour.*
Hall, Harry Alvan	*Law.*		Hanrahan, John	*Pub.*
Hall, Howard	*Act.*		Hansen, Carl Fisher	*Law.*
Hall, O.L.	*Writ.*		Hansen, Harry	*Jour.*
Hall, Roger G.	*Mgr.*		Harbach, Otto	*Dram.*
Hall, Thurston	*Act.*		Harbury, Charles	*Act.*
Hall, William A.	*Inv.*		Harcourt, William K.	*Act.*
Hall, William S.	*Auth.*		Hardenbergh, William P.	*Mnfr.*
Hallet, Jack	*Act.*		Hardenburgh, Henry J.	*Arch.*
Hallock, Robert	*Art.*		Hardie, Robert Gordon	*Art.*
Hallowell, Thomas Jewett	*P.O.A.*		Hardigg, James M.	*P.O.A.*
Halpern, John A.	*P.O.A.*		Harding, Lyn (H.M.)	*Act.*
Halpern, Nathan	*Prod.*		Hardwicke, Cedric	*Act.*
Halpern, Wilfred J.	*M.O.T.*		Hardy, Arthur Sherburne	*Auth.*
Halstead, Richard H.	*Bnkr.*		Hardy, Hugh	*Arch.*
Halton, Charles	*Act.*		Hardy, Samuel B.	*Act.*
Ham, Harry	*Mgr.*		Hare, Francis Lumsden	*Act.*
Hambleton, T. Edward	*Prod.*		Hare, Montgomery	*Writ.*
Hamer, Gerald	*Act.*		Hargous, Robert	*P.O.A.*
Hamer, Joseph	*Act.*		Hargrove, Marion	*Writ.*
Hamill, Ernest A.	*Bnkr.*		Haring, Forrest C.	*Mgr.*
Hamill, Laurence	*Writ.*		Harkins, Daniel H.	*Act.*
Hamilton, Allen McLane	*Phys.*		Harkness, Albert	*Arch.*
Hamilton, Clayton	*Writ.*		Harlow, Arthur, Jr.	*P.O.A.*
Hamilton, Davis	*Pub.*		Harlow, Harrington	*Law.*
Hamilton, Donald Clayton	*Mgr.*		Harmon, Lewis	*PrR.*
Hamilton, Edward P.	*Pub.*		Harney, George E.	*Arch.*
Hamilton, Frank	*Act.*		Harper, Henry Sleeper	*Pub.*
Hamilton, Gordon Clayton	*Edit.*		Harper, Horatio R.	*Pub.*
			Harper, J. Henry	*Pub.*

Harper, John	*Pub.*	Harwood, Harry	*Act.*
Harper, W.A.	*Pub.*	Harwood, Raymond C.	*Pub.*
Harrigan, Anthony Hart	*Phys.*	Haskell, Ernest	*Art.*
Harrigan, Edward	*Act.*	Haskell, Stevens	*Arch.*
Harrigan, William D.	*Act.*	Hassam, Childe	*Art.*
Harriman, Karl Edwin	*Edit.*	Hassell, George	*Act.*
Harrington, Davis	*P.O.A.*	Hastings, Cuyler	*Act.*
Harrington, Jerome	*Act.*	Hastings, Ernest	*Act.*
Harrington, John D.	*Act.*	Hastings, John R.	*Edit.*
Harrington, Phillip	*Phot.*	Hastings, Thomas Jr.	*Arch.*
Harris, Andrew	*Edu.*	Hastings, Wells S.	*Auth.*
Harris, Elmer	*Dram.*	Haswin, Carl A.	*Act.*
Harris, Frank	*Mnfr.*	Hatch, Denison	*Writ.*
Harris, Julian La Rose	*Edit.*	Hatch, Eric	*Writ.*
Harris, Leonard R.	*Pub.*	Hatch, Frank B.	*Act.*
Harris, Michael	*Pub.*	Hatch, Henry Prescott	*Bnkr.*
Harris, Mitchell	*Act.*	Hatch, Roger	*Act.*
Harris, Wadsworth	*Act.*	Hatfield, Byron	*Act.*
Harris, William	*Act.*	Hatfield, Dalzell	*P.O.A.*
Harris, William	*Mgr.*	Hatfield, Hurd	*Act.*
Harris, William, Jr.	*Mgr.*	Hatton, Frederick	*Dram.*
Harrison, Alfred E.	*Mgr.*	Haugaard, William E.	*Arch.*
Harrison, Bertram	*Act.*	Haven, George G.	*Bnkr.*
Harrison, Birge	*Art.*	Havens, Munson A.	*Writ.*
Harrison, Burton N.	*Law.*	Haverlin, Carl	*Pub.*
Harrison, Harry	*Writ.*	Haviland, Paul B.	*Mer.*
Harrison, Henry Sydnor	*Writ.*	Hawes, John Tilten	*Pub.*
Harrison, Louis	*Act.*	Hawes, William Holbrook	*Act.*
Harrison, Rex	*Act.*	Hawk, William S.	*Ho.*
Harrison, Thomas		Hawkes, Wells	*Writ.*
Alexander	*Art.*	Hawkins, Rush C.	*Law.*
Harriss, Louis	*Writ.*	Hawkins, Stuart	*Writ.*
Hart, Bernard	*Prod.*	Hawkins, W. W., Jr.	*Writ.*
Hart, Charles Henry	*Law.*	Hawley, H. Dudley	*Act.*
Hart, Charles S.	*Pub.*	Hawley, Howard O.	*P.O.A.*
Hart, Everett	*Prod.*	Hawley, Hughson	*Art.*
Hart, Gordon	*Act.*	Haworth, Joseph	*Act.*
Hart, Harold Burton	*Acct.*	Hawthorne, Charles W.	*Art.*
Hart, Lorenz II	*Jour.*	Hay, Austin	*Act.*
Hart, Louis Bret	*Surr.*	Haycraft, Howard	*Writ.*
Hart, Moss	*Dram.*	Hayden, J. Alexander	*Mnfr.*
Hart, William Howard	*Art.*	Hayden, John	*Dir.*
Hartig, Herbert	*Act.*	Haydon, James C.	*Mer.*
Hartley, George D.	*Bnkr.*	Hayes, Henry R.	*P.O.A.*
Hartley, J. Scott	*Sclp.*	Hayes, Joseph A	*Dram.*
Hartman, Lee Foster	*Edit.*	Hayes, Peter Lind	*Act.*
Hartswick, F. Gregory	*Edit.*	Hayes, Ralph	*Jour.*
Harvey, Harry B.	*Mus.*	Hayes, Richard Somers	*R.R.*
Harvey, James Clarence	*Writ.*	Hayes, Timothy	*Writ.*

Hayman, Alf	*Mgr.*	Hendrick, Ellwood	*Chem.*
Haynes, Eldridge	*Pub.*	Hendrick, James P.	*Law.*
Haynes, Storrs	*TvX.*	Hendrick, Robert E.P.	*Art.*
Hays, Austin	*Sclp.*	Hendrickson, Robert A.	*Law.*
Hays, Donald C.	*Law.*	Hendrix, Joseph C.	*Bnkr.*
Hays, Harvey	*Act.*	Hendryx, Shirl W.	*Writ.*
Hays, Lee	*Prod.*	Henniker-Heaton, Raymond	*Writ.*
Hays, Tim	*Jour.*	Henry, Frank C.	*Pub.*
Hayton, Lennie	*Cond.*	Henry, Philip S.	*Mer.*
Hayward, Leland	*Prod.*	Henry, William A.	*Act.*
Hayward, Louis	*Act.*	Herald, Robert S.	*Art.*
Hazeltine, Mayo W.	*Jour.*	Herbert, Carl	*Act.*
Hazeltine, William O.	*Act.*	Herbert, Don	*Prod.*
Hazelton, George C.	*Act.*	Herbert, Henry	*Act.*
Hazen, David W.	*Jour.*	Herbert, Holmes E.	*Act.*
Hazen, Edward J	*Mer.*	Herbert, Joseph W.	*Act.*
Hazen, George H.	*Pub.*	Herbert, Sidney	*Act.*
Hazlitt, Henry	*Writ.*	Herbert, William	*Brkr.*
Head, Alfred H.	*Mgr.*	Herd, Richard T.	*Prod.*
Head, Thomas	*Act.*	Herford, John B.	*Law.*
Hearn, Frank	*Act.*	Herford, Oliver	*Art.*
Hearne, Douglass D.	*Law.*	Hering, Henry	*Sclp.*
Hearst, Austin	*Prod.*	Hering, Oswald C.	*Art.*
Hebard, Alfred P.	*Art.*	Heriot, Wilton	*Act.*
Heckscher, August	*Eng.*	Herlihy, Edward	*Act.*
Hedges, Job E.	*Law.*	Herlihy, Edward J.	*Bro.*
Heflin, Van	*Act.*	Herman, Gilbert O.	*Act.*
Heggie, O.P.	*Act.*	Herman, Robert	*M.O.T.*
Heigham, Montague H.B.	*P.O.A.*	Herold, Don	*Auth.*
Heiman, Marcus	*Mgr.*	Herrick, Howard	*Writ.*
Heimemann, William	*Pub.*	Herrick, John F.	*Jour.*
Heiskell, Morgan	*Art.*	Herrick, Sanford S.	*P.O.A.*
Heitman, Robert	*Act.*	Herrick-Cragin, Charles	*Act.*
Helfenstein, J.M.	*Mus.*	Herrmann, Edward	*Act.*
Heller, Franklin M.	*Prod.*	Herrmann, Harry	*Writ.*
Heller, James G.	*Mus.*	Hersey, David	*Act.*
Hellerman, Fred	*Mus.*	Hersholt, Jean	*Act.*
Hellman, Geoffrey	*Auth.*	Hertzberg, Michael Lee	*Law.*
Helmuth, William Tod	*Phys.*	Hertzler, John	*Act.*
Hemenway, Augustus	*P.O.A.*	Herz, William Jr	*Act.*
Hemingway, Ernest	*Auth.*	Herzbrun, Bernard	*Arch.*
Hemphill, Newton A.	*Mnfr.*	Hess, John D.	*Writ.*
Hendee, Harold	*Edit.*	Hetzler, Edwart T.	*Writ.*
Henderson, Charles R.	*Mer.*	Hewett, Charles D.Jr	*P.O.A.*
Henderson, David	*Mgr.*	Hewett, Erskine	*Law.*
Henderson, Harold G.	*Law.*	Hewitt, Abram S.	*Law.*
Henderson, Lucius J.	*Act.*	Hewitt, Ashley C., Jr.	*Dipl.*
Henderson, Skitch	*Comp.*	Hewitt, Ashley C.	*Eng.*
Hendrick, Arthur Pomeroy	*P.O.A.*	Hewitt, Edward Ringwood	*Chem.*
Hendrick, Burton J.	*Edit.*	Hewitt, Peter Cooper	*Mnfr.*

Heydt, Louis Jean	*Act.*	Hoff, Edwin	*Act.*
Hickey, John	*Des.*	Hoffbauer, Charles	*Art.*
Hickman, Alfred	*Act.*	Hoffman, Arthur S.	*Edit.*
Hickman, Norman	*M.O.T.*	Hoffman, Harold M.	*Act.*
Hickok, Guy	*Writ.*	Hoffman, Harry Leslie	*Art.*
Hicks, Charles T.	*P.O.A.*	Hoffmann, Richard	
Hicks, Russell	*Act.*	Wyndham	*Writ.*
Higgins, Colin	*Prod.*	Hoffman, Samuel Verplanck	*P.O.A.*
Higgins, R.H., Jr.	*Bnkr.*	Hoffman, William H.	*Arch.*
Highman, John A. E.	*Pub.*	Hoffman, Richard H.	*Phys.*
Higley, Philo	*Auth.*	Hogan, Charles Beecher	*Prof.*
Hilder, John Chapman	*Edit.*	Hogan, J.P.	*Writ.*
Hill, Barton	*Act.*	Hogan, James P.	*P.O.A.*
Hill, Frank E.	*Writ.*	Hogan, John V.l.	*Writ.*
Hill, Frederick Trevor	*Law.*	Hogan, Michael	*Writ.*
Hill, George B.	*Auth.*	Hogan, Robert	*Act.*
Hill, George H. B.	*P.O.A.*	Hogue, John Roland	*Act.*
Hill, Henley	*Edit.*	Hohl, Arthur	*Act.*
Hill, Lawrence	*Pub.*	Hohman, Charles	*Act.*
Hill, Robert E. Lee	*Act.*	Holbrook, Hal	*Act.*
Hill, W.E.	*Art.*	Holcombe, Armstead R.	*Edit.*
Hiller, Lejaren'a	*Art.*	Holden, Arthur	*Arch.*
Hilliard, John Northern	*Auth.*	Holden, E.B.	*Mer.*
Hilliard, Robert	*Act.*	Holden, Raymond P.	*Edit.*
Hills, Laurence	*Edit.*	Holder, Frank T.	*Mnfr.*
Hilly, John	*P.O.A.*	Holland, C. Maurice	*Prod.*
Himmell, Samuel S.	*P.O.A.*	Holland, Edmund M.	*Act.*
Hines, Dixie	*Writ.*	Holland, F. Raymond	*Art.*
Hinson, Harry Lee	*Art.*	Holland, George	*Act.*
Hinton, John H.	*Phys.*	Holland, Joseph	*Act.*
Hipper, Charles H.	*Act.*	Holland, Joseph J.	*Act.*
Hirsch, Jeffrey	*Dir.*	Holland, Richard W.	*Act.*
Hirsch, Michael	*Act.*	Hollander, Jacob H.	*Prof.*
Hirschfeld, Al (H.M.)	*Art.*	Hollerith, Charles, Jr.	*Prod.*
Hirshan, Leonard	*Agt.*	Holliday, Robert Cortes	*Writ.*
Hitchcock, Frank H.	*P.G.*	Hollister, Paul M.	*Writ.*
Hitchcock, Raymond	*Act.*	Holloway, Joseph	*Prod.*
Hitchcok, Alfred	*Dir.*	Holm, John Cecil	*Dram.*
Hobson, Burton	*Pub.*	Holmes, Taylor	*Act.*
Hobson, Francis Thayer	*Pub.*	Holmes, William David	*Comp.*
Hobson, Henry A. (Hon)	*Cons.*	Holms, Burton	*Lec.*
Hodge, Albert E.	*Act.*	Holmgren, John	*Art.*
Hodge, J. Aspinwall Jr	*Law.*	Holt, Edwin	*Act.*
Hodges, Charles E.	*Ins.*	Holt, Elliot	*Pub.*
Hodges, Harrison Blake	*R.R.*	Holtzman, Edward	*Phys.*
Hodges, John K.	*Bnkr.*	Holtzmann, David M.	*Law.*
Hodges, Leigh Mitchell	*Writ.*	Holz, Leffert	*Law.*
Hoe, Robert	*Mnfr.*	Hood, Raymond	*Arch.*
Hoeber, Arthur	*Art.*	Hood, William J.	*Writ.*
Hoeber, Paul B.	*Pub.*	Hook, Ted	*M.O.T.*
Hoey, John	*P.O.A.*		

Hooker, Brian	*Auth.*
Hooley, Richard M.	*Mgr.*
Hooper, C.E.	*Writ.*
Hooper, Parker M.	*Arch.*
Hoover, Ellison	*Cart.*
Hoover, Herbert (H.M.)	*Pres.*
Hopkins, Arthur (H.M.)	*Prod.*
Hopkins, Charles Roberts	*Act.*
Hopkins, Lindsey	*Bnkr.*
Hopkins, Milton	*Law.*
Hopper, Charles H.	*Act.*
Hopper, De Wolf	*Act.*
Hopper, James Michael	*M.O.T.*
Hopper, James M.	*Writ.*
Hopper, Michael James	*M.O.T.*
Hoppin, Tracy	*Art.*
Hornak, Richard	*M.O.T.*
Hornblow, Arthur, Jr.	*Prod.*
Horowitz, David H.	*P.O.A.*
Horton, Edward Everett	*Act.*
Horton, John	*Act.*
Horwitz, Murray Lee	*Act.*
Hough, Emerson	*Auth.*
Houghton, A. C.	*Mnfr.*
Houghton, C. Norris	*Prod.*
Houghton, Francis X.	*P.O.A.*
Houghton, George C.	*Cler.*
Houghton, George H.	*Cler.*
Houghton, Harry E.	*Pub.*
Houghton, William Morris	*Edit.*
Hourwich, George Kennan	*Law.*
House, Fred C.	*Act.*
House, Henry Arthur	*Dram.*
Houseman, John (H.M.)	*M.O.T.*
Hovey, Carl	*Writ.*
Howard, Bronson	*Dram.*
Howard, Charles Stewart	*Mgr.*
Howard, Francis	*Arch.*
Howard, Harold	*Act.*
Howard, John Galen	*Arch.*
Howard, Leslie	*Act.*
Howard, Michael	*Act.*
Howard, Oscar F.	*Art.*
Howard, Peter B.	*P.O.A.*
Howard, Roy W.	*Jour.*
Howard, Sidney	*Writ.*
Howe, Frank, Jr.	*Mgr.*
Howe, Frederic C.	*Writ.*
Howe, Hartley E.	*Edit.*
Howe, Leonard	*Act.*
Howe, Thorndike Dudley	*P.O.A.*
Howe, W. T. H.	*P.O.A.*
Howe, Walter	*Act.*
Howells, Henry	*M.O.T.*
Howland, C.	*Mer.*
Howland, Gardiner	*P.O.A.*
Howland, Henry E.	*Law.*
Howland, Hewitt H.	*Pub.*
Howland, Louis M.	*Mnfr.*
Hoyns, Henry	*Pub.*
Hoyt, Charles H.	*Dram.*
Hoyt, Palmer	*Jour.*
Hoyt, Walter S.	*Mer.*
Hu, Shih (H.M.)	*Auth.*
Hubbard, Elijah Kent, Jr.	*Mnfr.*
Hubbard, George	*Auth.*
Hubbard, Grosvenor	*Law.*
Hubbard, Louis De Koven	*Mnfr.*
Hubbard, William P.	*Law.*
Huber, Paul D.	*Act.*
Hubert, Russell M.	*Act.*
Huddleston, David	*Act.*
Hudson, Eric	*Art.*
Hudson, Robert	*Act.*
Huett, Richard	*Pub.*
Huff, Matthew Brooks	*Eng.*
Hughes, Barnard	*Act.*
Hughes, Del	*Act.*
Hughes, Henry Douglas	*P.O.A.*
Hughes, J. Lawrence	*Edit.*
Hughes, J. J.	*Writ.*
Hughes, Rupert	*Auth.*
Hughes, Sidney	*P.O.A.*
Hughes, Stanley C.	*P.O.A.*
Hughes, William	*Act.*
Hughston, Regan	*Act.*
Hugo, Laurence Victor Sr	*Act.*
Hugo, Laurence V. Jr	*M.O.T.*
Huie, Irving Van Arnan	*Eng.*
Hull, Henry	*Act.*
Hull, Howard	*Act.*
Hull, Shelley	*Act.*
Hulswit, Mart	*Act.*
Humphrey, William J.	*Act.*
Humphreys, Edward Walsh	*P.O.A.*
Humphreys, John S.	*Arch.*
Humphreys, Robert	*Edit.*
Hundley, John Walker	*M.O.T.*
Hungerford, Edward	*Writ.*
Hunt, Frazier	*Writ.*

Hunt, John Cummings	*Pub.*	Irvin, Rea	*Art.*
Hunt, Joseph Howland	*Arch.*	Irvine, J. Harry	*Act.*
Hunt, Richard Howland	*Arch.*	Irving, Alexander Duer	*Ins.*
Hunt, Richard M.	*Arch.*	Irving, George S.	*Act.*
Hunter, Charles Bates	*Writ.*	Irving, Henry	*Act.*
Hunter, Ernest R.	*Pub.*	Irving, Louis du Pont	*Bnkr.*
Hunter, Fenley	*Exp.*	Irwin, Benoni	*Art.*
Hunter, James B.	*Surg.*	Irwin, Godfrey	*Jour.*
Hunter, Kenneth	*Act.*	Irwin, Robert	*R.E.*
Hunter, Rollo W.	*Dir.*	Irwin, Robert Easton	*Mer.*
Hunting, Gardner	*Auth.*	Irwin, Wallace	*Writ.*
Hunting, Roger Bryant	*P.O.A.*	Irwin, Will	*Writ.*
Huntington, Archer M.	*Writ.*	Isham, Samuel	*Art.*
Huntington, Charles P.	*Arch.*	Ittelson, Alvin	*Prod.*
Huntington, Charles R.	*P.O.A.*	Ivanowski, Sigismund de	*Art.*
Huntington, John	*Prod.*	Ives, Brayton	*Bnkr.*
Huntingnton, Joseph Selden	*P.O.A.*	Ives, Fred M.	*Phys.*
Hurd, Peter	*Art.*	Ives, H. Davis	*Aarch*
Hurja, Emil	*Jour.*	Ivins, William M.	*Law.*
Hurlbut, Frank M.	*Bnkr.*	Ivo, Alexander	*Act.*
Hurlbut, Harold	*Sing.*	Jaccaci, August F.	*Art.*
Hurley, Arthur	*Act.*	Jack, Edwin B.	*Act.*
Hurst, William Lonsdale	*Act.*	Jackson, Alan R.	*Edit.*
Hussung, Will	*Act.*	Jackson, Charles J.	*Act.*
Huston, John	*Dir.*	Jackson, Joseph H.	*Edit.*
Huston, Walter	*Act.*	Jackson, Martin	*P.O.A.*
Hutchens, John K.	*Jour.*	Jackson, Ray Lee	*Phot.*
Hutchinson, Gardiner	*Mnfr.*	Jacobi, Lou	*Act.*
Hutt, Henry	*Art.*	Jacobs, Bernard B.	*Prod.*
Hutt, William	*Act.*	Jacobs, Elias A.	*Law.*
Hutton, G. M.	*P.O.A.*	Jacobs, Max	*P.O.A.*
Hutton, Hugh	*Cart.*	Jacobs, Victor	*Law.*
Hutton, Laurence	*Auth.*	Jacobsen, John E.	*Dir.*
Hyde, A. F.	*P.O.A.*	Jacobson, Irving	*Act.*
Hyde, William H.	*P.O.A.*	Jacobson, Sol	*PrR.*
Hylan, Donald	*Act.*	Jacoves, Felix	*Act.*
Hyman, Earle	*Act.*	Jagel, Frederick	*Sing.*
Iams, Jack	*Jour.*	Jakes, John	*Writ.*
Ievers, R. W.	*Mer.*	James, Beau	*M.O.T.*
Illian, George	*Art.*	James, Clifton	*Act.*
Imison, Michael	*Art.*	James, Hal	*Prod.*
Ingalls, W. B. B.	*R.E.*	James, Henry F.	*Mer.*
Ingersol, William	*Act.*	James, Hibbard	*Act.*
Inglis, James S.	*Art.*	James, W. Stephen	*Act.*
Innes-Brown, H. Alwyn	*Jour.*	Jameson, House B.	*Act.*
Ireland, Alleyne	*Writ.*	Jamison, Marshall	*Dir.*
Ireland, Joseph N.	*Auth.*	Janney, Ben	*Mgr.*
Irish, Loomis	*M.O.T.*	Janney, Lëon	*Act.*
Irons, Robert B.	*P.O.A.*	Jaques, George B.	*Mer.*

Jarrett, Henry C.	*Mgr.*	Johnson, Owen	*Auth.*
Jayme, William N.	*Writ.*	Johnson, Robert	
Jayne, Horace Howard	*P.O.A.*	Underwood	*Edit.*
Jeayes, Allan	*Act.*	Johnson, S. Whittlesey	*P.O.A.*
Jebb, Gladwyn	*Amb.*	Johnson, Tefft	*Act.*
Jefferson, Charles B.	*Mgr.*	Johnson, William Martin	*Art.*
Jefferson, Frank	*Brkr.*	Johnston, Alva	*Writ.*
Jefferson, George D.	*Prof.*	Johnston, Moffat	*Act.*
Jefferson, Joseph	*Act.*	Johnstone, Gordon	*Act.*
Jefferson, Joseph Warren	*Act.*	Johnstone, Will B.	*Cart.*
Jefferson, Thomas L.	*Act.*	Jolley, James	*Act.*
Jefferson, William Winter	*Act.*	Jonas, Charles H. J. Jr.	*P.O.A.*
Jeffries, Bowen	*Act.*	Jones, Allen A.	*Eng.*
Jeffries, Will	*Act.*	Jones, Barry	*Act.*
Jehlinger, Charles	*Dir.*	Jones, Benjamin M.	*Mer.*
Jehlinger, Charles (H.M.)	*Prof.*	Jones, Carl W.	*Pub.*
Jenkins, Allen	*Act.*	Jones, Ellis O.	*Writ.*
Jenkins, Frank	*Brkr.*	Jones, Elmer R.	*P.O.A.*
Jenkins, George	*S.A.*	Jones, Francis C.	*Art.*
Jenkins, Herbert F.	*Pub.*	Jones, Franklin	*Act.*
Jenkins, John W. R.	*Prod.*	Jones, Grahame	*Writ.*
Jenkins, Richard Leas	*Phys.*	Jones, George W.	*Edit.*
Jenkins, Robert O.	*Act.*	Jones, Grover	*Writ.*
Jenkins, William	*Writ.*	Jones, H. Bolton	*Art.*
Jenks, Charles T.	*Mer.*	Jones, H. Madison	*P.O.A.*
Jennings, Allyn	*Arch.*	Jones, Henrik	*P.O.A.*
Jennison, Peter Saxe	*Pub.*	Jones, Henry	*Act.*
Jensen, Frode	*Phys.*	Jones, Henry Arthur	*Dram.*
Jepson, Edwin C.	*Mgr.*	Jones, James Earl	*Act.*
Jepson, Eugene	*Act.*	Jones, John P.	*P.O.A.*
Jerome, Edwin	*Act.*	Jones, Jonathan Jefferson	*Pub.*
Jessop, George K.	*Dram.*	Jones, Lee	*Mus.*
Jewett, Henry	*Act.*	Jones, Oliver	*A.F.*
Jewett, Rutger Bleecker	*Pub.*	Jones, Paul	*Writ.*
Joel, George N.	*Pub.*	Jones, Paul Guildford	*Act.*
Joels, Merrill E.	*Act.*	Jones, Richard B.	*P.O.A.*
Joffe, Irwin	*P.O.A.*	Jones, Richard Lloyd	*Edit.*
Johansen, John C.	*Art.*	Jones, Robert Edmond	*S.A.*
Johnson, Alvin S.	*Edit.*	Jones, Stanley B.	*Writ.*
Johnson, Benjamin	*Act.*	Jones, Tommy Lee	*Act.*
Johnson, Burges	*Writ.*	Jones, Waring	*Writ.*
Johnson, Eastman	*Art.*	Jones, Whitworth	*Act.*
Johnson, Edward	*Mgr.*	Jordan, Lee A.	*Bro.*
Johnson, Harry J.	*P.O.A.*	Jorgulesco, Jonel Eugene	*S.A.*
Johnson, Herbert	*Art.*	Josephson, Marvin A.	*Agt.*
Johnson, James D.	*Writ.*	Josephy, Alvin, Jr.	*Jour.*
Johnson, Malcom	*Pub.*	Joslin, William L.	*P.O.A.*
Johnson, Martyn	*Edit.*	Joslyn, Allyn	*Act.*
Johnson, Nunnally	*Writ.*	Jostyn, Jay	*Act.*
Johnson, Orrin	*Act.*	Joyce, Henry	*Educ.*

Joyce, William H.	*R.R.*	Kegley, Kermit	*Act.*
Julia, Raul	*Act.*	Keightley, Cyril	*Act.*
Julian, Frederick	*Act.*	Keith, Boudinot	*Law.*
Jusserand, J. J.	*Amb.*	Keith, David Lemuel	*Act.*
Justin, George	*Prod.*	Keith, Ian	*Act.*
Kaempffert, Waldemar	*Writ.*	Keith, Lawrence	*Act.*
Kafer, John C.	*Eng.*	Kelcey, Herbert	*Act.*
Kahler, Hugh McNair	*Auth.*	Kelland, Clarence B.	*Auth.*
Kahn, James M.	*Writ.*	Kelland, Thomas Smith	*Writ.*
Kahn, Julius	*Act.*	Kellar, Henry	*Mag.*
Kail, Robert	*Act.*	Kelley, Albert Bartram	*Law.*
Kaland, William J.	*Prod.*	Keller, Arthur	*Art.*
Kalbfleisch, Charles	*Law.*	Kelley, J. D. J.	*Navy*
Kalem, Theodore E.	*Jour.*	Kelley, Kenneth	*Phys.*
Kalkhurst, Eric Stanley	*Act.*	Kellock, Harold	*Writ.*
Kampmann, Eric	*Pub.*	Kellogg, Luther Laflin	*Law.*
Kane, S. Nicolson	*P.O.A.*	Kellogg, Paul U.	*Edit.*
Kane, Tom	*Prod.*	Kelly, Eugene, Jr.	*Law.*
Kane, Whitford	*Act.*	Kelly, Fred C.	*Writ.*
Kanev, Sydney Mark	*Phys.*	Kelly, Gregory	*Act.*
Kanfer, Stefan	*Jour.*	Kelly, Hugh	*Pub.*
Kanin, Garson	*Dir.*	Kelly, Laurence C.	*Eng.*
Kantor, MacKinlay	*Auth.*	Kelly, P. J.	*Act.*
Kaplan, Frederic M.	*Pub.*	Kelly, Thomas H.	*P.O.A.*
Karen, James	*Act.*	Kelly, William J.	*Act.*
Karen, Reed	*Writ.*	Kelsey, Fenton, Jr.	*Pub.*
Karl, Arthur Martin	*P.O.A.*	Kelvey, Henry Warwick	*Act.*
Karlen, Arno	*Writ.*	Kemmer, George W.	*Mus.*
Karloff, Boris	*Act.*	Kemp, George W.	*Mer.*
Karp, David	*Writ.*	Kendal, William H.	*Act.*
Karp, Richard	*Jour.*	Kendall, Messmore	*Law.*
Kates, Henry	*P.O.A.*	Kendall, William B.	*Mer.*
Katz, Oscar	*TvX.*	Kendall, William B.	*Brkr.*
Kaufman, George S.	*Dram.*	Kendall, William Sargeant	*Art.*
Kaup, William	*Dir.*	Kendrick, Richard	*Act.*
Kayes, Alan	*M.O.T.*	Kennaday, Paul	*Edit.*
Kean, Julian H.	*Law.*	Kennard, Joseph Spencer	*Auth.*
Keane, Edward	*Act.*	Kennedy, Adam	*Writ.*
Keane, Thomas W.	*Act.*	Kennedy, Burt	*Prod.*
Kearney, Patrick	*Dram.*	Kennedy, Charles O'Brien	*Writ.*
Keating, Fred	*Mag.*	Kennedy, Charles Runn	*Dram.*
Keating, Joseph	*Act.*	Kennedy, David A.	*Art.*
Keefe, Robert S.	*Jour.*	Kennedy, E. G.	*Art. Dir.*
Keefer, Don H.	*Act.*	Kennedy, Valentine E.	*Mgr.*
Keefer, Henry	*Act.*	Kennelly, Norman	*Writ.*
Keeler, O. B.	*Writ.*	Kennicott, Donald	*Jour.*
Keena, Thomas	*Act.*	Kent, Atwater	*Eng.*
Keep, William B.	*Law.*	Kent, Edgar	*Act.*
Keese, William L.	*Auth.*	Kent, Henry Watson	*P.O.A.*
Kegerreis, Robert B.	*Act.*		

Kent, Rikel	*Act.*	Kirk, William W.	*P.O.A.*
Kerker, Gustave A.	*Comp.*	Kirkland, Hardee	*Act.*
Kerker, Michael A.	*M.O.T.*	Kirkwood, James	*Act.*
Kerman, Sheppard	*Act.*	Kirshon, Paul	*Writ.*
Kern, Jerome	*Comp.*	Kislik, Richard	*Pub.*
Kernan, Thomas	*Pub.*	Kissel, Howard	*Jour.*
Kerney, James, Jr.	*Edit.*	Klarnet, Philip	*Writ.*
Kernochan, Marshall R.	*Comp.*	Klavun, Walter	*Act.*
Kerr, Chester	*Pub.*	Kleeman, Arthur S.	*Bnkr.*
Kerr, Geoffrey	*Act.*	Klein, Charles	*Dram.*
Kerr, Walter (H.M.)	*Jour.*	Klein, Matthew	*Art.*
Kerrigan, J. M.	*Act.*	Klein, Sidney	*P.O.A.*
Kester, Paul	*Dram.*	Klemperer, Werner	*Act.*
Ketcham, Edward C.	*Pub.*	Kline, John M.	*Act.*
Key, Ted	*Cart.*	Kline, Kevin	*Act.*
Keys, C. M.	*Bnkr.*	Klineman, Robert D.	*Edu.*
Kibbee, Guy	*Act.*	Kling, Saxon	*Act.*
Kieffer, Paul	*Law.*	Klonis, Stewart	*Art.*
Kilduff, James	*Bnkr.*	Klotz, John R. MacPherson	*Eng.*
Kiley, Richard	*Act.*	Knapp, Joseph Palmer	*Pub.*
Kilgour, Joseph T.	*Act.*	Knight, Augustus S.	*Ins.*
Killgore, H. Scott	*Eng.*	Knight, Clayton	*Art.*
Kilmer, Christopher	*Auth.*	Knight, Frank	*R An.*
Kilmer, Kenton	*Writ.*	Knight, John	*Act.*
Kilty, Jerome	*Act.*	Knight, Raymond	*Auth.*
Kimball, Arthur G.	*Comp.*	Knoblock, Edward (H.M.)	*Dram.*
Kimball, Benjamin	*Law.*	Knopf, Alfred, Jr	*Pub.*
Kimball, David	*Act.*	Knopf, Edwin	*Edit.*
Kimball, Francis H.	*Arch.*	Knott, Frederick	*Dram.*
Kimball, H.I., Jr.	*Pub.*	Knowles, Edwin	*Act.*
Kimball, Robert	*Edit.*	Knowles, Frederick Milton	*Jour.*
King, Clarence	*Auth.*	Knowlton, Perry	*Art.*
King, Claude	*Act.*	Knox, Alexander	*Act.*
King, David W.	*Writ.*	Knox, Henry Hobart	*Eng.*
King, Dennis	*Act.*	Knox, John Jay	*Bnkr.*
King, Emmett C.	*Act.*	Kobbe, Philip	*Writ.*
King, Herbert G.	*Brkr.*	Kober, Arthur	*Dram.*
King, John C.	*Act.*	Kochman, Robert	*Prod.*
Kingdon, Frank	*Act.*	Koehler, Charles	*Act.*
Kingsbury, John A.	*P.O.A.*	Kolker, Henry	*Act.*
Kingsford, Walter	*Act.*	Kontopoulos, Demetrios	*Prod.*
Kingsley, Sidney	*Dram.*	Koopman, Augustus	*Art.*
Kinkead, C.G.	*Dram.*	Korff, Arnold	*Act.*
Kinnell, Murray	*Act.*	Korper, Fordham	*M.O.T.*
Kinney, M. Curtis	*Arch.*	Kortlucke, Frederick F. Jr.	*Phys.*
Kinsey, Harold C.	*Pub.*	Kraft, Randolf Jr.	*Act.*
Kinsolving, Charles M.	*Writ.*	Kramer, John Wright	*Act.*
Kinsolving, William Lee	*Act.*	Kramer, Mandel	*Act.*
Kinstler, Everett Raymond	*Art.*	Kramer, Wright	*Act.*
Kirby, Rollin	*Art.*	Kraus, Philip	*Act.*

Krembs, Felix	*Act.*	Lane, John	*Pub.*
Kresel, Lee	*Act.*	Lane, John A.	*Act.*
Krishner, Bernard	*Jour.*	Lang, Stephen	*Act.*
Krolik, Jeff	*M.O.T.*	Langan, Glenn	*Act.*
Kronenfeld, Ivan	*Act.*	Langmuir, Dean	*Writ.*
Kruger, Otto	*Act.*	Langner, Lawrence	*Prod.*
Krumgold, Joseph Q.	*Prod.*	Langton, Basil	*Act.*
Kullers, John R. "Red"	*Act.*	Lanier, Charles	*Bnkr.*
Kuney, Jack	*Prod.*	Lanier, Charles D.	*Edit.*
Kuntz, Daniel	*Mus.*	Lanier, Henry Wysham	*Auth.*
Kuralt, Charles	*Jour.*	Lanier, Sidney	*M.O.T.*
Kurnitz, Harry	*Writ.*	Lansing, Robert	*Act.*
Kuroemon, Onoe II	*Act.*	Lantz, Robert	*Art.*
Kuss, Richard	*Act.*	Lardner, John	*Writ.*
Kyle, Howard	*Act.*	Lardner, Ring W.	*Writ.*
L'Estrange, Julian	*Act.*	Larimore, Earle	*Act.*
La Curto, James	*Act.*	Larkin, Peter	*S.A.*
La Farge, John	*Art.*	LaRovere, Ray	*Mus.*
La Farge, C. Grant	*Arch.*	Larremore, Thomas A.	*Mus.*
La Gatta, John	*Art.*	Larsen, Lars	*P.O.A.*
La Guardia, Fiorello H.	*Mayor*	Larsen, Milton	
La Guardia, Michael	*Act.*	Larsen, Ray	*P.O.A.*
Laas, William	*Writ.*	Lask, George Edwin	*Mgr.*
Labatt-Simon, Malcolm	*Writ.*	Latham, Frederick G.	*Mgr.*
Lackaye, Wilton	*Act.*	Latham, Harold S.	*Auth.*
Lackland, Ben	*Act.*	Latham, Joseph W.	*Act.*
Lackner, Francis J. Jr.	*M.O.T.*	Latham, Maxton	*Act.*
Lacy, Harry	*Act.*	Latham, Thomas W.	*Writ.*
Ladd, Schuyler	*Act.*	Lathrop, Barbour	*Jour.*
Laffan, William M.	*Edit.*	Lathrop, Francis	*Art.*
Lahr, Bert	*Act.*	Lathrop, George Parsons	*Auth.*
Laidlaw, James Lees	*Bnkr.*	Laughlin, Robert A.	*P.O.A.*
Laighton, Paul de Blois	*R.E.*	Laughton, Charles	*Act.*
Laird, Philip D.	*Brkr.*	Laurence, William L.	*Jour.*
Laire, Judson	*Act.*	Lauriat, Charles E., Jr.	*Pub.*
Laite, Charles William	*Act.*	Lavery, Emmet	*Dram.*
Lalley, Edward Patrick	*P.O.A.*	Lavezzo, Dan III	*P.O.A.*
Lally, F.E.	*Mer.*	Law, Henry H.	*P.O.A.*
Lamb, Frank E.	*Act.*	Law, Mouzon	*Dir.*
Lamb, William J.	*M.O.T.*	Law, Walter W., Jr	*Mer.*
Lambert, John, Jr.	*Art.*	Law, Walter W.	*Mer.*
Lambuth, David	*Prof.*	Lawder, Donald	*Writ.*
Lamont, Frederick F., Jr.	*Prod.*	Lawder, Wallace	*Jour.*
Lamont, Thomas William	*Bnkr.*	Lawes, Lewis E.	*Auth.*
Lance, Henry W.	*Phys.*	Lawford, Ernest	*Act.*
Landau, Jack	*Dir.*	Lawler, T. Jerome	*Act.*
Lande, Nathaniel	*Prod.*	Lawliss, Charles R.	*Jour.*
Landers, George M.	*P.O.A.*	Lawrence, Arthur R.	*Act.*
Lane, Charles	*Act.*	Lawrence, Edmund	*Act.*
Lane, Frank	*Act.*	Lawrence, Jerome	*Dram.*

Lawrence, John T.	*Pub.*
Lawrence, Mark	*Prod.*
Lawrence, Richard Hoe	*Bnkr.*
Lawrence, Thomas J.	*Act.*
Lawrence, William L.	*Prod.*
Lawrence, William W.	*Prof.*
Lawson, Steve	*M.O.T.*
Lax, Michael	*Art.*
Lay, Wilfrid	*Auth.*
Lazarus, Reuben A.	*Law.*
Leaf, Martin	*Law.*
Leaf, Munro	*Writ.*
Leamy, Hugh	*Edit.*
Leary, David	*Act.*
Leavitt, Ted	*Act.*
LeBaron, William	*Dram.*
Leberman, Joseph	*Act.*
Leberthon, H. Ginnel	*Art.*
Lechich, Anthony	*Phys.*
Lechner, Herman	*Act.*
Ledoux, Louis V.	*Dram.*
Lee, Charles N.	*P.O.A.*
Lee, Clark	*Jour.*
Lee, Gerald Stanley	*Auth.*
Lee, Henry Walsh	*Jour.*
Lee, Jack	*Act.*
Lee, Jack	*Mus.*
Lee, Jon	*Act.*
Lee, Kenneth	*Act.*
Lee, Robert E.	*Dram.*
Lee, W.H.L.	*Law.*
Leeds, Theodore E.	*Law.*
Lees, Robert	*Prod.*
LeFaucheur, Albert Randolph	*Eng.*
Leib, G. Bruce	*P.O.A.*
Leiber, Fritz	*Act.*
Leigh, Philip	*Ct*
Leighton, Fred	*Writ.*
Leiman, Eugene A.	*Law.*
Lemay, Harding	*Writ.*
LeMoyne, William J.	*Act.*
Lenahan, Patrick	*Pub.*
Lennen, Philip W.	*Writ.*
Lent, Henry B.	*Writ.*
Lenthall, Franklyn	*Act.*
Leon, Joseph	*Act.*
Leonard, George Herbert	*Act.*
Leonard, Hugh	*Dram.*
Leonard, Richard	*Writ.*
Lerman, Omar K.	*Dir.*
Lerner, Alan Jay	*Dram.*
Leslie, Bertram	*P.O.A.*
Leslie, F. Andrew	*M.O.T.*
Leslie, Frank H.	*Writ.*
Leslie, George W.	*Act.*
Leslie, Jack	*Act.*
Leslie, Laurence	*Act.*
Lesser, Sol	*Prod.*
Lessey, George A.	*Act.*
L'Estrange, Julian	*Act.*
LeSueur, Robert	*Act.*
Levering, Richmond	*P.O.A.*
Leverton, Garrett	*Edit.*
Levin, Gerald M.	*Jour.*
Levingson, Lester	*Phys.*
Levy, Newman	*Auth.*
Lewers, William	*Act.*
Lewis, Arthur	*Mgr.*
Lewis, Arthur	*Act.*
Lewis, Earle R.	*P.O.A.*
Lewis, Eugene H.	*Law.*
Lewis, Frederick	*Act.*
Lewis, Horace	*Act.*
Lewis, Howard C.	*Pub.*
Lewis, James	*Act.*
Lewis, Jerry D.	*Writ.*
Lewis, Michael	*Act.*
Lewis, N. Sheldon	*Act.*
Lewis, Walter	*Act.*
Lewis, William	*Act.*
Lewishon, Sam	*Law.*
Leyden, Leo	*Act.*
Lieb, Charles H.	*P.O.A.*
Lieb, Robert P.	*Act.*
Lienau, Paul F.	*P.O.A.*
Liff, Samuel (Biff)	*Prod.*
Light, Alan	*Edu.*
Lilley, Edward Clarke	*Dir.*
Lillie, T.W.	*P.O.A.*
Lilly, Joseph C.	*Writ.*
Lincoln, Charles M.	*Edit.*
Lincoln, E. K.	*Act.*
Lincoln, John L.	*P.O.A.*
Lincoln, Joseph C.	*Writ.*
Lindberg, Lawrence W.	*Prod.*
Lindeberg, H.T.	*Arch.*
Lindermann, Jan	*Dir.*

Lindley, David Howell	*Act.*
Lindley, Denver	*Edit.*
Lindquist, Robert J.	*Pub.*
Lindsay, Howard	*M.O.T.*
Lindsay, John V. (H.M.)	*Law.*
Lindsay, Nicholas Vachel	*Auth.*
Ling, Richie	*Act.*
Lingane, David	*Jour.*
Linington, Argyle	*Writ.*
Lippincott, David McCord	*Writ.*
Lippincott, J. Bertram	*Pub.*
Lippman, Monroe	*Edu.*
Lippmann, Walter	*Auth.*
Lipscomb, H. Bernard III	*Edu.*
Lipscomb, Thomas H.	*Pub.*
Lipson, Paul	*Act.*
Liss, Alan R.	*Pub.*
Lissauer, Geoffrey R.	*M.O.T.*
Lissauer, Robert	*Mus.*
Lissner, Will	*Edit.*
Litel, John	*Act.*
Littell, Edmund M.	*Writ.*
Little, Joseph J.	*Prin.*
Little, S. George	*Edit.*
Littlefield, C.W.	*Navy*
Livingston, Goodhue	*Arch.*
Livingston, Norman	*Dir.*
Livingston, Robert E.	*Writ.*
Lloyd, David Demarest	*Writ.*
Lloyd, Eric	*Jour.*
Lloyd, Frederick M.	*M.O.T.*
Lloyd, Frederick W.	*Act.*
Loane, Kenneth	*M.O.T.*
Locke, Edward	*Auth.*
Locke, Irving	*Act.*
Lockhart, Gene	*Act.*
Lockridge, Richard	*Writ.*
Lodeesen, Marius	*Writ.*
Lodge, George Cabot	*Auth.*
Loeb, James	*Bnkr.*
Loewe, Frederick	*Comp.*
Lofting, Hugh	*Auth.*
Logan, John Gordon	*Edit.*
Logan, Joshua L.	*Prod.*
Logan, Robert R.	*Law.*
Logan, Stanley	*Act.*
LoGiudice, A. Jack	*Act.*
Lonergan, Michael	*Prod.*

Long, Birch Burdette	*Art.*
Long, Johnny	*Mus.*
Long, Orie W.	*Prof.*
Long, Ray	*Writ.*
Longman, Edward G.	*Act.*
Loraine, Robert	*Act.*
Lorayne, Harry	*Act.*
Lord, James Brown	*Arch.*
Lordan, John	*Act.*
Lordan, Lee A.	*M.O.T.*
Lorentz, Pare	*Edit.*
Lorimer, George Horace	*Edit.*
Lorimer, Graeme	*Writ.*
Lorimer, Wright	*Act.*
Lorrillard, Louis L.	*P.O.A.*
Losee, Frank	*Act.*
Lothian, Charles E.	*Mgr.*
Lothian, Joseph	*Act.*
Lott, George Gilbert	*Art.*
Lott, Laurence C.	*Act.*
Loud, Grover	*Jour.*
Louden, Thomas	*Act.*
Lounsberry, Richard K.	*Brkr.*
Love, Montagu	*Act.*
Love, Samuel Alphonso	*Writ.*
Lovejoy, Albert R.	*Dir.*
Loveland, Gilbert	*Pub.*
Loveland, Ralph	*Mer.*
Low, Carl	*Act.*
Low, H. Burton	*P.O.A.*
Low, Will H.	*Art.*
Lowe, David, Jr.	*TvX.*
Lowe, Jacques	*Pub.*
Lowe, James	*M.O.T.*
Lowe, James (Jim)	*Sing.*
Lowell, James Russell	*Auth.*
Lowell, Orson	*Art.*
Lowenstein, Ralph	*Act.*
Lowrie, John M.	*Law.*
Lowry, George S.	*P.O.A.*
Lowther, George	*Act.*
Lubow, Oscar B.	*M.O.T.*
Lucas, Herbert	*Arch.*
Lucas, John Dearborn	*Writ.*
Luckinbill, Lawrence	*Act.*
Lucy, Arnold	*Act.*
Ludlowe, Henry	*Act.*
Ludlum, Robert	*Act.*
Ludwig, John	*M.O.T.*

Ludwig, William	*Writ.*	Mackay, William A.	*Art.*
Luescher, Mark A.	*Mgr.*	MacKaye, Milton	*Writ.*
Lum, Alvin K. U.	*Act.*	Mackaye, Percy	*Auth.*
Lunt, Alfred	*Act.*	MacKenna, Kenneth	*Act.*
Lunt, Storer B.	*Pub.*	Mackenzie, Cameron	*Edit.*
Luria, Sydney A.	*Law.*	Mackenzie, Compton	*Auth.*
Lurie, Richard	*Writ.*	MacKenzie, Ian	*Pub.*
Lurie, Walter	*Dir.*	Mackie, Fergus	*Sclp.*
Lurton, Douglas E.	*Edit.*	MacLaren, Donald	*Act.*
Lyman, Frank	*Mer.*	MacLaughlin, Don	*Act.*
Lynch, Dermot	*M.O.T.*	MacLean, Charles Agnew	*Edit.*
Lynch, Mark	*Act.*	MacLean, Joseph Talbot	*Phys.*
Lyndall, Percy	*Act.*	MacLeod, Gavin	*Act.*
Lynes, Stephen C.	*R.E.*	MacMahon, Horace	*Act.*
Lyon, George H.	*Edit.*	MacMillan, Robert	*Jour.*
Lyon, Michael Corey	*Jour.*	Macmonnies, Frederick	*Sclp.*
Lyon, Richard	*Art.*	MacMurray, John Van	
Lyons, Frank T.	*Bnkr.*	Antwerp	*Writ.*
Lytell, Bert	*Auth.*	MacNeil, Neil	*Edit.*
MacAlarney, Robert	*Writ.*	MacRae, Cuyler	*Edit.*
Macalister, William	*R.E.*	Macrae, Elliott B.	*Edit.*
MacArthur, Charles	*Dram.*	Macrae, John	*Pub.*
MacArthur, James	*Edit.*	Macy, Carleton	*Act.*
MacArthur, James	*Act.*	Macy, Nelson	*Eng.*
Macauley, Joseph	*Act.*	Madden, Richard J.	*Agt.*
MacBain, Alastair	*Writ.*	Madigan, Tom	*Prod.*
MacBryde, John	*Act.*	Maeder, Frank	*Mgr.*
MacCarter, Henry	*Art.*	Maeder, Jay	*Jour.*
MacCarthy, Justin Huntly	*Writ.*	Magee, Frank M. Jr.	*M.O.T.*
MacColl, James A.	*Act.*	Maginnis, Martin	*P.O.A.*
Macdonald, Charles	*Eng.*	Magonigle, Harold Van	
Macdonald, Charles B.	*Brkr.*	Buren	*Arch.*
MacDonald, James A.	*Ins.*	Magonigle, J. H.	*Mgr.*
MacDonald, John D.	*Writ.*	Magoun, Francis P.	*P.O.A.*
MacDonough, Glen	*Dram.*	Magrath, George Burgess	*Phys.*
MacFayden, John	*Arch.*	Mahin, John Lee	*Writ.*
Macgowan, Kenneth	*Writ.*	Mahler, Frank	*Mgr.*
MacGrath, Harold	*Writ.*	Mahoney, John	*Mus.*
MacGregor, Edgar	*Mgr.*	Mahoney, John	*Act.*
MacGregor, George P.	*M.O.T.*	Mahony, Thomas F.	*Pub.*
MacGregor, Kenneth	*Dir.*	Mair, Charles A.	*P.O.A.*
Machamer, Jefferson	*Art.*	Maitland, Thomas	*P.O.A.*
Mack, William Basil	*Act.*	Major, Ralph H. Jr.	*Edit.*
Mackall, Lawton	*Writ.*	Malchien, Richard	*Act.*
Mackay, Charles D.	*Act.*	Malcom, George Ide	*Brkr.*
Mackay, Edward J.	*Act.*	Mali, H. W. T.	*P.O.A.*
Mackay, F. F.	*Act.*	Mallery, Otto T.	*Prof.*
MacKay, John	*Edu.*	Mallon, George Barry	*Edit.*
MacKay, John W.	*Bnkr.*	Mallory, Bolton	*Edit.*
Mackay, Robert	*Act.*	Mallory, M. H.	*Mgr.*

Malone, John T.	*Act.*	Marshall, Oswald	*Act.*
Maloney, Peter	*Act.*	Marshall, Tully	*Act.*
Mamet, David	*Writ.*	Martello, John	*Act.*
Manber, David	*Writ.*	Martin, A. N.	*Bnkr.*
Manchester, Harland	*Writ.*	Martin, Barney	*Act.*
Mandelstam, Abraham	*P.O.A.*	Martin, Ben	*Edit.*
Maney, Michael	*Law.*	Martin, Benjamin Ellis	*Phys.*
Manfred, Frederick	*Writ.*	Martin, Drelincourt M.	*Bibl.*
Manheim, Frank J.	*Bnkr.*	Martin, Dwight	*Jour.*
Mankiewicz, Joseph	*Prod.*	Martin, Edward S.	*Writ.*
Manley, James	*P.O.A.*	Martin, Elliot	*Prod.*
Manley, William Ford	*Auth.*	Martin, George	*Edit.*
Mann, Cameron	*Bish.*	Martin, George N.	*Act.*
Mann, Parker	*Art.*	Martin, Harold G.	*P.O.A.*
Manners, J. Hartley	*Dram.*	Martin, Jacques	*Act.*
Manning, Bruce	*Writ.*	Martin, John Williams	*Army*
Manning, Dick	*Mus.*	Martin, John Sayre	*P.O.A.*
Mansfield, Howard	*Law.*	Martin, Lewis	*Act.*
Mansfield, Richard	*Act.*	Martin, Marc David	*Act.*
Manship, Paul	*Sclp.*	Martin, Milward W.	*Writ.*
Manson, Day	*Act.*	Martin, Neil M.	*Act.*
Manson, Thomas L. Jr.	*P.O.A.*	Martin, Peter	*P.O.A.*
Mantell, R. B.	*Act.*	Martin, Robert Dale	*Act.*
Mantle, Burns	*Writ.*	Martindale, Joseph B.	*Bnkr.*
Mapes, Charles V.	*Mer.*	Martinelli, Giovanni	*Sing.*
Mapes, Victor	*Dram.*	Martinsen, Dick	*Act.*
March, Frederic	*Act.*	Martland, Harrison S., Jr.	*Phys.*
Marchbanks, Hal	*Prin.*	Marx, Samuel	*Prod.*
Marcosson, I. F.	*Edit.*	Mascott, Richard A.	*Edit.*
Marek, Frederick Kane	*P.O.A.*	Mason, Brewster	*Act.*
Marek, George R.	*Auth.*	Mason, Edward Tuckerman	*Auth.*
Markey, Morris	*Writ.*	Mason, F.H.	*Art.*
Markle, John	*P.O.A.*	Mason, Frank E.	*Edit.*
Marks, Leonard	*Law.*	Mason, Gaylord C.	*Act.*
Marland, Douglas	*Act.*	Mason, Gregory	*Writ.*
Marlow, David A.	*Law.*	Mason, Harding T.	*Edit.*
Marlowe, Arthur	*Mgr.*	Mason, Henry Lowell	*Mer.*
Marquis, Don	*Writ.*	Mason, John B.	*Act.*
Marriott, B. Rodney	*Dir.*	Mason, Marion Otis	*P.O.A.*
Marrow, Macklin	*Mus.*	Mason, Marshall	*M.O.T.*
Marsh, Edward Clark	*Pub.*	Mason, Norman	*Art.*
Marsh, Frederick Dana	*Art.*	Mason, Robert T.	*Jour.*
Marsh, George Tracy	*Law.*	Masqueray, Emanuel L.	*Arch.*
Marsh, Reginald	*Art.*	Massen, Louis F.	*Act.*
Marshall, Alexander	*Writ.*	Massey, Raymond	*Act.*
Marshall, Anthony	*Prod.*	Massoletti, Henry E.	*P.O.A.*
Marshall, Herbert	*Act.*	Massoletti, Joseph D.	*P.O.A.*
Marshall, John	*Act.*	Masson, William Charles	*Act.*
Marshall, Mortimer	*Act.*	Masters, Edgar Lee	*Writ.*

Masters, Hilary	*Writ.*
Matesky, Jared	*Act.*
Mather, Stephen Tyng	*Writ.*
Matheson, Martin	*Pub.*
Mathews, Wilbur Knox	*Bnkr.*
Mathewson, Brockholst	*Writ.*
Mathieu, Carl	*Mus.*
Matson, Harold	*Writ.*
Matthews, Brander	*Auth.*
Matthews, Thomas S.	*Jour.*
Matz, Charles Albert, Jr.	*Writ.*
Maude, Cyril	*Act.*
Maule, Harry E.	*Pub.*
Maurice, Arthur B.	*Edit.*
Maurice, Charles F.	*P.O.A.*
Mavis, Paul	*Prod.*
Mawson, Edward R.	*Act.*
Maxwell, Lloyd R.	*Writ.*
Maxwell, Robert	*Act.*
May, Earl C.	*Writ.*
May, Frank	*Act.*
Mayer, Lloyd	*Edit.*
Mayes, Herbert R.	*Edit.*
Mayforth, Leland	*Act.*
Maynard, Duff Green	*Mnfr.*
Maynard, George W.	*Art.*
Mayo, Frank	*M.O.T.*
Mazzaluppo, Vincent	*Arch.*
McAdams, John V.	*Writ.*
McCallister, Paul	*Act.*
McAlpin, Benjamin B.	*Law.*
McAlpin, Charles W.	*Mer.*
McAlpin, George L.	*Mnfr.*
McAndrew, William R.	*Jour.*
McAnney, B.O.	*Edit.*
McArdle, Frank J.	*Dir.*
McAvity, Thomas A.	*Prod.*
McBride, Clifford	*Cart.*
McBride, Robert M.	*Pub.*
McCabe, John	*Writ.*
McCaffrey, John K.M.	*Edit.*
McCaffrey, William	*Agt.*
McCall, John C.	*Ins.*
McCarthy, C.J.	*Art.*
McCarthy, Charles	*Act.*
McCarthy, John C.	*Writ.*
McCarthy, John J.	*Writ.*
McCarthy, John R.	*Eng.*
McCarty, Barclay	*Writ.*
McCauley, William	*Act.*

McCaw, Raymond	*Edit.*
McClain, John	*Writ.*
McClane, John	
McClintic, Guthrie	*Dir.*
McClung, Garet Wilson	*Prof.*
McClure, Bruce Holme	*Edit.*
McClure, Robert Bruce	*Pub.*
McCobb, Paul	*Art.*
McConnell, Frederic	*Dir.*
McConnell, Frederick C.	*P.O.A.*
McConnell, Gerald	*Pub.*
McCord, Bert	*Writ.*
McCord, Lewis	*Act.*
McCorkle, David	*M.O.T.*
McCormack, Frank	*Act.*
McCormack, Thomas J.	*Pub.*
McCormick, Alexander Agnew	*Edit.*
McCormick, Ken	*Pub.*
McCormick, Myron	*Act.*
McCormick, Robert S.	*P.O.A.*
McCouch, Gordon M.	*Art.*
McCracken, Richard	*Edit.*
McCullough, Allen	*Act.*
McCullough, Andrew	*Dir.*
McCullough, Patrick	*Act.*
McCurdy, Allen W.	*Cler.*
McCurry, R. Blayne	*P.O.A.*
McCutcheon, George Barr	*Auth.*
McCutcheon, John T.	*Cart.*
McCutcheon, Wallace	*Act.*
McDade, Matt	*Jour.*
McDermott, George	*Mer.*
McDermott, Tom	*Act.*
McDonald, Earl	*Act.*
McDonough, Justin Kilderry	*Act.*
McDougall, Rex	*Act.*
McDowell, Henry Burden	*Writ.*
McDowell, William Melbourne	*Act.*
McEntee, Jervis	*Art.*
McEvoy, Dennis	*Writ.*
McEvoy, J.P.	*Writ.*
McEvoy, Renny	*Act.*
McFadden, John H.	*Mer.*
McFadden, Parmalee	*Edit.*
McGann, Michael John	*Act.*
McGavin, Darren	*Act.*
McGaw, Baldwin	*Dir.*

McGee, Harold	*Act.*	McPherrin, John W.	*Pub.*
McGeehan, W. O.	*Writ.*	McPherson, Logan G.	*R.R.*
McGinn, Francis D.	*Act.*	McPherson, Ross	*Phys.*
McGiver, John	*Act.*	McQuade, John	*Act.*
McGivern, William	*Auth.*	McRae, Bruce	*Act.*
McGlinn, John A.	*Mus.*	McSweeney, Denis F.	*Mgr.*
McGovern, John	*Act.*	McVey, Patrick	*Act.*
McGovern, John T.	*Writ.*	McVicar, Harry Whitney	*Art.*
McGowan, John	*Act.*	McWade, Robert	*Act.*
McGrath, Paul	*Act.*	McWilliams, Shirrell Norten	*Mer.*
McGraw, Curtis W.	*Pub.*	Mead, Edward S.	*Pub.*
McGuiness, James K.	*Writ.*	Mead, William R.	*Arch.*
McGuire, W. S.	*Law.*	Meader, George	*Act.*
McHale, Joseph	*Pub.*	Meador, John E.D.	*Writ.*
McHugh, Frank	*Act.*	Mealand, Richard L.	*Edit.*
McHugh, Peter	*Edu.*	Mearian, Mike	*Act.*
McIntyre, Alfred R.	*Pub.*	Medina, Edward	*M.O.T.*
McIntyre, Frank	*Act.*	Meech, Henry L.	*Mgr.*
McKay, Alexander	*Pub.*	Meech, Owen	*Act.*
McKee, Elmore H.	*Cler.*	Meek, Donald	*Act.*
McKee, Robert T.	*Arch.*	Megrue, Roi Cooper	*Agt.*
McKee, Thomas J.	*Coll*	Meighan, James	*Act.*
McKelway, St. Clair	*Writ.*	Meiselman, Ben	*P.O.A.*
McKeogh, Arthur	*Edit.*	Melamed, Fred	*Act.*
McKeown, Robert	*P.O.A.*	Melamed, Louis	*Prod.*
McKeown, Robert	*Art.*	Melchers, Gari	*Art.*
McKesson, Malcolm Forbes	*Art.*	Melchers, Richard	*Mnfr.*
McKim, Charles F.	*Arch.*	Melfo, Frank	*Act.*
McKim, Clarence	*Bnkr.*	Meloney, William Brown, II	*Writ.*
McKinlay, David A.	*Pub.*	Melrose, Wilson	*Act.*
McKinley, Kent	*Jour.*	Melville, Frank	*Pub.*
McKinney, Duane	*S.A.*	Menser, Clarence L.	*Dir.*
McKnight, Charles	*Bnkr.*	Menus, Justin A.	*Law.*
McKnight, Thomas	*Writ.*	Menzies, William C.	*Art.*
McLanahan, M. Hawley	*Arch.*	Mercer, John	*Comp.*
McLean, George H.	*Ins.*	Meredith, Burgess	*Act.*
McLearn, Frank C.	*Writ.*	Merivale, John Herman	*Act.*
McLeod, Keith	*Mus.*	Merivale, Philip	*Act.*
McMartin, John	*Act.*	Merrell, Richard	*Writ.*
McMaster, Gilbert Totten	*Surg.*	Merrick, Duff	*Jour.*
McMichael, Walter	*Jour.*	Merrill, Charles E., Jr.	*Pub.*
McMorrow, Thomas	*Writ.*	Merrill, George V.	*Law.*
McNair, William	*Dec.*	Merrill, Stuart F.R.	*Writ.*
McNamara, Brooks	*Edu.*	Merrill, W. Bradford	*Edit.*
McNamara, Edward	*Act.*	Merritt, Abraham	*Edit.*
McNaughton, Harry	*Act.*	Merritt, Carroll B.	*Pub.*
McNerney, Eugene, Jr.	*Art.*	Merton, Richard G.	*P.O.A.*
McNulty, John	*Writ.*	Mervale, Gaston	*Act.*
McNutt, Patterson	*Writ.*	Merwin, Samuel	*Edit.*
McNutt, William S.	*Writ.*	Meservy, George P.	*Law.*

Mesier, Louis	*P.O.A.*	Mills, Charles J.	*Pub.*
Metcalf, James A.	*Mer.*	Mills, Edgar	*Mus.*
Metcalf, Willard L.	*Art.*	Mills, Edward E.	*Pub.*
Meyer, E. Pennington	*Pub.*	Mills, Edward S.	*Edit.*
Meyer, Eugene	*P.O.A.*	Mills, Frank R.	*Act.*
Meyer, G. Von L.	*Mer.*	Mills, Frederic C.	*Bnkr.*
Meyer, Josh	*Art.*	Mills, Grant	*Act.*
Meyer, Matthew A.	*Pub.*	Millward, Charles A.	*Act.*
Meyer, Sheldon	*P.O.A.*	Milton, Robert D.	*Dir.*
Meyer, Josh	*M.O.T.*	Miner, Karl R.	*Law.*
Meyers, Gerald F.	*Art.*	Miner, Worthington C.	*Act.*
Meylan, Paul Julien	*Art.*	Mines, Flavel Scott	*Writ.*
Meyn, Heinrich	*Sing.*	Minnigerode, Fitzhugh Lee	*Writ.*
Mich, Daniel D.	*Edit.*	Minskoff, Jerome	*Prod.*
Michel, Theodore	*P.O.A.*	Miscione, Michael T.V.	*M.O.T.*
Mickelson, Sig	*News.*	Mitchell, Albert Post	*Act.*
Middleton, Drew	*Jour.*	Mitchell, Dodson L.	*Act.*
Middleton, Edwin	*Act.*	Mitchell, Earle	*Act.*
Middleton, George	*Dram.*	Mitchell, Edwin Valentine	*Auth.*
Middleton, Scudder	*Auth.*	Mitchell, Grant	*Act.*
Mielziner, Jo	*S.A.*	Mitchell, John A.	*Edit.*
Miers, Earl S.	*Writ.*	Mitchell, John D.	*Prof.*
Mikules, T. Leonard	*Writ.*	Mitchell, Julian	*Dir.*
Milan, Frank	*Act.*	Mitchell, Langdon Elwyn	*Auth.*
Milburn, John G.	*Law.*	Mitchell, Loften	*M.O.T.*
Miles, Dudley Howe	*Auth.*	Mitchell, Morton D.	*Jour.*
Miles, David	*Act.*	Mitchell, S. Weir	*Phys.*
Miles, William	*Act.*	Mitchell, Thomas	*Act.*
Milestone, Lewis	*Dir.*	Mitchell, William Avery	*M.O.T.*
Miley, John	*Prof.*	Mitchell, William H.	*Pub.*
Miller, Arthur (H.M.)	*Dram.*	Mittenthal, Richard Alan	*Edit.*
Miller, Charles Wooster	*Mer.*	Mittenthal, Richard	*Edit.*
Miller, Charles F.	*Act.*	Mockridge, Norton	*Jour.*
Miller, Charles F.	*Art.*	Modaff, Robert	*Arch.*
Miller, Frank E.	*Phys.*	Moehring, Jason J.	*Act.*
Miller, Gilbert Heron	*Act.*	Moffat, William D.	*Edit.*
Miller, H.B.	*Jour.*	Moffet, Harold	*Act.*
Miller, Henry	*Act.*	Moffett, Clemens	*Writ.*
Miller, Jahu De Witt	*Lec.*	Moffett, Cleveland	*Writ.*
Miller, James R.	*Writ.*	Moffett, Samuel E.	*Edit.*
Miller, J. P.	*Writ.*	Mokae, Zakes	*Act.*
Miller, Lawrence McK.	*Brkr.*	Molloy, Thomas J.	*Act.*
Miller, M. Hughes	*Pub.*	Moloney, Patrick Noel	*P.O.A.*
Miller, Russell	*P.O.A.*	Monahan, James	*Writ.*
Miller, Sigmund S.	*Dram.*	Monks, John Jr.	*Prod.*
Miller, Warner	*Mer.*	Monroe, Augustin	*Law.*
Millet, Francis D.	*Art.*	Montgomery, A.W.	*Mnfr.*
Milli, Robert	*Act.*	Montgomery, Edward	
Millis, Walter	*Writ.*	Livingston	*Bnkr.*
		Montgomery, J. Lynch	*Ins.*

Montgomery, John Howard	*Law.*	Morse, Frank P.	*Mgr.*
Montgomery, Robert	*Act.*	Morse, Harry W.	*Prof.*
Montgomery, Robert H., Jr.	*Law.*	Morse, Herbert J.	*Mgr.*
Montgomery, T.H.	*Mus.*	Morse, Samuel	*Jour.*
Montgomery, William, Jr.	*Law.*	Mortimer, Henry	*Act.*
Moody, William Vaugh	*Writ.*	Morton, Howard E.	*Writ.*
Moody, Winfield S.	*Edit.*	Morton, Michael	*Dram.*
Mooney, William P.	*Act.*	Morton, Thomas H.	*Art.*
Moore, Dick	*Act.*	Moscowitz, David Z.	*P.O.A.*
Moore, Don W.	*Writ.*	Mosel, Tad	*Dram.*
Moore, Douglas		Moses, Robert	*Writ.*
Stuart (H.M.)	*Auth.*	Moses, Theodore W.	*Prof.*
Moore, John C.	*Mer.*	Mosher, Gregory	*Prod.*
Moore, Joseph, Jr.	*Bnkr.*	Moskoff, John C.	*Act.*
Moore, Mechlin	*Writ.*	Moss, Arnold	*Act.*
Moore, Percival T.	*Act.*	Moss, Courtlandt D	*Mer.*
Mora, F. Luis	*Art.*	Mott, Jordan L., Jr.	*Mnfr.*
Moran, Joseph A.	*Act.*	Mott, Valentine	*Phys.*
Moran, Neil	*Act.*	Mottet, Frederic	*Mer.*
Mordaunt, Frank	*Act.*	Moulton, Harold	*Act.*
Mordecai, Randolph	*Act.*	Moulton, Henry H.	*Law.*
Morgan, Brewster	*Edit.*	Moulton, Robert H.	*Arch.*
Morgan, Clayland T.	*Pty*	Mowbray, H. Siddons	*Art.*
Morgan, Edward J.	*Act.*	Moyer, Albert	*Writ.*
Morgan, Frank	*Act.*	Moynihan, Arthur	*Law.*
Morgan, Henry L.	*Arch.*	Mueller, Carl	*Art.*
Morgan, J. Pierpont	*Bnkr.*	Mueller, John C.	*Law.*
Morgan, Ralph	*Act.*	Mueller, Merrill F.	*Edit.*
Morgan, Wallace	*Art.*	Muirdoch, James E.	*Act.*
Morley, Malcolm	*Act.*	Mulhare, Edward	*Act.*
Morrell, Harry E.	*Pub.*	Mulholland, John	*Mag.*
Morrell, Henry	*Act.*	Mullaney, William J.	*P.O.A.*
Morris, Felix	*Act.*	Mulligan, Hugh	*Jour.*
Morris, George E.	*R.E.*	Mullin, Michael	*Edu.*
Morris, Gouverneur	*Writ.*	Mullins, William J.	*P.O.A.*
Morris, Harrison Smith	*Auth.*	Munn, George F.	*Art.*
Morris, John H.	*M.O.T.*	Munro, David A.	*Pub.*
Morris, Robert, Jr.	*Act.*	Munro, Wallace	*Act.*
Morris, William	*Act.*	Munroe, Frederick M.	*Pub.*
Morrison, George Austin,		Munsell, Warren P.	*A.F.*
Jr.	*Law.*	Munshin, Jules	*Act.*
Morrison, George Austin	*Mer.*	Munson, Gorham	*Auth.*
Morrison, Hobe	*Jour.*	Murdoch, James E.	*Act.*
Morrison, Jack S.	*M.O.T.*	Murkland, Harry B.	*Writ.*
Morrison, Lewis	*Act.*	Murphy, Arthur R., Jr.	*Pub.*
Morrison, Priestly	*Dir.*	Murphy, Edgar Gardner	*Auth.*
Morrissey, Thomas Edward	*Act.*	Murphy, George	*Act.*
Morrow, Don	*Act.*	Murphy, John Daly	*Act.*
Morrow, William	*Edit.*		

Murphy, John D.	*Prof.*	Newman, Robert H.	*Writ.*
Murphy, Joseph E.	*Eng.*	Newman, William G.	*Mgr.*
Murphy, Myles	*Act.*	Newson, Henry D.	*Pub.*
Murphy, Patrick H.	*Dir.*	Newton, A. Edward	*Auth.*
Murphy, Ralph	*Act.*	Newton, Edward P.	*Cler.*
Murphy, Richard	*Writ.*	Newton, Francis	*Art.*
Murphy, Tim	*Act.*	Newton, Robert Safford	*Phys.*
Murray, Brian	*Dir.*	Newton, Theodore	*Act.*
Murray, Evaristo	*Pub.*	Niblo, Fred	*Act.*
Murray, Feg	*Art.*	Nicander, Edwin	*Act.*
Murray, George M.	*Writ.*	Nichols, Arthur B.	*Dec.*
Murtaugh, Paul	*Writ.*	Nichols, Guy	*Act.*
Muscio, U. V.	*Pub.*	Nichols, Humphrey T.	*Writ.*
Musson, Bennet	*Act.*	Nichols, J. Osgood	*Law.*
Myers, Fred	*Jour.*	Nichols, Lyman	*Mer.*
Myers, George Hewitt	*P.O.A.*	Nichols, Robert E.	*M.O.T.*
Myers, John R.	*P.O.A.*	Nicholson, Frederick	*Law.*
Myers, Kenneth	*M.O.T.*	Nicholson, John E.	*Arch.*
Myers, Paul	*Edu.*	Nicholson, Meredith	*Auth.*
Naish, J. Carrol	*Act.*	Nickell, Paul	*Dir.*
Napoli, Vincent A.	*Act.*	Nicol, Alexander I.	*Act.*
Nash, John McL	*Law.*	Niehaus, Charles H.	*Sclp.*
Nash, Ogden	*Writ.*	Nielsen, Thomas J.	*Edit.*
Nassivera, John	*Prod.*	Nielson, Thomas G.	*Act.*
Nast, Cyril	*Agt.*	Nobles, Milton	*Act.*
Nast, Thomas	*Art.*	Nock, Albert J.	*Writ.*
Nastasi, Frank	*Act.*	Nolan, Lloyd	*Act.*
Naughton, Jack	*Act.*	Nolan, Norman	*P.O.A.*
Nedell, Bernard	*Act.*	Nolen, John	*Arch.*
Needham, Henry Beach	*Jour.*	Nolte, Charles	*Act.*
Neeson, Andrew L.	*Mer.*	Norman, F.S.	*Pub.*
Neff, John C.	*Wirt*	Norman, Nathaniel Cruse	*Phot.*
Neidlinger, S. Travers	*Art.*	Norris, Charles Gilman	*Auth.*
Neill, James	*Act.*	Norris, Ernest E., Jr.	*Writ.*
Neilly, Andrew H., Jr.	*Pub.*	Norris, Frank	*Phys.*
Neilson, Francis	*Act.*	Norris, Frank C.	*Jour.*
Nelson, George Harold	*Art.*	Norris, Henry S.	*Phys.*
Nelson, Henry Loomis	*Auth.*	Norris, William	*Act.*
Nelson, Herbert	*Act.*	North, Alan	*Act.*
Nelson, James H.	*Prod.*	North, Frederick O.	*Mgr.*
Nelson, Louis	*Art.*	North, John Ringling	*Cir.*
Nelson, Ralph	*Prod.*	North, Sterling	*Writ.*
Nettleton, Walter	*Art.*	North, Wilfrid	*Act.*
Neuwirth, Frank	*P.O.A.*	Northcote, H.O.,	*Bnkr.*
Newbold, Thomas	*Law.*	Northrup, Harry S.	*Act.*
Newcastle, The Duke Of	*P.O.A.*	Northshield, Robert	*Prod.*
Newcomb, Thomas	*Writ.*	Norton, Elliott	*Jour.*
Newell, George C.	*Ins.*	Norton, John W.	*Mgr.*
Newlin, A. Chauncey	*P.O.A.*	Norton, Karl Benton, Jr.	*Prod.*
Newman, Barry	*Act.*	Norton, Roy E.	*Auth.*
Newman, Ralph G.	*Writ.*		

Norton, W.W.	*Pub.*	Ogden, James L.	*P.O.A.*
Norton, William A.	*Act.*	Ohira, Kazuto	*PrR.*
Norvelle, Lee	*Prof.*	Okolowitz, Frederick	*Art.*
Norwood, Robert	*Cler.*	Olcott, Chauncey	*Act.*
Nourse, Alan E.	*Phys.*	Olcott, George M.	*P.O.A.*
Novell, Arthur	*Jour.*	Olin, Stephen H.	*Law.*
Noyes, James B.	*Pub.*	Olivier, Laurence	*Act.*
Noyes, Thomas Ewing	*Prod.*	Olmstead, Clarence	*Prod.*
Nugent, Elliott	*Dram.*	Olsen, Moroni	*Act.*
Nugent, J.C.	*Act.*	Olyphant, Robert	*Mer.*
O'Boyle, William B.	*Prod.*	Oman, William M.	*Pub.*
O'Brien, Dennis F.	*P.O.A.*	Oneal, Frederick	*Act.*
O'Brien, Eugene	*Act.*	Ongley, Byron	*Act.*
O'Brien, M.J.	*P.O.A.*	Oppenheimer, George	*Writ.*
O'Brien, Pat	*Act.*	Opper, Frederick Burr	*Art.*
O'Brien, Paul D.	*Law.*	Ormerod, C. Berkeley	*Writ.*
O'Brien, Thomas J.	*Cler.*	Ormonde, Eugene	*Act.*
O'Connell, Arthur	*Act.*	Orofino, Francis X.	*P.O.A.*
O'Connell, Hugh V.	*Act.*	Orr, Forrest	*Act.*
O'Connor, Andrew	*Sclp.*	Orrick, David	*Act.*
O'Connor, Carroll	*Act.*	Orton, Vrest	*Auth.*
O'Connor, John	*Pub.*	Osborn, Chase S.	*Writ.*
O'Connor, John Joseph	*Jour.*	Osborn, Reynold Ted	*Act.*
O'Day, Daniel, Jr.	*Bnkr.*	Osbourne, George	*Act.*
O'Donnell, Jack	*Writ.*	Osbourne, Lloyd (H.M.)	*Writ.*
O'Hara, Geoffrey	*Comp.*	Osgood, Charles	*Jour.*
O'Hara, John	*Auth.*	Osgood, James R.	*Pub.*
O'Higgins, Harvey	*Auth.*	Osgood, John C.	*Mer.*
O'Malley, Frank Ward	*Writ.*	Otis, John	*Act.*
O'Malley, Neill	*Act.*	Otis, William K.	*Surg.*
O'Meara, Walter	*Writ.*	Ottenheimer, Albert M.	*Act.*
O'Morrison, Kevin	*Dram.*	Oudin, Eugene	*Sing.*
O'Neal, Frederick	*Act.*	Oursler, Fulton	*Wirt*
O'Neill, Arthur	*Phot.*	Oursler, William Charles	*Writ.*
O'Neill, Eugene (H.M.)	*Dram.*	Overman, Lynne	*Act.*
O'Neill, Henry	*Act.*	Overton, Charles	*Act.*
O'Neill, James	*Act.*	Owen, Russell	*Writ.*
O'Rourke, Thomas	*Act.*	Owen, William F.	*Act.*
Oakley, Henry A.	*Ins.*	Oz, Steven	*Act.*
Ober, Harold	*Lit.*	Pace, Julian V.	*M.O.T.*
Ober, Robert	*Act.*	Pack, Richard M.	*Bro.*
Obolenksy, Ivan	*Pub.*	Packard, Frank	*P.O.A.*
Obts, Hans A.	*Prin.*	Padgett, Billy	*Act.*
Ocko, Daniel	*Act.*	Page, Arthur W.	*Edit.*
Odell, C.P.	*Prin.*	Page, Stanley Hart	*Writ.*
Odell, George C.D.	*Auth.*	Page, Thomas Nelson	*Writ.*
Odell, George D.	*Sing.*	Paget, F.M.	*Act.*
Oelrichs, Hermann	*Bnkr.*	Paine, Albert Bigelow	*Auth.*
Oenslager, Donald	*Art.*	Paine, Henry Gallup	*Edit.*
Ogden, J.Bergen	*Phys.*	Painter, Clarke	*Act.*

Paisner, Bruce	*M.O.T.*	Patten, Joseph	*Act.*
Palian, Peter	*Dir.*	Patten, Moultrie	*Act.*
Palmer, A.M.	*Mgr.*	Patten, Thomas G.	*Brkr.*
Palmer, Charles G.	*Mnfr.*	Patten, Walter R.	*Brkr.*
Palmer, Dudley B.	*Writ.*	Patterson, Edward	*Law.*
Palmer, Elisha L.	*Mnfr.*	Patterson, James J.	*Jour.*
Palmer, Francis J.	*Writ.*	Patterson, Russell	*Art.*
Palmer, Fredrick	*Writ.*	Pattullo, George	*Auth.*
Palmer, Harry Buchanan	*P.O.A.*	Paul, Howard	*Writ.*
Palmer, Irving	*M.O.T.*	Paulton, Harry	*Act.*
Palmer, Loren	*Edit.*	Paulus, Robert J.	*M.O.T.*
Palmer, Morton M.	*Bnkr.*	Pauncefore, George	*Act.*
Palmer, Paul	*Edit.*	Paval, Philip	*Art.*
Palmer, Sheldon	*Law.*	Pavetti, Francis J.	*Law.*
Palmer, Stephen S.	*Bnkr.*	Payette, William C.,	*Jour.*
Palmer, Thomas	*Act.*	Payne, B. Iden	*Act.*
Pancosast, Archer V.	*Mer.*	Payne, George Henry	*Auth.*
Pantaleoni, Guido	*Mus.*	Payne, Will	*Auth.*
Pape, Eric	*Art.*	Payson, William F.	*Auth.*
Papp, Frank	*Prod.*	Peabody, Arthur J.	*P.O.A.*
Pardoll, David M.	*Mgr.*	Peabody, Augustus	*Bnkr.*
Park, Bruce R.	*Edu.*	Peacock, Roscoe	*Pub.*
Parke, William	*Act.*	Pearce, George C.	*Act.*
Parkenham, T. Compton	*Writ.*	Pecht, Michael	*Pub.*
Parker, Austin	*Auth.*	Pecile, Jordan	*Edu.*
Parker, Everett C.	*Cler.*	Peck, Benjamin M.	*Mer.*
Parker, George D.	*Act.*	Peck, Gregory	*Act.*
Parker, Gilbert	*Auth.*	Peck, Howard M.	*Arch.*
Parker, Raymond C.	*Bio*	Peckham, W.G.	*Law.*
Parker, W.B.	*Pub.*	Peet, Charles B.	*Ins.*
Parker, Willard D.	*P.O.A.*	Pegler, Westbrook	*Writ.*
Parker, Willard, Jr.	*Mnfr.*	Peirce, James Mills	*Prof.*
Parks, Paul	*Mus.*	Peirce, Thomas Mitchell	*Art.*
Parmentier, Douglas	*Pub.*	Peixotto, Ernest C.	*Art.*
Parr, Charles Mckew	*Writ.*	Peixotto, Florian	*Art.*
Parrish, James C.	*P.O.A.*	Pelletier, Wilfred	*Mus.*
Parrish, Maxfield	*Art.*	Pellew, George	*Writ.*
Parrish, Samuel L.	*Law.*	Pemberton, Brock	*Prod.*
Parshall, Dewitt	*Art.*	Pembroke, George	*Act.*
Parson, Geoffrey	*Edit.*	Pendleton, Edmund	*Auth.*
Parson, George B.	*Brkr.*	Penfield, Frederic C.	*Auth.*
Parsons, John E.	*Law.*	Penn, David	*Jour.*
Parsons, Schuyler L.	*Mer.*	Pennell, Daniel	*Mgr.*
Parsons, Thomas William	*Auth.*	Pennell, Joseph	*Art.*
Partington, Rex	*Prod.*	Pennington, William	*Law.*
Parton, Lemuel F.	*Writ.*	Penzner, Seymour	*Act.*
Patrell, Donald	*P.O.A.*	Peple, Edward H.	*Dram.*
Patrell, Oliver	*P.O.A.*	Peploe, Fitzgerald	*Sclp.*
Patrick, Leonard	*Act.*	Percyval, T. Wigney	*Act.*
Patrick, Vincent	*Writ.*	Perin, Bradford	*Art.*

Perkins, C. Lawrence	*Mer.*	Pierce, Charles S.	*Sci.*
Perkins, Donald	*Act.*	Pierce, Henry H.	*Art.*
Perkins, E.H.	*Bnkr.*	Pierce, Richard A.	*Act.*
Perkins, Francis Davenport	*Writ.*	Pierrot, George	*Edit.*
Perkins, James N.	*Writ.*	Pietsch, Charles F.	*Writ.*
Perkins, Thomas C.	*Edit.*	Pilcher, Lewis F.	*Arch.*
Perrin, Dwight S.	*Edit.*	Pileggi, Nicholas	*Jour.*
Perrin, Will	*Art.*	Pinchot, James W.	*P.O.A.*
Perrotta, Fioravante	*Law.*	Pine, Ralph	*Pub.*
Perry, Charles M.	*P.O.A.*	Pinero, Arthur Wing Hon.	*Dram.*
Perry, Lawrence	*Writ.*	Pinkham, Edward W. Hy	*Phys.*
Perry, Oliver Hazard	*P.O.A.*	Pinza, Ezio	*Sing.*
Perry, Philip	*Act.*	Pitcher, James R.	*Ins.*
Perry, Roland Hinton	*Sclp.*	Pitkin, Walter, Jr.	*P.O.A.*
Perry, William A.	*Eng.*	Pitman, James Richard	*Act.*
Pershing, John J. (H.M.)	*Army*	Pitman, Stephen Minot	*Bnkr.*
Perugini, Giovanni	*Sing.*	Pitou, Augustus	*Mgr.*
Peters, Charles Rollo	*Art.*	Pitt, Charles D.	*Act.*
Peters, House	*Act.*	Pixley, Frank	*Auth.*
Peters, Rollo	*Act.*	Plagemann, Bentz	*Writ.*
Peters, Samuel T.	*Mer.*	Planco, Johnnie	*Agt.*
Petrie, George	*Act.*	Plante, William C.	*Art.*
Pettolina, Anthony	*M.O.T.*	Platt, C.A.	*Art.*
Pew, Marlen E.	*Edit.*	Platt, George Foster	*Dir.*
Pezet, A.W.	*Auth.*	Platt, Isaac Hull	*Phys.*
Pfaff, Warren	*M.O.T.*	Platt, John	*Eng.*
Pfeiffer, Joseph C.	*Pub.*	Plimmer, Harry	*Act.*
Pfeiffer, Timothy N.	*Law.*	Plummer, Christopher	*Act.*
Phares, Frank H.	*Writ.*	Plunkett, Charles	*Act.*
Phelps, Charles	*Phys.*	Pocock, A. J.	*Prod.*
Phelps, William Lyon	*Prof.*	Pocock, James	*M.O.T.*
Philbrick, Norman	*M.O.T.*	Pogostin, S. Lee	*Dram.*
Philiber, John	*Act.*	Poland, Edward	*Act.*
Philips, Judson	*Writ.*	Polhemus, Millard F.	*P.O.A.*
Phillips, Alphonso	*Act.*	Polisar, Jonathan Marc	*P.O.A.*
Phillips, Henry Albert	*Auth.*	Polk, Ralph, Jr.	*P.O.A.*
Phillips, James, Jr.	*Jour.*	Pollock, Allan	*Act.*
Phillips, John S.	*Edit.*	Pollock, Bernard	*Act.*
Phillips, Joseph B.	*Writ.*	Pollock, Channing	*Dram.*
Phillips, Paul J.	*M.O.T.*	Pollock, Thomas C.	*Writ.*
Phillips, Randy	*Act.*	Pomroy, H.K.	*Brkr.*
Phillips, Robert S.	*Writ.*	Pond, Walter	*Law.*
Phipps, Edward H.	*Eng.*	Pool, Frank Jean	*Coll*
Picaza, Julian De	*Writ.*	Poole, Ernest C.	*Auth.*
Piccirilli, Attilio	*Sclp.*	Poole, William M.	*Edit.*
Pichel, Irving	*Dir.*	Poor, Henry W.	*Bnkr.*
Pickering, Loring	*Edit.*	Pope, Alexander	*Art.*
Pickering, M.J.	*Mer.*	Pope, Charles Macauley	*Act.*
Pickett, John E.	*Edit.*	Pope, Charles R.	*Cons.*
Piel, David	*M.O.T.*	Pope, John Russel	*Arch.*

Porter, Cole	*Comp.*	Proctor, Charles E.	*Art.*
Porter, Harold E.	*Auth.*	Proctor, David G.	*Act.*
Porter, Horace	*Army*	Proctor, Joseph	*Act.*
Porter, William Deering	*Mnfr.*	Proctor, Thomas R.	*Bnkr.*
Porter, William F.	*Law.*	Prode, Gordon	
Porterfield, Robert	*Act.*	Proser, Leopold	*Writ.*
Posner, Stephen	*M.O.T.*	Prout, Charles	*Jour.*
Post, Guy Bates	*Act.*	Puccio, Thomas A.	*Law.*
Post, Langdon W.	*Writ.*	Pulitzer, Ralph	*Edit.*
Post, William, Jr.	*Act.*	Pullen, Stanley T.	*P.O.A.*
Postley, Clarence A.	*P.O.A.*	Pulsifer, Harold Trowbridge	*Auth.*
Potter, Asa P.	*Bnkr.*	Purcell, John F.	*Jour.*
Potter, Frank Hunter	*Mus.*	Purdie, Francis B.	*P.O.A.*
Potter, Henry C.	*Bish.*	Purdum, Ralph	*Act.*
Potter, Julian	*P.O.A.*	Purrington, William A.	*Law.*
Potter, Mark W.	*Law.*	Putnam, Boyd	*Act.*
Potter, Philip B.K.	*Prof.*	Putnum, George P.	*Mfgr.*
Poulton, A.G.	*Act.*	Putnum, James	*Pub.*
Poupart, Homer	*M.O.T.*	Pyle, Howard	*Art.*
Powell, Francis	*Act.*	Pyre, Walton	*Act.*
Powell, Hickman	*Writ.*	Queenan, Reginald O.	*Phys.*
Powell, Richard Dick	*Act.*	Quigley, Jack	*Mgr.*
Power, Littledale	*Act.*	Quinby, George H.	*Dir.*
Power, Tyrone	*Act.*	Quinby, Henry C.	*Law.*
Power, William H.	*Mgr.*	Quinlan, Francis J.	*Phys.*
Powers, Eugene	*Act.*	Quinn, Edmond T.	*Sclp.*
Powers, James T.	*Act.*	Quinn, Stanley J., Jr.	*Prod.*
Powers, John M. Jr.	*P.O.A.*	Quinn, Thomas	*Writ.*
Powers, Tom	*Act.*	Quintero, Jose	*Dir.*
Prall, Robert H.	*Dir.*	Rabb, Maxwell M.	*Prod.*
Pratt, Lee	*Prod.*	Rachow, Louis A.	*Edu.*
Presbrey, Gene W.	*Mgr.*	Racusin, M. Jay	*Jour.*
Prescott, John	*Act.*	Radcliffe, Vernon	*Dir.*
Preston, Robert	*Act.*	Rae, William E.	*Edit.*
Price, Allonzo	*Act.*	Raffael, Jack	*Act.*
Price, Bruce	*Arch.*	Rafferty, John D.	*Writ.*
Price, Garrett	*Art.*	Raffetto, Michael	*Act.*
Price, Mark	*Act.*	Ragland, William H.	*Plant.*
Price, Michael P.	*Prod.*	Rahr, Frederic H.	*Art.*
Price, Vincent	*Act.*	Raiguel, George Earle	*Auth.*
Price, Walter	*Brkr.*	Raiken, Lawrence	*Act.*
Price, William Meade	*Art.*	Raine, William MacLeod	*Auth.*
Prichette, James	*Art.*	Rainey, John Crews	*P.O.A.*
Prideaux, Tom	*Jour.*	Rainey, William S.	*Dir.*
Primrose, William	*Mus.*	Rains, Claude	*Act.*
Prince, Harold	*Prod.*	Rainsford, W.S.	*Cler.*
Prince, Morton Peabody	*Writ.*	Ralston, Gilbert	*Act.*
Probert, George S.	*Act.*	Ramsdell, Clifford	*Writ.*
Proctor, A. Phinister	*Sclp.*	Ramsdell, James A.P.	*P.O.A.*
		Ramsey, Gordon	*Act.*

Ramsey, Walden	*Act.*	Reid, Whitelaw	*Dipl.*
Rand, Calvin	*P.O.A.*	Reidy, Peter J.	*P.O.A.*
Randall, Kenn	*Act.*	Reiland, Karl Hon	*Cler.*
Randall, William R.	*Act.*	Reilley, Thomas M.	*Mgr.*
Ranson, Herbert	*Act.*	Reilly, James F.	*Mgr.*
Rapp, Martin	*Pub.*	Reinhart, Charles S.	*Art.*
Rapport, Samuel	*Pub.*	Reinhart, Joseph W.	*R.R.*
Rasely, George	*Sing.*	Reinold, Bernard A.	*A.F.*
Rathbone, Basil	*Act.*	Relph, George	*Act.*
Rauscher, William V.Jr	*Cler.*	Relyea, Charles M.	*Art.*
Rawlins, Lester	*Act.*	Remington, Frederic	*Art.*
Rawson, Mitchell	*Writ.*	Remsen, Ira Mallory	*Art.*
Ray, Randolph Hon	*Cler.*	Renaud, Ralph E.	*Edit.*
Rayburn, Gene	*Act.*	Renick, Kyle	*Prod.*
Raymond, C.M.	*P.O.A.*	Rennie, Frank	*Art.*
Raymond, Charles Henry	*Phot.*	Rennie, Hugh	*Act.*
Raymond, Gene	*Act.*	Rennie, James	*Act.*
Raymond, George B.	*Ins.*	Renthal, Charles H.	*P.O.A.*
Raymond, George L.	*Prof.*	Repass, Richard R.	*Writ.*
Raymond, William	*Act.*	Repp, Guy	*Act.*
Reach, James	*Writ.*	Revere, Eugene	*Act.*
Read, Edward C.K.	*Writ.*	Reynal, Eugene	*Pub.*
Read, William A.	*Bnkr.*	Reynolds, Charles	*Act.*
Readick, Frank	*Act.*	Reynolds, Edward, Jr.	*Pub.*
Reagan, Allan	*Writ.*	Reynolds, Patrick J.	*Jour.*
Reardon, Mark	*Writ.*	Reynolds, Paul R.	*Lit. Agt.*
Reber, J. Howard	*Law.*	Reynolds, Quenton	*Jour.*
Rector, Harlan	*Act.*	Rheims, Gaston R.	*Mel.*
Redding, Joseph D.	*Law.*	Rhind, J. Massey	*Sculpt.*
Redfield, Edward Willis	*Art.*	Rhodes, Erik	*Act.*
Redmond, Henry S.	*Bnkr.*	Rhodes, Joseph	*Prod.*
Redmund, William	*Act.*	Ribalow, Meier Z.	*Edu.*
Reed, Alex	*Act.*	Rice, Chester	*Jour.*
Reed, Daniel	*Act.*	Rice, Clarence C.	*Phys.*
Reed, Henry H.	*Ins.*	Rice, Edmund C.	*Dram.*
Reed, Joseph Verner	*Prod.*	Rice, Grantland	*Writ.*
Reed, Luther A.	*Dram.*	Rich, Charles H.	*Army*
Reed, Roland	*Act.*	Rich, Edwin G.	*Auth.*
Rees, Roger	*Act.*	Richard, F.T.	*Cart.*
Reese, Edward B.	*Act.*	Richards, Houston	*Act.*
Reese, William Willis	*P.O.A.*	Richards, Martin	*Prod.*
Reeve, Christopher	*Act.*	Richardson, Donald M.	*Dir.*
Reeves, Earl	*Writ.*	Richardson, Frank C.	*Phys.*
Reeves-Smith, H.	*Act.*	Richardson, Frank W.	*Dec.*
Regan, Walter	*Act.*	Richardson, Frederick A.	*Edit.*
Reice, Edmund C.	*Edit.*	Richardson, Lee	*Act.*
Reichert, James	*Mus.*	Richardson, Locke	*Lec.*
Reid, Ogden	*Edit.*	Riche, Robert	*Writ.*
Reid, Robert	*Art.*	Richman, Charles J.	*Act.*
		Richter, Charles Manton	*P.O.A.*

Ricketts, Thomas	*Act.*	Roberts, Tony	*Act.*
Riddell, George E.	*Act.*	Roberts, William Carmen	*Edit.*
Riddell, H.S.	*Mgr.*	Robertson, Cliff	*Act.*
Riddle, George	*Lec.*	Robertson, Guy	*Act.*
Riddle, George	*Mus.*	Robertson, T.S.	*Phys.*
Riddle, George	*Act.*	Robins, Edward H.	*Act.*
Rideing, William H.	*Auth.*	Robins, T.E.	*Edit.*
Ridges, Stanley C.	*Act.*	Robinson, Bertrand	*Dram.*
Rigby, Edward	*Act.*	Robinson, Boardman	*Art.*
Rigby, Paul	*Art.*	Robinson, Charles K. III	*Act.*
Rigdon, Walter	*Pub.*	Robinson, Charles K.	*Dram.*
Rigg, Edgar T.	*Pub.*	Robinson, Forrest	*Act.*
Riggs, George C.	*Mer.*	Robinson, Francis	*M.O.T.*
Riggs, Siydney	*Act.*	Robinson, Frank B.	*Mnfr.*
Riley, Allan J.	*P.O.A.*	Robinson, Frank Tracy	*Mer.*
Riley, Thomas	*Law.*	Robinson, Kenneth Allan	*Writ.*
Riley, Thomas L.	*Dir.*	Robinson, Moncure	*Law.*
Rimington, Critchell	*Pub.*	Robinson, Thomas L.	*Pub.*
Ringling, Alfred T.	*Cir.*	Robson, Stuart	*Act.*
Ringwalt, Ralph C.	*Law.*	Roche, Arthur Somers	*Writ.*
Ripple, Pacie	*Act.*	Roche, Eugene H.	*Act.*
Ritchie, Franklin	*Act.*	Rockwell, Norman	*Art.*
Ritchie, George	*News.*	Roddie, Stewart W.	*Writ.*
Riter, Joseph	*Mgr.*	Rodgers, Richard	*Comp.*
Ritner, George E.	*Prod.*	Roebling, Ferdinand W.	*Mnfr.*
Rittenberg, Morris	*TvX.*	Roeder, Benjamin F.	*Dram.*
Ritter, Theodore	*Mgr.*	Roerick, William	*Act.*
Rives, George L.	*P.O.A.*	Roessle, T.E.	*Ho.*
Rivkin, Allen	*Auth.*	Rogers, Archibald	*P.O.A.*
Rizzo, Dick	*Act.*	Rogers, Benjamin G.	*Act.*
Rizzuto, Phil	*Bro.*	Rogers, Brooks	*Act.*
Robards, Jason, Jr.	*Act.*	Rogers, G. Vernor	*Pub.*
Robb, J. Addison	*Auth.*	Rogers, Gil	*Act.*
Robb, J. Hampden	*Coll*	Rogers, James Gamble	*Arch.*
Robb, James	*Bio*	Rogers, Kipp	*Law.*
Robb, Scott Hall	*M.O.T.*	Rogers, Leigh	*Writ.*
Robbin, Irving	*Mus.*	Rogers, Loraine	*Mgr.*
Robbins, Chandler	*P.O.A.*	Rogers, Lorlys Elton	*Law.*
Robbins, Rowland A.	*P.O.A.*	Rogers, Ronald	*Act.*
Robbins, Russell H.	*P.O.A.*	Rogers, William A.	*Art.*
Roberts, Doug	*Jour.*	Rogerson, Philip C.	*Dir.*
Roberts, Edward Barry	*Writ.*	Rokenbaugh, Henry Scott	*Law.*
Roberts, Frank	*Act.*	Roland, Edward J.	*P.O.A.*
Roberts, Franklyn	*Act.*	Roman, Charles P.	*P.O.A.*
Roberts, Joseph W.	*Bro.*	Rome, Harold	*Comp.*
Roberts, Kenneth	*Act.*	Ronalds, George L.	*P.O.A.*
Roberts, Kenneth L.	*Writ.*	Roof, Stephen W.	*Phys.*
Roberts, Lloyd Douglas	*Act.*	Roohan, James E.	*Edit.*
Roberts, Milton	*Act.*	Roope, Fay	*Act.*
Roberts, Roy	*Act.*	Roosevelt, Frank	*P.O.A.*

Roosevelt, James	*Ins.*
Roosevelt, Robert B.,Jr	*R.E.*
Root, Elihu	*Law.*
Roper, Elmo	*Writ.*
Rork, Samuel E.	*Mgr.*
Rorke, Hayden	*Act.*
Rosa, Philip	*Edit.*
Rose, Carl	*Cart.*
Rose, Norman	*Act.*
Rosebault, Charles J.	*Pub.*
Roselle, William	*Act.*
Roseman, Ralph	*Prod.*
Rosen, Martin	*Agt.*
Rosen, Victor	*Writ.*
Rosenberg, Bernard	*P.O.A.*
Rosenberg, Conrad	*Phys.*
Rosenthal, A.M.	*Jour.*
Rosenthal, Arthur J.	*Edit.*
Ross, Clinton	*Auth.*
Ross, David	*M.O.T.*
Ross, Gordon	*Art.*
Ross, Harold	*Edit.*
Ross, James	*Eng.*
Ross, Lanny	*Sing.*
Ross, Robert F.	*Act.*
Ross, Sydney	*Arch.*
Ross, Thomas W.	*Act.*
Rossetti, Dominick	*Dir.*
Rotch, Arthur	*Arch.*
Roth, Harold	*Den.*
Roth, Herb	*Art.*
Roth, Otto	*Mus.*
Rothenberg, Marvin	*Dir.*
Rothschild, Alfred	*Writ.*
Roudebush, J. Heywood	*Sclp.*
Roulet, William	*Pub.*
Rounds, Ralph S.	*Law.*
Rowan, Bayard F.	*Edu.*
Rowan, Ernest	*Act.*
Rowsome, Frank H.,Jr.	*Edit.*
Royce, Brigham	*Act.*
Royce, Julian	*Act.*
Royle, Edwin Milton	*Act.*
Royle, J.C.	*Writ.*
Ruben, Paul A.	*Act.*
Rubinstein, John	*Act.*
Rublee, George	*Writ.*
Ruegg, Fred F.	*Bro.*
Ruffner, Edmund Birch	*Sing.*
Ruggles, James F.	*P.O.A.*
Ruml, Beardsley	*Writ.*
Rumsey, C.C.	*Sclp.*
Rupp, Gerald	*Law.*
Ruppaner, A.	*Phys.*
Russ, Zachary	*Prod.*
Russak, Ben	*Jour.*
Russell, Alexander	*Mus.*
Russell, Andrew H.	*Army*
Russell, E.G.W.	*Art.*
Russell, Horace	*Law.*
Russell, James Townsend	*Cler.*
Russell, John E.	*Writ.*
Russell, Peter H.	*SMg.*
Russell, R. H., Jr.	*Pub.*
Russell, Sol	*Act.*
Russell, T. McDonough	*Eng.*
Russell, William H.	*Arch.*
Ruth, M. L.	*Surg.*
Rutherford, John	*Act.*
Rutherford, John A.	*Bnkr.*
Rutman, Laurence	*Edit.*
Ruxton, Philip	*P.O.A.*
Ryan, Edmon	*Act.*
Ryan, J. Timothy	*Jour.*
Ryan, John Paul	*Writ.*
Ryan, Maxwell D.	*Phys.*
Ryan, Royal W.	*P.O.A.*
Ryle, William T.	*Mer.*
Ryley, J. H.	*Act.*
Ryskind, Morrie	*Dram.*
Saalburg, Allen	*Art.*
Sabin, N. Henry	*P.O.A.*
Sabine, Martin	*Act.*
Sacco, John	*Mus.*
Sachs, James	*Jour.*
Sack, Victor	*Prod.*
Sacket, Francis	*P.O.A.*
Sackett, Hubert	*Act.*
Safford, Charles L.	*Mus.*
Safford, Ray J.	*Pub.*
Sage, Dean	*Mer.*
Sage, Percy	*Act.*
Sage, William	*Bnkr.*
Sage, William H.	*Mer.*
Sainpolis, Johh	*Act.*
Saint-Gaudens, Augustus	*Sclp.*
Saint-Gaudens, Homer	*Edit.*
Salisbury, Harrison E.	*Writ.*
Salisbury, Philip	*Pub.*
Salkin, Herbert M.	*Art.*

Salmi, Albert	*Act.*	Schaffner, Franklin	*Dir.*
Salter, Harold	*Act.*	Schalk, Rudolph	*P.O.A.*
Salvini, Alexander	*Act.*	Schary, Dore	*Dram.*
Salvini, Tommaso	*Act.*	Schary, Jeb	*Mgr.*
Sampson, Charles E.	*Mer.*	Schauffler, Robert H.	*Writ.*
Sampson, E. Pope	*Mer.*	Schecter, A. A.	*Writ.*
Sampson, William	*Act.*	Scheeder, Louis	*Act*
Samrock, Victor	*M.O.T.*	Scheer, George	*Writ.*
Sams, William	*Act.*	Schelling, Ernest	*Mus.*
Samstag, Nicholas	*Mgr.*	Schenck, Elliot	*Mus.*
Samuel, Ray	*Writ.*	Schenker, Joel W.	*Prod.*
Samuels, Arthur H.	*Mus.*	Scherick, Edgar	*Prod.*
Samuels, Neil	*Act.*	Scherman, Harry	*Edit.*
Sanders, Sydney A.	*Agt.*	Scherman, Thomas K.	*Cond.*
Sanderson, Percy	*Cons.*	Scheuer, Steven	*Prod.*
Sanderson, Rob F.	*Writ.*	Schey, Robert	*P.O.A.*
Sanger, Eugene B.	*Act.*	Scheyer, Daniel	*P.O.A.*
Sanger, Francis W.	*Art.*	Scheyer, Daniel	*Law.*
Sanger, William C.	*P.O.A.*	Schieffelin, George M.	*Pub.*
Santley, Joseph	*Act.*	Schier, Ernest	*Jour.*
Santley, Joseph Sawyer	*Writ.*	Schiffman, S. Fred	*Agt.*
Sardi, Vincent, Jr.	*M.O.T.*	Schloss, Edwin W.	*Prod.*
Sargent, Franklin	*Prof.*	Schlotterer, Raymond C.	*Jour.*
Sargent, John Singer	*Art.*	Schmidt, Arthur P.	*Pub.*
Satterlee, F. L.	*Phys.*	Schmidt, Jack	*Act.*
Saudino, Bruno B.	*Moa*	Schmidt, Karl	*Edit.*
Sauer, Hans	*Art.*	Schnabel, Stefan	*Act.*
Saunders, Allen	*Writ.*	Schnebbe, F. H.	*Mgr.*
Saunders, Dero	*Jour.*	Schneider, Herman	*Writ.*
Saunders, Donald L.	*P.O.A.*	Schneider, Irving	*Prod.*
Sauter, William	*Act.*	Schnitzer, Robert C.	*Act.*
Savage, Henry W.	*Mgr.*	Schoedsack, Ernest B.	*Prod.*
Saville, John G.	*Act.*	Schoen, Lee	*Arch.*
Sawhill, John C.	*Edu.*	Schoenfeld, Gerald	*Prod.*
Sawyer, Spencer L.	*Act.*	Schofield, Charles I.	*Act.*
Saxton, Eugene F.	*Pub.*	Schoonover, Frank E.	*Art.*
Sayler, Oliver M.	*Auth.*	Schreiber, Charles J.	*Jour.*
Saylor, Henry H.	*Edit.*	Schrier, Herman	*Law.*
Sayre, Joel	*Writ.*	Schroeder, Edwin A.	*Mer.*
Scaglione, Robert Phillip	*P.O.A.*	Schroeder, Gilliat	*Mer.*
Scaife, Lauriston L.	*Law.*	Schuck, John	*Act.*
Scaife, Roger L.	*Pub.*	Schuler, Eric	*Agt.*
Scanlon, Walter	*Sing.*	Schull, Richard B.	*Act.*
Scarborough, George	*Dram.*	Schulman, Jack	*Pub.*
Schable, Robert	*Act.*	Schultz, Albert	*Mer.*
Schaefer, George	*M.O.T.*	Schulz, Ralph	*Jour.*
Schaefer, Stanley	*Pub.*	Schuster, Alan	*M.O.T.*
Schaefer, William P.	*Art.*	Schuster, M. L.	*Pub.*
Schaeffer, Frederick C.	*Law.*	Schwartz, Alan U.	*Law.*
Schaeffer, Phillip H.	*Law.*		

Schwartz, Arthur	*Comp.*	Senber, Henry	*Writ.*
Schwartz, Samuel H.	*Mgr.*	Sendax, Victor	*P.O.A.*
Schwarz, Sanford	*Pub.*	Senfeld, Matthew M.	*P.O.A.*
Schweitzer, Albert	*Phys.*	Senour, Roy R. Jr.	*Edu.*
Scibetta, Anthony	*Mua*	Serra, Raymond	*Act.*
Sclesinger, Frank	*Mer.*	Serrano, J. V,	*Act.*
Scott, Barry	*Writ.*	Seward, Clarence	*Law.*
Scott, Cyril	*Act.*	Seydel, Victor	*TvX.*
Scott, Donald	*Pub.*	Seymour, Dan	*M.O.T.*
Scott, Frank H.	*Pub.*	Seymour, James W.	*Writ.*
Scott, James L.	*Law.*	Seymour, John D.	*Act.*
Scott, Justin	*Writ.*	Seymour, Whitney North	*Law.*
Scott, Leroy	*Auth.*	Seymour, Whitney North	
Scott, Lester, Jr.	*Mgr.*	Jr.	*Law.*
Scott, Temple	*Pub.*	Seymour, William	*Mgr.*
Scott, W. E. D.	*Orn.*	Shaine, Frederick M.	*Jour.*
Scott, Walter F.	*Act.*	Shainwald, Herman	*R.E.*
Scourby, Alexander	*Act.*	Shanks, Robert	*Jour.*
Scribner, Charles	*Pub.*	Shanks, William B.	*Act.*
Scribner, Samuel	*Mgr.*	Shannon, J. J.	*Art.*
Scudder, M. L., Jr.	*P.O.A.*	Shannon, Joseph W.	*Act.*
Scull, Guy H.	*Writ.*	Shannon, Palmer	*M.O.T.*
Seabrooke, Thomas	*Act.*	Sharkey, Samuel M.	*Edit.*
Seagram, Wilfred	*Act.*	Shaughnessy, J. J.	*Art.*
Seale, Ervin	*Cler.*	Shaw, A. W.	*Edit.*
Seaman, Louis L.	*Phys.*	Shaw, Alfred	*Arch.*
Seaton, George	*Writ.*	Shaw, Brinsley	*Act.*
Seaver, Edwin	*Writ.*	Shaw, Chet	*Jour.*
Seawell, Brockman	*Act.*	Shaw, Francis	*P.O.A.*
Seawell, Donald R.	*Law.*	Shaw, Harold	*Art.*
Seay, Charles M.	*Act.*	Shaw, John M.	*Brkr.*
Sebastian, John	*Mus.*	Shaw, Ken	*Prod.*
Sedgewick, Russell	*Act.*	Shaw, Percy L.	*Edit.*
Sedgewick, Theodore	*Cler.*	Shaw, Robert A.	*Pub.*
See, Edward	*Act.*	Shaw, Robert J	*Writ.*
Seebach, Julius	*Mus.*	Shear, Michael	*P.O.A.*
Seelen, Arthur	*P.O.A.*	Sheean, Vincent	*Auth.*
Seerle, Carl	*Act.*	Sheehan, Timothy E.	*Prod.*
Segal, Martin E.	*P.O.A.*	Sheffield, Justus	*Law.*
Segel, Harold	*P.O.A.*	Sheldon, E. Lloyd	*Mgr.*
Seitz, George	*Writ.*	Sheldon, Edward	*Dram.*
Selby, John	*Writ.*	Sheldon, Edwin B.	*Brkr.*
Selden, Albert	*Comp.*	Sheldon, Herman A.	*Act.*
Selden, Geoffrey	*TvX.*	Sheldon, Richard D.	*P.O.A.*
Selinsky, Wladimir	*Mus.*	Sheldon, Richard K.	*P.O.A.*
Sellew, Frederic	*Phys.*	Shelley, Harry	*Comp.*
Selton, Morton	*Act.*	Shelley, William	*Act.*
Selwyn, Edgar	*Act.*	Shelton, Reid	*Act.*
Semans, James Hustead	*Phys.*	Shepard, Charles R.	*Phys.*
Semple, Lorenzo, Jr.	*Dram.*	Shepard, Morgan	*Edit.*

Shepherd, William G.	*Writ.*	Simpson, Alexander	*Writ.*
Sherer, John A.	*P.O.A.*	Simpson, Ivan F.	*Act.*
Sheridan, John E.	*Art.*	Simpson, John W.	*Law.*
Sherley, Douglas	*P.O.A.*	Simpson, Kenneth F.	*P.O.A.*
Sherman, A.S.	*Bnkr.*	Sinatra, Frank	*Act.*
Sherman, George	*Bnkr.*	Singer, Cecil M.	*P.O.A.*
Sherman, William T.	*Army*	Singer, Paris	*Arch.*
Sherwin, Louis	*Writ.*	Singer, William H. Jr.	*Art.*
Sherwood, Arthur M.	*Brkr.*	Singerman, Herman	*P.O.A.*
Sherwood, Garrison P.	*Writ.*	Sinnott, Arthur J.	*News.*
Sherwood, Robert E.	*Writ.*	Sirola, Joseph	*Act.*
Shevelove, B.G.	*Dir.*	Sisley, Ray	*Art.*
Shine, Ezra	*Law.*	Sisson, Edgar	*Edit.*
Shine, Giles	*Act.*	Siwek, Manuel	*Pub.*
Shine, John L.	*Act.*	Sjome, Go es	*Act.*
Shipman, Louis F.	*Dram.*	Skiddy, W.W.	*Mer.*
Shirley, Alfred	*Act.*	Skinner, Neil	*Act.*
Shoemaker, Charles C.	*Edit.*	Skinner, Otis	*Act.*
Shook, John Euclid	*Art.*	Slate, Sam	*Dir.*
Short, H. Hassard	*Act.*	Slater, W. Stuart F.	*Pub.*
Showalter, Max	*Act.*	Sloan, Gary	*Act.*
Shreve, J. Nelson	*P.O.A.*	Sloane, William	*Pub.*
Shugio, Heromich	*Art.*	Sloane, William M.	*Auth.*
Shull, Richard B.	*Act.*	Sloat, Howard G.	*M.O.T.*
Shuman, Edwin L.	*Auth.*	Sloccum, Thomas W.	*Mer.*
Shuman, I.	*Edit.*	Slomanson, Lloyd	*Arch.*
Shust, William	*Act.*	Slon, Sidney	*Writ.*
Shuster, George N.	*Auth.*	Sloser, Michael	*Pub.*
Shuttleworth, Jack	*Edit.*	Sloves, Marvin	*P.O.A.*
Shyre, Paul	*Act.*	Slutsker, Peter	*Act.*
Sidenberg, George M.	*Mer.*	Small, Herbert	*Pub.*
Silberman, James H.	*Pub.*	Small, Milton	*M.O.T.*
Silha, Otto A.	*Jour.*	Smalley, Webster	*P.O.A.*
Sill, Stephen R.	*Chem.*	Smart, J. Scott	*Act.*
Sills, Milton	*Act.*	Smedley, W.T.	*Art.*
Sills, Stephan	*Chem.*	Smiga, Brian	*Act.*
Silver, Ron		Smiley, David E.	*Edit.*
Silverman, Dennis	*P.O.A.*	Smith, Adon	*Mnfr.*
Silverstone, Jonas T.	*Law.*	Smith, Alexander	*Bnkr.*
Silvestri, Martin	*Act.*	Smith, Arthur	*Auth.*
Simmons, Edward E.	*Art.*	Smith, Beaumont	*Act.*
Simmons, J. Edward	*Nbkr*	Smith, Beverly	*Writ.*
Simmons, William B.	*P.O.A.*	Smith, Bradish J.	*R.E.*
Simon, Alfred E.	*Mus.*	Smith, C. Aubrey	*Act.*
Simon, David L.	*Phys.*	Smith, C. Howard	*Jour.*
Simon, Gerald	*Act.*	Smith, Chard	*Auth.*
Simon, Peter	*Act.*	Smith, Charles	*P.O.A.*
Simon, Richard	*TvX.*	Smith, Datus C., Jr	*Pub.*
Simon, Robert	*Pub.*	Smith, E.A.	*Pub.*
Simon, Robert A.	*Writ.*	Smith, E.J.	*R.N.*

Smith, Edward C.	*R.P.*	Sommers, James P.	*M.O.T.*
Smith, Eugene	*Act.*	Soper, James G.	*Art.*
Smith, F. Berkley	*Arch.*	Sorel, Edward	*Art.*
Smith, F. Hopkinson	*Auth.*	Sorel, Guy	*Act.*
Smith, G. Albert	*Act.*	Sorvino, Paul	*Act.*
Smith, George M.	*Edit.*	Sorzano, Julio F.	*P.O.A.*
Smith, Gordon A.	*Writ.*	Sothern, Edward H.	*Act.*
Smith, H. Ben	*Act.*	Sothern, Harry	*Act.*
Smith, Harrison	*Auth.*	Sothern, Sam	*Act.*
Smith, Harry	*Auth.*	Sousa, John P.	*Comp.*
Smith, Harry B.	*Dram.*	Southard, Bennett	*Act.*
Smith, Harry M.	*Law.*	Soutter, James T.	*P.O.A.*
Smith, Harvey H.	*Writ.*	Spacey, Kevin	*Act.*
Smith, Henry	*Pub.*	Sparkes, Boyden	*Writ.*
Smith, J. Ascher	*Act.*	Sparks, Harry L.	*Bnkr.*
Smith, James W.	*Writ.*	Sparks, Robert	*Writ.*
Smith, James D.	*Bnkr.*	Sparks, Robert W.	*P.O.A.*
Smith, Jay J.	*Art.*	Sparling, Earl	*Jour.*
Smith, Lloyd E.	*Pub.*	Spaulding, Charles A.	*Mgr.*
Smith, Lou	*Pty*	Spaulding, Eugene R.	*Pub.*
Smith, Mark	*Act.*	Speaks, Charles	*Writ.*
Smith, Mark, III	*Act.*	Spear, Peter M.	*Law.*
Smith, Milton	*Dir.*	Spears, Harry G.	*Brkr.*
Smith, Oliver	*S.A.*	Speed, John	*Writ.*
Smith, R. Berkeley	*Arch.*	Speirs, Russell F.	*Dram.*
Smith, Rowland C.	*Cler.*	Spence, Hartzell	*Writ.*
Smith, S. Mark	*Prod.*	Spencer, Bonnell	*Writ.*
Smith, St. Clair	*Phys.*	Spencer, Creighton	*Cler.*
Smith, Stafford	*Law.*	Spencer, E. Bogart	*P.O.A.*
Smith, Sydney	*Act.*	Spencer, Girard	*P.O.A.*
Smith, T. Guilford	*Mer.*	Sperber, Alan B.	*Phys.*
Smith, W.H., Jr.	*Mer.*	Spewack, Samuel	*Dram.*
Smith, Wallter	*Writ.*	Speyer, James	*Bnkr.*
Smith, Walter B.	*Army*	Spicer, Bart	*Writ.*
Smith, William P.	*Bnkr.*	Spier, Lester C.	*Surg.*
Smith, Winchell	*Act.*	Spire, William M.	*Dir.*
Snibbe, Richard	*Arch.*	Spitzer, J. George	*M.O.T.*
Snow, Wilbert	*Prof.*	Sprague, Arthur C.	*Auth.*
Snyder, Arlen Dean	*Act.*	Sprague, Clarence H.	*Prof.*
Snyder, Bill	*Mus.*	Sprague, Franklin K.	*Writ.*
Snyder, Henry M.	*Pub.*	Sprecher, Ben	*Prod.*
Snyder, John S.	*Pub.*	Springer, John	*PrR.*
Snyder, Martin	*M.O.T.*	Springs, Elliott	*Auth.*
Snyder, Mat B.	*Act.*	Spungin, Gardner	*Pub.*
Snyder, Robert	*Prod.*	St. James, Maximilian	*Act.*
Sobel, Stanford L.	*Writ.*	Stafford, Linley M.	*M.O.T.*
Sobiloff, Hyman J.	*Writ.*	Stahl, Ben	*Art.*
Somerville, Randolph	*Prof.*	Stallard, Ernest	*Act.*
Somerville, Warren	*Prod.*	Stallings, Laurence	*Dram.*
Sommers, Harry G.	*Mgr.*	Stancliff, H.T.	*Navy*

Standing, Guy	*Act.*	Stern, Donald M.	*P.O.A.*
Stanford, Antony	*Act.*	Stern, Henry	*Law.*
Stanford, Harry B.	*Act.*	Stern, Milton R.	*Writ.*
Stang, Arnold	*Act.*	Stern, Paul	*M.O.T.*
Stanley, Frederic	*Art.*	Sternbach, Maurice C.	*Mer.*
Stanley, James	*Mus.*	Sterner, Albert E.	*Art.*
Stanton, Edmund C.	*Mgr.*	Sterner, Frederick J.	*Arch.*
Stanton, Walter	*Mer.*	Sternroyd, Vincent	*Act.*
Stapleton, John	*Dram.*	Sterrett, Cliff	*Cart.*
Stark, John M.	*Prod.*	Sterrett, Paul	*Mus.*
Starling, Lynn	*Dram.*	Sterry, John	*Mer.*
Starnes, Richard	*Edit.*	Stetson, Joseph	*Law.*
Starr, Reginald	*Law.*	Steuer, Gary	*Prod.*
Starr, Roger	*Writ.*	Stevens, Alden	*Writ.*
Starrett, William	*Art.*	Stevens, Byam K.	*P.O.A.*
Staton, Harry	*News.*	Stevens, Clifford	*M.O.T.*
Staton, Harry F. Jr.	*Writ.*	Stevens, Dalton	*Art.*
Stearns, John A.	*M.O.T.*	Stevens, Edwin	*Act.*
Stearns, Michael	*Jour.*	Stevens, Horace P.	*Phys.*
Stearns, Monroe,	*Edit.*	Stevens, J. Burton	*Art.*
Stebbins, Roland	*Bnkr.*	Stevens, Thomas	*Dir.*
Stedman, Edmund	*Auth.*	Stevens, William	*Art.*
Stedman, Marshall	*Act.*	Stevenson, Charles A.	*Act.*
Steele, Asa	*Dram.*	Stevenson, Donald M.	*Pub.*
Steele, Charles M.	*Pub.*	Stevenson, Gordon	*Art.*
Steele, Frederic	*Art.*	Stevenson, John S.	*Mer.*
Steele, Milford	*Writ.*	Stevenson, Richard W.	*Act.*
Steele, Porter	*Mus.*	Stevenson, Robert	*Prof.*
Steele, Vernon	*Act.*	Steward, Grant	*Act.*
Steep, Thomas	*Writ.*	Stewart, Andrew	*Pub.*
Steffens, Loncoln	*Writ.*	Stewart, Charles	*Mgr.*
Steger, Julius	*Act.*	Stewart, Don	*Act.*
Stehli, Edgar	*Act.*	Stewart, Donald. O.	*Auth.*
Stein, Arthur	*Pub.*	Stewart, George W.	*Pub.*
Stein, Ronald J.	*Art.*	Stewart, Graham	*Act.*
Steinbeck, John	*Auth.*	Stewart, Grant	*Art.*
Steinman, Barry J. W.	*M.O.T.*	Stewart, James	*Act.*
Steinway, John H.	*Writ.*	Stewart, Jeff	*Pub.*
Steinway, Theo. E.	*Comp.*	Stewart, Percy M.	*R.E.*
Steinway, William R.	*Mnfr.*	Stewart, S.H. Gardyne	*Bnkr.*
Stelling, William	*Act.*	Stewart, George	
Stepanek, Kahel	*Act.*	Woodbridge	*Writ.*
Stephens, James	*Act.*	Stewart-Gordon, James	*Edit.*
Stephens, Norman	*Prod.*	Stickney, Joseph	*P.O.A.*
Stephens, Thomas E.	*Art.*	Stiefel, Bernard	
Stephenson, Henly	*Act.*	Stieglitz, Alfred	*Art.*
Sterling, J.A.	*Mnfr.*	Stiers, David Ogden	*Act.*
Sterling, Jack	*RAn.*	Stiller, Jerry	*Act.*
Sterling, Philip	*Act.*	Stillman, Henry B.	*Act.*
Sterling, Richard	*Act.*	Stimson, Daniel M.	*Phys.*

Stimson, F.J.	*Auth.*	Strong, Richard A.	*P.O.A.*
Stitt, Jese	*Cler.*	Strong, William E.	*Bnkr.*
Stix, Thomas	*Writ.*	Strother, E. French	*Edit.*
Stix, Thomas C.	*Agt.*	Stroud, Jerry	*Pub.*
Stix, Thomas L.	*Agt.*	Strunsky, Robert	*Writ.*
Stix, Thomas L. Jr	*Law.*	Stryker, Llloyd	*Law.*
Stockton, Richard	*Farm.*	Stuarrt, Henry	*Writ.*
Stockton, Richard	*Dram.*	Stuart, Alexander H.	*Act.*
Stoddard, Henry L.	*Edit.*	Stuart, Henry L.	*Writ.*
Stoddard, Lorimer	*Act.*	Stuart, Ian J.	*Act.*
Stoddart, James H.	*Act.*	Stuart, Kenneth	*Art.*
Stoeckel, Carl	*P.O.A.*	Studley, J.B.	*Act.*
Stogo, Donald	*Art.*	Sturgell, Jack	*Edu.*
Stoker, Bram	*Writ.*	Sturges, Arthur	*P.O.A.*
Stokes, Henry	*Act.*	Sturges, Johnathan	*Auth.*
Stokes, Horace W.	*Pub.*	Sturges, Preston	*Auth.*
Stone, Edward D.	*Arch.*	Sturgis, Danford N.b.	*Arch.*
Stone, Herbert S.	*Pub.*	Sturgis, Edward B	*Eng.*
Stone, Louis A.	*P.O.A.*	Sturgis, Frank K.	*P.O.A.*
Stone, Melville	*Pub.*	Sturgis, Russell	*Arch.*
Stone, Speed	*P.O.A.*	Suckley, Robert B.	*Law.*
Stoneburner, Samuel G. Jr	*Act.*	Sudarsky, Peter	*Prod.*
Stoner, Harry	*Art.*	Sullivan, Frank	*Writ.*
Stopp, Gerald D.	*Dir.*	Sullivan, John M.	*Act.*
Storey, John P.	*Army*	Sullivan, John F.	*Law.*
Story, Douglas	*Auth.*	Sullivan, John T.	*Act.*
Story, Ted	*Act.*	Sullivan, Mark	*Edit.*
Stout, Loren	*Art.*	Sullivan, Thomas	*Auth.*
Stow, John A.	*P.O.A.*	Sullivan, Warren	*Pub.*
Stowwell, Calvin L.	*Bnkr.*	Sultan, Donald	*Art.*
Straight, Willard	*P.O.A.*	Sulzberger, Arthur H.	*Pub.*
Straka, Jerome A.	*P.O.A.*	Sumner, Mark Reese	*Dir.*
Strange, Robert	*Act.*	Sundberg, Clinton	*Act.*
Stransky, Charles	*Act.*	Suraci, Patrick J.	*M.O.T.*
Strasser, Alfred C.	*Art.*	Surette, Thomas W.	*Mus.*
Strater, Henry	*Art.*	Suss, Gregory	*Prod.*
Strater, Nicholas A.	*Dram.*	Sutherland, A. Edward	*Prod.*
Stratton, Chester	*Act.*	Sutherland, Don Page	*Edu.*
Stratton, Leslie C.	*Writ.*	Sutphen, W.G.	*Edit.*
Stratton, Sidney V.	*Arch.*	Sutphin, Donald R.	*P.O.A.*
Straus, Roger W., Jr	*Pub.*	Suydam, Edward	*Art.*
Stravinsky, John	*Act.*	Svenson, Andrew Jr.	*P.O.A.*
Street, Julian	*Writ.*	Swackhamer, E. W.	*Dir.*
Strickler, Jerry	*Act.*	Swafford, Thomas J.	*Bro.*
Stringer, Wilson	*RaX.*	Swan, Oliver G.	*Agt.*
Strohm, John	*Auth.*	Swan, William	*M.O.T.*
Stromenger, W. Harry	*Law.*	Swayne, George B.	*Mer.*
Strong, Austin	*Arch.*	Swayze, John Cameron	*Jour.*
Strong, Charles E.	*Law.*	Sweatnam, Willis P.	*Act.*
Strong, Cyrus M	*P.O.A.*		

Sweeney, James	*Writ.*	Taylor, Charles	*Edit.*
Sweeny, Thompson	*Phys.*	Taylor, Charles J.	*Art.*
Sweeny, Tyler	*Bnkr.*	Taylor, Deems	*Mus.*
Sweet, George	*Act.*	Taylor, Douglas	*Prin.*
Sweets, William Mc.D.	*Writ.*	Taylor, Dwight	*Art.*
Swenson, Eric P.	*Auth.*	Taylor, F. Walter	*Art.*
Swett, Herbert L.	*Mgr.*	Taylor, Francis	*Coll*
Swezey, Robert D.	*RaX.*	Taylor, Frederic	*Bnkr.*
Swing, Raymond	*Writ.*	Taylor, H.S.	*Mgr.*
Swire, R. Derek	*M.O.T.*	Taylor, Henry F.	*Act.*
Swire, Willard	*Act.*	Taylor, Henry J.	*Auth.*
Swope, Herbert	*Auth.*	Taylor, James	*Act.*
Sword, Carl R.	*Cler.*	Taylor, John W.	*Ins.*
Sydney, Basil	*Act.*	Taylor, Longley	*Act.*
Syers, Robert J.	*P.O.A.*	Taylor, Louis C.	*Art.*
Sykes, C.H.	*Art.*	Taylor, Norman	*Writ.*
Sykes, Jerome	*Act.*	Taylor, Peter	*Writ.*
Sykes, Mccready	*Law.*	Taylor, W.B.	*Act.*
Sykes, T.F.	*Pub.*	Teague, Donald	*Art.*
Sylvester, Frank L.	*Act.*	Teague, Walter D.	*Art.*
Sylvester, Harry	*Writ.*	Tearle, Conway	*Act.*
Sylvester, Robert	*News.*	Tebbel, John	*Writ.*
Szarabajka, Keith	*Act.*	Tebbel, Robert	*Writ.*
Taber, Richard	*Act.*	Tefft, F. Griswold	*Mer.*
Taber, Robert	*Act.*	Tefft, William E.	*Mer.*
Tabor, Francis H.	*Prof.*	Teinway, Theodore E.	*Comp.*
Tabori, Kristoffer	*Act.*	Telesco, Michael	*Act.*
Tachau, William G.	*Arch.*	Telford, David D.	*Mnfr.*
Taft, Joseph H.	*Arch.*	Temkin, Victor	*Pub.*
Taggert, William S.	*P.O.A.*	Templeton, Alec	*Mus.*
Tainter, Frank	*Eng.*	Ten, Eyck Baflent	*Lwy.*
Tait, Samuel	*Writ.*	Terhune, Albert P.	*Writ.*
Taliaferro, Henry III	*M.O.T.*	Terle, Conway	*Act.*
Talley, Truman	*Pub.*	Terrell, James M.	*Pub.*
Tallmadge, Frederick S.	*Law.*	Terrell, St. John	*Prod.*
Tally, Ted	*M.O.T.*	Terriss, Thomas	*Act.*
Tanner, Frederick C.	*Law.*	Terry, Paul H.	*Art.*
Tappan, Frederick D.	*Bnkr.*	Tesla, Nikola	*Inv.*
Taraci, Thomas	*Art.*	Tetlow, Edwin	*Jour.*
Tarbell, Edmund C.	*Art.*	Thalenberg, Marvin	*Phys.*
Tarkington, Newton	*Auth.*	Thanhouser, Edwin	*Act.*
Tarleton, Ernest	*Act.*	Thatcher, Robert Osborn	*P.O.A.*
Tarr, Horace G.	*Eng.*	Thayaer, Stephen H.	*Bnkr.*
Tasker, J. Dana	*Edit.*	Thayer, Henry W.	*Art.*
Tassin, Algernon	*Act.*	Thayer, N.. Townsend	*Bnkr.*
Tate, Alfred O.	*Inv.*	Thayer, Raymond L.	*Art.*
Tatham, Edwin	*Mnfr.*	Thayer, Stephen	*Bnkr.*
Taub, Robert M.	*Prod.*	Thiel, Robert R.	*Prod.*
Taubkin, Irvin S.	*Jour.*	Thomas, A.E.	*Auth.*
Taws, David	*Art.*	Thomas, Augustus	*Auth.*

Thomas, C.N.	*P.O.A.*	Tinling, Ted	*Act.*
Thomas, Charles W.	*Mgr.*	Tinney, Cal	*Act.*
Thomas, Earl B.	*Writ.*	Tippit, Wayne	*Act.*
Thomas, Ellis J.	*Law.*	Tippy, William B.	*P.O.A.*
Thomas, Frank M.	*Act.*	Tirrell, George L.	*Writ.*
Thomas, G.R.	*Phot.*	Tisdalae, Archibald	*Law.*
Thomas, Henry T.	*Pub.*	Tober, Donald G.	*P.O.A.*
Thomas, John	*Auth.*	Tobey, Fred	*Art.*
Thomas, John Charles	*Sing.*	Tobey, Kenneth	*Act.*
Thomas, John A.	*Writ.*	Todd, H. David	*Art.*
Thomas, John E.	*Mer.*	Todd, James	*Act.*
Thomas, Lowell	*Auth.*	Tolan, Michael	*Act.*
Thomas, Rhys	*Act.*	Toland, Hugo	*Act.*
Thomas, Richard	*Act.*	Toler, Sidney S.	*Act.*
Thomas, W.J., Jr	*Writ.*	Tolhurst, Fred	*Comp.*
Thomas, Walter	*Act.*	Tomalin, Arthur	*Edit.*
Thomas, Walter G.	*Arch.*	Tombs, Lee	*M.O.T.*
Thomas, William H.	*P.O.A.*	Tomlinson, Edward	*Auth.*
Thomas, William, Jr. C.	*Writ.*	Tomlinson, Robert Michael	*Act.*
Thommpson, William H.	*Act.*	Tompkins, E.F.	*Edit.*
Thompson, Denman, II	*Writ.*	Tompkins, Eugene	*Mgr.*
Thompson, Frank, Jr.	*Law.*	Tone, Franchot	*Act.*
Thompson, Frederic	*Mgr.*	Tonetti, Francis M.l.	*Sclp.*
Thompson, J. Walter	*P.O.A.*	Tony, Roberts	
Thompson, J.S. Barbour	*R.R.*	Toohey, John P.	*Auth.*
Thompson, Lewis	*Writ.*	Toohey, Richard	*Pub.*
Thompson, Robert M.	*Mer.*	Toole, John L.	*Act.*
Thompson, W.P.	*P.O.A.*	Toombs, Allen Lee	
Thomson, Frederick A.	*Act.*	Toomey, Regis	*Act.*
Thomson, James F.	*Sing.*	Toritch, Waldemar	*Mer.*
Thomson, John D.	*Law.*	Torrence, David	*Act.*
Thomson, Kenneth	*Act.*	Torrey, Volta	*Edit.*
Thomson, William H.	*Art.*	Toscanini, Arturo	*Mus.*
Thorn, Philip	*Writ.*	Totheroh, Dan	*Dram.*
Thorne, Frederick	*Act.*	Tourney, Herman L.	*Mgr.*
Thornton, Richard	*Act.*	Tours, Frank	*Mus.*
Thornton, Richard H.	*Edit.*	Tovrov, Orin	*Writ.*
Thorpe, Courtenay	*Act.*	Towle, Frank F.	*P.O.A.*
Thorpe, Merle	*Edit.*	Towne, Charles	*Edit.*
Thorpe, Warren	*Writ.*	Townsend, Antony M.	*Prod.*
Thorson, Robert	*Arch.*	Townsend, Arthur F.	*Mer.*
Throne, Malachi	*Act.*	Townsend, Arthur R.	*Dram.*
Thulstrup, Thure De	*Art.*	Townsend, Issac	*P.O.A.*
Thurber, James	*Writ.*	Townsend, James B.	*Edit.*
Tibbett, Lawrence	*Mus.*	Townsend, Ralph M.	*Writ.*
Tiffany, Louis Comfort	*Sty*	Townsend, Robert C.	*P.O.A.*
Tilden, Freeman	*Writ.*	Townsend, Smith	*Cler.*
Tillett, William S.	*Writ.*	Townsend, Stephen	*Act.*
Tilton, Arthur C.	*P.O.A.*	Townshend, Arthur B.	*Phys.*
Tilton, George	*Act.*	Tows, Coe D.	*P.O.A.*

Tows, Ferrars H.	*Law.*	Turner, Webb William	*P.O.A.*
Trachtman, Joseph	*Law.*	Tyhg, Stephen Jr.	*Broker*
Tracy, Evarts	*Arch.*	Tylo, Michael	*Act.*
Tracy, Spencer	*Act.*	Uhl, Richard	*Mus.*
Traeger, Henry	*Act.*	Ullett, Nicholas	*Act.*
Trafton, Clark	*Edu.*	Ullmen, Allen	*Writ.*
Train, Arthur	*Auth.*	Ullman, E. R.	*P.O.A.*
Trapani, Salvatore	*Act.*	Ullman, James R.	*Writ.*
Travis, Edmund C.	*P.O.A.*	Ulman, Robert	*P.O.A.*
Travis, John C.	*Law.*	Underhill, Jacob	*P.O.A.*
Travolta, John	*Act.*	Underhill, John G.	*Auth.*
Trefflich, Henry	*Writ.*	Underwood, Drury	*Writ.*
Tregaskis, Richard	*Writ.*	Underwood, H. G.	*Law.*
Tregor, Nicholas A.	*Sclp.*	Upham, G. B.	*P.O.A*
Treidler, Adolph	*Art.*	Urbanski, Douglas	*M.O.T.*
Trevor, John	*Act.*	Urmy, Ralph B. Jr.	*Act.*
Triolo, Anthony	*Art.*	Urskali, William	*Writ.*
Tripp, David E.	*Art.*	Vail, Lester	*Act.*
Tripp, John		Valenta, Leonard	*Act.*
Tripp, Paul	*Act.*	Valentine, Charles A.	*Arch.*
Trotti, Lamar	*Writ.*	Valentine, De Alton	*Art.*
Troy, Thomas H.	*Law.*	Vance, Arthur T.	*Edit.*
Truex, Ernest	*Act.*	Vance, Louis Joesph	*Auth.*
Truex, Philip E.	*Act.*	Vandegrift, George W.	*Phys.*
Truman, Harry S.	*Pres.*	Vanderbilt, Cornelius	*R.R.*
Trumball, Walter	*Auth.*	Vanderbilt, George W.	*P.O.A.*
Truro, Victor	*Act.*	Vanderbilt, W. K.	*R.R.*
Tryon, Thomas	*Arch.*	Vandercook, John. W.	*Auth.*
Tucker, Frank	*Writ.*	Vanderlip, Frank A.	*Bnkr.*
Tucker, John Bartholomew	*Act.*	Van de Water, F. F.	*Writ.*
Tucker, Preble	*Law.*	Van Alen, J. J.	*P.O.A.*
Tuckerman, Lucius C.	*Lec.*	Van Allen, William H.	*Cler.*
Tunney, Gene	*P.O.A.*	Van Antwerp, Ted	*M.O.T.*
Turgeon, Peter	*Act.*	Van Buren, Frederick T., Jr.	*Phys.*
Turbull, Hector	*Auth.*	Van Der Marck, Alfred	*M.O.T.*
Turner, Paul N.	*Lawr.*	Van Doren, Carl	*Edit.*
Tuttle, Day	*Act.*	Van Doren, Peter	*Edit.*
Twachtman, John H.	*Art.*	Van Dyke, Charles S.	*Writ.*
Tweed, Chas. H.	*Lawy.*	Van Dyke, Henry	*Prof.*
Twigg, Gilbank	*Sculpt.*	Van Dyke, William	*Law.*
Twinem, Levl.	*Clar.*	Van Dyke, John C.	*Lib.*
Twitchell, Art C.	*Prod.*	Van Emburgh, D. B.	*P.O.A.*
Twombley, H. Mc.	*Bank.*	Van Geuns, Jean-Rene	*P.O.A.*
Twyford, A. A.	*Prof.*	Van Horne, Franklin M.	*Mer.*
Tyler, Alfred	*P.O.A.*	Van Horne, Richard B.	*Eng.*
Tyler, C. C.	*Lawy.*	Van Loon, Hendrik	*Auth.*
Tyler, Harry	*Act.*	Van Norden, Theodore L.	*Bnkr.*
Tyler, Geo. C.	*Mgr.*	Van Rooten, Courtlandt	*Edu.*
Tyler, S. B.	*Ins.*	Van Rooten, Luis D'Antin	*Act.*
Tymun, J. B.	*Act.*	Van Santvoord, Charles T.	*P.O.A.*

Van Slyke, Warren C.	*Law.*	Wakefield, Earle	*P.O.A.*
Van Voorhis, C.W.	*M.O.T.*	Walbridge, Henry	*P.O.A.*
Van Voorhis, Westbrook	*M.O.T.*	Walburn, Ramond	*Act.*
Van Wart, James	*M.O.T.*	Walck, Henry Z.	*Pub.*
Van Werveke, George	*Art.*	Walcot, Charles	*Act.*
Van Zile, Edward S.	*Auth.*	Waldo, Earl	*Mus.*
Varley, Harry	*Writ.*	Waldo, George	*Art.*
Varner, Van der Veer	*Writ.*	Waldron, John	*Act.*
Varnum, James M.	*Law.*	Waldron, Webb	*Edit.*
Varrey, Edwin	*Act.*	Wales, Edward H.	*Bnkr.*
Vaughan, Stuart	*Dir.*	Walker, Clifford	*Act.*
Veiller, Anthony	*Auth.*	Walker, George H.	*Mgr.*
Ver Dorn, Jerry	*Act.*	Walker, Henry O.	*Art.*
Vermilyea, Harold	*Act.*	Walker, John T. Jr.	*Arch.*
Vernon, Grenville	*Writ.*	Walker, Robert J.C.	*Mer.*
Vesey, Arthur H.	*Auth.*	Walker, Roberts	*Law.*
Victor, Alexander F.	*Inv.*	Walker, Stanley	*Edit.*
Vidor, King	*Dir.*	Walker, Thomas W.	*News.*
Viehman, Theodore	*Dir.*	Walker, William H.	*Art.*
Viele, Herman K.	*Auth.*	Wallace, David	*Writ.*
Vincent, Claude	*Act.*	Wallace, Edward C.	*Mer.*
Vincent, George G.	*Mus.*	Wallace, James G.	*P.O.A.*
Vincent, Leon H.	*Lec.*	Wallace, Mike	*Act.*
Vincent, Walter	*Mgr.*	Wallace, W.C.	*Law.*
Vir Den, Ray	*Mus.*	Wallace, W.H.	*P.O.A.*
Vitelli, Vincent	*M.O.T.*	Wallach, Eli	*Act.*
Vivanti, F.A.	*Mer.*	Wallack, J. Lester	*Act.*
Voelker, John D.	*Writ.*	Waller, Lewis	*Act.*
Vogel, Karl	*Coll.*	Wallis, Frank E.	*Arch.*
Voigts, Richard C.	*M.O.T.*	Walling, William	*Pub.*
Von Gaertner, Louis A.	*Comp.*	Walliser, Blair A.	*Prod.*
Von Glehn, W.G.	*Art.*	Wallower, Ted Paul	*Bro. X.*
Von Mitzel, Max	*Act.*	Walsh, George	*P.O.A.*
Von Seebeck, George	*Mus.*	Walsh, Harry	*Pub.*
Von Utassey, George	*Pub.*	Walsh, James Anthony	*Act.*
Voskovec, George	*Act.*	Walsh, Lionel	*Act.*
Vroom, Frederic	*Act.*	Walsh, M. Emmet	*Act.*
Vroom, Lodewick	*Writ.*	Walsh, Martin J.	*Act.*
Wachtel, Jeffrey	*Act.*	Walsh, Richard	*Edit.*
Wadelton, T.D.	*Arch.*	Walsh, Robert H.	*Farm.*
Wadsworth, W. Austin	*P.O.A.*	Walsh, Tony	*Act.*
Wagenhals, L.A.	*Mgr.*	Walsh, Townsend	*Jour.*
Waggner, George	*Prod.*	Walston, Ray	*Act.*
Wagner, Carl F.	*Bnkr.*	Walter, Wilmer	*Act.*
Wagner, Oscar	*Mus.*	Walters, H.	*Mer.*
Wagner, Otto	*Bnkr.*	Walthall, Henry	*Act.*
Wagner, Rob	*Art.*	Wang, Arthur	*Pub.*
Wagner, Walter	*Act.*	Wanger, Walter F.	*Mgr.*
Waid, Everett	*Arch.*	Waram, Percy Carne	*Act.*
Waissman, Kenneth	*M.O.T.*		

Warburton, John	*Act.*	Webster, Bryon	*Act.*
Ward, Edmund A.	*P.O.A.*	Webster, Harold McCloud	*Act.*
Ward, James H.	*Law.*	Webster, Harold T.	*Art.*
Ward, John G.	*Mer.*	Webster, Henry Titchell	*Writ.*
Ward, LeRoy P.	*Arch.*	Webster, Richard Morgan	*Army*
Ward, Samuel	*Phys.*	Weed, Clive	*Art.*
Ward, Williard P.	*Eng.*	Weed, Raphael A.	*Art.*
Warden, Jack	*Act.*	Weed, Robert L.	*Act.*
Ware, Harlan	*Writ.*	Weeks, Francis H.	*Law.*
Warfield, David	*Act.*	Weeks, Willet	*Pub.*
Waring, George E, Jr.	*P.O.A.*	Weel, Gordon J.	*Pub.*
Waring, Todd	*Act.*	Weidner, Frederick III	*Act.*
Warner, Charles Dudley	*Auth.*	Weinstein, H. David	*Prod.*
Warner, George H.	*Auth.*	Weir, Walter	*Writ.*
Warner, Frank H.	*Law.*	Weiss, William H.	*R.R.*
Warner, Henry B.	*Act.*	Weissman, Jack	*P.O.A.*
Warren, Carlton	*Act.*	Weist, Dwight	*Act.*
Warren, E. Walpole	*Cler.*	Weitzenhoffer, Max Jr.	*M.O.T.*
Warren, Joseph	*Act.*	Welch, Edward M.	*Art.*
Warren, Joseph W.	*Prof.*	Weld, Arthur C.G.	*Mus.*
Warren, Lloyd	*Arch.*	Weld, Francis M.	*Phys.*
Warren, Ralph F.	*Dir.*	Weld, John	*Writ.*
Warren, Whitney	*Arch.*	Weldon, Nathaniel W. Jr.	*Prod.*
Warrin, Frank L. Jr.	*Law.*	Weldon, Warren	*Prod.*
Wartels, Nat	*Pub.*	Weller, Cedric	*Act.*
Washburn, Ives	*Edit.*	Weller, Samuel MacLeary	*Writ.*
Wasserman, Dale	*Dram.*	Weller, Charles B.	*Act.*
Waterbury, James M.	*P.O.A.*	Welliver, Judson C.	*Writ.*
Waterhouse, Archibald	*Ins.*	Wells, Frederic DeWitt	*Law.*
Waterston, Samuel A.	*Act.*	Wells, J.M.	*Arch.*
Watkins, Thomas C.	*Bnkr.*	Wells, Linton	*Writ.*
Watson, Neale W.	*Pub.*	Wells, Maurice	*Act.*
Watson, R.C.	*Ins.*	Wendell, Evert Jansen	*P.O.A.*
Watson, Henry S.	*Art.*	Wendell, Howard	*Act.*
Watson, Minor	*Act.*	Wendell, Jacob Jr.	*Act.*
Watts, G. Graham	*Phys.*	Wenk, Burton	*Art.*
Waxman, Percy	*Writ.*	Wenman, Henry	*Act.*
Way, Nelson	*P.O.A.*	Wenning, Thomas H.	*Writ.*
Wayne, David	*Act.*	Wendt, Edmund C.	*Phys.*
Weaver, Henry Jr.	*Act.*	Wentworth, John Sr.	*M.O.T.*
Weaver, Joseph W.	*Act.*	Werrenrath, Reinald	*Sing.*
Webb, J. Louis	*Art.*	Wershba, Joseph	*Jour.*
Webb, Kenneth	*Dram.*	West, Percy	*Act.*
Webb, Peter R.	*Jour.*	Westerton, Frank H.	*Act.*
Webb, W. Seward	*R.R.*	Westervelt, Leonidas	*Auth.*
Webb, Peter W.	*Dram.*	Westley, John	*Act.*
Webber, James Plaisted	*Dir.*	Wetmore, Charles W.	*Law.*
Weber, Karl		Wetmore, Edmund	*Law.*
Weber, William C.	*Edit.*	Wever, Edward H.	*Act.*

Weybright, Victor	*Pub.*	Whitlock, Brand	*Writ.*
Weyl, Walter E.	*Auth.*	Whitman, Herbert S.	*P.O.A.*
Weyr, Thomas	*Writ.*	Whitman, James Spurr	*Mer.*
Wheat, Lawrence	*Act.*	Whitman, Roger B.	*Auth.*
Wheatcroft, Nelson	*Act.*	Whitman, Roger C.	*Writ.*
Wheeler, Claude L.	*Phys.*	Whitman, Stephen French	*Writ.*
Wheeler, Dunham	*Arch.*	Whitmore, James	*Act.*
Wheeler, Edward J.	*Edit.*	Whitney, Caspar	*Edit.*
Wheeler, Henry Dwight	*P.O.A.*	Whitney, Frederick C.	*P.O.A.*
Wheeler, Howard D.	*Edit.*	Whitney, Steven	*M.O.T.*
Wheeler, Thomas M.	*P.O.A.*	Whitney, W.C.	*P.O.A.*
Wheeler, William Ogden	*P.O.A.*	Whitridge, Frederick W.	*Law.*
Wheeler, William L. Jr.	*Phys.*	Whittaker, Herbert	*M.O.T.*
Wheelock, Joseph	*Act.*	Whittemore, Richard D.	*M.O.T.*
Wheelock, Joseph Jr.	*Act.*	Whorf, Richard	*Act.*
Wheelwright, John T.	*Law.*	Whytal, A. Russ	*Act.*
Whelpey, James D.	*Jour.*	Wickersham, George W.	*Law.*
Whiffen, Thomas	*Act.*	Wickes, Joseph	*S.A.*
Whitaker, Jack	*M.O.T.*	Wickstead, McIntyre	*Act.*
White, Edward E. Jr.	*Pub.*	Widdecombe, Wallace	*Act.*
White, Frank K.	*Pub.*	Widmark, Richard	*Act.*
White, George C.	*M.O.T.*	Wien, Lawrence	*Act.*
White, Gilbert	*Art.*	Wiener, John A.	*Law.*
White, Horatio Clarke Jr.	*Pub.*	Wieser, George J.	*Pub.*
White, Nathaniel	*Act.*	Wiggam, Albert E.	*Writ.*
White, Owen P.	*Writ.*	Wilber, Allen S.	*Pub.*
White, Roderick	*Mus.*	Wilby, Joseph	*Law.*
White, S.V.	*Bnkr.*	Wilcox, Arthur V.	*Art.*
White, Stanford	*Arch.*	Wilcox, Frank	*Act.*
White, Stewart Edward	*Auth.*	Wilder, Clinton	*Prod.*
White, Watson	*Act.*	Wilder, Thornton	*Dram.*
White, William A.	*P.O.A.*	Wilde, Percival	*Dram.*
White, William Allen	*Edit.*	Wilder, James A.	*Art.*
White, William Lindsay	*Jour.*	Wildhack, Robert J.	*Art.*
Whitehead, O.Z.	*Act.*	Wilds, Walter	*Writ.*
Whitehead, Paxton	*Act.*	Wiley, William Bradford	*Pub.*
Whitehead, Robert	*Prod.*	Wilk, Max	*Writ.*
Whitehead, Russell	*Arch.*	Wilkens, H.A.J.	*Eng.*
Whitehouse, Frederick Cope	*P.O.A.*	Wilker, Lawrence J.	*M.O.T.*
Whitehouse, George M.	*Bnkr.*	Wilkie, John L.	*Law.*
Whitehouse, J. Henry	*Bnkr.*	Wilkinson, Lupton A.	*Writ.*
Whitelam, Peter	*Writ.*	Wilkison, W.M.	*Mgr.*
Whitelaw, Arthur	*Prod.*	Willard, D. Seymour	*Bnkr.*
Whitelock, William Wallace	*Auth.*	Willard, E.S.	*Act.*
Whitesell, John P. II	*M.O.T.*	Willard, John	*Auth.*
Whitfield, Henry D.	*Arch.*	Willard, Thomas H.	*Phys.*
Whiting, Arthur	*Mus.*	Willauer, Arthur E.	*Arch.*
Whiting, Joseph E.	*Act.*	Willet, Peter S.	*Writ.*
Whiting, Judson	*Dir.*	Willets, Howard	*Mer.*
Whiting, Robert Rudd	*Writ.*	Willey, John Coffin	*Pub.*

Willey, Leonard	Act.	Wilstach, Paul	Dram.
William, Warren	Act.	Wiman, Dwight Deere	Mgr.
Williams, Alexander H.	Writ.	Winant, Forrest	Act.
Williams, Charles D.	Art.	Winant, William III	P.O.A.
Williams, Churchill	Auth.	Winchester, Robert	Phys.
Williams, Earle	Act.	Windom, William	Act.
Williams, F. Bryan	Writ.	Windust, Bretaigne	Act.
Williams, Frederick	Mgr.	Windheim, Marek	Sing.
Williams, Frederick C.	Dir.	Winer, Elihu	Writ.
Williams, Fritz	Act.	Wing, Paul	Dir.
Williams, George C.F.	Mnfr.	Wingfield, H. Conway	Act.
Williams, Henry Meade	Edit.	Winslow, E.F.	R.R.
Williams, Herschel V., Jr.	Writ.	Winslow, James Norton	Ins.
Williams, J. Randall, III	Pub.	Winsmore, Robert	Auth.
Williams, Jesse Lynch	Auth.	Winston, Gustavus S.	P.O.A.
Williams, Joe	Edit.	Winston, J.O.	Eng.
Williams, John Daniel	Writ.	Winter, Erza	Art.
Williams, John L.B.	Pub.	Winternitz, Robert	P.O.A.
Williams, Joseph R.	Mgr.	Winters, Jerry	Dir.
Williams, Mervin	Act.	Winters, Roland	Act.
Williams, Michael	Edit.	Wirsig, Woodrow	Edit.
Williams, N. Winslow	Law.	Wise, Thomas	Act.
Williams, Palmer	Prod.	Wister, Owen	Law.
Williams, R.H.	Mer.	Wiswell, Andrew M.	Mus.
Williams, Rhys	Act.	Withers, D.D.	P.O.A.
Williams, Robert Neff	Edu.	Witt, Andrew M.	Act.
Williams, Sidney	Writ.	Witt, Peter	Agt.
Williams, T.C.	Phys.	Wolcott, Edward Oliver	P.O.A.
Williams, Wythe	Writ.	Wolcott, Henry	Bnkr.
Williamson, Douw D.	Chem.	Wolfington, Iggie	Act.
Wilmer, Sidney	Act.	Wohlforth, Robert	Pub.
Willmore, Joseph	M.O.T.	Woitach, Richard	Mus.
Wilson, Andrew C.	Cler.	Wolf, Jack	PrR.
Wilson, Douglas	Prod.	Wolff, Ira	Art.
Wilson, Edward A.	Art.	Wolff, Julian	Writ.
Wilson, Elmo C.	P.O.A.	Wolff, Richard	M.O.T.
Wilson, Francis	Act.	Wolff, Sanford	M.O.T.
Wilson, Frederic	Art.	Wolff, William I.	Phys.
Wilson, George W.	Act.	Wolhandler, Joseph	PrR.
Wilson, Gill Robb	Writ.	Woloshin, Sid	Mus.
Wilson, Harry Leon	Writ.	Wood, Arnold	Pub.
Wilson, J. Plumpton	Act.	Wood, Charles G., Jr.	Mer.
Wilson, James E.	Act.	Wood, Douglas	Act.
Wilson, John C.	Prod.	Wood, H. Duncan	Bnkr.
Wilson, Lanford	Dram.	Wood, Meredith	Pub.
Wilson, Morrow	Act.	Wood, Roland	Act.
Wilson, Russell	Law.	Wood, W. Clifford	Bnkr.
Wilson, Trey	Act.	Wood, William T.	P.O.A.
Wilson, William J.	Writ.	Woodberry, George E.	Prof.
		Woodbridge, William B.	Ins.

Woodburn, John	*Edit.*	Wyler, William	*Dir.*
Woodford, Walter E.	*Mer.*	Wylie, Max	*Dir.*
Woodhouse, L.G.	*P.O.A.*	Wylie, Porter	*Pub.*
Woodruff, Arthur	*Mus.*	Wyndham, Charles	*Act.*
Woodruff, Frank D.	*Pub.*	Wyngate, Charles	*Act.*
Woodruff, Henry	*Act.*	Wynne, Gerald	*Jour.*
Woodruff, Stanley	*P.O.A.*	Yang, Jay	*Art.*
Woods, George D.	*P.O.A.*	Yarnell, Richard	*Act.*
Woods, James	*Act.*	Yellen, Barry	*M.O.T.*
Woods, John J.	*Jour.*	Youmans, Vincent Jr.	*Pub.*
Woods, Donald	*Act.*	Young, Ernest S.	
Woods, Richard M.	*Mnfr.*	Zaldivar, Gilbert	*Prod.*
Woods, Robert	*Act.*	Zalduondo, J.A.	*P.O.A.*
Woods, Stuart C.	*Writ.*	Zebley, John F.	*Bnkr.*
Woodson, William	*Act.*	Zeigon, James	*P.O.A.*
Woodward, George	*Act.*	Zelenko, Norman	*Law.*
Woodward, George B.	*Ins.*	Ziegler, Fred J.	*Auth.*
Woodwars, Stanely	*Edit.*	Ziman, Jerrold	*Act.*
Woolett, Sidney	*Edit.*	Zimbalist, Efrem Jr.	*Act.*
Wooley, Edgar M.	*Act.*	Zimet, Philip	*M.O.T.*
Worlock, Frederic	*Act.*	Zimmer, Lee	*M.O.T.*
Worsley, Wallace	*Act.*	Zimmermann, Edwin	*Act.*
Worthing, Frank	*Act.*	Ziolkowski, Korczak	*Sclp.*
Wortman, Denys	*Art.*	Zion, Sidney	*Jour.*
Wrather, Jack Devereaux, Jr.	*Prod.*	Zirato, Bruno	*Prod.*
Wray, Henry Russell	*Art.*	Zitrin, Arthur	*Phys.*
Wray, John	*Act.*	Zoffer, Berthold	*Phys.*
Wreden, Nicholas	*Auth.*	Zogbaum, Rufus F.	*Art.*
Wrenn, John H.	*Bnkr.*	Zuckerman, Henry	*Bnkr.*
Wright, Ben	*Ann.*	Zweig, Jack	*Phys.*
Wright, Bob	*Act.*		
Wright, Dan	*Agt.*		
Wright, Daniel	*Agt.*		
Wright, Edward A.	*Prof.*		
Wright, Ernest H.	*Auth.*		
Wright, Frank Lloyd	*Arch.*		
Wright, Hamilton W.	*Writ.*		
Wright, Herb	*Prod.*		
Wright, Herb, III			
Wright, Herbert Carelton	*Law.*		
Wright, James	*Law.*		
Wright, Norman Soreng	*Mus.*		
Wright, Richardson	*Auth.*		
Wright, Robert	*Writ.*		
Wright, Stephen	*Act.*		
Wright, William Spencer	*Art.*		
Wright, Wynn	*Prod.*		
Wrubel, David	*Law.*		
Wunderman, Lester	*Adv*		
Wykes, Hunter	*Bnkr.*